GOD'S WORD
FOR LIFE

ADULT LESSON GUIDE

VOLUME 2

2022–2023

LESSON GUIDE

© 2022 Pentecostal Publishing House

36 Research Park Court
Weldon Spring, MO 63304
www.pentecostalpublishing.com
All rights reserved.
Manufactured in USA, September 2022, 6912245

EDITORIAL STAFF

Editor in Chief: Robin Johnston
Associate Editor, Curriculum: Lee Ann Alexander
Adult Editor, Curriculum: LJ Harry

WRITERS

Gayla Baughman	Scott Graham	Jeremy Painter
Terry Baughman	LJ Harry	Chris Paris
Ryan Bundren	Jonathan Mohr	Johnnie Peyton
Johnny Celey	Jonathan Mullings	Tes Stewart
Richard Davis	G. Glenn Murphy	Ron Wofford

www.pentecostalpublishing.com

THIS BOOK
BELONGS TO

_____

_____

_____

GOD'S WORD
FOR LIFE

*****AN** indicates All Nations Sunday.

*****CS** indicates Christmas Sunday.

SPRING 2023 CONTENTS

***ES** indicates Easter Sunday.

HOW TO USE THIS LESSON GUIDE

GETTING STARTED

The first page of each lesson gives pertinent information that will be foundational for teaching the lesson. Here you will find the Lesson Title, the Truth about God, the Truth for My Life, and both the Focus Verses and Lesson Text. In addition, a callout box will either give an overview of the series (the first lesson of each series contains this information) or will connect students with their daily devotional activity from the previous week.

SEPTEMBER 4, 2022   SERIES 1: THE GOD OF DELIVERANCE

1.1 SLAVES CAN BE DELIVERED

FOCUS VERSE
Hebrews 3:14
For we are made partakers of Christ, if we hold the beginning of our confidence stedfast unto the end.

LESSON TEXT
Exodus 2:1–10;
Hebrews 3:1–19

TRUTH ABOUT GOD
God circumvents efforts that seek to keep us enslaved.

TRUTH FOR MY LIFE
I will act on God's provision of deliverance.

Series Overview:
This series, "The God of Deliverance," will follow the Israelites on their journey out of slavery in Egypt to the building of the Tabernacle in the wilderness. We will watch as Moses grows up in the palace of Pharaoh and have a closeup view of the plagues that ultimately led to the Israelites' freedom. We will follow them through the Red Sea to the mountain where they received the commandments, and we will end up watching the glory of the Lord fill the Tabernacle. This series will show us a God who delivers and allow each of us to experience that deliverance in our own lives.

8

LESSON 1.1

SG TEACHING OUTLINE

Icebreaker: Have you ever repeated a story you just knew was true only to discover it was not? Describe what happened.

Lesson Connection: Share the Lesson Connection.

I. THE HEBREWS WERE SLAVES IN EGYPT
   » What are the "spiritual thermometers" in your life that help indicate the spiritual atmosphere you are in?
   A. Governments May Forget Their History
      » What measures signal that the past has been forgotten? These might be changes in someone's personal life or in the world in general.
   B. Pharaoh's Daughter Rescued Moses from Death
   C. Discovering God's Unstoppable Plan for My Deliverance
      » What are some testimonies of God's deliverance in your life and others' lives?

II. ANOTHER DELIVERER LIKE MOSES
   A. Moses Was a Type of the Messiah, Jesus Christ
   B. I Will Choose Grace and Truth
      » How would you tell a friend or coworker about God's grace and truth?

III. OLD COVENANT VERSUS NEW COVENANT
   A. The New Covenant Accomplished What the Old Covenant Only Symbolized
      » What did you see and understand better after you received the Holy Spirit that you could not understand before?
   B. I Will Believe in Jesus and Experience Deliverance from Sin

Internalizing the Message

Prayer Focus
Lead the group in prayer and consider the following topics of focus:
• Pray for God to help you to know what spiritual atmosphere you are in and if He wants you to continue therein.
• Ask God to help you be and do what He wants you to as you grow stronger in your faith.

9

SG TEACHING OUTLINE

The SG (Small Group) Teaching Outline is the lesson content in outline form. Each lesson main point is listed along with suggested discussion questions. Although the outline can be used to teach the lesson in a large group setting, the "SG" indicates the content is also designed to be used in a Small Group. Because of this, an icebreaker question has been provided to help jump-start interaction in the Small Group meeting.

FALL: LESSON 1.1

LESSON CONNECTION

On March 22, 2018, an ordinary family said goodbye to an extraordinary man. He wasn't just extraordinary because he had reached the age of 107. He wasn't even extraordinary simply because he had served in government for over twenty-five years or because he'd won a chess tournament at age ninety-nine. Johan van Hulst was remarkable because he saved over six hundred Jewish children from Nazi genocide.

In 1940 van Hulst had been appointed deputy principal of the Reformed Teacher Training College, a seminary in Amsterdam, as World War II swept across Europe. Van Hulst's first contributions included helping convert the college into a shelter for Dutch teachers in danger for refusing to sign the oath of loyalty to Germany. By 1942 van Hulst began an even more radical means of rescuing Jews in the Netherlands.

Nazis used a theater across the street from the college as a deportation center for Jewish families. As part of the process, children were separated from their parents and sent to a crèche (a nursery) next door. The nursery shared a back garden with the college, and van Hulst seized the opportunity to step in and save the children.

By secretly coordinating operations with nursery workers, van Hulst and his colleagues helped smuggle children out of the city. These courageous individuals canvassed potential adoptive families who could take the endangered children into their homes without detection. Then partnering nursery workers covertly removed the names of the children from the Nazi's registry.

Van Hulst and the network of secret deliverers then arranged for the children to be hidden in containers such as laundry baskets and sacks. Deliverers would time their clandestine mission for when a tram passed, blocking the view of Nazi guards so another resistance worker could hide away with the hidden child. The rescued toddlers would live out the rest of the war in hiding.

The covert deliverance efforts lasted until 1943 when the nursery was closed and its Jewish director was sent to the death camp at Auschwitz. Van Hulst continued to help other Jews in danger until he was forced to go into hiding just three weeks before the liberation. On March 8, 1972, Yad Vashem (the World Holocaust Remembrance Center) recognized Johan van Hulst as Righteous Among the Nations (an honor to describe non-Jews who risked their lives to save Jews from genocide).

In an age when most North Americans enjoy relative safety, it may be difficult to understand the depths of van Hulst's sacrifice. Yet we can acknowledge with appreciation the high cost of deliverance and the glorious freedom his efforts purchased for at least six hundred children.

10

LESSON CONNECTION

Most often the Lesson Connection will be a story or illustration designed to give students a glimpse of the overall theme of the lesson. Since stories often appeal to the heart and emotions, this portion of the lesson seeks to engage the heart to receive the truth that will be taught. You are encouraged to personalize this section and include your own testimony to help students connect to the lesson.

BIBLE LESSON

The Bible Lesson is a manuscript of the entire lesson. The lessons are written by various Apostolic authors who not only skillfully explain the truths of Scripture but also share ways we can apply these truths to our lives. The lesson contains discussion questions to stimulate thought and media callouts (videos and images available in the Adult Resource Kit) to connect with students of all learning styles.

BIBLE LESSON

I. THE HEBREWS WERE SLAVES IN EGYPT

The children of Israel were in a position they never saw coming. It happened slowly over time as evil forces exerted more and more power in their lives. Through time and circumstance, the enemy slowly took away their rights. By the time the Israelites realized what had happened to them, they were entrenched in bondage. Hope seemed a million miles away.

These events are a perfect example of how Satan draws many people into spiritual slavery, and especially how believers can backslide. The devil tries to chip away at our conscience and eliminate small disciplines in our lives. We begin to think, *Maybe this aspect of godly living isn't important or this small sin surely won't hurt me that badly; after all, it's not as bad as those other sins.* Eventually, through gradual regression, the devil can put us back into the same slavery from which God delivered us.

A. Governments May Forget Their History

The Egyptians had not always oppressed the Hebrews. In fact, Joseph once held a position of authority in their government; he was second only to Pharaoh himself. However, governments may forget their history (Exodus 1:8). The Egyptians did not remember God's miraculous provision through Joseph's supernatural ability to interpret Pharaoh's dreams. They did not remember how the God of the Hebrews had provided for them for seven years through Joseph's exceptional God-given ability to manage and administrate. And then, because they forgot previous blessings, they committed egregious sins.

What are the "spiritual thermometers" in your life that help indicate the spiritual atmosphere you are in?

As Christians we must not forget the blessings God has poured out on us in the past. When seasoned Christians fall into sin, it is mainly because they have forgotten or discounted the many miracles and blessings God has given them in the past. How can someone who is filled with the Holy Spirit and baptized in Jesus' name backslide? The answer is simple: by slowly and gradually forgetting over time.

What indicators signal that the past has been forgotten? These might be changes in someone's personal life or in the world in general.

B. Pharaoh's Daughter Rescued Moses from Death

Fortunately, God saw the Israelites in their distress and had a plan to deliver them (Exodus 2:1-10). Even while Pharaoh was trying to kill all the Hebrew baby boys, God protected many of their children. One of these children was named Moses, whose infancy was exceptional. After his birth, his mother hid him for three months. When she could hide him no longer, she formed a floating basket and sent him down the river. Undoubtedly the basket left her hands with a prayer as she sent her child downstream.

God heard her prayer and demonstrated His saving power. Providentially, the person to save the baby Moses was Pharaoh's

---

INTERNALIZING THE MESSAGE

If you have ever seen an elephant perform in a circus or at a zoo, you might be amazed at the handler's ability to control the massive creature that might be one hundred times heavier than the trainer. The elephant will perform tricks and stunts with complete submission, even though the elephant could easily crush the trainer with one movement. However, the most impressive stunt is probably when the performance is over and the handler walks away. Sometimes the handler ties a small rope around the elephant's ankle and attaches the rope to a small stake in the ground, leaving the elephant for a long period of time. The elephant could easily break the rope or pull up the stake, but often it remains perfectly docile, not aware that freedom is just one choice away.

The reason for this is the similar to the fable of the frog. When the elephant was an infant, the trainers attached large, heavy chains to the baby elephant's ankle so it could not break free. Eventually, the baby elephant stopped resisting. When the elephant gives up, the trainers no longer need the heavy chains but can lead it around with a small rope, no matter how large the elephant grows.

The brutal attacks of the enemy are designed to wear us down over time. They are designed to cause us to lose hope and give in to the lie that we are not strong enough to resist. The devil would like us to believe that the only option is bondage. In truth, we are not strong enough to break free based on our own strength alone. However, when we have Christ living inside of us, we become like the massive elephant, and the heavy chains that bound us become like weak ropes. We can now live a life free from sin and bondage. However, if we allow the tricks of the devil to deceive us into thinking we are still weak and powerless, we might still allow ourselves to remain in spiritual slavery.

Do not be like the frog who is comfortable in the boiling water, and do not be like the massive elephant being led around by a small rope. Receive Jesus Christ and claim your liberty in Him today.

Prayer Focus
Lead the group in prayer and consider the following topics of focus:
• Pray for God to help you to know what spiritual atmosphere you are in and if He wants you to continue therein.
• Ask God to help you be and do what He wants you to as you grow stronger in your faith.

INTERNALIZING THE MESSAGE

The end of each lesson will offer a final call to action to apply the lesson's content. The goal of each lesson is not just to share biblical information, but to show what must be done with the information, challenging students to apply God's Word to their lives. You are encouraged to use the Prayer Focus to end the lesson with a time of consecration.

LEGEND

The following icons and boxes are used to aid leaders in navigating the content.

Contains a suggested discussion question

Gives direction regarding a media callout that is available

SG Signals the information can be used in a Small Group setting.

V Shows a video component is available to help illustrate the lesson information.

I Indicates an image is available to help illustrate the lesson information.

WHAT IT IS

Every leader should have tools to help the vital mission of ensuring spiritual growth for your church. My Growth Toolkit is a full-service web-based portal to empower leaders in the teaching and leadership ministry of the church. It features growth tracking, record keeping, and management tools for groups or classes along with training materials and attendance tracking for the entire church. This solution enables the church and leadership to stay more connected and helps foster spiritual growth.

My Growth Toolkit offers a full array of resources to help lead your group effectively including:

Admin Dashboard:
- Easily view and track attendance of members and guests
- Monitor the spiritual health of your church with strategic assessments
- Track conversion metrics (i.e., number of baptisms, Holy Ghost filled, etc.)

Group Leader Dashboard:
- Easily access digital curriculum resources
- Provide training for group leaders and staff
- Monitor effectiveness of teachers and group leaders with individual assessments
- Track attendance for groups

Additional Resources:
- Child Check-in technology to improve security
- My Growth area for members that includes daily devotionals, daily Bible reading, spiritual growth assessments, and much more
- Apostolic Study Bible digital access

Visit **www.mygrowthtoolkit.com** for more information and to access any digital resources of God's Word for Life you have purchased.

PODCAST

The God's Word for Life Podcast presents portions of Scripture with fresh insight and urges adults to think deeply about how the Bible impacts their lives. Each week episodes will encourage listeners to engage with God's Word through reflection and prayer, further develop their personal relationship with Jesus Christ, and live out God's Word in their lives.

CONNECT ON SOCIAL MEDIA

 @GodsWordforLife   @GodsWordforLife   @GWFLife

DIGITAL RESOURCE KIT

The Adult Resource Kit offers a wide array of materials to help expand the impact of each lesson. From videos that inspire discussion to social media tools to help encourage adults to join your group or class, this kit provides tools to help leaders grow their group and make teaching time more effective. Some resources include:

A Video to Accompany Each Lesson to Prompt Discussion or Further Thought

Small Group Teaching Outlines and Participant Guides

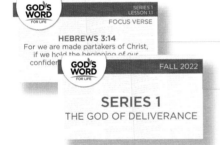

A Powerpoint to Accompany Each Lesson

NEW

Lesson Leaves and a Printable Version of the Scripture Text

NEW

Social Media Graphics, Tips, and Sample Posting Calendar

DAILY DEVOTIONAL GUIDE

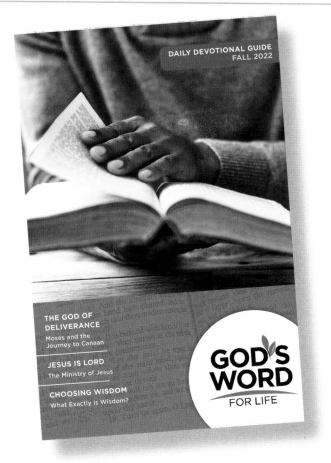

Becoming lifelong Apostolic disciples takes more investment than just an hour on Sunday or Wednesday. Now you can dig into God's Word every day. This guide gives an overview of the biblical text presented in the Lesson Guide each week and is then divided into smaller portions for daily study. Each day offers brief insight about the Bible passage, a devotion that challenges readers to apply Scripture, and then space to reflect and pray over the principles presented.

GOD'S WORD FOR FAMILIES

God's Word for Families is a wholly Apostolic discipleship tool designed to help your entire family grow in relationship to God and each other. By exploring a biblical passage from Sunday to Saturday, daily ten-minute activities use a variety of learning styles to engage family members to hear God's voice. Tap in to God's plan for your family by committing to daily discipleship with *God's Word for Families*.

Weekly Overview:

- Sunday — Intrtoduction to the Bible Passage
- Monday — "Why?"
- Tuesday — Analytic Learning
- Wednesday — Worship
- Thursday — Real-life Application
- Friday — Discussion
- Saturday — Family Project

DISCIPLES COME IN ALL AGES

God's Word for Life is more than just a resource for seasoned saints like you; it is a discipleship program to help every member of the church, no matter how young or old, become a lifelong follower of Jesus Christ. With the teaching materials for children aligned to follow the same Bible passage as the adults each week, everyone in the church can grow together in united focus on God's Word.

MATERIALS FOR CHILDREN'S CLASSES

Activity Pages, Leader Guides, and Resource Kits are available for interactive classes based on multiple learning styles:

Little Learners
Ages 2-3

Kindergarten
Ages 4-5

Early Elementary
Grades 1-3

Late Elementary
Grades 4-6

Children's Church
Ages 4-12

www.GodsWordForLife.faith

ENGAGE YOUR YOUTH WITH GOD'S WORD

Your investment in an Apostolic resource like this book reflects your commitment to spiritual growth. You can expand that investment to also empower youth and young adults to become lifelong Apostolic disciples.

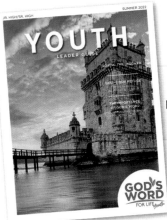

Leader Guide

Everything a teacher needs to lead students in an engaging class

Daily Devotional Guide

A game-changing tool to lead students into Scripture each day of the week

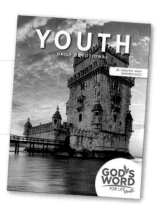

Resource Kit

Special features including social media aids and a supplement for ministering to students with special needs

www.GodsWordForLife.faith

GOD'S WORD

FOR LIFE

ADULT LESSON GUIDE
FALL 2022

TABLE OF CONTENTS

*AN indicates All Nations Sunday.

SERIES 1: THE GOD OF DELIVERANCE

1.1

SLAVES CAN BE DELIVERED

FOCUS VERSE
Hebrews 3:14
For we are made partakers of Christ, if we hold the beginning of our confidence stedfast unto the end.

LESSON TEXT
Exodus 2:1–10;
Hebrews 3:1–19

TRUTH ABOUT GOD
God circumvents efforts that seek to keep us enslaved.

TRUTH FOR MY LIFE
I will act on God's provision of deliverance.

Series Overview:

This series, "The God of Deliverance," will follow the Israelites on their journey out of slavery in Egypt to the building of the Tabernacle in the wilderness. We will watch as Moses grows up in the palace of Pharaoh and have a closeup view of the plagues that ultimately led to the Israelites' freedom. We will follow them through the Red Sea to the mountain where they received the commandments, and we will end up watching the glory of the Lord fill the Tabernacle. This series will show us a God who delivers and allow each of us to experience that deliverance in our own lives.

SG TEACHING OUTLINE

Icebreaker: Have you ever repeated a story you just knew was true only to discover it was not? Describe what happened.

Lesson Connection: Share the Lesson Connection.

I. THE HEBREWS WERE SLAVES IN EGYPT
    » *What are the "spiritual thermometers" in your life that help indicate the spiritual atmosphere you are in?*

    A. Governments May Forget Their History
        » *What indicators signal that the past has been forgotten? These might be changes in someone's personal life or in the world in general.*

    B. Pharaoh's Daughter Rescued Moses from Death

    C. Discovering God's Unstoppable Plan for My Deliverance V
        » *What are some testimonies of God's deliverance in your life and others' lives?*

II. ANOTHER DELIVERER LIKE MOSES

    A. Moses Was a Type of the Messiah, Jesus Christ

    B. I Will Choose Grace and Truth
        » *How would you tell a friend or coworker about God's grace and truth?*

III. OLD COVENANT VERSUS NEW COVENANT

    A. The New Covenant Accomplished What the Old Covenant Only Symbolized
        » *What did you see and understand better after you received the Holy Spirit that you could not understand before?*

    B. I Will Believe in Jesus and Experience Deliverance from Sin

Internalizing the Message I

Prayer Focus
Lead the group in prayer and consider the following topics of focus:
- Pray for God to help you to know what spiritual atmosphere you are in and if He wants you to continue therein.
- Ask God to help you be and do what He wants you to as you grow stronger in your faith.

LESSON CONNECTION

On March 22, 2018, an ordinary family said goodbye to an extraordinary man. He wasn't just extraordinary because he had reached the age of 107. He wasn't even extraordinary simply because he had served in government for over twenty-five years or because he'd won a chess tournament at age ninety-nine. Johan van Hulst was remarkable because he saved over six hundred Jewish children from Nazi genocide.

In 1940 van Hulst had been appointed deputy principal of the Reformed Teacher Training College, a seminary in Amsterdam, as World War II swept across Europe. Van Hulst's first contributions included helping convert the college into a shelter for Dutch teachers in danger for refusing to sign the oath of loyalty to Germany. By 1942 van Hulst began an even more radical means of rescuing Jews in the Netherlands.

Nazis used a theater across the street from the college as a deportation center for Jewish families. As part of the process, children were separated from their parents and sent to a crèche (a nursery) next door. The nursery shared a back garden with the college, and van Hulst seized the opportunity to step in and save the children.

By secretly coordinating operations with nursery workers, van Hulst and his colleagues helped smuggle children out of the city. These courageous individuals canvassed potential adoptive families who could take the endangered children into their homes without detection. Then partnering nursery workers covertly removed the names of the children from the Nazi's registry.

Van Hulst and the network of secret deliverers then arranged for the children to be hidden in containers such as laundry baskets and sacks. Deliverers would time their clandestine mission for when a tram passed, blocking the view of Nazi guards so another resistance worker could ride away with the hidden child. The rescued toddlers would live out the rest of the war in hiding.

The covert deliverance efforts lasted until 1943 when the nursery was closed and its Jewish director was sent to the death camp at Auschwitz. Van Hulst continued to help other Jews in danger until he was forced to go into hiding just three weeks before the liberation. On March 8, 1972, Yad Vashem (the World Holocaust Remembrance Center) recognized Johan van Hulst as Righteous Among the Nations (an honor to describe non-Jews who risked their lives to save Jews from genocide).

In an age when most North Americans enjoy relative safety, it may be difficult to understand the depths of van Hulst's sacrifice. Yet we can acknowledge with appreciation the high cost of deliverance and the glorious freedom his efforts purchased for at least six hundred children.

BIBLE LESSON

I. THE HEBREWS WERE SLAVES IN EGYPT

The children of Israel were in a position they never saw coming. It happened slowly over time as evil forces exerted more and more power in their lives. Through time and circumstance, the enemy slowly took away their rights. By the time the Israelites realized what had happened to them, they were entrenched in bondage. Hope seemed a million miles away.

These events are a perfect example of how Satan draws many people into spiritual slavery, and especially how believers can backslide. The devil tries to chip away at our conscience and eliminate small disciplines in our lives. We begin to think, *Maybe this aspect of godly living isn't important or this small sin surely won't hurt me that badly; after all, it's not as bad as those other sins.* Eventually, through gradual regression, the devil can put us back into the same slavery from which God delivered us.

> What are the "spiritual thermometers" in your life that help indicate the spiritual atmosphere you are in?

A. Governments May Forget Their History

The Egyptians had not always oppressed the Hebrews. In fact, Joseph once held a position of authority in their government; he was second only to Pharaoh himself. However, governments may forget their history (Exodus 1:8). The Egyptians did not remember God's miraculous provision through Joseph's supernatural ability to interpret Pharaoh's dreams. They did not remember how the God of the Hebrews had provided for them for seven years through Joseph's exceptional God-given ability to manage and administrate. And then, because they forgot previous blessings, they committed egregious sins.

As Christians we must not forget the blessings God has poured out on us in the past. When seasoned Christians fall into sin, it is mainly because they have forgotten or discounted the many miracles and blessings God has given them in the past. How can someone who is filled with the Holy Spirit and baptized in Jesus' name backslide? The answer is simple: by slowly and gradually forgetting over time.

> What indicators signal that the past has been forgotten? These might be changes in someone's personal life or in the world in general.

B. Pharaoh's Daughter Rescued Moses from Death

Fortunately, God saw the Israelites in their distress and had a plan to deliver them (Exodus 2:1–10). Even while Pharaoh was trying to kill all the Hebrew baby boys, God protected many of their children. One of these children was named Moses, whose infancy was exceptional. After his birth, his mother hid him for three months. When she could hide him no longer, she formed a floating basket and sent him down the river. Undoubtedly the basket left her hands with a prayer as she sent her child downstream.

God heard her prayer and demonstrated His saving power. Providentially, the person to save the baby Moses was Pharaoh's daughter. When she came down to the river to bathe, she saw the child and immediately had compassion on him. As she swaddled the baby, Moses' sister ran from the bushes and offered to find a Hebrew woman to nurse and raise the child. Of course, Moses' sister went right back to their mother. Even though Pharaoh tried to have all the Hebrew babies killed, Moses was raised by his own mother with the protection of the Egyptian government.

C. Discovering God's Unstoppable Plan for My Deliverance

Few, if any, of us have experienced literal slavery, but many of us have experienced spiritual, emotional, or psychological slavery. Many have experienced trauma, either by circumstances of life or by the wickedness of humanity, that has left them tortured by doubt and fear. Others have committed such great sin that has left them overwhelmed by guilt and self-condemnation. However, no matter the size or cause of the spiritual bondage, our God can deliver us. There are probably many testimonies in this very room of God's miraculous deliverance from a wide variety of situations. The same God who delivered the Israelites and who delivered our elders and leaders can deliver us as well.

Teacher Option: *A supplemental video is available in the Resource Kit.* [V]

What are some testimonies of God's deliverance in your life and others' lives?

II. ANOTHER DELIVERER LIKE MOSES

After Moses' providential protection in the river as a baby (Exodus 2), he grew up and fled from the household of Pharaoh after killing an Egyptian. Moses then lived in Midian where he received his formal calling to deliver the Hebrews from their slavery in Egypt (Exodus 3). He returned to Egypt where the miraculous work of God delivered the Hebrews from their bondage through ten supernatural plagues (Exodus 11–12).

After the Hebrews were delivered, God gave them the Law—a series of commandments for them to follow. This was not just because God wanted to have control over them. Rather, the Law was given to keep the Israelites in healthy relationship with God and prevent them from falling back into slavery ever again. While giving them these commandments, the Lord also gave them a prophecy of another deliverer like Moses. (See Deuteronomy 18:15–19.)

A. Moses Was a Type of the Messiah, Jesus Christ

Even though Moses was used by God to deliver the Hebrews, God knew in His divine foreknowledge that this was not the last time the Israelites would need to be delivered. Since God exists outside of space and time, He understood that Israel would continue to sin, turn to false gods, and fall into slavery. Moses was a precursor and type of the ultimate deliverer who would deliver all people for all time. Of course, this deliverer would be Jesus Christ.

In Acts 3:22–26, Peter preached a sermon confirming that Jesus Christ was indeed the Prophet foretold in Deuteronomy 18:15–19. However, the deliverance Jesus offered through His death on the cross was greater than anything Moses ever did. This is why we no longer look to the law of Moses for salvation. Jesus offered a more complete salvation; therefore, we are no longer bound by the Law.

The writer of John's gospel phrased it like this: "For the law was given by Moses, but grace and truth came by Jesus Christ" (John 1:17). The Law was not sufficient to keep us out of slavery like the "grace and truth" of Jesus Christ. The grace Jesus offers is unmerited favor. Although we deserve slavery, God has given us an opportunity to receive freedom. Truth refers to reality and fact. We can only experience ultimate truth in Jesus Christ. Biblically, truth is not an abstract concept, but the person of Jesus (John 14:6).

B. I Will Choose Grace and Truth

Both the truth and grace that Jesus Christ offers are freely available to us. The problem is not availability but our willingness to accept what Jesus is freely offering. In the familiar fable of a frog who sits passively while water gradually heats to a boil, the frog always has an opportunity to jump out. However, a frog that is comfortable where it is might not choose that freedom. Instead, it may slowly perish. The frog is only one choice away from life, freedom, and salvation.

Similarly, we are only one choice away from salvation. We can choose today to receive the grace and truth that Christ is offering. We can repent of our sins, submit to baptism in the name of Jesus, and receive the gift of the Holy Ghost with the sign of speaking in other tongues. By choosing salvation, we are choosing to receive the unmerited favor and blessings of the Lord (grace) and to live an overcoming life in the higher reality that God desires for us (truth).

How would you tell a friend or coworker about God's grace and truth?

III. OLD COVENANT VERSUS NEW COVENANT

Sometimes when Christians speak of the experiences in the Old Testament versus the New Testament, we speak in terms of the Old Covenant versus the New Covenant. Both were established by God and were appropriate for the time when they were given.

However, the Old Covenant was never intended to be permanent. Paul wrote that the Law was a "schoolmaster" to keep us until Christ came (Galatians 3:24). When Christ died and rose again, He established the New Covenant. Under the Old Covenant, many sacrifices had to be made for all kinds of different problems. Under the New Covenant, Christ sacrificed Himself "once for all" (Hebrews 10:10). His singular sacrifice was efficacious enough to cover all sins for all time. We are still living under that New Covenant and the effects of Jesus' eternally atoning sacrifice.

A. The New Covenant Accomplished What the Old Covenant Only Symbolized

The Old Covenant was never the end goal. The writer of Hebrews made it clear: the Law was a "shadow of good things to come, and not the very image of the things" (Hebrews 10:1). The Law could never make people perfect. Instead, when the children of God regularly came forward to make sacrifices, their sins were rolled forward year after year, waiting for the ultimate sacrifice that could only come through the Messiah.

Ironically, when people still try to live by the Mosaic law, they submit themselves once again to slavery. Paul said when people only live by the Old Testament, it is as if they are living with a veil draped over their hearts (II Corinthians 3:14–15).

Thankfully, the veil over one's heart does not have to be permanent. When sincere people turn their hearts over to the Lord, "the vail shall be taken away. Now the Lord is that Spirit: and where the Spirit of the Lord is, there is liberty" (II Corinthians 3:16–17). When we receive the Holy Spirit that was poured out on the Day of Pentecost, we can experience the full liberty Christ desires for us.

What did you see and understand better after you received the Holy Spirit that you could not understand before?

B. I Will Believe in Jesus and Experience Deliverance from Sin

The Pharisee Nicodemus was well versed in the law of Moses. When he came to Jesus secretly by night, he recognized immediately that Jesus was "a teacher come from God" (John 3:2). However, Jesus was more than just a special teacher; He was the Messiah. Jesus answered a question Nicodemus never asked and told him, "Except a man be born again . . . of water and of the Spirit, he cannot enter into the kingdom of God" (John 3:3, 5). For all his knowledge and training, Nicodemus could not understand what Jesus was saying. Could there really be freedom from the constraints of the Law, which they had followed rigorously for thousands of years? Could there really be hope for the Messiah at this point in history?

Nicodemus seemed genuinely curious, so Jesus revealed to Nicodemus a part of His nature in the now-famous John 3:16–17. "For God so loved the world, that he gave his only begotten Son, that whosoever believeth in him should not perish, but have everlasting life. For God sent not his Son into the world to condemn the world; but that the world through him might be saved." Jesus had not come to bring death. Jesus had not come to condemn. Jesus had not come to keep people in slavery. Jesus had come to bring freedom and life.

Each one of us has an opportunity today to choose Jesus and the life and freedom He offers. No longer must we be slaves to our situations. We can respond today and start the journey to receive all God desires for us. However, the impetus is on us to respond. God is a gentleman and will not force His grace and truth on anyone. He will wait patiently for us to choose Him. Let us not delay; let us choose Him now while we have the chance.

INTERNALIZING THE MESSAGE

A supplemental image is available in the Resource Kit. (I)

If you have ever seen an elephant perform in a circus or at a zoo, you might be amazed at the handler's ability to control the massive creature that might be one hundred times heavier than the trainer. The elephant will perform tricks and stunts with complete submission, even though the elephant could easily crush the trainer with one movement. However, the most impressive stunt is probably when the performance is over and the handler walks away. Sometimes the handler ties a small rope around the elephant's ankle and attaches the rope to a small stake in the ground, leaving the elephant for a long period of time. The elephant could easily break the rope or pull up the stake, but often it remains perfectly docile, not aware that freedom is just one choice away.

The reason for this is the similar to the fable of the frog. When the elephant was an infant, the trainers attached large, heavy chains to the baby elephant's ankle so it could not break free. Eventually, the baby elephant stopped resisting. When the elephant gives up, the trainers no longer need the heavy chains but can lead it around with a small rope, no matter how large the elephant grows.

The brutal attacks of the enemy are designed to wear us down over time. They are designed to cause us to lose hope and give in to the lie that we are not strong enough to resist. The devil would like us to believe that the only option is bondage. In truth, we are not strong enough to break free based on our own strength alone. However, when we have Christ living inside of us, we become like the massive elephant, and the heavy chains that bound us become like weak ropes. We can now live a life free from sin and bondage. However, if we allow the tricks of the devil to deceive us into thinking we are still weak and powerless, we might still allow ourselves to remain in spiritual slavery.

Do not be like the frog who is comfortable in the boiling water, and do not be like the massive elephant being led around by a small rope. Receive Jesus Christ and claim your liberty in Him today.

Prayer Focus
Lead the group in prayer and consider the following topics of focus:
- Pray for God to help you to know what spiritual atmosphere you are in and if He wants you to continue therein.
- Ask God to help you be and do what He wants you to as you grow stronger in your faith.

1.2

LEAVING SLAVERY

FOCUS VERSES
Exodus 15:1–2
¹ Then sang Moses and the children of Israel this song unto the LORD, and spake, saying, I will sing unto the LORD, for he hath triumphed gloriously: the horse and his rider hath he thrown into the sea. ² The LORD is my strength and song, and he is become my salvation: he is my God, and I will prepare him an habitation; my father's God, and I will exalt him.

LESSON TEXT
Exodus 7:1–7; 12:11–17, 50–51; 14:26–31; 15:1–2

TRUTH ABOUT GOD
The Lord is more powerful than things holding us in bondage.

TRUTH FOR MY LIFE
I will celebrate my deliverance from being a slave to sin.

Thinking about Last Week:

Have students refer to their Daily Devotional Guide to answer the following questions:
1. What most affected you as you read through the the Lesson Text and Biblical Insights?
2. How did it shape your prayers and thoughts throughout the week?
3. Do you feel you grew closer to the Lord this past week? Why or why not?

(SG) TEACHING OUTLINE

Icebreaker: Have you ever had to make a difficult move (e.g., a new home, a new job)? Explain what made it difficult.

Lesson Connection: Share the Lesson Connection.

I.   THE PLAGUES EXPOSED EGYPT'S FALSE GODS (I)
    » *What are some of the false gods this world serves today?*

   A. The Plagues Made the Lord Known to Egypt

   B. I Will Fear and Believe the Lord
       » *What does the fear of God look like in your life?* (V)

II. THE LORD MADE A DISTINCTION BETWEEN ISRAEL AND EGYPT
    » *What are some of the major distinctions between the people of God and the world?*

   A. Effects of the Plagues

   B. The Blood of the Lamb Protected Those Who Applied It

   C. I Will Apply the Blood of the Lamb to My Life
       » *What do you think about when you think of the blood of Christ?*

III. THE PASSOVER COMMEMORATED ISRAEL'S DELIVERANCE

   A. The Lord Spoiled the Egyptians and Destroyed Their Army

   B. I Will Celebrate My Deliverance from Sin
       » *What testimonies of God's deliverance in your life do you share the most?*

Internalizing the Message

Prayer Focus
Lead the group in prayer and consider the following topics of focus:
• Praise God for the testimonies in your life and others.
• Ask God to continue to work miracles to give more people testimonies of His goodness and greatness.

LESSON CONNECTION

Marcus will never forget when he first met Randy. Marcus was teaching Bible school at the time, and he and Randy were in a couple of the same classes. Randy was certainly not a traditional student. He was almost thirty years old, while most of his classmates were teenagers or in their early twenties. His clothes were nice but not expensive. He was quiet and reserved and not the first person to speak up. Academically he was certainly not the best student in class, but he was the hardest worker. He spent countless hours in the library receiving special tutoring just to eke out Cs in his classes, but he was proud of himself just for passing.

When Randy moved to the area to attend college, he began attending the same church Marcus attended. Randy immediately formed a special connection with the pastor. Not long after Randy arrived, the pastor invited him to preach a main service. He stumbled through the Scripture reading; it was clear that reading was not his strong suit. He got lost in his notes and was sometimes hard to follow. However, while few could recall the title of his sermon or the text from which he preached, everyone seems to remember Randy telling the story of his conversion. Tears flowed down his cheeks, his voice began to tremble, but he spoke with confidence and conviction.

"Just a few years ago, I was homeless," Randy shared. "I was pushing shopping carts for a living at a grocery store in a little town in the middle of nowhere. I would spend my days pushing carts in front of the store and my evenings and nights behind the store doing any drug I could get my hands on. All my friends were alcoholics, smokers, and drug addicts. Then one day I was laying in the grass by the store when a man approached me and began to tell me about Jesus. The man told me that I didn't have to live that way anymore, and I could be free from all my addictions. That night he gave me a ride to church. I was so desperate that I went right down to the altar and raised my hands and prayed for deliverance. That night, God filled me with the Holy Ghost and instantly freed me from all my addictions. I never smoked, drank, or did drugs again, and I never had a desire to either. Not only did God set me free, but He shielded me from any withdrawals. God showed me that day He is stronger than any addiction or sin that would try to keep me in bondage. Now, I will never stop telling the story of how God delivered me. He set me free, and He can set you free too."

BIBLE LESSON

I. THE PLAGUES EXPOSED EGYPT'S FALSE GODS

Teacher Option: *A supplemental image is available in the Resource Kit.* **I**

God delivered Israel out of Egypt with signs and wonders no one could deny. Through His servant Moses, God sent ten plagues upon Egypt. The first plague turned the Nile River into blood, which destroyed their primary water source and killed all the fish (Exodus 7:14-24). Not to be outdone, the Egyptian magicians used dark magic to also turn water into blood. The same thing happened with the second plague (Exodus 8:1-15). At Moses' command, an overabundance of frogs invaded Egypt with such force that the filthy creatures could be found in every bedroom and kitchen cabinet in Egypt. Once again, the Egyptian magicians used dark magic to conjure up even more frogs. The Egyptians were determined to prove that their gods were stronger.

However, the third plague was different (Exodus 8:16-19). Moses struck the ground, and the dust of the air became gnats that tormented every human and animal in Egypt. The Egyptian magicians tried as they might to replicate this plague, but they could not. Just three rounds into the battle, the God of the Israelites had already proven He was superior. By the sixth plague, the magicians could not even stand on their feet. By the eighth plague, all the servants of Pharaoh were actively begging Pharaoh to let Moses and the Israelites go. They realized how much more powerful the God of Moses was over all their pagan gods.

Through the ten plagues, God demonstrated how weak and false these Egyptian gods were. For every plague, the Egyptians had a corresponding deity that failed to perform when the Egyptians needed it most. When God sent swarms of flies as the fourth plague, He established the inadequacy of Khepri, the Egyptian god of creation who had the head of an insect. When God sent hail as the seventh plague, He proved that Nut, the Egyptian goddess of the sky, was unable to protect them. When God sent the ninth plague, darkness, He demonstrated the falsehood of Ra, the Egyptian god of the sun, one of the oldest and most important Egyptian deities.

In modern times, few people serve literal idols of wood and stone. However, many still worship at the altars of money, career, fame, or other worldly standards of success. God has no problem proving any of these gods as weak and insufficient. If we will allow Him to, God can demonstrate Himself as the only God worth serving.

What are some of the false gods this world serves today?

A. The Plagues Made the Lord Known to Egypt

God used the plagues to demonstrate Himself as real and powerful in the lives of the Egyptians. The ten plagues also helped make God known to the Israelites. Truthfully, the Israelites had not been living in the freedom God desired for them. The plagues on Egypt revealed to the Hebrews that God was still on their side and fighting for them, even during their darkest hour. The plagues reminded them that God was still in control and working for their deliverance. God sent Moses to remind them of God's message. Today, God has given us pastors, preachers, and other spiritual leaders to guide us and remind of God's power and plan for our lives.

B. I Will Fear and Believe the Lord

At any point, the Hebrews could have chosen not to believe God and remain in slavery. On the other hand, the Egyptians could have repented and humbled themselves before God, and the plagues would have ceased. Thankfully, Exodus 14:31 records that the Israelites "saw that great work which the LORD did upon the Egyptians: and the people feared the LORD, and believed the LORD, and his servant Moses." This type of fear does not mean they were scared or anxious about what God might do. In this context, to fear God means to revere and respect God with a sense of awe and wonderment, recognizing His great power and sovereignty over the world and our lives.

What does the fear of God look like in your life?

II. THE LORD MADE A DISTINCTION BETWEEN ISRAEL AND EGYPT

Teacher Option: A supplemental video is available in the Resource Kit. **V**

Later during the ten plagues, only the oppressive Egyptians were affected because God made a distinction between His people and their enemies. Plague after plague, God shielded the Israelites, their land, and their possessions from the effects. The Egyptians got weaker and weaker while God's children grew stronger and stronger. God powerfully demonstrated His justice by rightly judging the difference between the righteous and the unrighteous.

With this knowledge, we can be confident that the God of the Israelites is actively working on our behalf to free us from sin and bondage with which the enemy would try to oppress us. Even when it seems like the wicked are prevailing, we must remember that God sees the situation perfectly and hears our prayers to Him. He has already made a distinction between His children and the enemy, and He is fighting for us.

What are some of the major distinctions between the people of God and the world?

A. Effects of the Plagues

In the fourth plague, God pronounced through His servant Moses that the land of Goshen—where the Israelites dwelt—would be protected from the plague of flies about to descend on the land (Exodus 8:22-24). While the Egyptians spent the entire plague slapping at flies and watching flies destroy their food supplies, the Israelites did not need to reach for the flyswatter once. In the fifth plague, a grave sickness came upon the Egyptian livestock, devastating them, but the Israelite animals remained safe and healthy. In the seventh plague, God perfectly bisected the sky so that not a single hailstone landed in Goshen, even though neighboring Egypt was pounded by the worst hail their land had ever seen. The ninth plague is especially incredible (Exodus 10:21–29). In Egypt, complete and total darkness engulfed the people, so much so that no one could travel or even see each other. But in Goshen, the normal rising and setting of the sun did not change at all. How could this be? Theoretically, one could have stood on the border between Egypt and Goshen and hopped back and forth between normal sunlight and pitch-black darkness. This miracle only further demonstrated the power of the God of the Israelites.

B. The Blood of the Lamb Protected Those Who Applied It

The tenth and final plague did not affect the Israelites, but God issued a special caveat to this final plague (Exodus 12:12–13). Earlier, the Israelites were automatically protected from the plagues. However, in the tenth plague, God purposed to kill the firstborn of every household, but God gave special instructions for how the Israelites were to protect themselves from this suffering. Each household was commanded to slaughter a lamb and smear the blood on the doorframe of the house. When God would pass through the land to enact the final plague, He would see the blood covering the household and pass over that house. Everyone in the house would be spared.

Of course, the blood of the lamb was a foreshadowing of the blood that another Lamb would shed one day. When John the Baptist first saw Jesus, he cried out, "Behold the Lamb of God, which taketh away the sin of the world" (John 1:29). John understood prophetically that the coming Messiah would be sacrificed, and His blood would provide atonement and protection from eternal death and punishment.

C. I Will Apply the Blood of the Lamb to My Life

The blood Jesus, the ultimate Lamb, shed on Calvary is still efficacious to this day. When we apply Jesus' blood to our lives, we too can experience freedom, protection, and deliverance. John said we are to submit to God and "walk in the light," and then the blood of Jesus Christ will cleanse us from sin (I John 1:7). Paul wrote that in Christ "we have redemption through his blood, the forgiveness of sins, according to the riches of his grace" (Ephesians 1:7). Peter wrote that believers have been "redeemed" by "the precious blood of Christ, as of a lamb without blemish and without spot" (I Peter 1:18–19).

Just as the Israelites applied the blood to the doorposts of their houses, so the New Testament believers applied the blood of Jesus to their souls when they repented, were buried in baptism, and received the Holy Spirit. We also now have the chance to apply the blood of Jesus to our lives. Since the death of Christ was "once for all" (Hebrews 10:10), we must believe that His blood is still effective to this day. We can still apply His blood to our lives and experience redemption, cleansing, and deliverance.

What do you think about when you think of the blood of Christ?

21

III. THE PASSOVER COMMEMORATED ISRAEL'S DELIVERANCE

At the same time God gave the Israelites instructions to protect themselves during the Passover, He also gave them instructions to make the remembrance of the event an annual celebration. In Exodus 12:14, God instructed them to make this day "a memorial." The Passover would be a time to feast and celebrate, but also to worship and honor God. To this day, devout Jews still celebrate Passover to collectively remember God's divine deliverance and protection.

A. The Lord Spoiled the Egyptians and Destroyed Their Army

On the Israelite's way out of Egypt, God added another blessing on top of their deliverance. The Egyptians were so weak from the plagues that God allowed the Hebrews to plunder the Egyptians on their way out of town. They took precious metals, jewelry, and clothing. Whatever they wanted from the Egyptians, the Hebrews simply asked, and the Egyptians gave it to them (Exodus 12:35–36).

When the Israelites reached the Red Sea, some of them thought God's divine favor they had experienced until this point was about to cease. The Red Sea was too wide and treacherous to cross with so many people, and the Egyptian army was hot on their trail. However, God was not done delivering His children. Moses lifted his staff and the Red Sea parted, revealing a path straight across the sea with a wall of water on either side (Exodus 14:26). Miraculously, the Israelites crossed on dry ground. When the Egyptians attempted to pursue them, Moses lifted his hand and the water returned, destroying the entire Egyptian army.

God had not brought the Israelites out of Egypt just to allow them to perish at the Red Sea. Similarly, God has not delivered us from our sins and transgressions to allow us to spiritually perish when we encounter various trials. God would not start us on a path unless He planned on walking with us every step of the way.

B. I Will Celebrate My Deliverance from Sin

When the Israelites were truly free from the Egyptians, Exodus 15 records a song that Moses and the children of Israel sang in worship to God. In this song, they sang about God's destruction of the Egyptians in the Red Sea.

What testimonies of God's deliverance in your life do you share the most?

Just like the Israelites sang this song in Exodus 15 and celebrated their deliverance annually with the Passover celebration, we should also regularly celebrate the fact that we have been saved. Even if we don't have a formal feast, we should make a point to share our testimony as often as possible. By doing so, we memorialize the monumental change God has wrought in our lives. When we share our testimonies, we encourage others and strengthen ourselves by keeping God's delivering power at the forefront of our minds.

INTERNALIZING THE MESSAGE

Randy's sermon at the beginning of this lesson was not the last one he would ever preach. Randy did not graduate from Bible school, but shortly after he arrived there, he received his ministry license and was asked to pastor a church near where he was saved. He moved back home and took over a church of only five people, who were renting a tiny storefront that could only seat a dozen or so people. Randy did not care how big the church was, and he knew the church could not afford to pay him. He just wanted to tell people about the same God who delivered him from his addictions and spiritual bondage all those years ago.

A few years passed, and Marcus and his wife were planning on traveling overseas on a mission trip. When Randy heard about this, he invited them to minister at his church so they could be a support. When Marcus walked into the church, he was flabbergasted. The church of five people had grown to almost a hundred. The church now rented three storefronts in a strip mall. They were trying to buy the entire plaza. When Randy and his wife treated Marcus and his wife to a meal afterward, Randy handed Marcus one of the largest checks he had ever received up to that point to help fund their missions trip.

Marcus sat in that small-town buffet and stared at Randy in amazement. Marcus began to gush at how well the church was doing. Randy was as humble as ever and redirected all the praise and glory back to God. "I have to ask," Marcus said. "What was your secret to growing this church? Did you use any special tools or programs?"

Randy smiled. His eyes brimmed with tears as he began to speak. "Do you remember my testimony I told all those years ago at Bible school? Well, my pastor told me that I just needed to keep on telling that story. He told me that the world needed to hear about the saving and delivering power of Jesus Christ. When I came to pastor this church, I just kept telling people about how God saved me. Sometimes I even post pictures on social media and on the screen at church of myself before I was saved. When people see those photos and hear those stories, they realize there is hope for them too. Now almost all the people in my church are former drug addicts and alcoholics. I cannot tell you how many people God has delivered from addictions, either instantaneously or over time. And every time I see another soul set free, it reminds me: I have to keep telling people about a God who can deliver."

Prayer Focus

Lead the group in prayer and consider the following topics of focus:
- Praise God for the testimonies in your life and others.
- Ask God to continue to work miracles to give more people testimonies of His goodness and greatness.

SERIES 1: THE GOD OF DELIVERANCE

1.3

THE TEN COMMANDMENTS

FOCUS VERSE
Romans 16:26
But now is made manifest, and by the scriptures of the prophets, according to the commandment of the everlasting God, made known to all nations for the obedience of faith.

LESSON TEXT
Exodus 20:1-17; Matthew 22:37-40; Romans 16:25-27

TRUTH ABOUT GOD
God loves us enough to create safeguards for our good.

TRUTH FOR MY LIFE
I will follow the commands of Scripture and experience the spiritual protection they provide.

Thinking about Last Week:

Have students refer to their Daily Devotional Guide to answer the following questions:
1. What most affected you as you read through the the Lesson Text and the Biblical Insights?
2. How did it shape your prayers and thoughts throughout the week?
3. Do you feel you grew closer to the Lord this past week? Why or why not?

SG TEACHING OUTLINE

Icebreaker: Do you find you are naturally a rule follower, or do you tend to march to the beat of your own drum?

Lesson Connection: Share the Lesson Connection. [I]

I. TWO VERSIONS OF THE TEN COMMANDMENTS

> *Think back to when you first learned about the Ten Commandments. Which one stood out to you most? Which is hardest for you to follow?*

A. The Most Significant Difference

B. The Ten Commandments and the First and Second Commandments [V]

C. The Relationship between Faith and the Ten Commandments

> *When you think of faith versus Law, what do you think of? How can we walk by faith on a daily basis instead of living legalistically?*

D. Believing in Jesus and Obeying the Gospel

II. LOVE GOD

> *Think about these four aspects of completely loving God: heart, soul, mind, and strength. What are some examples of loving God in each of those aspects of your life? For you, which aspect is easiest to love God? Which is the hardest?*

A. The First Four Commandments

B. Loving God and Finding Spiritual Protection

III. LOVE YOUR NEIGHBOR

> *How do you respond in love to people who are not kind to you in return?*

A. The Last Six Commandments

B. Loving My Neighbor and Finding Spiritual Protection

> *Think about examples of evangelizing, performing acts of service, speaking uplifting words, and being a peacemaker. How are these ways in which we love our neighbors?*

Internalizing the Message

Prayer Focus
Lead the group in prayer and consider the following topics of focus:
• Thank God for His Word that shows us how to live pleasing to Him.
• Ask God for help in following His commands to love Him and love others.

LESSON CONNECTION

A supplemental image is available in the Resource Kit. (I)

Between 2017 and 2019, John and Jen were excited to spend ten months in the South Pacific as AIM (Associate in Missions) workers in the country of Vanuatu. They served under Peter and Robyn Gration, veteran missionaries who previously ministered in the Solomon Islands and Papua New Guinea. John and Jen were excited for the opportunity to serve the mission work and to learn from the missionaries' wise and experienced leadership.

One Friday evening in Vanuatu, the missionaries invited the younger couple to their house for homemade pizza and fellowship. The Grations began to regale them with stories of their mission ministry around the South Pacific. They told stories of protection from sickness and disease. They spoke about working with cannibals and children of cannibals in Papua New Guinea. They recalled the many sacrifices of Western comfort they voluntarily gave up in order to reach the wonderful inhabitants of the South Pacific with the gospel. John and Jen sat in wonder, amazed at the privilege to hear such great stories of faith firsthand, while eating some of the best homemade pizza on the planet.

They were full of questions for these veterans of the faith. At one point John asked if they had ever feared for their safety or if they would have rather stayed and pastored in a Westernized country closer to family, with modern medicine and conveniences. Missionary Peter Gration did not have to think for long. He responded, "One thing I have discovered is you are always safer in the will of God than anywhere else. When you follow God's will and His commandments, there is nowhere else that could possibly be safer. Yes, we could have pastored in a Westernized country in a safe suburb, but that wouldn't have been God's will. We would have been in more spiritual and physical danger there because we were outside of God's plan for our lives. So when you are in God's will and following His commandments, it doesn't matter if you're in the most remote island or even a war-torn, oppressive country; you will always be safer in God's will than anywhere else in the world."

BIBLE LESSON

I. TWO VERSIONS OF THE TEN COMMANDMENTS

Often we hear about the "Ten Commandments." In reality, God gave them many more than ten. There are 613 distinct commandments throughout the entire Law. However, the Ten Commandments are significant because they are the first ten listed after Moses came down off Mount Sinai. These Ten Commandments are still godly guidelines all believers should follow.

Think back to when you first learned about the Ten Commandments. Which one stood out to you most? Which is hardest for you to follow?

The Ten Commandments are recorded twice in the Old Testament law. They are recorded first in Exodus 20:1–17. The second time the Ten Commandments are listed is in Deuteronomy 5:5–22. The Book of Deuteronomy contains a recounting and review of the laws and teachings in Exodus, Leviticus, and Numbers. The name Deuteronomy literally means "second law."

A. The Most Significant Difference: Exodus Connects the Sabbath with Creation; Deuteronomy Connects It with Israel's Deliverance from Egypt

Although these two accounts of the Ten Commandments are virtually identical, there is one important, complementary difference between the two of them. Both versions list the fourth commandment as a directive to "remember the sabbath day, to keep it holy" (Exodus 20:8). (See also Deuteronomy 5:12.) The Sabbath was the day the Israelites rested from their labor to focus on their relationship with God. God wanted to make sure the Israelites were resting regularly to spend time with their God and remember that He was their ultimate provider.

In Exodus, Israel was to remember the Sabbath because that was the example God gave at Creation. God created the world in six days and rested the seventh. If God Himself rested, who are we to think we can outwork God?

In Deuteronomy, the Israelites were told to spend the Sabbath thinking about their deliverance out of the land of Egypt. By resting on the Sabbath, the Israelites could remember the conditions from which God delivered them. The Sabbath is also an opportunity to remember that we cannot deliver ourselves by our own efforts, no matter how hard we work, just as the Israelites could not work hard enough to free themselves from Egypt.

B. The Ten Commandments and the First and Second Commandments

Teacher Option: *A supplemental video is available in the Resource Kit.* **V**

The Ten Commandments, just ten of the larger 613, caused a lot of questions on how exactly the Law should be followed. In fact, by the time Jesus showed up, several different religious sects had differing interpretations on how the various commandments should be followed. When Jesus walked the earth, many sought to challenge Him on His knowledge of the Law, not knowing He was the one who wrote it. A group called the Pharisees were some of the most confrontational. One of them, a lawyer, challenged Jesus one day and asked Him, "Master, which is the great commandment in the law?" (Matthew 22:36).

Jesus' answer stunned them. Jesus replied, "Thou shalt love the Lord thy God with all thy heart, and with all thy soul, and with all thy mind. This is the first and great commandment. And the second is like unto it, Thou shalt love thy neighbour as thyself. On these two commandments hang all the law and the prophets" (Matthew 22:37–40).

The first great commandment to which Jesus referred was from the *Shema* in Deuteronomy 6:4-5. The second is from a more obscure passage in Leviticus 19:18. Jesus said that every prophecy and commandment in the Old Testament depended on these two commandments: love God and love your neighbor. Together they have been called the "joint love commandments."

The first four of the Ten Commandments all have to do with how we love God; the remaining six all demonstrate ways in which we love our neighbor. In fact, some would argue that the overwhelming majority of the remaining 603 commandments have to do with loving one's neighbor (since they mostly address civil procedures), how to treat foreigners, and how to settle disputes. Since Jesus said the Law and Prophets rested on these two commandments, all of the Old Testament either teaches us how to love God or how to love our neighbor. When we seek to love God and love our neighbor, we will fulfill the Law. (See Galatians 5:14.)

C. The Relationship between Faith and the Ten Commandments

Some find it difficult to understand the relationship between faith and the Ten Commandments. However, the Law was never designed to save the Israelites. Paul wrote that no one could be "justified by the works of the law, but by the faith of Jesus Christ, even we have believed in Jesus Christ, that we might be justified by the faith of Christ, and not by the works of the law: for by the works of the law shall no flesh be justified" (Galatians 2:16). Paul also wrote, "For therein is the righteousness of God revealed from faith to faith: as it is written, The just shall live by faith" (Romans 1:17).

Living by faith is not a New Testament idea. The well-known phrase "the just shall live by faith" that appears in Romans 1:17, Galatians 3:11, and Hebrews 10:38 is actually a quote from Habakkuk 2:4—an Old Testament book written by the prophet Habakkuk. It is evident that the Law was never designed to be followed as an end-all to salvation, but as a guideline to teach the Israelites how to live by faith.

When you think of faith versus Law, what do you think of? How can we walk by faith on a daily basis instead of living legalistically?

D. Believing in Jesus and Obeying the Gospel

The Old Testament was not designed to be permanent. Paul wrote, "Wherefore the law was our schoolmaster to bring us unto Christ, that we might be justified by faith. But after that faith is come, we are no longer under a schoolmaster" (Galatians 3:24-25). In another place, Paul said that the "scriptures of the prophets" brought us to the place where all people of every nation could know "the obedience of faith" (Romans 16:26). Faith and obedience go hand in hand. It is impossible to say one has faith without following the commands of Scripture and the words Jesus spoke.

II. LOVE GOD

Jesus said the first great commandment was to "love the Lord thy God with all thy heart, and with all thy soul, and with all thy mind" (Matthew 22:37). The Book of Mark adds the phrase "and with all thy strength" (Mark 12:30). Basically, we are to love God with everything we have within us. These four elements—heart, soul, mind, and strength—give us a good picture of how complete our devotion must be to God.

A. The First Four Commandments

Think about these four aspects of completely loving God: heart, soul, mind, and strength. What are some examples of loving God in each of those aspects of your life? For you, which aspect is easiest to love God? Which is the hardest?

The first four of the Ten Commandments teach us an important aspect of how we are to love God. The first command forbade the Israelites from having any other god before Jehovah (Exodus 20:3). The second command is related to the first: the Israelites were not to make any images or idols to serve and worship in place of Jehovah (Exodus 20:4-6). Today the "gods" that come between us and the one true God might not be physical idols of marble or precious metals; sometimes our contemporary idols are work, money, or an individual who distracts us from serving God completely.

The third commandment cautioned the Israelites not to "take the name of the LORD thy God in vain" (Exodus 20:7). Many have correctly interpreted this as a directive not to use God's name flippantly or blasphemously as a byword or a curse, but the concept also entails much more than this. We also should not misuse God's name with things that are not holy or consistent with God's nature. When someone proclaims the name of God over things that are clearly sinful and unrighteous to justify them, that is another form of using God's name in vain.

The fourth commandment was already mentioned extensively above. The Sabbath day must be kept regularly as a time to reflect and commune with God, free from the distractions of this life. This time of rest causes us to grow closer to Him week by week.

B. Loving God and Finding Spiritual Protection

The commandments to love God are not for God's benefit only; rather, all of the commandments—including the first four—are for our benefit. When we prioritize loving God, we discover the peace, rest, and comfort He desires for us. Even more than this, we will find spiritual protection and deliverance when we submit in obedience to God. As the Gration missionary family said, "You are always safer in the will of God and following His commands."

III.   LOVE YOUR NEIGHBOR

The second great commandment Jesus said was to "love thy neighbour as thyself" (Matthew 22:39). This directive is especially difficult because of the added phrase "as thyself." In other words, it is not enough to simply love others; we must love them as much as we love our own selves.Of the two great commandments Jesus referenced, this second one might be hardest to follow. While God is perfect and holy and righteous, people are not. It seems easier to love a perfect God who loves us back and desires good things for us. It is much harder to love imperfect, flawed people, who might horribly wound and harm us. This is why the phrase "as thyself" is so important. If we expect to receive love, mercy, grace, and forgiveness from others, we must freely give that to others as well.

How do you respond in love to people who are not kind to you in return?

A. The Last Six Commandments

Each of the last six commandments within the Ten Commandments falls under the category of "love thy neighbor." For this, Thou shalt not commit adultery, Thou shalt not kill, Thou shalt not steal, Thou shalt not bear false witness, Thou shalt not covet; and if there be any other commandment, it is briefly comprehended in this saying, namely, Thou shalt love thy neighbour as thyself."

The fifth commandment calls God's people to honor their father and mother. For some who have had abusive or unloving parents, this can be hard to comprehend. However, the love and honor we are called to give our parents is not dependent on their treatment of us. This does not mean we allow ourselves to be abused or continually taken advantage of. (In situations of abuse, seek counsel from the appropriate authorities.) However, the point in this passage is to love and honor parents.

Obviously, it is difficult to commit murder or cheat on one's spouse while loving the person we are sinning against. Stealing, lying, and being envious are also not conducive to loving one's neighbor properly. While stealing and telling lies seem like obvious offenses, covetousness seems less severe. But envy is dangerous because of its connections to resentment, dissatisfaction, frustration, and anger.

Think about examples of evangelizing, performing acts of service, speaking uplifting words, and being a peacemaker. How are these ways in which we love our neighbors?

B. Loving My Neighbor and Finding Spiritual Protection

Just like loving God offers safety and protection for the Christian, so does loving one's neighbor. If love is our primary motivation in how we treat one another, we will experience healthier and more wholesome relationships. We can better assess all our actions toward others if we measure whether or not we are acting out of love. As Paul said, "Love worketh no ill to his neighbour: therefore love is the fulfilling of the law" (Romans 13:10).

INTERNALIZING THE MESSAGE

Living in the small country of Vanuatu taught John and Jen much about the important connection between the joint love commandments to love God and love their neighbor. When they sat down around a fire with friends to eat new and unique foods they had never heard of before, they were loving God and loving their neighbors. When they visited the marketplace or visited the homes of the locals to fellowship, they were loving God and loving their neighbors. When they visited the local hospital to pray for the child of one of the saints in the church, they were loving God and loving their neighbors. When they spent the Sabbath day relaxing with church members, eating plantains and mangoes and reflecting on the goodness of God, they were loving God and loving their neighbors.

The longer this young couple worked, the more they realized how these two commandments—love God and love your neighbor—could not be separated. We love God by loving our neighbors. The two commandments are like two sides of the same coin. When we honor God, we find the strength to love our neighbors like we should. When we love our neighbors, we honor God by demonstrating the transformative work He has performed in our lives.

This does not mean that living out the joint love commandments is always easy, nor that we always perform them with perfection. All of us have experienced people who are hard to love. These are typically the people who do not treat us nicely no matter how kind we are to them. Sometimes they are friends and family members who betrayed us even though we did nothing to deserve such poor treatment. In these situations the love of God inside of us is tested. We can keep coming back to these joint love commandments to evaluate how we are doing. Loving God and loving our neighbors cannot be perfected in a day but can be continually practiced over time. Let us all seek to learn new, meaningful ways every day to love God and love our neighbors.

Prayer Focus
Lead the group in prayer and consider the following topics of focus:
- Thank God for His Word that shows us how to live pleasing to Him.
- Ask God for help in following His commands to love Him and love others.

SERIES 1: THE GOD OF DELIVERANCE

1.4

FILLED WITH GOD'S GLORY

FOCUS VERSES
Exodus 40:34–35
³⁴ Then a cloud covered the tent of the congregation, and the glory of the LORD filled the tabernacle.
³⁵ And Moses was not able to enter into the tent of the congregation, because the cloud abode thereon, and the glory of the LORD filled the tabernacle.

LESSON TEXT
Exodus 35:30–36:7; 40:33–38; Hebrews 9:6–14, 23–28

TRUTH ABOUT GOD
The Holy Spirit dwells in believers who are the Temple of God.

TRUTH FOR MY LIFE
I will let the glory of the Lord fill my life.

Thinking about Last Week:

Have students refer to their Daily Devotional Guide to answer the following questions:
1. What most affected you as you read through the Lesson Text and the Biblical Insights?
2. How did it shape your prayers and thoughts throughout the week?
3. Do you feel you grew closer to the Lord this past week? Why or why not?

SG TEACHING OUTLINE

Icebreaker: If you could add anything to our existing church building, what would it be?

Lesson Connection: Share the Lesson Connection.

I.   THE TABERNACLE WAS BUILT BY SPIRITUALLY GIFTED MEN I

   A.   Bezaleel, Aholiab, and Other Artisans

   B.   I Will Do What God Enables Me to Do

     » *In what areas has God gifted you that you will use for His glory? In what other areas would you like to grow and learn?*

II. THE TABERNACLE WAS SYMBOLIC

   A.   Pointing to Covenant

     » *What things are easier under the New Covenant? What things might be harder?*

   B.   I Will Embrace the New Covenant

     » *How can we perform each of the three above elements every day? Give practical examples of each.*

III. THE TABERNACLE WAS FINISHED

   A.   The Glory of the Lord

     » *Maybe you don't see a physical glory cloud, but what signs do you look for from day to day to remind yourself that God's presence dwells within you?*

   B.   I Will Let the Glory of the Lord Fill My Life V

     » *What daily choices can we make to ensure we actively dwell in Christ and allow Him to dwell in us every day?*

Internalizing the Message

Prayer Focus
Lead the group in prayer and consider the following topics of focus:
• Thank God for the gifts He has given you and the church family.
• Pray for God to use you for His glory.
• Ask God to show all of us what gifts we are able to use for Him.

LESSON CONNECTION

When Johnnie was a child, the church his father pastored was growing rapidly. The average-sized building was quickly becoming too small to fit everyone. What a wonderful problem to have! The children's and youth departments were growing the fastest, quickly outgrowing the few classrooms in the church building. The pastor had a vision to expand. The church had a large property with room to build another structure behind the existing one. With faith in his heart, he poured out his vision to the church and began to raise funds. They needed a larger space to accommodate the influx of souls God was going to send.

As the church sacrificially gave, the time to build came. Many of the congregants worked as professional laborers. The majority worked in agriculture, operating heavy machinery; some were plumbers; others were electricians; many of the saints were simply strong, solid workers. Left and right, God began to place burdens for the new building on the hearts of the congregation. Some volunteered to lay the metal roofing. Others volunteered to hang sheetrock. When the carpet arrived, people in the church who worked as professional floorers volunteered to cut and lay the material. As the interior was finished, several volunteers helped decorate. In no time the new building, known forever and always as simply "The Annex," stood tall and proud in the back of the church property. It boasted twelve hundred square feet and multiple large, modern classrooms, ready to receive the first group for children's church.

Before the first group of young people ever had class in the new building, the congregation gathered in the parking lot to formally pray over and dedicate the new facility. The many builders and decorators stood together, glowing with happiness. Each worker could identify the beam, window, electrical outlet, PVC pipe, or sheet of insulation they helped install. Every person who contributed was able to recognize and celebrate the fact that God had called and anointed them for this mission. Aside from the foundation, the rest of the building was 100% built by members of the church volunteering their time.

Their efforts would not be in vain. Within a few years, all children's and youth programs in the church exploded in size. Almost one hundred attendees every Sunday morning were under the age of eighteen, outnumbering even the adult class. The faithful sacrifice of these workers is a perfect example of what can happen when God's people bind together as a unified body to use their unique gifts and talents to advance the kingdom of God.

BIBLE LESSON

I. THE TABERNACLE WAS BUILT BY SPIRITUALLY GIFTED MEN

Teacher Option: *A supplemental image is available in the Resource Kit.* **①**

The building of the Tabernacle is one of the most powerful and symbolic stories in the entire Old Testament. Filled with foreshadowing of things to come, the very materials used to construct the portable building would have implications for millennia. Much of the Tabernacle was constructed of acacia wood—a rough, prickly material—overlaid with precious gold.

In addition to the materials of the building being spiritually significant, the men who built the Tabernacle were also of great importance. The Israelites at that time were a mobile people. They could not simply plant a temple in the ground in an arbitrary spot. Furthermore, in the day and age they lived, contractors and professional building companies were essentially nonexistent. Even if there were a local construction company, many of the inhabitants of the land were hostile toward the Israelites and would not have desired to help them build anything. Hence it was necessary for God to raise up spiritually gifted men from among them to oversee the building of His holy Tabernacle.

A. Bezaleel, Aholiab, and Other Artisans

Before the construction of the Tabernacle could begin, God selected wise and skilled workers to oversee the process. These men were not only talented in their professions; they were anointed by God to do the work of the Kingdom. Two of the men God chose to lead the work were Bezaleel and Aholiab. Their calling is recorded in Exodus 35:30–35.

Bezaleel is the first worker listed. Although it is not certain, the wording of the text seems to indicate he had every skill set Aholiab had, but Bezaleel had even more. Bezaleel could cut and set stone and carve wood. Both men had complimentary skill sets and were the perfect choice to lead the work.

However, these men were not just skilled in their specific areas of labor. The Bible also makes a special note that these two men were also granted a God-given ability to teach others how to do this work as well. This is an important lesson for anyone desiring to be in leadership today. When God guides people into leadership roles, He will typically also give them the ability to train others, thereby exponentially increasing their ministry.

Exodus 36:1–7 records that Bezaleel, Aholiab, and all the other skilled artisans were granted wisdom and understanding as well as the skills and abilities to do the work necessary to build the Tabernacle. However, the workers were not the only ones with responsibilities to contribute to the process. All of Israel was called to help the work through giving offerings. Their giving was so generous that eventually the workers reported to Moses that they had way more than was needed to complete the work of the Tabernacle. What a wonderful problem to have! We should pray that every church, including ours, receives such a burden to give offerings freely and without compulsion until every need is more than filled.

B. I Will Do What God Enables Me to Do

This story provides an excellent analogy for the way every church should operate in terms of supporting and contributing to the work of the church. Some are called to senior leadership, like Moses. Just like God gave Moses to be Israel's God-called spiritual leader, God has given us a pastor to lead and oversee the work of His church. God has also granted other leaders to oversee specific sections of the church, like Bezaleel and Aholiab did. These men could be seen as analogous to department leaders, like the youth pastor, Sunday school director, or outreach coordinator. God has also provided workers just like the many skilled laborers without any title who worked under the direction of Moses, Bezaleel, and Aholiab. The church needs many faithful laborers who show up week after week. Even if you do not fall into any of the above categories, this story lets us know that everyone is responsible for giving offerings to support the work of God. Even those who cannot work can give in the offering.

In what areas has God gifted you that you will use for His glory? In what other areas would you like to grow and learn?

We all should pray about how we can contribute in the church. God has given everyone unique abilities, and there is no such thing as too many laborers. God is calling all of us to work in His church in the areas in which He has gifted and called us. Certainly there is some area of ministry where you can labor and help advance the kingdom of God. To be certain, everyone is called to be a giver. If you are not sure what areas you are called to work in, pray and ask God to reveal those things to you. Ask your pastor and church leadership for guidance. God will hear the sincere prayers of those who seek to serve.

II. THE TABERNACLE WAS SYMBOLIC

A. Pointing to Covenant

Every aspect of the Tabernacle and its construction—the materials, the workers, the function and use of the Tabernacle—can teach us important lessons still applicable to life in the church today. The Tabernacle served as an important foreshadowing of Christ and the New Covenant. Christ Himself was the ultimate fulfillment of the Tabernacle. When John recorded that "the Word was made flesh, and dwelt among us" (John 1:14), the imagery is the same as the Tabernacle that dwelt in the central part of the Israelite camp. The original Greek text paints this picture: "the Word became flesh, and did tabernacle among us" (John 1:14, Young's Literal Translation).

The writer of Hebrews used the analogy of the Tabernacle extensively to demonstrate the importance of understanding and embracing the New Covenant in Jesus Christ. One passage records, "But Christ being come an high priest of good things to come, by a greater and more perfect tabernacle, not made with hands, that is to say, not of this building" (Hebrews 9:11). Because Christ's sacrifice was more complete and more perfect than any lamb or dove offered under the Old Covenant, the New Covenant He established was "greater and more perfect."

This second covenant no longer requires physical offerings at a physical tabernacle, but it does require an internal, spiritual connection with God. The Bible records these words of God: "This is the covenant that I will make with them after those days, saith the Lord, I will put my laws into their hearts, and in their minds will I write them; and their sins and iniquities will I remember no more. Now where remission of these is, there is no more offering for sin" (Hebrews 10:16–18).

What things are easier under the New Covenant? What things might be harder?

B. I Will Embrace the New Covenant

After his lengthy explanation of the New Covenant, the writer of Hebrews encouraged his readers, "Let us draw near with a true heart in full assurance of faith. . . . Let us hold fast the profession of our faith without wavering; . . . and let us consider one another to provoke unto love and to good works: not forsaking the assembling of ourselves together, as the manner of some is; but exhorting one another" (Hebrews 10:22–25).

This passage contains three basic exhortations. The first is for us to draw near to God. This includes receiving God into our hearts through repentance, baptism in Jesus' name, and the infilling of the Holy Spirit. The second is for us to remain faithful, without wavering. We must also continue to grow and mature in Christ every day. The third is for us to remember we are part of the body of Christ and to encourage and strengthen one another. We are not just called to be saved alone; we must also work to disciple the lost and build up our fellow believers.

How can we perform each of the three above elements every day? Give practical examples of each.

III. THE TABERNACLE WAS FINISHED

The workers were unified. The materials were gathered. The labor was grueling, but soon the work was finished. The Tabernacle was erected. Its mobile design allowed it to be disassembled and reassembled whenever the Lord instructed the Israelites to move. Finally, the Tabernacle was ready to receive sacrifices. Their place of worship was ready to receive the priests who would minister daily before the Lord. All of Israel had a central focus point, right in the middle of the camp, to focus their eyes and remind themselves where their ultimate protection and provision came from.

A. The Glory of the Lord

After the Tabernacle was finished, a miraculous event occurred that reaffirmed the Lord's blessing over all the work they had done. As Moses and the children of Israel looked on, "a cloud covered the tent of the congregation, and the glory of the LORD filled the tabernacle" (Exodus 40:34). The glory cloud was so thick, Moses could not even enter inside the Tabernacle structure

This supernatural, visible manifestation of God's presence was not a one-time occurrence. In fact, the glory cloud overshadowing the Tabernacle was forevermore an indicator when it was time for them to move. If the glory cloud surrounded the Tabernacle, the Israelites did not move camp; they stayed as long as God's Spirit was in their midst. However, when the cloud lifted, the Israelites packed up camp and left. God's Holy Spirit dictated when and how often they moved.

The glory cloud provides appropriate instruction for how we follow God's Spirit today. When God's holy presence descends and fills our lives, we can be confident we are exactly in the place God wants us to be. However, if we sense the absence of God's glory, we have either moved out of God's will, or it is time for us to move to be in God's will. We must continually seek God's presence and abide wherever His Spirit dwells.

Maybe you don't see a physical glory cloud, but what signs do you look for from day to day to remind yourself that God's presence dwells within you?

Teacher Option: *A supplemental video is available in the Resource Kit.* **V**

B. I Will Let the Glory of the Lord Fill My Life

The Tabernacle provides us another important symbol and foreshadowing. In the New Covenant, God's Spirit no longer dwells in the Ark of the Covenant, in an ornate box surrounded by a physical tent. Now, God's Spirit lives inside of us. Each one of us is an individual "tabernacle" in which the Holy Spirit longs to dwell. This was confirmed by Paul when he asked the question, "Know ye not that your body is the temple of the Holy Ghost which is in you, which ye have of God, and ye are not your own?" (I Corinthians 6:19). The Temple was the permanent, single-site dwelling of God built after the Tabernacle. Now, in an era when tabernacles and temples are no longer required, we are God's holy dwelling place. In Ephesians 2:22, Paul recorded that God has collectively built His church into a "habitation" or "dwelling place" in which He can abide.

However, God will not force His Spirit upon anyone. God has chosen all of us to be tabernacles in which He dwells, but we must choose to allow Him to abide within us. Peter called us to repent and be baptized for the remission of our sins, and God will fill our lives with His Holy Spirit and cleanse us from all unrighteousness. (See Acts 2:38; I John 1:9.) Let us choose every day to allow God's Spirit to "tabernacle" within us.

What daily choices can we make to ensure we actively dwell in Christ and allow Him to dwell in us every day?

INTERNALIZING THE MESSAGE

When Johnnie grew older, he had the opportunity to be a very small part of another church building program. In 2017 and 2018, he and his wife traveled to the South Pacific island country of Vanuatu as Associate in Missions workers. In 2015, just a couple years prior to their arrival, Cyclone Pam tore across the nation and destroyed the flagship church building for the United Pentecostal Church International of Vanuatu. The roof collapsed and the entire structure sustained massive water damage. However, in the midst of the destruction, the missionaries, local ministers, and churchgoers refused to see only the destruction. Instead, they saw opportunity.

The church sat at the base of a large hill on the property the church owned. When the rubble was cleared, the foundation was found to be solid. The local workers drew up some plans to turn the site of the church into an outdoor amphitheater. This would allow far more people to come and experience the presence of God and for their services and music to be heard far beyond the walls of a physical building. By the time Johnnie and Jen arrived in 2017, the majority of the work had been completed. A small portion of their budget was used to renovate some classrooms in the basement below the amphitheater, which are now used for Sunday school and Bible school classrooms.

As Johnnie sat in that massive theater for the first time during their national conference, he thought of the devastating story of Cyclone Pam and the inspirational tale of the new amphitheater rising from the rubble. Now he had a chance to observe faithful saints and ministers from all around the country gathered to the site of the amphitheater to worship God in unity. He stood on the platform and looked over the congregation. They filled the ground floor to maximum capacity, and beyond them, attendees could be seen all the way up the hillside—hundreds and hundreds of precious souls hungry for the gospel of Jesus Christ.

Johnnie could not help but be moved to tears as he reflected on the goodness and blessings of God. The Holy Spirit descended on that conference meeting as people worshiped and praised. It was clear God had chosen that ground as a place to dwell, and no gale force winds or cyclonic destruction could stop God's plan for the nation of Vanuatu. God has chosen His dwelling place—us—and now we can worship Him together.

Prayer Focus
Lead the group in prayer and consider the following topics of focus:
• Thank God for the gifts He has given you and the church family.
• Pray for God to use you for His glory.
• Ask God to show all of us what gifts we are able to use for Him.

SERIES 2: JESUS IS LORD

2.1

A HOUSE DIVIDED

FOCUS VERSE
Mark 3:35
For whosoever shall do the will of God, the same is my brother, and my sister, and mother.

LESSON TEXT
Mark 3:20–35

TRUTH ABOUT GOD
Jesus recast what "family" looks like.

TRUTH FOR MY LIFE
I will be born again and faithfully live for Jesus.

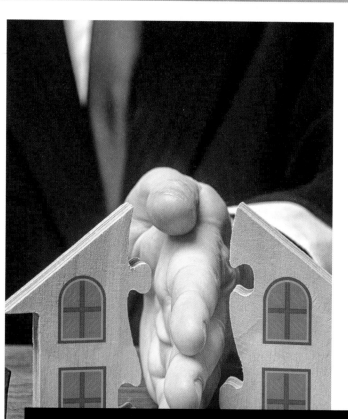

Series Overview:

This series, "Jesus Is Lord," will look closely at the claim that Jesus is the one true God. After hearing His teachings and seeing the miracles He performed, many in Scripture came to express faith in Jesus Christ as the Son of God. They watched Him cast out devils. The disciples were there when He calmed the storm. He delivered the demoniac in Gadara and set a woman free from a twelve-year-long disease. This series will not only remind us of the power of God that was at work in Jesus' day, but it will challenge us to have faith that His power is still available to us today. Truly, Jesus is Lord of all.

SG TEACHING OUTLINE

Icebreaker: What one trait describes your family the best?

Lesson Connection: Share the Lesson Connection.

I. THE FOUNDATION OF GOD'S FAMILY

    A. God's Family Members Share His Traits

    B. I Want to Be a Member of God's Family

       » *In addition to obedience, what are other traits we see in the family of God?*

II. JESUS' FAMILY AND FRIENDS CRITICIZED HIM

    A. Jesus' Response to His Critics

       » *Why do you suppose the scribes and others hated Jesus so much?*

    B. Jesus' Previous Encounter with the Strong Man

    C. I Will Follow Jesus Alone Because He Bound the Strong Man

       » *How does Jesus' victory over temptation give you power over temptation?*

III. THE FOUNDATION OF JESUS' FAMILY

    A. Being in Jesus' Family Is Not Always Popular **V**

       » *Recount a time when following Jesus caused you to be "outside."*

    B. Jesus' Family Members Share His Traits **I**

       » *Which of Jesus' family traits do you wish you had more of in your life?*

    C. I Will Be Born Again and Faithfully Live for Jesus

Internalizing the Message

Prayer Focus
Lead the group in prayer and consider the following topics of focus:
- For us to be bold and unashamed to live for Jesus
- To help others be born again into God's family

LESSON CONNECTION

I t was just past noon. After a remarkable show of masculine strength and valor, a refugee from Canaan known as "Usurper" hit it off with a local's daughter. A servant ran ahead of the freshly minted couple and informed her father back home. But we get to watch the best part.

As you can hear, there is quite a commotion behind the door. Inside, we will see the girl's father somewhat confused and a little excited by the news. Life is suddenly out of sync for him. "A younger daughter cannot marry before the older daughter," he mutters, "but he is my wealthy sister's son." The father scurries around, looking for his hat, quietly singing the word opportunity over and over again as his wife tries to find his coat and put something on the stove.

"They are right outside, sir," says one of the servants.

The father still cannot find his hat, so he licks his fingers, pats down his hair, and reminds himself to erase his silly smile and put on his best serious face. "I am to be feared," he reminds his face.

Here is the moment. Watch the door. The middle-aged man opens the door with calm and grandeur and looks toward the road with a cool, undisturbed gaze. After a few moments of pretense, the calm persona falls to pieces, and he takes off running toward the couple.

The refugee holds out his hand for a handshake. The girl belatedly warns her friend, "Dad's a hugger." But it is too late. Still at full speed, her father ignores the outstretched hand, takes up the stranger in a rapturous embrace, and kisses him on the cheek. "And he's a kisser," she adds.

"Dad, this is Usurper. Usurper, this is my dad."

"Usurper. Interesting name. How did you get it? What brings you to our country? I understand your mother is my sister. It has been a long time since I've seen her. How is she?"

"She's well," says the visitor. "I need to tell you my whole story. It will answer all your questions." The visitor tells a story of deceit, of how he took advantage of his brother and tricked his own invalid father, and how his mother helped him do it all. Then he tells of one recent night as he was seeking refuge, the starlit sky opened, and he saw angels walking up and down a hidden staircase.

The girl's father listens intently. With each twist in the plot, with each elaborate web of deception successfully deployed, the father draws an inch closer and smiles a little more. Soon the girl's father signals that he has heard enough. He is satisfied. He recognizes in Usurper a familiar soul, a fellow schemer. The father puts his hands on the visitor's shoulders, shakes them, and says with the greatest excitement, "Surely thou art my bone and flesh."

BIBLE LESSON

I. THE FOUNDATION OF GOD'S FAMILY

We have just heard a snapshot from the story of Jacob, Rachel, and Laban near the roots of God's human family Israel. Members of a family share certain traits. Some of these traits are transmitted physically. Some traits are learned. Our physical traits often betray our family identity. Someone may associate us with a certain family merely by looking at us or hearing us talk. But learned traits can be equally telling. Honesty or dishonesty can easily identify us with our family.

A. God's Family Members Share His Traits

Scripture frequently enumerates God's traits. He is holy, He is faithful, He is merciful, He is truthful, and so on. Likewise, God's children are holy, faithful, merciful, and truthful, among other things. Jesus once said that children of God would be recognized and identified by the way they make peace (Matthew 5:9). The sons of God, Paul wrote, are distinguished by the fact that they are led by the Spirit. Just as a boy begins to manifest his father's traits in time, those who are born of God will increasingly take on the characteristics of God as they mature.

B. I Want to Be a Member of God's Family

Although God's family was founded on Jacob as the forefather, we are allowed to be part of His family as we obey God. In our day, we are not excluded because we cannot trace our lineage back to one of the tribes of Israel; we are included through obedience. We might even say that obedience is the "DNA" of the kingdom of God, the mechanism by which we grow to resemble God. In Genesis 3, the serpent promised Eve divinity by disobedience. Jesus Christ, however, was exalted to lordship through obedience. (See Philippians 2:9.) We too are elevated by obedience.

In addition to obedience, what other traits do we see in the family of God?

II. JESUS' FAMILY AND FRIENDS CRITICIZED HIM

Mark's Gospel frequently nests stories of Jesus within other stories. Mark 3 provides one of the Gospel's earlier examples of the technique. In verse 20, we see Jesus inside a house teaching His followers, while His mother and brothers were outside, worried that the family's eldest son had lost His mind. In verse 21, they literally complained that He was "beside himself," which to this day is a claim that one has said goodbye to reason and common sense. We have what appears to be a division within the earthly household of the Messiah. Jesus was in a house and thought to be "outside his mind," but in truth, His earthly household was physically outside, and they were outsiders to Jesus' divine mission.

A. Jesus' Response to His Critics

Following Mark's pattern of storytelling, the second story is about a division within a household. The scribes accused Jesus of casting out devils by the power of Beelzebub (Satan). Jesus responded by saying that "a house . . . divided against itself . . . cannot stand" (Mark 3:25). If Satan was casting out his own wicked allies, his "household" had fallen, and his power was at an end.

Jesus' reply exposed the trouble with their accusation. If Satan was giving Jesus the power to bind devils, Satan's kingdom was being destroyed from within, and Jesus was the agent of that destruction. But if Jesus was not using satanic power to cast out devils, Jesus must have been binding devils by a power higher than Satan's, whose kingdom was being destroyed from without. If Jesus was casting out demons by a higher power, that higher power was the Holy Ghost. And if the Holy Ghost was casting out demons, the ruler of the house of demons had been tied up and his house plundered. In either scenario, the rule of the kingdom of Satan was over.

Jesus' rebuttal also exposed their blasphemy. And herein lies the reason for the stern warning Jesus gave for all time. If the scribes accused Jesus of casting out demons by the Spirit of God, they were attributing to God Himself the work of Satan. In their minds, the God of Israel had become the devil to their plans. Jesus called this blasphemy an unforgivable sin.

Jesus manifested what was in men's hearts. The manifestation of God in Christ revealed a long-standing hatred for God harbored in men's hearts, and the scribes' false accusation of Jesus merely confirmed what they thought of God all along. Fallen humanity is at war with God. When the scribes saw evidence of the Spirit's work, they knowingly and willfully sought to kill it. In the end, they would push God off the edge of the world He made and onto the cross—the Son of Man orphaned from the human race.

Why do you suppose the scribes and others hated Jesus so much?

After Jesus' remarks, Mark's narrative shifts back to the story that began the episode. Jesus' followers inside the house told Him that His family would like to meet Him outside. He gestured to the people listening to Him and said that His mother and brothers were those who obey the will of God. If Jesus was casting out devils, His exorcisms were examples of Satan's house being plundered as he sat helplessly by, bound and gagged. Jesus was claiming as His people those who were once members of the devil's household.

B. Jesus' Previous Encounter with the Strong Man

As readers of Mark's Gospel, we are invited to remember that Jesus already had an encounter with the devil. After Jesus defeated the devil in the wilderness, His first words (which are His first words in Mark's Gospel) were: "The time is fulfilled, and the kingdom of God is at hand; repent ye, and believe the gospel" (Mark 1:15). Jesus then went to Capernaum where He called His first disciples, cast demons out of a demoniac, and entered the house of Simon and Andrew. As Jesus was beginning His ministry, Herod bound and imprisoned John the Baptist.

Jesus immediately began preaching John's message and casting out devils as evidence that He was binding the "strong man." These exorcisms at Capernaum carried long-term consequences. People began lauding Jesus as one who taught with authority, unlike the scribes. For this cause, the next time the scribes encountered Jesus, they were ready with a slander even more vicious than earlier. The scribes could not deny that He taught with more authority than they did, so they attempted to attribute His authority to Satan. Their slander was an unwitting admission that they themselves were powerless wherever the devil laid his claim. In attributing Jesus' power to Satan, these political and religious leaders of Israel admitted their impotence against their enemy.

C. I Will Follow Jesus Alone Because He Bound the Strong Man

Jesus' victory over Satan in the wilderness was a cosmic reversal, an undoing of Adam's fatal act of disobedience. Throughout this temptation period, Jesus defined "whoever does the will of God" as a member of God's family. Interestingly but not coincidentally, Jesus did not call any disciples before His wilderness temptation. But He called Peter, James, John, and Andrew immediately afterward. The basis of His holy family is obedience: first His obedience to follow God and then His disciples' obedience to follow Him. We too can embrace our calling as sons and daughters of God, following Him and being free from what would bind us.

How does Jesus' victory over temptation give you power over temptation?

III.   THE FOUNDATION OF JESUS' FAMILY

Mark 3:13–19 chronicles the twelve disciples Jesus appointed to preach the gospel. When God began His mission of redemption, He appointed twelve men from the family of Abraham and gave their descendants a Law to obey. Likewise, by appointing twelve men to accompany Him and preach the gospel, Jesus made a clear statement that He was establishing a family—whose Father is God—for the redemption of the world. The twelve disciples then stood with Jesus while the leaders of Judea accused Him of heinous crimes, while devils confronted Him, and while Jesus' earthly family verbally abused Him. They even attempted to apprehend Him because they viewed Him as "beside Himself," or out of His mind.

Teacher Option: *A supplemental video is available in the Resource Kit.* **V**

A. Being in Jesus' Family Is Not Always Popular

Jesus and His new family appeared to be greatly outnumbered, but Jesus did not seem to mind.

Recount a time when following Jesus caused you to be "outside."

Following Jesus often calls us to join the one others view as "beside Himself." Following Jesus and being part of His family does not always make sense to others watching our lives. To join Him in His house is to go "outside," to leave behind the safety and normality of our social matrix and follow Him. But that is often the call of God to us. He does not call us to understand it or even agree with it, just to follow.

B. Jesus' Family Members Share His Traits

A biological family shares certain unique and fundamental characteristics. These fundamental characteristics are generated by shared genes. A man's telltale head, jawline, or vocal timbre will often show up in his son. Yet other traits are learned, like a father's mannerisms, the way he conveys irritation, clears his throat, or sways his shoulders when he walks. During the son's formative years, he unconsciously assimilates these subtleties from his father and mirrors them until they become his own. But these too are family traits and signs of his father's paternity.

What family traits does a son of God inherit from his Father? Jesus is God's true Son. The fundamental similarity between Jesus and the Father was so striking that Jesus' words were only those the Father had spoken; His actions were only those of His Father. When you saw Jesus, you had seen the Father. This is why Jesus could respond to Philip, "He who has seen Me has seen the Father" (John 14:9, NKJV). Jesus is the "express image of [the Father's] person" (Hebrews 1:3). Jesus taught that He "came down from heaven, not to do mine own will, but the will of him that sent me" (John 6:38). God's Son bears the family traits, and this is true of all God's sons and daughters. While we are not the incarnation of God Almighty like Jesus was, we are called to be His sons and daughters as we are born again into His family.

Which of Jesus' family traits do you wish you had more of in your life?

C. I Will Be Born Again and Faithfully Live for Jesus

This gift was not reserved for those in the Bible alone. We also may be members of God's family. Jesus taught obedience to the will of God is the basis of being part of God's family. (See John 1:12–13.) The will of God is the "midwife," as it were, the catalyst of our birth into this family. The call to obedience is simultaneous with our new birth, beginning with a call to repentance and water baptism in the name of Jesus Christ. The Spirit of God completes the birthing process, whereby we emerge from the world, as an infant emerges from the womb, crying Abba Father—our first cries announcing our new paternity.

After this new birth, the new child of God is no more finished growing into the characteristics of our heavenly Father than newborn babies are done being raised and trained by their mother and father. New children of God begin to take on a new nature, but they need time spent observing their heavenly Father through the life of Christ, learning from Him, practicing His characteristics (His holiness), and obeying His commandments. And in time, this newly born-again son of God will be conformed to the image of God's true Son, Jesus Christ (Romans 8:29).

INTERNALIZING THE MESSAGE

Obedience to the will of God is a lifelong occupation, and our kinship to Jesus is often revealed in the way we face adversity and even death. One man in particular emulated (followed) Jesus so closely that he died like Jesus died. We know him. He is Simon Peter. Jesus told Peter that following Him would mean Peter would be carried where he did not want to go, and there he would stretch forth his hands when he was old. Peter instinctively knew this meant he would be crucified for following his Lord. Peter objected. But one day later in life, he did indeed come to that promised "cross" road.

Like the Good Shepherd who lays down His life for His sheep, Peter, who was asked to feed Jesus' sheep, laid down his life in an act of ultimate obedience. He was carried where he did not want to go—to a cross—and his persecutors stretched forth his hands. By his crucifixion, Peter glorified the Lord. He then possessed the most unmistakable trait of the family of Jesus. Peter joined the one who was "beside Himself," outside the camp, pushed off the edge of the world and onto the cross. In the end, Peter did look quite a bit like his Father.

Prayer Focus
Lead the group in prayer and consider the following topics of focus:
- For us to be bold and unashamed to live for Jesus
- To help others be born again into God's family

2.2

CALMING THE STORM

FOCUS VERSE
I Timothy 3:16
And without controversy great is the mystery of godliness: God was manifest in the flesh, justified in the Spirit, seen of angels, preached unto the Gentiles, believed on in the world, received up into glory.

LESSON TEXT
Psalm 65:5–7; 89:8–9; Mark 4:35–41; I Timothy 3:16

TRUTH ABOUT GOD
Jesus is God manifest in the flesh.

TRUTH FOR MY LIFE
I will put my faith exclusively in Jesus.

Thinking about Last Week:

Have students refer to their Daily Devotional Guide to answer the following questions:

1. What most affected you as you read through the Lesson Text and the Biblical Insights?
2. How did it shape your prayers and thoughts throughout the week?
3. Do you feel you grew closer to the Lord this past week? Why or why not?

(SG) TEACHING OUTLINE

Icebreaker: What is the most frightening storm you have ever lived through?

Lesson Connection: Share the Lesson Connection.

I.   THE DAY JESUS PROVED HIS DEITY
>   *Do you ever have moments of confusion where it's difficult to understand what God is doing? What do you do in those times?*

A.   Even the Wind and Sea Obey Him ⬜I
>   *What would you have done if you were one of the disciples?*

B.   Who Is This Jesus?
>   *Can you describe a prayer God answered that caused you to be in awe of His power?*

C.   I Believe Jesus Is Who He Said He Is ⬜V

II. JESUS' TRUE IDENTITY
>   *In one sentence, describe the Incarnation to someone who has never heard of it.*

A.   Jesus Is God in Flesh

B.   I Will Trust Jesus to Calm My Storms

Internalizing the Message
>   *Are there any God-sized storms in your life that only God can calm? If so, let us ask Him to calm those storms as He calmed the storm upon the sea and the storm within the soul.*

Prayer Focus
Lead the group in prayer and consider the following topics of focus:
• For us to believe Jesus is who He says He is
• For Jesus to calm our storms and calm our fears

LESSON CONNECTION

I t was a pretty full day. By the time dusk was dawning, Jesus was back on the shore with the multitudes. He asked His disciples to take Him over to the other side. As the crowds turned to head home, someone who had seen Jesus' works and heard His words lingered for an interview with Jesus about being a disciple. Perhaps they sat down next to the sea to chat, resting against a piece of driftwood while the quiet waves lapped the stony shore. Sleep, that blessed state, that harbor for tired bodies at evening, must have been heavy on Jesus' mind. You can hear the fatigue in His response. As He watched the last families headed back to their lives and homes and beds, He said to the curious candidate, "The foxes have holes, and the birds of the air have nests; but the Son of man hath not where to lay his head" (Matthew 8:20).

The disciples took Jesus "even as he was in the ship" (Mark 4:36). This means Jesus was sleeping before He was taken into the ship. That entire day had been taken up with Jesus working and serving, but at the end of the day, He no longer worked. He slept. His disciples lifted the collapsed body of the Son of God, whose compassion had driven Him over the edge of consciousness.

The picture is almost maternal, perhaps one of the most tender in all of Scripture. One fisherman called to the others, asking for help, "Help me out. Take His arms. I'll get His feet."

"Don't wake Him up."

"One, two, three. Watch the oars."

"Hold His head. Good. Let's lay Him in the back."

"John, grab the pillow from Dad's boat."

Knee-deep in the Galilee, they shuffled the motionless Nazarene into the boat. Under the gathering clouds, they tenderly laid His head upon the pillow and covered Him. Away they sailed across the darkening waters. Perhaps Jesus slept just because He was unbothered by the storm. But most likely Jesus slept because He was bone-tired. He was so tired that even a tempest could not penetrate His sleep.

BIBLE LESSON

I. THE DAY JESUS PROVED HIS DEITY

Aside from the narrative of the Passion, no account gives so complete an itinerary of a single day in Jesus' life as the Gospels give of the day leading up to Jesus calming the stormy sea. The day was so full that it ended with Jesus falling into an otherworldly sleep on a pillow the disciples laid under His head. This is the only account we have of Jesus sleeping. On that day, needy men and women surrounded Him, touched Him, begged Him, and brought their children to Him. He wrested demons from men's souls, and for His troubles, He was accused of being in league with the devil. He blessed the broken, cleansed a leper, healed Peter's mother-in-law, healed a paralytic, listened to a centurion, and healed the man's servant. Jesus climbed a small mountain and commissioned twelve disciples.

He withstood the withering doubt of His own blood brothers. Before He ever sailed upon the sea that evening, He had already spent the day in the deep—the deep of humanity; a sea of people; waves of disease; the tests of enemies; a thousand hands reaching out to Him, clawing at Him, sapping His body of strength, one desperate request at a time. They pushed and pulled in every direction, straining the furthest limits of human endurance. At one point, the crowds were so dense and drew in so close that Jesus was backed onto the shore of the Galilee, right up to the edge of the water. Out of space and needing to spend time teaching, He had to get into a boat and push off a little from shore to create a little separation between Himself and the multitude so that everyone could hear. After He was done speaking and evening was near, He found that His work was still not done. His disciples were puzzled by His parables, so they asked their wearied Master to teach it again, but this time with detailed commentary.

Do you ever have moments of confusion where it's difficult to understand what God is doing? What do you do in those times?

A. Even the Wind and Sea Obey Him

Before we watch Jesus rise up out of sleep and calm the storm, we should consider the sea carefully. We should not assume that the sea represents to us what it represented to the ancient mind. For ancient Israelites, the sea represented chaos, a place under the dominion of forces hostile to God. Though the sea was ultimately under the sovereignty of God, the Israelites tended to fear the sea and avoid it as much as possible. To some degree, the sea seemed to resist the orderliness of Creation. In the beginning, the sea had to be divided in order for Creation to unfold.

The apocalyptic beast of Revelation is said to rise up out of the sea, as if to indicate the beast is empowered by Satan to bring chaos. When John heard the voice of Christ, John compared Christ's voice to the "voice . . . of many waters" (Revelation 1:15).

After hearing this voice, John fell at Christ's feet "as dead." To convey the idea of the kind of peace that prevails in Heaven, John wrote in apocalyptic symbolism that a sea like glass surrounds God's throne. In other words, there is no chaos or disorder or disharmony where God rules in His fullness.

Teacher Option:
A supplemental image is available in the Resource Kit. Ⓘ

The sea on which Jesus and His disciples sailed was not a figurative sea; it was the Sea of Galilee. This sea is essentially a modest-sized lake. The Jewish people were more willing to sail and fish this body of water. But although the Sea of Galilee is a lake, snow-cooled winds from nearby Mount Hermon frequently roll into the lake and clash with the dry, warmer winds coming from the Jordanian desert. The result is violent windstorms. Fishermen generally knew when and when not to sail. No doubt they had seen the signs, but Jesus asked them to sail. They must have believed they would be okay, since Jesus knew things they did not. But once the storm arose and tossed their small ship around, they thought their moments were numbered.

What would you have done if you were one of the disciples?

One disciple pulled in the sails. Another used buckets to bale the water coming in over the gunwale. Yet others grabbed an oar in hand to try to keep the bow of the boat facing the waves. They shouted, but the thunder and wind and heavy rain drowned them out. In between storms of darkness, such as might have been in the void before the creation of light, strobes of lightning, like the sky's bony fingers, electrified the sea. The white-blue light flashed on panicked faces as they saw a wave mount to the height of a city wall and loom over the boat. With an angry snatch, the jaws of the sea tore an oar from one of the men's hands. The mast of the small ship splintered down the middle. A disciple waited for the next flash of lightning to see how the Master was handling this. He was still asleep, almost comatose. The desperate disciple crawled over the seats and shook Him.

"Master, carest thou not that we perish?" (Mark 4:38).

From somewhere deep in the dreams of God in flesh, Jesus awakened. The disciples saw the lightning etched on the Master's pupils. Jesus lifted His head off the pillow and stood to His feet. The disciples, who had just given up hope of being saved by their own skill, looked back at Jesus as the wind whipped through His hair and pulled at His wet robe. More flashes of light streaked the sky. His mouth shaped the words, "Peace, be still" (Mark 4:39). And it was.

The disciples had seen leprosy retreat from sick bodies and demons leech out of men's souls at just Jesus' command. But who controls the wind? Where is the switch in nature that turns off a storm? And who has access to it? Anyone can tell the wind to be at peace. Three hundred years earlier on a narrow passage of the Mediterranean connecting the continents of Asia and Europe, Xerxes the son of Darius, emperor of Persia, rebuked the sea. He gave it three hundred lashes and inserted molten swords into the water as punishment for not yielding to his commandment for a smooth voyage. But the wind does not listen, not even to emperors.

Yet on the Sea of Galilee, suddenly the storm ceased. It was not because it had spent its force or someone had prayed an impressive prayer. The storm ceased from three short words from the lips of Jesus. Like a deafening stadium speaker going out in the middle of a song as the singers still try to sing, the storm's small voices now only faintly reached the distant ear. The lightning, thunder, and wind lost their amplitude. Moments earlier, waves threatened the men, but those selfsame waves now tumbled prostrate before the Lord as they cradled the boat in kindness.

B. Who Is This Jesus?

The disciples' eyes turned back to the Master. Their mouths fell agape. It slowly dawned on them that the Christ with them in the boat was far more powerful and fearful than the storm they had just escaped. They had gone from dread to an even greater dread. "What manner of man is this, that even the wind and the sea obey him?" (Mark 4:41).

They knew Jesus was a man. They had just watched Him spend Himself like a man. They had carried His unresponsive body to a pillow and place of slumber. But what kind of man? Psalm 107 in Israel's songbook taught them that God, not a man, calms the sea. What kind of man could do this? No mere man could, but Jesus did. Therefore, Jesus was no mere man. As His followers would soon come to more fully understand, Jesus was the God-man: very man and very God (God incarnate)—Jesus was God in flesh.

Can you describe a prayer God answered that caused you to be in awe of His power?

C. I Believe Jesus Is Who He Said He Is

In our age, some people have a difficult time believing that Jesus was God. Many in our day believe He came as a man. They have no trouble believing Jesus was a carpenter, a rabbi, a prophet, even a miracle worker. But they cannot muster the faith to declare He is God. But in the early Christian era, people tended to have a more difficult time believing Jesus was a man. Many of them believed He was God, and His humanity was just a matter of appearances. But both of these are errors. Gospel accounts such as Mark's take pains to declare that Jesus' humanity was true humanity, and His deity was true deity. We can build a deep relationship with this one true God, knowing He is everything His Word promises.

Teacher Option: *A supplemental video is available in the Resource Kit.* **V**

II. JESUS' TRUE IDENTITY

The disciples did not see God out of character; the Incarnation was God in character. The humanity of Christ did not hide God; it revealed God. When Jesus wept, He was not betraying His "fleshly weakness." The Incarnation gave God a body that was capable of suffering uniquely physical pains, but there are pains that transcend the body. Jesus wept not just because he had physical tears; He wept because God has always wept. When we see the Son of God, we are seeing God at His most authentic, not His least. The flesh of God was not a veil, hiding God's essence. Instead, God's incarnational flesh was a window through which we could see God clearly. God's flesh does not reveal God's weakest side, His best side, or any "side." The Incarnation shows us God's most complete self (Hebrews 1:2).

In one sentence, describe the Incarnation to someone who has never heard of it.

A. Jesus Is God in Flesh

The Incarnation is the beating heart of the Christian faith. We have been entrusted with the apostles' accounts of Jesus. In these accounts, Jesus clearly suffered the weakness of humanity, but He also very clearly worked as only He can. It is interesting that Mark painted Jesus in such human colors in this story—a story when a problem arose that only Deity could solve. It is almost as if the clash of human frailty and divine omnipotence was intentional. But maybe the way Mark framed the calming of the sea with Jesus' human weariness was intended to give the reader a sense of what this event must have been like for the disciples. They had just carried Jesus asleep into the boat, and then they faced a mighty tempest, a power beyond human reckoning. What could the man they just watched collapse do? Yes, He performed many miracles earlier in the day, but prophets long ago had also performed similar miracles. But never had a man held the reins of the wild sea.

B. I Will Trust Jesus to Calm My Storms

We look back on the disciples with awe. How could they miss it? Jesus told them who He was. He even demonstrated through miracles and wonders that He was more than a carpenter, rabbi, or prophet. He was divine. But they did not see it. However, they knew Him as a carpenter. They followed Him as a rabbi. They listened to Him as a prophet. We have the benefit of the cross, an empty grave, and a full upper room to give us more context. However, we too must be careful lest life's illnesses, disappointments, and hardships cloud our view that Jesus really is able to calm all our storms because He is the Creator. When He speaks, the waves and wind He controls must calm. We are safe, whether He calms the storm or He calms our soul. Jesus is who He said He is. Today you can leave encouraged. We can rest in this hope.

INTERNALIZING THE MESSAGE

At the end of the day, there was at least one more sea to calm. Two sets of eyes watched the stormy sea and the strange, miraculous calm. These eyes watched from a sepulchre up on the hills that overlooked that sea. Two wild men, naked and disheveled, shifting from rock to rock, witnessed Holiness bridle the untamed seas. These men watched the ship come to the shore. A legion of devils trembled when Christ set foot on land. They knew Jesus, the Son of the Most High, was coming for them. There was nowhere to run and nowhere to hide. Their time had come.

The demon-haunted men ran and threw themselves at Jesus' feet. The once-powerful devils who stripped their hostages of all dignity and lacerated them were now so weak and deferential, begging Jesus not to torment them. If He did not grant that request for surrender, they begged Him not to send them completely out of the country. They had no question as to what manner of man this was. They knew even more than Jesus' own disciples knew. Jesus was the God-man, more dreadful and terrible than any storm upon a sea, more blessed than any cherub or seraph of Heaven. With a word, Jesus sent them into a herd of swine and set their prisoners free.

Are there any God-sized storms in your life that only God can calm? If so, let us ask Him to calm those storms as He calmed the storm upon the sea and the storm within the soul.

Prayer Focus
Lead the group in prayer and consider the following topics of focus:
• For us to believe Jesus is who He says He is
• For Jesus to calm our storms and calm our fears

SERIES 2: JESUS IS LORD

2.3

GO HOME TO YOUR FRIENDS

FOCUS VERSES
Mark 5:19–20
19 Howbeit Jesus suffered him not, but saith unto him, Go home to thy friends, and tell them how great things the Lord hath done for thee, and hath had compassion on thee. 20 And he departed, and began to publish in Decapolis how great things Jesus had done for him: and all men did marvel.

LESSON TEXT
Mark 5:1–20

TRUTH ABOUT GOD
Jesus is compassionate.

TRUTH FOR MY LIFE
I will tell my friends about Jesus.

Thinking about Last Week:
Have students refer to their Daily Devotional Guide to answer the following questions:
1. What most affected you as you read through the Lesson Text and the Biblical Insights?
2. How did it shape your prayers and thoughts throughout the week?
3. Do you feel you grew closer to the Lord this past week? Why or why not?

SG TEACHING OUTLINE

Icebreaker: What was your favorite bedtime story or nursery rhyme as a child?

Lesson Connection: Share the Lesson Connection.

I.   EVIL SPIRITS KNOW WHO JESUS IS

    A.   Jesus Is the Son of the Most High God

       » *How do you think the disciples reacted when they heard Jesus was going into Gentile territory?*

    B.   All Creation Will Confess That Jesus Christ Is Lord

II. JESUS HAD COMPASSION FOR GENTILES I

    A.   The Plight of the Demoniac

    B.   I Will Have Compassion for the Rejected

       » *Can you think of anyone who may feel rejected to whom you can show the compassion of Jesus Christ?*

III. GO HOME TO YOUR FRIENDS

    A.   Jesus Had Compassion on the Demoniac and Delivered Him

       » *What about God's call on your life makes you unique and uniquely valuable?*

    B.   I Will Tell Others My Story of the Lord's Compassion V

       » *Who needs to hear your testimony? How can you share it with them this week?*

Internalizing the Message

       » *What role do you play in the story of God's redemption in your world?*

Prayer Focus
Lead the group in prayer and consider the following topics of focus:
• For us to have confidence in God's power over evil
• For Jesus to give us compassion for the rejected

LESSON CONNECTION

Created holy and free and in communion with God, the earth and its citizens fell under a Satanic blockade at the Fall (Genesis 3). A dark veil fell over the world. Communication between Heaven and Earth was throttled as Earth became a silent planet. The world's memory of God grew dim, and what it did remember of Him was largely twisted and distorted—mere projections of lost humanity's lust for power and fame onto the screen of the sky. Humans still groped in the dark for God (Job 12:25), but fallen angels channeled this search away from God and offered them beasts to worship, ugly religions, and self-hating, self-harming rituals. Humanity, made in the image of God, languished in the shadows and silence, nearly becoming the beasts they worshiped.

But one day in the heart of the shadowlands, long under the dominion of devils, a man named Abram heard the forgotten voice of God as clear as the day (Genesis 12:1–3). Abram was almost a nobody among the powers of the world. No one really noticed when he left his homeland, but his departure from Ur marked the beginning of a two-thousand-year-long operation in which Heaven worked, often quietly and modestly, to rebel against and subvert the wicked powers of the world and break the Satanic blockade. Satan may have noticed a mighty empire forming, but Israel, the nation born from Abram, was tiny and overlooked. Holy men in Israel were blessed with hearing so sensitive, they could hear the still, small voice of God when others heard only silence. They preached, prophesied, and taught this nation long-lost knowledge of God. These men, usually strange and completely out-of-step with the ways of the world, were called *Nevi'im*, or prophets. They prepared the nation for the day Heaven would launch a full-scale invasion. They called this future day the Day of the Lord.

The prophets did their work behind the scenes while the eyes of the world watched the rise and fall of empires. Somewhere in the course of time, the Satanic realm grew wise to the danger Israel posed to their reign, so all the empires of the world took turns tempting, oppressing, and enslaving Israel. Nevertheless, no power could stop the countdown. Under the careful vigil of the Satanic blockade, the invasion came. While the principalities were nervously watching the rulers of the house of Israel for the one the prophets said would be the mighty Son of God, the invasion started in the womb of a common woman. Bethlehem became the beachhead, God's foothold in the world. A host of angels burst into the sky to announce His arrival (Luke 2).

BIBLE LESSON

I. EVIL SPIRITS KNOW WHO JESUS IS

But the years passed, and the world remained much as it was before. The dark powers kept track of the Son of God, but nothing of great significance seemed to happen. With impunity, they continued their reign of terror, corrupting men and women, afflicting them, and sometimes taking possession of their bodies. But things changed suddenly in the Son of God's thirtieth year. It started when He was baptized by a prophet (Matthew 3:13-17). He then immediately showed up at Satan's earthly headquarters in the desert (Matthew 4:11-11)—as if to deliver a notice of the end of Satan's rule, take down its flag, and hoist the flag of the kingdom of God in its place. The demonic powers knew that the virtual silence between Heaven and Earth was broken, and God's voice was being broadcast to the masses. He was preaching from mountains and teaching by the seaside in parables of the Kingdom.

A. Jesus Is the Son of the Most High God

A massive shudder of fear went through the Satanic kingdom when the Son of God faced down a demon in a synagogue (Luke 4:33-37). The devil had full possession of a man—his grip so firm and complete that he could sit with no fear of losing control over the man at any point, even in a holy place where religious authorities read the Scriptures. Suddenly the devil found himself looking squarely into the Son's eyes. Without warning, he was being effortlessly extracted from the man's life with nowhere to go.

For the first time since the day humanity fell into sin and under Satan's tyrannical rule, the kingdom of darkness was in retreat. Men and women were starting to rebel against the powers of the world. The devil's only recourse was to work with the religious leaders and convince them—irony of ironies—that this messianic figure was actually operating under the power of Satan.

Things got even worse for the demonic rulers of this age. It was one thing to lose influence in the land of the prophets and Abram's descendants, but the most devastating sign of the collapse of Satan's dominion would be the loss of a Gentile in Gentile lands.

How do you think the disciples reacted when they heard Jesus was going into Gentile territory?

B. All Creation Will Confess That Jesus Christ Is Lord

After teaching and healing many in Israel, the Son of God told His followers that it was time to pass over to the other side—to the land of the Gentiles on the other side of the sea (Luke 8:22). The Son was on His way with every intention of humiliating Satan in his stronghold among the Gentiles too. On this trip, the devastation to the devil's kingdom was almost total. Although a storm raged on the sea on which they sailed, Jesus spoke a handful of words to turn the storm into a testimony of His power.

Teacher Option:
A supplemental image is available in the Resource Kit. ❶

II. JESUS HAD COMPASSION FOR GENTILES

In Galilee there were sordid stories of the powers of this world having possession of a human's body, and there were even stories where several demons would control a man at once. But this story seemed to top all other stories. On the other side of the Galilee was a man who served as a military camp for a legion of devils (Matthew 8:28–32). (A legion consists of anywhere from two thousand to five thousand soldiers.) These were not just any soldiers; they were highly skilled, professional soldiers capable of subduing any opposition. This legion of devils dragged this wretched man down to the lowest state a man can experience.

A. The Plight of the Demoniac

Sleep escaped him (he cried out day and night). He lived in nightmares and cut himself severely, possibly to know whether he was even yet alive. He was so completely at the mercy of this expert demon force that he could not answer in his own name. He sought shelter, but not from the rain, the wind, or the elements. No. He lived in tombs as one of the dead, seeking shelter from the living, shelter from the clean. But he was Legion's man, and as an example of his supernatural power, he was able to break metal chains. This was the demonic force—the Satanic SEAL team, if you will—that the Son of God, weary from a full day of work, was coming after. Jesus was going straight for the jugular. The disciples and the crowd would soon see that if the Son of God could dispatch Legion, He could defeat anyone.

B. I Will Have Compassion for the Rejected

Everyone was terrified of this man, but no one could do anything about him. The people in town did not feel safe with him anywhere near their homes. He was too strong for Gadara's strongest men. They tried to bind him with chains, but he snapped the chains like twigs. They tried to tame him, but he was untamable because he was possessed.

The Gadarenes just wanted peace and quiet, but they could not ignore one piercing truth. This man was not an animal; he was a son. He was probably a brother, possibly a father. He needed what we all need: compassion. Let us have compassion on those who feel rejected in our world. Let us look for those who need someone to notice them, to care for them. We may not be able to meet all their needs, but we can smile and greet them. In doing so, we may help restore their humanity. Everyone is created in the image of God.

Can you think of anyone who may feel rejected to whom you can show the compassion of Jesus Christ?

III. GO HOME TO YOUR FRIENDS

When Jesus came to shore, thousands of devils rushed toward Him. They found themselves reluctantly bowing down, as if under the power of a far greater force. They panicked because they knew they only had moments of relative freedom left. Legion cried out with a loud voice, "What have I to do with thee, Jesus, thou Son of the most high God? I adjure thee by God, that thou torment me not" (Mark 5:7). It was an act of pure desperation. Legion was trying in the name of God to cast out God in the flesh.

A. Jesus Had Compassion on the Demoniac and Delivered Him

These devils were not just in the middle of a defeat; they were being routed on three levels. First, they were caught in the embarrassing posture of worshiping a human being like the humans they had been toying with for thousands of years. This human, though, was crowned with glory and honor and dominion. In the Garden of Eden, Adam was given dominion over everything (Genesis 1:26), but he forfeited that dominion when he sinned. Jesus sinlessly wielded that dominion Adam was created to wield.

Second, the demons found themselves disparaging their own leader, Satan, by acknowledging that Jesus is the Son of the Most High God. The figure standing before them was higher than the lord they served. Third, the only source of hope for this demonic force was to retreat into a herd of pigs. How the mighty had fallen!

The narrative betrays the confusion the demon-possessed man wrestled with. In one place he spoke saying "I," "me," and "my." These are all singular pronouns in reference to himself. Then in the very same sentence, he referred to himself in the plural: "My name is Legion, for we are many" (Mark 5:9). It seemed like the chaos and disorder in the Sea of Galilee minutes earlier were also in the possessed man. Satan's kingdom is a kingdom of disorder and confusion.

We may remember from the last lesson that the sea was often thought to be symbolic of chaos and disorder. Perhaps that is one reason the demons asked Jesus to send them into the swine. As soon as He did, they compelled the animals to take them to the sea. They could not abide in a state of God-ordained order. God was there, and He is here to restore the order that He intended. When the man who was possessed was freed, Scripture's next scene shows him sitting with Jesus, clothed and in his right mind (Mark 5:15). When he spoke after being set free, we see order was restored. He spoke as one person.

In Mark's Gospel, being clothed or being naked is sometimes symbolic of one's nearness to or distance from Jesus. Nakedness was associated with disorder, chaos, and isolation. Being clothed was associated with being in fellowship with God and humanity. When the possessed man was far from Jesus, he was naked, but when Jesus reclaimed him, he was clothed.

The man's identity was lost and submerged beneath the identity of the enemy. Our enemy seeks to destroy human identity and the dignity God gave us when He made us in His image. It is easy to sometimes think that an individual becomes more distinct and unique in practicing sin. But in our sinfulness, we are all dreadfully similar. All the sins, crimes, and faults bear a tedious resemblance to one another, the world over. The stories of dictators and tyrants are all mind-numbingly the same. When we sin, we fall into the same patterns and cycles of selfishness, suffering, and despair, and we lose what makes us unique.

What about God's call on your life makes you unique and uniquely valuable?

When Christ comes into our lives, He reestablishes our identity. The sins that once bound us, took away the freedom of our will, and chained us to addictions and destructive behavior no longer have the same power over us. We are free to become more fully ourselves, sons and daughters of God. The apostle Paul spoke of being fully known once we stand face to face with Jesus (I Corinthians 13:12). Our true identity will become fully realized once we are transformed in glory. The apostle John heard the glorified Jesus say that the one who overcomes sin and the world will be given a "new name . . . , which no man knoweth saving he that receiveth it" (Revelation 2:17). Our identity will be so completely unique that we will be given a name that is shared only between ourselves and Jesus.

B. I Will Tell Others My Story of the Lord's Compassion

The newly freed man was so thankful, he offered to follow Jesus from town to town. He wanted to be one of Jesus' disciples. But Jesus refused to allow him to come with Him and His followers. Rather, Jesus commissioned him to go home to tell his friends what the Lord had done for him. Jesus had compassion on the man and expected that compassion would inspire him to testify to his friends and family of the goodness and power of God. While the demonic forces did not allow the man to speak, Jesus commissioned him to speak, but He did not commandeer the man. In other words, the kingdom of the enemy and the kingdom of God are fundamentally different in their regard for human beings.

Teacher Option: *A supplemental video is available in the Resource Kit.* **V**

The man had a very real testimony that God had changed his life and his eternity, and God commissioned him to tell his story to the people who knew him best. No one knows us like our family and friends. And no one needs to hear our testimony like our family and friends. Perhaps God gave you the job you have, not just so you could put food on your table, but perhaps people at your job know who you are now and who you used to be. While they may not be able to figure out what happened to you or how, they need you to testify.

Who needs to hear your testimony? How can you share it with them this week?

Take the witness stand at work or at school or in the teller line and testify to your family and friends what you have seen God do in your life and in others. Nothing testifies more powerfully of the power of God than our testimony. The man from Gadara was one of the first missionaries Jesus ever sent. He did not know theology and had not been in a Sunday school class, but he could tell his story. And he did, and so must we. Today you can be part of God's great mission by sharing your testimony and telling others of God's grace and power.

INTERNALIZING THE MESSAGE

O ur lives are stories. Better yet, we place ourselves in a bigger story that was written before we existed. When we came along, we have become that story's latest edition. This story—the really big story, the story that everyone, including God, angels, and demons take part in—gives us meaning and makes our lives intelligible. The story is the standard by which we judge the rightness or wrongness of our actions.

The story of Jesus we read in the Bible was only the start of the invasion of righteousness into sinfulness. It started in Judea, then Samaria, and now we are bringing that invasion of Heaven to the uttermost parts of the Earth. Christ has empowered and commissioned us to continue the work He initiated. We are rebels against the high rulers of this world. We do not walk the way of the world.

In this story, there is no neutral. We are either for Jesus or against Him. Paul taught that the soldiers in the army of the Lord were once in darkness but are now "children of light" (Ephesians 5:8). When Scripture speaks in terms of children of light or of darkness, it is referring to spiritual warfare—the two sides of a cosmic war. Baptism in the name of Jesus is not merely a symbolic token of the remission of sins. It is spiritual warfare, a clear signal of what side we are on. Baptism means declaring to the principalities that we are now soldiers in the invading force, the rebellion against Satan's rule. Jesus taught us to pray, "Our Father which art in heaven, Hallowed by thy name" (Matthew 6:9). Our loyalty is to Him alone and not to the kingdom of this world. Jesus also told us to pray, "Thy will be done in earth, as it is in heaven" (Matthew 6:10). In other words, just as the rule of God is perfect in Heaven—perfect order, perfect love—we are in the process of making that perfect rule a reality here in this world. The enemy is defeated, but in his long retreat, he still seeks out those whom he might destroy.

It is important that we never lose sight of the role the Apostolic church plays. We must be careful lest we put ourselves into a story of our own making, imagining that it is better to be a hero in our own story than a servant and role player in God's. In the end, there will only be one story, one Hero, and one people of God. One day, God's kingdom will completely subvert the kingdoms of the enemy, and the kingdoms of this world will become the "kingdoms of our Lord, and of his Christ, and he shall reign for ever and ever" (Revelation 11:15).

What role do you play in the story of God's redemption in your world?

Prayer Focus
Lead the group in prayer and consider the following topics of focus:
• For us to have confidence in God's power over evil
• For Jesus to give us compassion for the rejected

AN

IN EVERY NATION

FOCUS VERSE
Acts 10:35
But in every nation he that feareth him, and worketh righteousness, is accepted with him.

LESSON TEXT
Acts 10:34–48; 15:6–17

TRUTH ABOUT GOD
God saves all who come to Him in faith, no matter their ethnicity.

TRUTH FOR MY LIFE
I will love and rejoice with all who are born into the kingdom of God.

Thinking about Last Week:

Have students refer to their Daily Devotional Guide to answer the following questions:
1. What most affected you as you read through the Lesson Text and Biblical Insights?
2. How did it shape your prayers and thoughts throughout the week?
3. Do you feel you grew closer to the Lord this past week? Why or why not?

[SG] TEACHING OUTLINE

Icebreaker: Have you ever had a vision from God? If so, what did it mean?

Lesson Connection: Share the Lesson Connection.

I. PETER'S VISION

    A. Peter's Struggle

      » *Have you ever received clear instructions from God but resisted obeying? What created that struggle within you?*

    B. I Will Obey God's Voice

II. PETER'S MESSAGE

    A. God Shows No Partiality [I]

      » *Peter spoke the will of God but still had to be taught how to live it out. How easy is it to know and speak the will of God without allowing it to penetrate our minds and transform how we live?*

    B. I Will Tell Everyone the Gospel

      » *Who are some of the people God has placed in your life for you to reach with the gospel? What can you do to reach them this week?*

III. PETER'S APPEAL

    A. The Jerusalem Council [V]

      » *In what ways can the Jerusalem Council serve as a template for resolving conflicts among believers?*

    B. I Will Love and Rejoice with All Who Are Born into the Kingdom of God

      » *In what ways could culture potentially impair someone's ability to receive or share the gospel?*

Internalizing the Message

Prayer Focus
Lead the group in prayer and consider the following topics of focus:
- For God to help us love and share the gospel with all people
- For God to help our church be multicultural

LESSON CONNECTION

W e have little insight into how Adam and Eve lived before the Fall. We do know both historically and through contemporary actions how people have lived since the Fall. Humans quickly became tribal. This tribal impulse deepened after Babel. Before long people were scattered geographically and socially. Boundaries were established and barriers to social interaction were created.

The world in which we live is an heir to these actions and decisions. Sin always separates what should be together. However, God desires something different. He came to not only reconcile the world to Himself but also to bring reconciliation between people.

The idea of a society that includes, embraces, and benefits all people is neither a contemporary ideal nor one born out of post-modern thinking, cultural enlightenment, or political correctness. The kingdom of God was designed to personify this ideal.

God's plan has always been to ultimately bless all nations and restore them to Him. In several instances in Genesis, God gave Abraham promises for the Jewish people, culminating with the promise that all the nations of the earth would be blessed through Abraham's seed.

Psalm 147 praises God for building up Jerusalem and bringing the people of Israel together. Verse 20 of the same psalm acknowledges that God had not dealt with any other nation in this way, and no other nation knew the judgments of God like Israel knew. In this context, judgment is to be understood as ordinances or laws. This reflects the place of privilege and relationship Israel enjoyed because of the covenant with God that largely excluded everyone else. Because of the sins of God's people through the Old Testament, the kingdom of God was not the universal body it was prophesied and destined to become.

However, Isaiah 42 brought hope in the midst of their seeming hopelessness. God promised the Messiah would bring forth judgment (laws) to the Gentiles. What was once only available to a select few would one day be available for all. The Messiah, of the seed of Abraham, is the one of whom the writer of Hebrews wrote, "He is the mediator of a better covenant, which was established upon better promises" (Hebrews 8:6). Through Jesus all humanity would be reconciled and welcomed into the kingdom of God.

The lasting portrait of this kingdom is found in Revelation 7:9. "After this I beheld, and, lo, a great multitude, which no man could number, of all nations, and kindreds, and people, and tongues, stood before the throne, and before the Lamb." This is what the people of God are destined to become.

BIBLE LESSON

I. PETER'S VISION

God pushed to open the doors of the church to the Gentile world by giving two devout men a series of visions. In Acts 10, Luke introduced us to Cornelius, a Roman centurion. Luke described him as a generous, God-fearing, and prayerful Gentile. God sent an angel to tell Cornelius his prayers and generosity stood as a memorial before God. Then the angel instructed him to send men to Joppa to invite the apostle Peter to Caesarea. Cornelius was assured Peter would come to Caesarea to tell him what he needed to do to draw closer to God.

God still needed to prepare Peter's heart through another vision. As the Roman delegation neared Joppa, Peter went up onto the rooftop around lunchtime. While there, he fell into a trance and saw a vision of Heaven opening. A sheet appeared to be descending to earth. On the sheet were a variety of animals, reptiles, and birds. Suddenly a voice commanded Peter to get up, kill, and eat these animals. Peter was appalled. He responded, "Not so, Lord; for I have never eaten any thing that is common or unclean" (Acts 10:14). The voice responded, perhaps more sternly, "What God hath cleansed, that call not thou common" (Acts 10:15). This exchange was repeated three times, impressing on Peter the intention and gravity of his vision.

A. Peter's Struggle

Peter was a relentless follower of God. His obedience to God even in the face of persecution is well documented. In Acts 5, Peter was thrown into prison by the high priest and the Sadducees for preaching the gospel. An angel opened the prison doors and commanded Peter to return to the Temple to preach. When the religious authorities learned Peter was preaching again, they confronted him for his disobedience. Under the real threat of death, he responded, "We ought to obey God rather than men" (Acts 5:29).

Yet in Peter's vision, he knew he was speaking to a voice from Heaven. He even acknowledged the voice as "Lord." However, Peter told the Lord that he could not obey His commandment because it was contrary to what he had always done. Peter struggled largely because his customs, culture, and beliefs made him resistant to obeying the voice of God.

Have you ever received clear instructions from God but resisted obeying? What created that struggle within you?

B. I Will Obey God's Voice

We are inundated by voices that may influence our thoughts and actions. Some voices are internal. We all live with the residue of what we may have been exposed to in our past. What we have heard about people of other cultures may have become our own presumptions. Negative experiences possibly tarnish our impression of entire groups of people. Embedded cultural stereotypes might also have some measure of an impact on our outlook of others.

Some voices are external. We live in a time of unprecedented exposure to information and misinformation. Secular and sometimes religious voices have a vested interest in the division and decay of society. The devil has also always used division as a primary tactic. He understands that any division within the church body thwarts its progress, so he will use every avenue available to foster it.

We must be committed to hearing and obeying the voice of God and blocking out every contrary voice. What does God say about my neighbor? How does God see my neighbor? God's will is that none should perish (II Peter 3:9). His will is that His church would reach all people with His gospel. It is central to our purpose.

In each of the Gospels' renderings of what we call the Great Commission, the writers proclaimed that Jesus called them to go to all nations or to all of creation. The New Testament church was designed to fulfill God's timeless will. Peter preached that the Spirit would be poured out on all flesh (Acts 2:17). However, God had to address those barriers and prepare His people (even Peter) to overcome them to begin the process of becoming the church He desired to build. The church today does not address these issues to be culturally or politically correct; we do so in order to fulfill our commission and do the will of our Father.

Ultimately, Peter was obedient to God. As he was still pondering the meaning of his vision, Cornelius's men from Caesarea arrived at his house. The Spirit told Peter that three men had arrived and he should not hesitate to go with them because God sent them. Peter obediently invited them into his home.

The next day the apostle Peter and some of the other believers traveled with Cornelius's delegation to Caesarea. When they arrived, they discovered Cornelius had gathered a large group of family and friends to hear the preacher. Peter acknowledged it was not customary for a Jew to visit a Gentile, but he testified that God had told him not to call any man common or unclean. That included Cornelius and all Gentiles. Cornelius then told Peter about his own vision and how God heard his prayers.

II. PETER'S MESSAGE

A. God Shows No Partiality

God heard the prayer of Cornelius. This surprised Peter somewhat, but when he realized God appeared to Cornelius during his time of prayer and fasting, Peter received a revelation that would shape his ministry for the rest of his life. He said, "Of a truth I perceive that God is no respecter of persons: but in every nation he that feareth him, and worketh righteousness, is accepted with him" (Acts 10:34–35). While that statement may seem obvious,

Teacher Option:
A supplemental image is available in the Resource Kit. **Ⓘ**

In what ways can the Jerusalem Council serve as a template for resolving conflicts among believers?

this was a radical message that defied all conventional wisdom and tradition Peter had ever been taught.

Peter should have realized this in Acts 2 as he declared the plan of God for the New Testament church, but it appears the reality of this universal gospel message pierced all cultural barriers and prejudices Peter had while he stood in the home of a Gentile Roman centurion. Just then Peter understood the eternal, true impact of the words he spoke in Acts 2:39, "For the promise is unto you, and to your children, and to all that are afar off, even as many as the Lord our God shall call." Beyond receiving the Holy Spirit, it is sobering to realize Peter needed additional edification to overcome his prejudicial, traditional, and cultural biases.

Peter spoke the will of God but still had to be taught how to live it out. How easy is it to know and speak the will of God without allowing it to penetrate our minds and transform how we live?

B. I Will Tell the Gospel to Everyone

Sociologists use the term manifest function. It is defined as "the anticipated and intended goals of an action or social structure; the reason something is done." The church has a manifest function, and we cannot afford to substitute it for any unintended functions, no matter how noble they may be. We are called to go into all the world and preach the gospel to all creatures. Like Peter, our mission is to tell the gospel to everyone. The commission of the New Testament church is still our commission. Our unchanging purpose is to glorify God and spread the gospel to all people.

Who are some of the people God has placed in your life for you to reach with the gospel? What can you do to reach them this week?

III. PETER'S APPEAL

A. The Jerusalem Council

Making God's vision for His church a reality was not easy. As more Gentiles were converted, certain cultural frictions manifested. Some of the Jews (known as Judaizers) contended that these converts had to be circumcised and adhere to the law of Moses. Because of their ingrained tradition and culture, it was difficult for them to accept that anyone could enter a covenant with God without observing the Law. Paul and Barnabas fiercely disputed this teaching in the New Testament church. Paul, Barnabas, and others traveled to Jerusalem to resolve this tension with the apostles and elders there.

We sometimes call this meeting the Jerusalem Council or the Apostolic Council. Passionate opinions on both sides quickly made the council contentious. Peter, probably to the surprise of some, began to share his testimony. He reminded them that God had chosen him to preach the gospel to the Gentiles, and God—who knows the heart—confirmed He accepted them by filling them with the Holy Spirit just as He filled the Jews on the Day of Pentecost. Peter's testimony proved God placed no difference between Jews and Gentiles. The Gentiles' salvation was just as complete as the Jews'.

Soon the people were willing to listen to Barnabas and Paul as they testified of the great work God was doing among other Gentiles in Antioch. James followed with their testimony and reminded the council that Peter's testimony agreed with the words of Amos and other prophets. James even quoted God's words through the prophets. "After this I will return, and will build again the tabernacle of David, which is fallen down; and I will build again the ruins thereof, and I will set it up: that the residue of men might seek after the Lord, and all the Gentiles, upon whom my name is called, saith the Lord, who doeth all these things" (Acts 15:16–17).

This inclusive message was not new to the New Testament church. The Jews were well aware of the prophecies that God would include the Gentiles in His plan. They were aware of the words spoken at the birth of the New Testament church in Acts 2. However, they struggled with the practical application when the time came. Thankfully, some believers courageously accepted the plan of God and withstood culture, tradition, and wrong thinking in the church when necessary.

In what ways can the Jerusalem Council serve as a template for resolving conflicts among believers?

Teacher Option: *A supplemental video is available in the Resource Kit.* **V**

B. I Will Love and Rejoice with All Who Are Born into the Kingdom of God

Culture can be a beautiful thing. We can celebrate and appreciate the diversity of our cultures and cultural experiences. However, no culture is universal or timeless. No culture is common to every person at any point in time, and no culture is changeless over time. This creates the possibility for culture to become a barrier that prevents people from truly connecting with each other.

The gospel is the opposite. Whereas culture cannot be universal and timeless, the gospel's very nature is universal and timeless. It must be common to every person anywhere at any time, and it cannot change over time or space. Just as culture can potentially divide, the gospel can unite all humanity. It is imperative that we do not confuse culture and the gospel.

We embrace every culture, but we preach a gospel that is not driven by cultural or traditional influence. The message of the death, burial, and resurrection of Jesus Christ and the new birth available because of it is a message that will work for any and all. As the apostles declared in Acts 15, we need to embrace anyone God embraces and love all who are born into God's kingdom regardless of ethnicity, background, social status, or any other distinction. We have all become fellow heirs of the promises of God.

n what ways could culture potentially impair someone's bility to receive or share the gospel?

INTERNALIZING THE MESSAGE

nity is one of the most fundamental requirements for the New Testament church to become what it is meant to be. Unity has a multi-faceted definition. The obvious root word is unit, which speaks to being single as well as complete. Unity speaks to the state or quality of being both one and whole. The goal of unity is to be one, to be everything we are meant to be, and to have everything we are meant to have.

Unity does not come easily to human nature because it requires selflessness, sacrifice, empathy, and bearing with one another in love. It obviously does not come easily even to those in the church because Paul charged us to endeavor to keep the unity of the Spirit. (See Ephesians 4:3.) Endeavoring means to try hard or to do one's utmost. Unity is hard but worthwhile work.

Paul knew the New Testament church had a lot to overcome. Free and bond, Jews and Gentiles, male and female, even those who formerly persecuted and killed Christians were all coming together to form one glorious body of believers: the church.

In that passage, Paul gave us the basis for our unity. It is all based on the Spirit of God. "Endeavouring to keep the unity of the Spirit in the bond of peace. There is one body, and one Spirit, even as ye are called in one hope of your calling; one Lord, one faith, one baptism, one God and Father of all, who is above all, and through all, and in you all" (Ephesians 4:3-6).

This unity is of the Spirit, and the Spirit makes it possible. It is not a simple unity of our spirits; it is a unity we can never manufacture on our own. Through the Holy Spirit, we can overcome our human nature and any impediments to true unity.

This weekend in churches all over the world, musicians will help lead congregations in worship. Organs, pianos, keyboards, horns, guitars, and other stringed instruments will assemble and be in perfect harmony. This harmony will not be achieved because all the musicians came together and attempted to be tuned to each other. On the contrary, harmony is achieved because all the instruments are tuned to a common standard, a master tuner.

The call of our hour is to have the mind of Christ, be tuned to Him, and not allow any traditional or cultural barriers to jeopardize the harmony of the kingdom of God. As we look to Him and draw near to Him, we will draw near to our brothers and sisters. Because of the Spirit of God that lives in us, we can love and embrace anyone and everyone.

Prayer Focus
Lead the group in prayer and consider the following topics of focus:
- For God to help us love and share the gospel with all people
- For God to help our church be multicultural

2.4

YOUR FAITH HAS MADE YOU WHOLE

FOCUS VERSE
Mark 5:34
And he said unto her, Daughter, thy faith hath made thee whole; go in peace, and be whole of thy plague.

LESSON TEXT
Mark 5:24–34

TRUTH ABOUT GOD
God responds to faith.

TRUTH FOR MY LIFE
Because it is never too late to touch Jesus, I will take my need to Him.

Thinking about Last Week:

Have students refer to their Daily Devotional Guide to answer the following questions:
1. What most affected you as you read through the Lesson Text and the Biblical Insights?
2. How did it shape your prayers and thoughts throughout the week?
3. Do you feel you grew closer to the Lord this past week? Why or why not?

SG TEACHING OUTLINE

Icebreaker: How was life different or the same for you twelve years ago?

Lesson Connection: Share the Lesson Connection.

I. THE WOMAN WITH THE ISSUE OF BLOOD SUFFERED FOR TWELVE YEARS

    A. She Sought Many Cures Without Improvement V

    B. I Will Reject Hopelessness in Favor of Faith

       » *When you feel hopeless or overwhelmed, what do you do?*

II. THE WOMAN DID NOT TOUCH JESUS, BUT SHE TOUCHED HIS CLOTHING

    A. Faith, Not Formulas, Produce Results

    B. She Was Not Deterred Because Jesus Was Busy

       » *Why do we sometimes feel like God is too busy to heal us or help us?*

    C. I Will Trust in God, Not Formulas

       » *Have you ever caught yourself trying to find a formula to cause God to work in your life, or do you simply put your faith in His knowledge and wisdom?*

III. JESUS HEALED THE WOMAN AND GAVE HER PEACE

    A. She Was Made Whole and Inspired Others

       » *If you were Daughter, how do you think Jairus or the disciples might have acted toward you? How do you think Jesus might have acted toward you?*

    B. Because It Is Never Too Late to Touch Jesus, I Will Take My Need to Him

Internalizing the Message I

       » *What is the balance between faith and works? How do we make sure we wait on God while reaching out to Him in faith?*

Prayer Focus

Lead the group in prayer and consider the following topics of focus:

• For us to have faith in Jesus for our need

• For Jesus to give us the courage to reach out to Him in faith

LESSON CONNECTION

"If I could just . . . ," said Daughter, a woman with a twelve-year-old sickness. Daughter paused on the central question of what she would have to do to be well. She made a series of proposals, but it seemed none of them would work out.

"If I could just ask Him to touch me. But He might not want to touch someone like me."

"If I could just ask Him to say a word of healing over me. But He might not even give a hearing to someone like me."

"If I could just touch His hands. But I'd have to get close, and His entourage will keep me away."

"If I could just touch His garment. But to get that close, I'd have to be stronger and more favored than all the worthy people there."

"If I could just touch the hem of His garment. That's it. If I could just touch the hem of His garment."

A little hope stirred in her and steeled her for the severe test of her newfound faith. If she could just touch the hem of His garment, she would be healed.

BIBLE LESSON

I. THE WOMAN WITH THE ISSUE OF BLOOD SUFFERED FOR TWELVE YEARS

This woman is the only woman in the Gospels whom Jesus called Daughter. She was afflicted with a chronic flow of blood from a woman's womb. This condition made life outside of a home almost impossible for women in any culture, but it was especially hard for Jewish women. For the woman, a discharge of blood from the womb over the course of many days meant she was unclean for as long as the discharge continued. While she was unclean, she was considered a potential threat to the sanctity of the Tabernacle or Temple. Therefore, she had to remain at home, and anyone who lived with her or even touched where she sat could also be considered unclean.

A. She Sought Many Cures Without Improvement

There were prescribed cures for her disease if she was willing to pay for them. Each doctor responded about the same way, "I know exactly what to do for you. The Talmud has listed over fifteen potential cures for your disease."

Surely, out of those fifteen plus potential cures, one of them would be just what the doctor ordered. Here are a few of the cures the Talmud recommended:

1. *Take of gum Alexandria, of alum, and of crocus hortensis, the weight of a zuzee each; let them be bruised together, and given in wine to the woman that hath an issue of blood. But if this fail,*

2. *Take of Persian onions nine logs, boil them in wine, and give it to her to drink: and say, Arise from thy flux. But should this fail,*

3. *Set her in a place where two ways meet, and let her hold a cup of wine in her hand; and let somebody come behind and affright her, and say, Arise from thy flux. But should this do no good,*

4. *Take a handful of cummin and a handful of crocus, and a handful of faenu-greek; let these be boiled, and given her to drink, and say, Arise from thy* flux. But should this also fail,

5. *Dig seven trenches, and burn in them some cuttings of vines not yet four years old; and let her take in her hand a cup of wine, and let her be led from this trench and set down over that; and let her be removed from that, and set down over another: and in each removal say unto her, Arise from thy flux.* (See *Bab. Shabb. fol. 110 [Talmud]* as quoted in Adam Clark's Commentary on the New Testament.)

Teacher Option: *A supplemental video is available in the Resource Kit.* **V**

If none of those worked, there were at least ten other remedies that could be prescribed for this one condition. But of course, that would be ten more doctor's visits and ten more doctor's bills. After her last doctor's visit, she reached into her purse only to realize she had just enough for this cure and no more. But sadly, she was no better. In fact, she was getting worse.

B. I Will Reject Hopelessness in Favor of Faith

It is easy to feel hopeless when all the cures and prescriptions we try do not work. We are still sick. We are still addicted. We are still bankrupt. But we do not have to feel hopeless; we can have faith. Our faith is not grounded in what we can do but in what our God can do. Jesus proved all throughout the Gospels, and namely here in the Gospel of Mark, that He is greater than nature, the devils, disease, and even death.

When you feel hopeless or verwhelmed, what do you do?

II. THE WOMAN DID NOT TOUCH JESUS, BUT SHE TOUCHED HIS CLOTHING

People sometimes find themselves "canceled" by society, as if they are a potential plague needing to be isolated from society. In what was supposed to be a secular age, we have awakened to find ourselves involved in what is a kind of religious movement, administering prescriptions that are not too far removed from those from three thousand years ago.

Daughter was considered a danger to the community because she could communicate her dangerous uncleanness to anyone she touched. But in faith she boldly left her isolation and determined within herself to touch Jesus.

A. Faith, Not Formulas, Produce Results

Daughter's faith led her to a proper understanding of Jesus. She did not need to be strong or favored; she did not need to say just the right words or catch Him when He was alone; she did not need to successfully move Him to pity with a display of her suffering. She did not have a magic formula; all she had was faith. And it was enough. Her faith gave her insight to the power of Jesus others did not have. She only needed to touch the merest fringes of Jesus' garment. She understood she could be healed even if Jesus had not intended to heal her. Jesus did not even have to know He was healing her in order to heal her. What faith!

B. She Was Not Deterred Because Jesus Was Busy

That day Daughter was not the only one in need of a miracle. Jairus, a ruler of the synagogue, was desperate. His precious, twelve-year-old daughter lay at death's door back at his home. If Jesus did not make haste, the girl may not make it. Although Jesus was busy walking toward Jairus' house to work a miracle, Daughter still came to the crowd because she knew Jesus was her only hope for healing.

Mark's Gospel intertwines these two episodes together so we can compare them. Jesus was on His way to attend to an important official's daughter. Any delay could mean the death of the daughter, so we must imagine Jairus was walking fast, as any father would, on high alert against anything that would delay them. But suddenly a lowly, anonymous woman, unclean because of her condition, had the audacity to break through a crowd of important people to touch Jesus.

Without any training, without a single Bible study, Daughter's understanding of Christ dwarfed that of the scholars of Israel, including even of Jairus. This is what faith can do. Faith is the greatest teacher, opening up vistas of knowledge in an instant.

Why do we sometimes feel like God is too busy to heal us or help us?

C. I Will Trust in God, Not Formulas

The apostle Paul said we are justified by faith (Romans 5:1). The Greek term under the English verb justified could also—if English would allow—be translated "righteoused." We are righteoused by faith. Faith in God makes us righteous. Faith puts a halt to all the corrupting influences of doubt—the doubt that leads our hearts astray, the questioning of God's faithful care for us, the questioning of God's boundaries, the questioning of God's truthful Word. Faith aligns our hearts with God's heart and gives us a glimpse of God's perspective.

Touching the hem of His garment or bringing Him physically to our house will not automatically affect the same wondrous outcome. Jesus was not moved by their formulas but by their faith. He is moved by the same for us. Do not seek special formulas as if they are sacred incantations. Rather seek Jesus with faith, knowing He knows how to heal us and help us.

Have you ever caught yourself trying to find a formula to cause God to work in your life, or do you simply put your faith in His knowledge and wisdom?

III. JESUS HEALED THE WOMAN AND GAVE HER PEACE

A dozen years of weakening health had sapped her strength. But if she could somehow get to Jesus, there was a chance He would show compassion and she would be healed. So with the memory of twelve long, hard years behind her and nothing to lose in front of her, she ventured into the mob. The Bible does not spell it out for us, but many believe she crawled through the crowd. As she expected, they kicked her and stepped on her and stomped on her. But she kept crawling and saying, "If I can just touch the hem of His garment."

A. She Was Made Whole and Inspired Others

After a short time or long time, she finally reached where Jesus was. She saw the tassels hanging from Jesus' robe. With all the faith and strength she could muster, she reached out and touched the hem of His garment, and suddenly, everything changed. What was wrong was made right. She felt strength like she had not felt in twelve years. She instantly knew she was healed. She would doubtless go to the doctor for a checkup, but she already knew what the doctor would discover. She was healed.

But she was not the only one who felt the power of Jesus to heal. As soon as she touched Jesus, He stopped walking and asked, "Who touched my clothes?" The disciples were confused. Jairus was probably anxious. The crowd stopped abruptly and bumped into each other, like a pileup on the interstate. Jesus' followers pointed out the obvious. "Thou seest the multitude thronging thee, and sayest thou, Who touched me?" (Mark 5:31).

But this touch was different. This person did not just rub shoulders with Him or accidentally bump into Him when He stopped. She came to the parade fully intending to leave differently than she came, and she did. It would have been tempting for her to hide. As far as the rest of the town knew, she was still unclean and unfit to be in public. They knew about her sickness. She was not permitted to touch anyone, especially a holy man. How dare she make Him unclean? She confessed, "Master, it was me." She did not know what to expect from Jesus. She just knew she came to Jesus sick, and she was leaving healed.

Daughter told Him everything. She told Him how she had been sick for twelve years. During those dozen years, she tried one doctor after another, one prescription after another, but she only got sicker and weaker. But she heard of Jesus. And she heard He was compassionate and powerful, and if she could just touch the hem of His garment, she would be healed. And that is exactly what happened.

If you were Daughter, how do you think Jairus or the disciples might have acted toward you? How do you think Jesus might have acted toward you?

Jesus called her Daughter. It had probably been a long time since she had been called anything that kind, that humane. And He said, "Thy faith hath made thee whole" (Mark 5:34). We know Jesus made her whole, but Jesus worked through her faith to make her whole. Jesus draws our attention to her faith, as if to say this kind of faith purifies us, guides us, and in the end, justifies us.

B. Because It Is Never Too Late to Touch Jesus, I Will Take My Need to Him

Perhaps you feel hopeless because of what you have been going through. Even if you have battled for twelve years or longer, this story is a testament to the power of God to work through our unrelenting faith. We may not know exactly how God will respond when we ask, but we know He knows, and He will always do what is right. Let us take our need to Jesus and see Him work for us like He worked for Daughter and for Jairus' daughter. In case you do not know the rest of that story, Jairus's daughter died while they were on the way to the house. But when Jesus arrived, He spoke to her, "Damsel, I say unto thee, 'Arise.'" (Mark 5:41). And she did. Even death bows its grisly knee at the word of Jesus.

INTERNALIZING THE MESSAGE

A supplemental image is available in the Resource Kit. (I)

A great physicist studied his whole life. He spent long hours in the lab, toiling for the merest hints of truth hidden in the mysteries of his formulas. He was an atheist in a field dominated by unbelief. He achieved awards, prizes, and recognition for his groundbreaking genius in the field. But as he came toward the end of his life, he found himself strangely tempted to faith in God. In hindsight, he said he had studied for so long and with such intensity, only to find what fragments of truth he had discovered near the end of his life, people of faith in God had discovered as children.

After hours of climbing the tallest mountains of science, one rock at a time, one cliff at a time, one summit after another, he finally reached the top of the mountain of truth only to find Moses, Jeremiah, and Paul playing a game of checkers and laughing at one another's jokes on the top of the mountain. How had they gotten to that summit? Thousands of hours of hovering over a microscope or behind a telescope? No. They had leapt there in an instant—by faith.

What is the balance between faith and works? How do we make sure we wait on God while reaching out to Him in faith?

Prayer Focus
Lead the group in prayer and consider the following topics of focus:
- For us to have faith in Jesus for our need
- For Jesus to give us the courage to reach out to Him in faith

3.1

WISDOM'S WORTH

FOCUS VERSE
I Corinthians 1:24
But unto them which are called, both Jews and Greeks, Christ the power of God, and the wisdom of God.

LESSON TEXT
Proverbs 3:5–26; I Corinthians 1:24–30

TRUTH ABOUT GOD
Godly wisdom is the most valuable asset we could ever obtain.

TRUTH FOR MY LIFE
I will deepen my relationship with Jesus Christ, the source of wisdom.

Series Overview:

This series, "Choosing Wisdom," will lead us on a trip through highlighted portions of Proverbs and Ecclesiastes. We will look at wisdom's worth, wisdom's works, the truth that wisdom waits, and then hear wisdom's warning. The Scripture passages we will study will help us to better understand the importance of choosing wisdom. Wisdom is not elusive or impossible to attain. If we will seek wisdom by seeking the God who gives wisdom, we will gain what we need to please the Lord and walk in His commandments.

(SG) TEACHING OUTLINE

Icebreaker: What is the most difficult stand you have ever made for your faith?

Lesson Connection: Share the Lesson Connection. (I)

I. HUMILITY IS REQUIRED TO OBTAIN WISDOM
    » *What is a proverb from the Book of Proverbs you rely on because it speaks to you?*

    A. Looking to God Instead of Ourselves (V)

    B. I Will Embrace Humility
       » *What are some steps we can take to be more humble in a world that values individualism, often at the cost of wisdom?*

II. WISDOM'S REWARD

    A. The Benefits of Wisdom
       » *What wise steps can you take to create more peace in your life?*

    B. I Will Pursue Godly Wisdom

III. TRUE WISDOM IS FOUND ONLY IN JESUS CHRIST
    » *Since wisdom is not always about gaining, what might we have to lose to be wise?*

    A. Worldly Wisdom Will Not Save Us

    B. I Will Deepen My Relationship with Jesus Christ, the Source of Wisdom
       » *What wise action plan can you make for your life? What steps will you take in making godly plans for the future?*

Internalizing the Message

Prayer Focus
Lead the group in prayer and consider the following topics of focus:
• For us to look to Jesus for the wisdom we need
• For us to live with faith and courage in the wisdom God provides

LESSON CONNECTION

A supplemental image is available in the Resource Kit. (I)

t was the kind of day that makes kids misbehave—all the pomp and circumstance signaled something out of the ordinary and inspired rowdiness. But the raucous sounds of children gave way to crescendos of horns, flutes, harps, and lyres as people from every station in life fell down before the massive gold image King Nebuchadnezzar's staff had set up.

Mishael glanced over at Hananiah, who looked over to Azariah. It was almost comical how they suddenly seemed so tall, towering over the rows and rows of magistrates and commoners folded flat before the idol. Any humor was quickly dismissed at the sound of a new scurry: staff members rushing to the side of the king, hissing their accusations and gesturing at the singled out Hebrews.

The emotion of it all—that feeling of many eyes lasered in on him—transported Hananiah back to another moment, this time in a room filled with fellow captives and a menu of alien rations. Earthly wisdom whispered, "Just eat the food like everyone else. Do what these new overlords say and don't rock the boat. Why endanger yourself for the teachings and ways of a now-destroyed kingdom?"

But Daniel had been there to insist on a different course and maintain that wisdom belonged to God and that His ways were best. And he was right. Following the ways of God resulted in explicable favor that won the day.

And so as the symphony apexed once more, Hananiah followed Mishael and Azariah to the furnace. Pushing past the inner voice of doubts, they stood alone. Although the Babylonians seemed to have a monopoly on wisdom, the faithful Hebrews did not let their current circumstances deter them from following the wisdom and will of God, and in so doing, they walked in the fire with the source of all wisdom.

BIBLE LESSON

I. HUMILITY IS REQUIRED TO OBTAIN WISDOM

We have all encountered know-it-alls in our lives. Sometimes others may have even thought of us in this way, especially when we discuss a topic about which we are quite knowledgeable. But knowledge does not always equal wisdom. As Irish rugby player Brian O'Driscoll is known for saying, "Knowledge is knowing a tomato is a fruit. Wisdom is knowing not to put it in a fruit salad." We need to acknowledge we do not know it all. We need humility to obtain wisdom.

We must humble ourselves like the great King Solomon. In I Kings 3, when the Lord promised to give Solomon whatever he asked, the young king did not ask for honor, riches, or long life. He recognized the daunting task ahead of him, so he asked for wisdom. Others may have treated the Lord like a genie in a bottle, appearing to grant them their wishes, but Solomon knew better than to waste all he could glean from the source of wisdom on mere gifts and gold. Rather than setting himself above them, he set aside his pedigree and his power, embracing humility to be the leader he knew God and the people needed him to be.

Sadly, we know Solomon did not always follow the ways of wisdom (I Kings 11:1–3). Although he reached the pinnacle of royalty on earth and was renowned for his acute understanding, at some point, wisdom became theory without proper application. As an older man, Solomon needed the humility he possessed as a young man to continue walking in all the wisdom God had given him. Thankfully, he had the wisdom to write and collect proverbs from around the world that we can use today to increase in wisdom.

What is a proverb from the Book of Proverbs you rely on because it speaks to you?

A. Looking to God Instead of Ourselves

Proverbs 3 contains some of the most oft-quoted verses on pursuing God, the source of all wisdom. Proverbs 3:5–6 commands, "Trust in the LORD with all thine heart; and lean not unto thine own understanding. In all thy ways acknowledge him, and he shall direct thy paths." These verses challenge us to override our human inclination to trust in ourselves. While God has granted us the ability to approach situations logically, we must have the humility to avoid leaning on our own understanding.

Proverbs 3:7 warns us not to be wise in our own eyes. Our perspective may not always be the correct one. Even if we think we are right, we should humble ourselves and seek the Lord. The wise will double-check. As carpenters say, "Measure twice; cut once." We must have the humility to pray for a God's eye view of our situation.

Following the wisdom of the Lord leads to great rewards. We have health when we humble ourselves and follow the will and wisdom of God. God increases us, giving us all we need and more. While Proverbs 3:10 speaks of new wine literally bursting forth from our presses, there is also a spiritual application. When we follow the wisdom of the Holy Spirit, we will see a great outpouring of revival. God will bless us spiritually, physically, emotionally, and financially.

If we are willing to receive these blessings, we must also be willing to receive correction from the Lord. It is one thing to humble ourselves to be wise, but it is quite another to accept the chastening of the Lord and admit when we have done wrong. When we face these situations, we should be thankful for the discipline of the Lord because it reveals His love for us. Remember it takes discipline to be a disciple.

B. I Will Embrace Humility

The me-first, individualistic world we live in makes it difficult to embrace humility and accept the discipline required to be a disciple. People are discussing which pronouns they prefer based on a demand for transgender rights as well as confusion about gender. If many people were honest, they would discover that humanity's preferred pronouns have nothing to do with gender. Instead, this confusion is rooted in pride. Many should declare their pronouns are "me, myself, and I" to admit the selfish and self-centered view we all often have.

Teacher Option: A supplemental video is available in the Resource Kit. **V**

While there is nothing wrong with self-care or pursuing godly goals, we must humble ourselves to advance in the right way. We would do well to remember I Peter 5:6, "Humble yourselves therefore under the mighty hand of God, that he may exalt you in due time." Humility respects the sovereignty of God and helps us recognize God's timing and our own timing may often differ. We must all embrace humility to stay faithful to the will and wisdom of God.

What are some steps we can take to be more humble in a world that values individualism, often at the cost of wisdom?

II. WISDOM'S REWARD

Following God's wise plans for our lives will ultimately lead to reward. While we should not behave wisely just for the sake of reward, we have a kind and loving Savior who desires to give us good things, including the desires of our hearts. But let us learn the lesson that wisdom is its own reward. Those who follow the path of the wise will have a greater chance of leading happier, healthier lives. Such rewards are natural by-products of wisdom.

Wisdom does not always lead to great riches because God may choose to bless us in other ways, but poor decisions often do lead to poverty. Proverbs 21:20 declares, "There is treasure to be desired and oil in the dwelling of the wise; but a foolish man spendeth it up." Many people just say, "A fool and his money are soon parted." Whether or not we have money, we should make a firm commitment to never part from wisdom.

A. The Benefits of Wisdom

However, we must be wary of focusing too much on the gifts that come from wisdom. We know Solomon's wives turned his heart away from God, but perhaps he forgot some of his own proverbs and started focusing on his wealth. Wisdom also has the benefit of bringing peace. Solomon's very name comes from the Hebrew word for peace, *shalom*. David likely chose this name for his son out of a strong desire to put his days of fighting behind him and give his son a formidable kingdom where he could maintain peace.

Since all of wisdom's paths are peace, we must be wise enough to recognize when we have deviated into unnecessary conflicts. (See Proverbs 3:17.) Solomon's taxation policies eventually led to the division of the kingdom. If the king had held on to his wisdom and the peace it provided, the kingdom could have maintained its unity. The word *shalom* also means "wholeness." Solomon did not fully live up to his own name or the plans his father had for him.

> What wise steps can you take to create more peace in your life?

B. I Will Pursue Godly Wisdom

During our lives, we may find ourselves on wild-goose chases, pursuing things that are not of God. We should pursue wisdom because it leads to many wonderful rewards. We have a wise Lord who is more concerned about meeting our needs than giving us gifts that might lead us astray from His plan. We often thank the Lord for all the blessings He gives us, but perhaps we should also thank Him for many unanswered prayers—prayers we prayed that God wisely did not grant because He knows what we truly need.

Many things in life appear wise or logical. However, Proverbs 3:21 speaks of "sound wisdom." In a world where many people offer advice and all forms of counsel, we must be careful to follow the right kind of wisdom. Worldly wisdom might have some benefits, but worldly wisdom alone will not lead to the ultimate success God has for us.

Essentially, sound wisdom is wisdom so effective that it leads to success. Godly wisdom may yield different definitions of success. The earliest mention of success in Scripture is found in Joshua chapter 1. Joshua found success in battle when he conquered the land of Canaan because Joshua meditated on the Word of God. (See Joshua 1:8.) If we are looking for a self-help book or a volume on wisdom, we should look to the Bible.

III. TRUE WISDOM IS FOUND ONLY IN JESUS CHRIST

When we look in the New Testament, we discover true wisdom can only be found through the life and teachings of Jesus. Some have called Jesus a wise philosopher, but we know He is so much more. Although Jesus provided many wise sayings, He led a life that defied logic and worldly wisdom.

Many people found the message of Jesus to be counterintuitive. He talked about saving your life by losing it. He talked about winning the ultimate battle through loss. His words made little sense to many of His followers. Some people left Him because of His hard sayings. Even the apostles often had difficulty understanding His message. (See Luke 18:34.) We must stay at the feet of Jesus to continue to glean from His teachings.

Since wisdom is not always about gaining, what might we have to lose to be wise?

A. Worldly Wisdom Will Not Save Us

The apostle Paul also spoke of the great reversals required to achieve wisdom. Paul wrote, "Let no man deceive himself. If any man among you seemeth to be wise in this world, let him become a fool, that he may be wise" (I Corinthians 3:18). Here, Paul spoke of the humility required to achieve wisdom.

As a learned man in Scripture, Paul realized he had acted like a fool when he pursued early Christians and put them to death. He had lacked the wisdom that could only come from an encounter with the God of all wisdom. His life forever changed when he met Jesus on the road to Damascus.

Paul wrote to the Corinthian church in an attempt to correct their foolish behaviors. He stated, "The foolishness of God is wiser than men; and the weakness of God is stronger than men" (I Corinthians 1:25). Through weakness, Jesus achieved victory over sin and death. In doing so, He defied humanity's logic. We must exercise great caution if we focus on worldly wisdom. To us, it may seem logical and profitable; to God, it may seem exceedingly foolish.

Paul ended I Corinthians 1 by reminding us of the strong connection between wisdom and humility. He warned us that no flesh should glory in the presence of God (I Corinthians 1:29). Instead we should be humble. This humility leads to us being made wise through Christ. In I Corinthians 1:30, Paul wrote, "But of him are ye in Christ Jesus, who of God is made unto us wisdom, and righteousness, and sanctification, and redemption" (I Corinthians 1:30). Christ is the beginning of a better life. That better life begins with wisdom.

B. I Will Deepen My Relationship with Jesus Christ, the Source of Wisdom

What wise action plan can you make for your life? What steps will you take in making godly plans for the future?

Today Jesus Christ is calling us to deepen our relationship with Him. Such a relationship goes beyond Him merely being our Savior. Jesus has not only saved us and redeemed us, but He is also ready to advise us as our wise counselor. Walking with Jesus Christ will make us wiser than we could ever hope to be on our own. A strong relationship with Jesus will help us to grow in wisdom.

INTERNALIZING THE MESSAGE

The man stood at the bus stop on a cold, snowy northern morning. Snowflakes kissed his cheeks as warm tears flowed from his eyes. He felt the desperation of making a difficult decision. His own human nature told him he should take the offer on the table, get out of his current situation, and journey on to something better. The wisdom of the Holy Spirit told him to wait.

But the new job offer came from a godly pastor, someone the man and his wife trusted. They had friends where they were going. If the couple made a pros and cons list, they could easily tilt the scales in favor of leaving. But remember, there is wisdom in patience. James wrote, "But let patience have her perfect work, that ye may be perfect and entire, wanting nothing" (James 1:4).

The couple wanted nothing more than to extricate themselves from their current situation. Time had run its course. They had served faithfully and now had an opportunity to serve elsewhere. They may even feel valued again. The decision loomed over the man's head like the chilly gray sky. It also seemed just as murky. Sometimes that happens when our hearts desperately desire something that seems reasonable and logical, but God says "no."

That moment helped the man more clearly understand the difference between human wisdom and godly wisdom. While he and his wife could make a strong case for leaving and pursuing the new opportunity, the wisdom of the Holy Ghost told him to wait. Just as the Spirit prevented Paul and his companions from doing the good work of preaching the word in Asia (Acts 16:6), the Lord was preventing this couple from doing something—not because the situation was not promising, but because it was the will and wisdom of God for them to wait.

As the man wiped the snow and tears off his face and boarded the bus, he knew he would not be traveling any farther than his current destination, at least for now. Soon the wisdom of God would lead him and his wife in a new and fruitful direction. Along their journey they would meet a couple who faced obstacles because they found themselves out of the will, timing, and wisdom of God. The man would remember that freezing, gloomy day at the bus stop. He would be thankful he had chosen godly wisdom over his own human logic and desires, while deepening his relationship with Jesus Christ: the true source of wisdom.

Prayer Focus
Lead the group in prayer and consider the following topics of focus:
- For us to look to Jesus for the wisdom we need
- For us to live with faith and courage in the wisdom God provides

3.2

WISDOM'S WORKS

FOCUS VERSE
Proverbs 31:31
Give her of the fruit of her hands; and let her own works praise her in the gates.

LESSON TEXT
Proverbs 31:10–31

TRUTH ABOUT GOD
God's wisdom produces tangible results in our lives.

TRUTH FOR MY LIFE
I will put God's wisdom into action by obeying His Word.

Thinking about Last Week:

Have students refer to their Daily Devotional Guide to answer the following questions:
1. What most affected you as you read through the Lesson Text and the Biblical Insights?
2. How did it shape your prayers and thoughts throughout the week?
3. Do you feel you grew closer to the Lord this past week? Why or why not?

(SG) TEACHING OUTLINE

Icebreaker: What is the wisest decision you have ever made?

Lesson Connection: Share the Lesson Connection. (I)

I.   WISDOM IS DISPLAYED THROUGH OUR ACTIONS (V)

   » *What bits of wisdom have others shared with you? Why did you find them so valuable?*

   A.   Attributes of Wisdom

   » *What will you do to follow the example of wisdom set by the Proverbs 31 woman?*

   B.   I Will Put God's Wisdom into Action through Obedience to His Word

   » *What are some of the major distinctions between the people of God and the world?*

II. MY FAITH IN JESUS IS DISPLAYED THROUGH MY ACTIONS

   » *What parts of your life need evaluating? Where could you use a little more wisdom in your daily life?*

   A.   Wisdom Is Proved Right by Her Deeds

   » *What are some keys for success that do not change over time?*

   B.   God So Loved That He Gave, Proving His Love through Action

   C.   I Will Show My Faith in God and Love for Him through My Daily Actions

   » *Whom do you know who is in need? How can you help to meet the spiritual needs and other needs they may have?*

Internalizing the Message

Prayer Focus
Lead the group in prayer and consider the following topics of focus:
• Praise to God for His wisdom He so willingly gives
• For God to continue to give us wisdom to do right for the right reasons

LESSON CONNECTION

A supplemental image is available in the Resource Kit. [I]

The book *Hidden Figures: The American Dream and the Untold Story of the Black Women Mathematicians Who Helped Win the Space Race* recounts the lives of forgotten pioneers who wisely and bravely overcame multiple obstacles to help others reach the stars. Known as calculators, these women demonstrated their skills by engaging in some of the most complex math even the most advanced computers of their day could not do. These human supercomputers helped to put an American into orbit around the earth.

At the height of the Cold War, their coworkers and their nation desperately wanted to beat the Russians, especially since the Soviet Union jumped out to an early lead in the space race, surging past the United States with the Sputnik satellite and the first human in space. However, these women dealt with another type of war on their home soil: they fought battles of prejudice and gender discrimination on a daily basis. The Langley Research Center was segregated and prescribed not only separate restrooms, but also a segregated table in the cafeteria for Black employees. If they were not belittled for their race, they were belittled for their gender.

Despite all these challenges, the women acted in wisdom, outperforming their male counterparts and finding solutions others simply could not find. As America reached for the stars, these women mathematicians reached far beyond what anyone else thought they could achieve. Without them, the United States would not have won the space race.

Their wisdom produced the tangible result of putting a man in earth's orbit. Amid the flare of rockets, flashing cameras, and a sea of prejudice, the worth of these ladies of wisdom was forgotten. Until one day someone told their story, and the world saw their sheer knowledge, composure, and persistence in the face of adversity. Although it took far too long for their success story to get off the ground, they proved that America could not soar unless these wise women helped their nation boldly go where it had never gone before.

BIBLE LESSON

I. WISDOM IS DISPLAYED THROUGH OUR ACTIONS

Teacher Option: A supplemental video is available in the Resource Kit. **V**

The fable of the ant and the grasshopper shows the importance of planning for the future. While the grasshopper played and wiled away the days, the ant gathered food for winter. During the summer, many might have viewed the grasshopper as the wiser of the pair. But come winter, the wisdom of the tiny ant stood tall. The grasshopper looked desperate and foolish along with anyone who chose to hop on his bandwagon.

We must not simply think ourselves to be wise; we must demonstrate the best practices of wisdom. We must choose right over wrong. We must prefer the eternal over the temporary. We must embrace wisdom and eschew foolishness.

What bits of wisdom have others shared with you? Why did you find them so valuable?

A. Attributes of Wisdom

The end of Proverbs 1 depicts wisdom as a woman. Known as Lady Wisdom, she cries out to the unwise in a desperate attempt to help them change their foolish ways. When we move to the end of the book, we see Proverbs 31 presents a woman embodying wisdom. She has many attributes worth following. Although many focus on this chapter's lessons for women, men can also glean from the woman's fine example.

Her first attribute is her strong relationship with her husband, built on trust. The couple have confidence in each other. He knows she will bring him good and not evil throughout his life. In a present-day world of broken marriages, separations, and divorce, we would do well to attend to the maintenance of good relationships.

Her second attribute is her strong work ethic that helps her prepare for the future. She makes garments and works diligently throughout the night, often getting little sleep before rising early the next day. She is often found at the spindle. The clothing she produces can be sold or used to clothe her household in scarlet as they brace for the winter snows. She herself wears strength and dignity and does not fear for the future.

Her third attribute reveals her superior acumen as a businesswoman. While some might think business transactions are only part of a man's world, the Bible says otherwise. The Proverbs 31 woman evaluates a field and purchases it. To increase the wealth of her family, she plants a vineyard. Whether trading in garments or her vineyard's yield, her business is profitable.

While most of these efforts center on her household, her fourth attribute shows how she cares for others in her community. She gives to the poor. The needy know she will be willing to offer them a helping hand. She also teaches others. In fact, she is renowned for her wisdom and faithful instruction. The needy who follow her wisdom and example may be able to use her assistance and teachings to get out of poverty.

The wise woman is lauded for her many abilities. Her children call her blessed. Her husband praises her because she fears the Lord. Others in the city gates honor her. Her life reveals patterns to which everyone can aspire, even though wisdom may manifest itself in different ways. Some may choose various methods to earn money or to meet the needs of others. All of us should follow the example of the Proverbs 31 woman and fear the Lord in everything we do.

What will you do to follow the example of wisdom set by the Proverbs 31 woman?

B. I Will Put God's Wisdom into Action through Obedience to His Word

We would all do well to seek the wisdom that comes from the Proverbs 31 woman and her fear of God. In a world full of life coaches, self-help books, and purveyors and peddlers of so-called common sense, we must diligently seek the wisdom of God. We discover this wisdom in Scripture. When we read and obey the Word of God, we find ourselves walking with the wise.

We share the wisdom and perseverance of Joseph when we refuse temptation. We learn from the mistakes of Moses, discovering that our motives may sometimes be good, but our methods may not yield the desired results. We strive to be faithful followers like Joshua, learning from one of the world's greatest leaders as we glean the knowledge required to take the children of slaves and turn them into one of the strongest fighting forces ever assembled. We see the power of prayer, fasting, and obedience to the Lord through the godly wisdom of Esther. We recognize the importance of timing when we determine that God has called us to the Kingdom for a specific season.

To acquire more wisdom, we read Proverbs where we find actionable items—many which are exemplified by the Proverbs 31 woman. We learn how to work with others more effectively. We find passages that teach us to develop healthy relationships. Although our time on this earth is short, we learn to prepare for the future by engaging in sound financial principles. The world has many books, but only one book—the Bible—has the breadth and depth of wisdom we truly need to navigate this life and the life to come. We should not allow the greatest book of wisdom to lie idly on our bookshelves collecting dust. We should pick it up, brush it off, and start collecting and enacting all its wisdom.

II. MY FAITH IN JESUS IS DISPLAYED THROUGH MY ACTIONS

The fear of the Lord is the beginning of wisdom. We display this reverence through faith in Jesus Christ. However, Jesus demands more of us than signing a church roll or shaking the pastor's hand. Even when we repent, are baptized in the name of Jesus, and receive the Holy Ghost, we still have work to do. Our reverence for the Lord must be displayed through real world deliverables such as our actions.

Texans have a saying about people who are all talk and no action. They take one look at some individuals and state, "He's all hat and no cattle." Many people can go down to the local Western store and buy the ten-gallon hat, the big belt buckle, and the sharpest pair of boots. They may look the part, but "the proof is in the pudding." When they fail to hold onto their hat, their buckle will not hold up their pants, and they forget to check for the snake that might be lurking in their boots. These pretenders may retreat as fast as their scrawny legs will carry them. They came to tame Texas, but Texas tamed them.

A lot of Christians are the same way. They may dress in their Sunday best, carry their Bible right next to their heart as they enter the church building, and spout off a few verses of Scripture. But appearances cannot hide their lack of humility and the deficit of inward holiness that no amount of outward holiness can cure. Like the disciples who could not abide Jesus' hard sayings, they put down the Bible when they read something that offends them. They quickly run out of popular verses of Scripture to quote because they have not engaged in diligent study of the Word.

What parts of your life need evaluating? Where could you use a little more wisdom in your daily life?

A. Wisdom Is Proved Right by Her Deeds

While we may say, "The proof is in the pudding," and Texans may say, "All hat, no cattle," Jesus said, "Wisdom is justified of her children." In other words, wisdom is justified by what it produces. Sometimes things seem to be wise or right, but they fizzle out. Wisdom always withstands the test of time. Like the Proverbs 31 woman, wisdom's children rise up and call her blessed.

We must not simply follow the theoretical teachings of wisdom; we must practically engage her teachings in our lives. When we come into the house of God, we may humbly realize we lack wisdom. Like the fake cowboy, we may even feel like pretenders. Like the rich young ruler, we may need to go a bit further in our walk with God. But if we continue to follow the Word of God and the preaching and teaching of the ministry, we can show ourselves to be faithful servants of the Most High God. It just takes time, effort, and putting our trust in the Lord.

Many of us stick around because we have tasted and seen that the Lord is good (Psalm 34:8). Chefs can work hard to use all the right ingredients to create the best dish, but taste ultimately matters. Sometimes the greatest chefs are beaten by the simplest recipes. Their quest to come up with some new concoction can be bested by the recipe Grandma received from her grandma. The recipe for success proves its wisdom over and over again.

The greatest technologies in the world seem amazing. Yet we cannot ignore that they were produced with the same spirit of ingenuity and diligence that led to the wheel, the wagon, the automobile, the electric car, and so forth. Although some parts of the formula may change and seem more innovative, essential parts of the recipe for success will always remain.

What are some keys for success that do not change over time?

B. God So Loved That He Gave, Proving His Love through Action

Some fail to learn the lesson of wisdom. They want the blessing now without any cost in the present or the future. Many in Jesus' day likely wanted a Messiah to give them an easy victory over the Romans. They expected a crushing defeat of their enemies and the inauguration of a new kingdom on earth. They reasoned that the divine power of the Messiah would require little sacrifice on His part or theirs. How wrong they were!

Jesus could have chosen the easy way out. He even prayed for the cup to pass from Him in Gethsemane. Jesus could have proclaimed all our sins were forgiven, but He knew that the Law required a sacrifice. Jesus proved His love by dying on the cross for us. He not only showed His love for us, but He also revealed that our actions should be motivated by love. It is essential for us to do right for the right reasons. In championing the values of wisdom, we can see that wisdom enacted and motivated by love can forever change the world.

C. I Will Show My Faith in God and Love for Him through My Daily Actions

We must show our faith in God and demonstrate our love for Him through consistent godly actions. Daily we must follow the wise path and develop our relationship with the Lord through prayer, reading and meditating on the Word, and faithful church attendance.

We must show our love for the Lord by loving others. We should love our brothers and sisters in Christ. Galatians 6:10 states, "As we have therefore opportunity, let us do good to all men, especially unto them who are of the household of faith." Like the Proverbs 31 woman, we should provide for our families and the household of faith.

Whom do you know who is in need? How can you help to meet the spiritual needs and other needs they may have?

We should also love our neighbors and help those in our community. We cannot simply worry about them being filled with the Holy Spirit without helping ensure their bellies are filled. James declared the importance of having faith with works. We must believe for their salvation and actively seek their betterment by meeting basic human needs. The Proverbs 31 woman did not simply feed the needy, she also taught the principles of wisdom that made her successful.

INTERNALIZING THE MESSAGE

The grocer often saw the older woman walking the aisles, pleasantly greeting other customers, and generally brightening everyone's day. Although her hair had grown a bit greyer over the years, her smile had never dimmed. She faced the passing of her husband with sadness and a courage to go on despite the loneliness. The local supermarket was a place for her to gather supplies for the week and to connect with others.

She willingly and kindly offered advice to young mothers looking for the right baby products, suggested recipes for young couples learning to cook, and even boldly cautioned people playing the lottery to save their money for a rainy day. Some heeded her wisdom; others ignored it. Those who disliked it grumbled under their breath, not wanting anyone to see them being unkind to a seasoned citizen.

As she advanced in years and began to decline, so did the neighborhood. She remembered the day she could not do her shopping due to the police caution tape hovering over the broken glass. The robbery drove the original owner out of business. He retired in fear, selling the shop to someone else. Aware of the rising crime rates and the drug deals happening behind the store, the woman stayed in the neighborhood because she loved it, and it held so many wonderful memories for her.

People were less friendly now. Some even talked back when she tried to offer her kind advice. "Grandma, my business is my business. Mind your own business." She wanted to help; she did not want to cause trouble. Her voice of wisdom grew faint from the feebleness that naturally accompanies the aging process, but mainly because no one wanted to hear her.

She knew well that her decline was inevitable, but she hoped her beloved neighborhood could be saved. Then the unthinkable happened. As she finished putting the groceries into her car, someone knocked her down, took her keys, and stole her vehicle. As she lay on the ground, bleeding from a head wound, the assailant said to his partner in crime, "She's just an old lady. Don't worry about her. She doesn't need this stuff anyway."

The assault led to her death, but she was not yet finished with life. People in the neighborhood were surprised to learn of the woman's wealth through saving, sewing clothes for others, and even tending a garden to limit the amount of produce she had to buy. Just as she had given vegetables to others, she donated her savings to the neighborhood. Her will provided funds for a community center, educational programs, and a remodel to the dilapidated library. The old woman so many ignored became a local celebrity. Even the man who knocked her down turned himself in, unable to bear the shame of hurting the wise, old woman. He only wished he had heeded the advice of Lady Wisdom before it was too late. Even though she had passed away, she continued to speak a wisdom that could not be dimmed by death.

Prayer Focus
Lead the group in prayer and consider the following topics of focus:
• Praise to God for His wisdom He so willingly gives
• For God to continue to give us wisdom to do right for the right reasons

3.3

WISDOM WAITS

FOCUS VERSE
Ecclesiastes 3:11
He hath made every thing beautiful in his time: also he hath set the world in their heart, so that no man can find out the work that God maketh from the beginning to the end.

LESSON TEXT
Ecclesiastes 3:1–15

TRUTH ABOUT GOD
God acts according to His sovereign timeline.

TRUTH FOR MY LIFE
I will patiently trust God's timing for my life.

Thinking about Last Week:

Have students refer to their Daily Devotional Guide to answer the following questions:

1. What most affected you as you read through the Lesson Text and the Biblical Insights?
2. How did it shape your prayers and thoughts throughout the week?
3. Do you feel you grew closer to the Lord this past week? Why or why not?

SG TEACHING OUTLINE

Icebreaker: What is the fastest you have ever driven to avoid being late?

Lesson Connection: Share the Lesson Connection.

I. THERE IS A TIME FOR EVERY PURPOSE AND ACTIVITY **V**
   » *How good are you at managing your time with God? What can you do to improve?*

   A. Seasons Are a Natural Part of Life
      » *What steps can we take to manage lifetime goals?*

   B. Wisdom Includes Knowing How to Wait Patiently for the Right Season

   C. I Will Follow God's Plan and Will for My Life
      » *Think about a time when God appeared to be silent. How did you make it through to hear His voice again?*

II. TIMING IS CRITICAL IN THE CHRISTIAN LIFE
    » *Why do you think God sometimes seems to delay things in our lives?*

   A. When the Time Was Right, God Sent Forth His Son **I**

   B. If We Patiently Labor, We Will Reap the Harvest "in Due Season"

   C. I Will Patiently Trust God's Timing for My Life
      » *How can we be more intentional about accepting God's timing in our lives?*

Internalizing the Message

Prayer Focus
Lead the group in prayer and consider the following topics of focus:
• For the discernment to know God's timing in our lives
• For the grace to trust God's timing in our lives

LESSON CONNECTION

The soldiers all remained in their ranks steadfastly standing at attention. If their legs hurt, they ignored the pain. If their arms ached, they gave no hint of discomfort. If a fly landed on their nose, they resisted the urge to shoo it away. They were all disciplined, but they seemed even more circumspect today. Their superior had demanded that every crease in their uniform be perfect and every weapon glisten in the sun. Today the great general Napoleon would pass through their midst.

The commanding officers hid any nervousness. If they could have held in the perspiration that beaded down their necks, they would have. They would have done nearly anything to please their commander-in-chief. Today was a day to stand out, but not in the wrong way. By lining up properly and adhering to every military protocol, the officers hoped they could advance in rank. If one of their comrades' regiments failed the test, they could take his position. Quiet ambition seethed through the army as each man, no matter his position, hoped to be the exemplar of the true warrior their general hoped to see.

Napoleon rode on a great steed, inspecting the troops. They remained quiet and disciplined. Then the unthinkable happened. Something spooked Napoleon's horse. The beast writhed and bucked, attempting to dislodge the great general. All the officers and soldiers held fast to their positions, unsure of what to do.

Then seemingly out of nowhere, a soldier broke rank and came to the aid of his general. He seized the horse by the reins, calming the animal. With great respect, he held out the reins to Napoleon. Napoleon took them from the low-ranking soldier and simply said, "Thank you, Captain."

Because the soldier saw a need and met it, he advanced when others remained still, stuck to rituals and protocols. The story proves that timing is everything. The soldier might have taken many years to reach the rank of captain, or he might never have achieved it. Timing made all the difference. The soldier's actions were not rash; they were born out of all the times the soldier had exercised patience through training, discipline, and following orders. Like him, we must serve the Lord patiently and wait for the opportunity to serve at a higher level. We must patiently trust God's timing for our lives.

BIBLE LESSON

I. THERE IS A TIME FOR EVERY PURPOSE AND ACTIVITY

Our daily lives are governed by time. Our alarm clocks jolt some of us out of bed, while others desperately slap at the snooze button to get a few more ZZZs. The early risers sip coffee peacefully, while the sleepyheads desperately try to put the coffee in a to-go cup. Appointments, coffee breaks, lunch breaks, and project deadlines dictate most of our activities. Even when the clock signals the end of the workday, we know we will have to do everything all over again the next day. Plus, we may have to carve out more time for kids' practices, grocery shopping, and meal planning and preparation. At the end of the day, we may ask ourselves, "Where did all the time go?"

Teacher Option: *A supplemental video is available in the Resource Kit.* **V**

Time flies, especially when we are having fun. We try to avoid being late by getting to work "in the nick of time." Sometimes we run out of time; other times we have some spare time. Time and time again, we realize we need to make more time for God, family, and friends. Yet we still have to work because time is money. We can waste time. We can kill time. We can have a whale of a time or a hard time. When we have a hard time, we hope the saying is true that time heals all wounds. In the end, we know that only time will tell. Hopefully, we will figure out this time thing because we cannot turn back the hands of time no matter how hard we try. Someday we will all be out of time and faced with eternity.

How good are you a managing your time with God? What car you do to improve?

A. Seasons Are a Natural Part of Life

The Preacher wrote, "To every thing there is a season, and a time to every purpose under the heaven" (Ecclesiastes 3:1). God ordered the times and seasons for us. Since God is eternal, He is timeless. Time did not exist at the beginning of Creation. Since the Almighty was an everlasting being not governed by time, time did not need to exist. In fact, for the first three days of Creation, there really was not such a thing as time. Then on the fourth day, the Lord created the sun as the greater light to rule the day and the moon as the lesser light to rule the night. These lights allowed there to be signs, seasons, days, and years. Although God did not need time, He knew His creation would.

Despite being governed by time, humans often fail to manage it as well as they should. While some succeed in this endeavor in the natural world, they fail spiritually. They neglect eternal things. Therefore, the psalmist wrote, "So teach us to number our days, that we may apply our hearts unto wisdom" (Psalm 90:12).

What steps can we take to manage lifetime goals?

B. Wisdom Includes Knowing How to Wait Patiently for the Right Season

Wisdom helps us to differentiate between various seasons in our lives and to patiently wait for the right one. The Preacher listed a number of seasons in Ecclesiastes chapter 3, starting with the big picture of a time to be born and a time to die. Along our journey on this earth, we must plant at the proper time, and we must patiently wait for the harvest. Sometimes we feel desperate for the produce our labors will bring, but God often allows His blessings to cultivate a bit longer to reward us greatly.

During times of struggle in our lives, we need time to heal. When things are broken down, we need to take time to mourn and give ourselves time to recover. But we must also realize we will build up again, dancing and rejoicing in the wonder-working power of God's restoration.

Throughout all these seasons, the cycle of life continues. Sometimes we have great prosperity in a time of getting. Then life becomes difficult, and we experience a season of loss. We might be tempted to rend our garments in times of loss and mourning, but in due time, we must pull ourselves together with the help of the Lord, family, and friends to realize it is a time to sew things back together.

C. I Will Follow God's Plan and Will for My Life

We must willingly make the commitment to follow God's plan and will for our lives—whether we think our timing is off or that the Lord has forgotten about us. While we revel in the happy seasons of life, we cannot escape those negative times and seasons that affect us all. Perhaps they are not completely bad; times of mourning are also times of remembrance. Although we feel sad at the loss of loved ones, we cherish all the special moments we had with them.

We must also realize that different seasons of life are more easily recognized than others. On many occasions, we will feel in tune with the plan and will of God. In these wonderful times, everything seems to click perfectly, working in harmony. At other times, we may find ourselves struggling to discern the will and plan of God. While we should always examine ourselves to ensure we are following the Lord to the best of our ability, we must also realize we all face times when God has chosen to be silent. Such seasons may be a test of our faithfulness. We must continue serving Him with all our might, waiting for that glorious time when He once again speaks a word into our lives.

Think about a time when God appeared to be silent. How did you make it through to hear His voice again?

II. TIMING IS CRITICAL IN THE CHRISTIAN LIFE

We cannot underestimate the importance of time. The saying "timing is everything" illustrates this key principle that governs the universe, our daily lives, and our eternity. We must appreciate God's timing and walk in it. Doing so is essential to a successful Christian life.

We may feel a strong desire to step out and embrace our calling and a specific ministry opportunity. While God and our leaders may appreciate our zeal, the timing may not be right. We may need to cultivate our gifts and exercise patience. In fact, many Christians have talked about their initial disappointment at not being able to participate in a particular ministry at a certain time. Later on, God opened the right door for them in His timing. Hindsight, as they say, is twenty-twenty. Often these Christians tell of realizing how unprepared they were until God gave them a season to learn more and enhance their gifts.

When we think about right timing in the Christian life, we must look to Jesus as our example. Many may have thought He should have begun His ministry at twelve years old when He answered the questions of the teachers in the Temple. Others may have thought eighteen or twenty-one was a good age. Jesus, however, patiently waited until His thirties for the right time. In fact, He came to earth with perfect timing.

Why do you think God sometimes seems to delay things in our lives?

A. When the Time Was Right, God Sent Forth His Son

Teacher Option: A supplemental image is available in the Resource Kit.

Galatians 4:4 tells us the importance of timing, "But when the fulness of the time was come, God sent forth his Son, made of a woman, made under the law." A great deal of history had to occur before the fullness of time could be reached and God could send forth His Son at just the right time.

A look at history reveals a good place to start watching God's clock is 586 BC with the destruction of the Temple by the Babylonians. The situation looked grim. King Nebuchadnezzar exiled many of the Jews to Babylon where they surprisingly prospered. But they needed to be back in their land to prepare for the Messiah. The Persians defeated the Babylonians, allowing the Jews to return home. They not only supported the Jewish effort to rebuild their Temple, but they also created roads and infrastructure that later proved critical to the spread of the gospel.

Then Alexander the Great conquered the Persians. This once-in-a-lifetime leader expanded the empire and spread Greek culture and language throughout the world. The New Testament would be written in Koine Greek. The Romans eventually became the superpower and added more roads and territories. They even went into Europe as far as Great Britain where many years later King James would have the entire Bible translated into English.

The Babylonians, Persians, Greeks, and Romans all had to arise to pave the way for Christ. They created the right time and place for Jesus to be born in a manger in Bethlehem when biblical prophecy was fulfilled through the decree of a Roman governor. This history lesson about the timing and power of God should help us exercise patience and show endurance.

B. If We Patiently Labor, We Will Reap the Harvest "in Due Season"

Heaven awaits in the next life, but a great harvest is coming in this life. We must continue to patiently labor to achieve all God has for us in due season. The nurturing aspects of being in the right place allow for solid growth. At the right season, the righteous produce fruit. We are known by the fruits we bear. Therefore, we must be patient and diligent.

In Galatians 6:9, Paul warned of us losing heart or even going so far as to give up: "And let us not be weary in well doing: for in due season we shall reap, if we faint not." Far too many have run the race only to stop at the last turn, allowing spiritual exhaustion to overcome them. If only they had rounded the bend to see the finish line in sight. Then they would have finished strong.

Sadly, some fail to even begin the race. In Acts 24, Paul witnessed to Felix very convincingly. Unfortunately, verse 25 tells us of Paul's strong pull for Felix's soul and the governor's sad response: "And as he reasoned of righteousness, temperance, and judgment to come, Felix trembled, and answered, Go thy way for this time; when I have a convenient season, I will call for thee."

C. I Will Patiently Trust God's Timing for My Life

The story of Felix is a cautionary tale about missing out on God's timing. For those who have yet to repent, be baptized in the name of Jesus, and receive the baptism of the Holy Spirit with the evidence of speaking in other tongues, today is the day of salvation. There is no time to delay.

As we follow the plan of salvation, we must patiently trust God's timing for our lives. We may have a great desire to jump into ministry, but we must trust God's perfect timing. We can certainly witness to our friends, share our testimony with them, and invite them to church, but we need time to grow in grace and in our knowledge of the Word of God before we move into certain areas of ministry. The more we grow, the more able we will be to enter those new areas.

How can we be more intentional about accepting God's timing in our lives?

Those who have served God for a while have learned the importance of God's timing. Their walk with God likely includes stories of becoming impatient and almost missing the will of God. Because they crucified the flesh and trusted in God's timing, the Almighty did a wonderful work in their lives. We must follow their examples of patience and have confidence in the Lord to orchestrate every season of life for us.

BIBLE LESSON

I. NOW IS THE TIME TO SERVE GOD

We may sometimes think of the world as being inconvenient, but we live in a time of convenience beyond the wildest dreams of previous generations. The ability for most people to place an online order and receive delivery within a day or two—sometimes within an hour or two—means our needs and wants can be met very readily. Even when we find ourselves faced with the annoying inconvenience of a traffic jam that will put us home too late to make dinner, we can safely log on to a mobile ordering site, make a quick stop along the way, and have a hot delicious dinner available for our family.

With all our modern conveniences, we still have trouble making time for all the things we need to do. Our devices provide us access to the world, yet they can cut us off from family and friends. Some of us might honestly prefer visiting with neighbors on the back porch, enjoying some good old-fashioned homemade ice cream and fun conversations, instead of eating a pint of Rocky Road by ourselves, battling loneliness while we attempt to keep up with our sea of Facebook "friends," some of whom we may not know that well.

In our comfortable, user-friendly world, we may think we have little time for God. We may even look for a more convenient season to serve the Lord. We would make time to seek the face of God, but many of us feel extremely busy despite our creature comforts. We would turn to God, but something else has caught our attention—well, at least for the next thirty seconds or so. Then it is on to something else. In the midst of all this convenience, we must realize that now is the time to serve God.

What steps can we take to make more time for the Lord?

A. Time Will Eventually Rob Us of Both Opportunity and Strength

Teacher Option: *A supplemental video is available in the Resource Kit.* **V**

The story is told of an old tribal chief who welcomed missionaries to his village. He decided to become a Christian, but perhaps he did not have a proper view of serving Jesus. He felt Christians could not do much because he equated being a Christian with being old. Such an attitude ignores the vitality of a vibrant life in Christ.

We cannot ignore the fact that age will someday sap our strength and rob us of opportunities. The Preacher in Ecclesiastes declared, "Remember now thy Creator in the days of thy youth, while the evil days come not, nor the years draw nigh, when thou shalt say, I have no pleasure in them" (Ecclesiastes 12:1). When we are young, we must remember our Creator because the aging process will radically change our lives later in our lives.

In Ecclesiastes 12, the Preacher gave us metaphorical ways of understanding how our eyes, ears, legs, and even our entire body will deteriorate with age. As we read through the passage, we can see age cause us to stoop over, lose our teeth, and struggle with fading vision. The passage speaks of death being nigh and may cause us to feel a bit depressed when we read it.

The Preacher, however, was not simply warning us about getting old; he wanted us not to forget God when we are still young. Older people may struggle to hear the sermon, while young people with perfect hearing ignore it. Older people may have a difficult time reading the Word of God due to declining eyesight, while teenagers may just choose not to read it.

This passage also helps us think about eternal things such as returning to our Creator at death. It encourages us to look past the here and now to prepare for the hereafter. Everyone is guaranteed to die, but only those who repent, are baptized in Jesus' name, and receive the gift of the Holy Spirit can receive life eternal with Jesus.

B. I Will Serve God Now

In deciding to serve God now, we are not merely making a decision out of fear. We should serve God willingly and faithfully instead of thinking of salvation as a fire insurance policy that will deliver us from the flames of Hell. Fearing and remembering our Creator is far more important than being afraid of dying.

What are some things you would like to accomplish in your lifetime? What is on your "bucket list"?

The fear of the Lord will help us to keep His commandments. When we respect the Lord and His ways, we will prosper. We will benefit from the wisdom God gives us. A healthy appreciation for the finality of this life and a strong faith in the Lord who has gone to prepare a place for us creates a good balance. We must all make the commitment to serve the Lord, whether we are just beginning our walk with God or we need to renew our faith.

II. GOD WILL RIGHTEOUSLY JUDGE EVERY WORK

We must all face Judgment Day when the Lord will review our lives. This reality should help us to have the fear of the Lord and to prepare for the future. Hopefully, we can all see the wisdom of thinking past the present and looking to eternity.

A woman was doing wrong, but she did not want to stop. However, she also disliked feeling judged by others. She boldly proclaimed to some friends, "Only God can judge me." One of her friends replied, "That's right. And that should make you very afraid."

A. Every Secret Will Be Revealed and Every Word Judged

Judgment seems very scary because all our unrepented secrets will be revealed. Every word we have spoken will be evaluated. Many people who greatly desire privacy will find that they cannot hide anything from the judgment of God. Jesus gave the warning about secrets being revealed in Luke 8:17, "For nothing is secret, that shall not be made manifest; neither any thing hid, that shall not be known and come abroad." In Luke 12:3, Jesus elaborated, noting that things spoken in darkness would be heard in the light, and things whispered in someone else's ear in a closet would be proclaimed on the housetop. No one can escape their words.

Even NASA and other scientific organizations know that words last forever. Often scientists pick up decades-old radio or television broadcasts from space. The vast expanse of the universe cannot keep these words from returning. This fact should teach us to measure our words before they are measured on the scales of God's justice.

All of us have spoken idle words that we regret. Unless we repent, God will judge us for every wrong word we have spoken. Our idle words will follow us to Judgment (Matthew 12:36), but that is only the beginning of our problems. The other issue lies in the fact that we do not always properly examine our words. Proverbs 16:2 states, "All the ways of a man are clean in his own eyes; but the LORD weigheth the spirits." Our words may seem right in our eyes, but God is our Judge, and His scales are accurate.

If you were allowed only one tweet or one paragraph for the world to remember you by, what would you write?

B. I Will Align My Words, Actions, and Motives to God's Word

Given the seriousness of Judgment Day, we must make the commitment to align our words, actions, and motives with God's Word. If we speak the Word of God and live by it, we can be sure we will not be judged for those utterances. In fact, they will help us to live a better life.

The Word of God causes us to weigh our actions. We may be tempted to do something wrong, but the Holy Spirit will bring a verse of Scripture to mind to send us in the proper direction. The Lord never meant to stop us from taking action; He just wants our actions to be in sync with His Word and wisdom.

Even if we think we are engaging in the right action, we must check our motives. Sometimes we may have the right idea but the wrong impetus for making a decision. Allowing the Word of God and the Holy Spirit to steer us in the right direction will help us to stay on course.

III. OUR HIGHEST PRIORITY IS TO FEAR GOD AND KEEP HIS COMMANDMENTS

We can find ourselves heading down the wrong paths because of incorrect priorities. Even though we know better, a spiritual self-examination can sometimes reveal that we are putting the pursuit of job satisfaction, wealth, or pleasure above the Lord. A man of wealth may like to fish on Sundays in his sleek new boat, while a poor man may miss church fishing on the bank with a beat-up rod and reel. No matter their station in life, both are failing to please God. Let us all prioritize fearing God and keeping His commandments.

Some go even further and quote verses from the Bible while blatantly disobeying the very Word of God they purport to preach and obey. God has not merely called us to give lip service to His commandments. While we are thankful when we hear the Word of God, we have not done enough. Even if we receive the Word with gladness, more is required. Obedience is the practical application of the Word of God.

Think of an example of someone who blatantly disobeyed the Word of God. What was the result?

A. Our Greatest Obligation in Life Is to God

We should have no greater commitment or obligation in life than to love God and keep His commandments. While we often think of sin getting in our way, sometimes life itself can prevent us from doing the right thing. We must work to provide for our families; Scripture declares the importance of fulfilling this loving obligation. (See II Thessalonians 3:10.) However, we cannot allow making a living to prevent us from living for God.

A man once testified of the great new job the Lord had given him at the car plant. The pay and benefits were good for a growing family, but the hours were long and hard. The man soon found himself missing multiple church services and lots of family events. He went to his pastor, seeking counsel. Rather than telling the church member exactly how he should proceed, the man of God looked him in the eyes and said, "You know what you need to do."

Knowing in his heart that the pastor had read the situation perfectly, the man quit his job and started his own business. The pay was less, but the rewards of time spent with God and family more than made up the difference. Asked today if he would go back to his old job, the man would resoundingly deny even the hint of that possibility. Some may wonder why the Lord gave him that high-paying job in the first place, but the man knows the reason beyond the shadow of a doubt. The Lord wanted him to more fully appreciate his walk with God and his relationship with his wife and his children. No job is worth the loss of our relationship with the Lord or our loved ones.

B. I Will Fear God and Keep His Commandments

Like the man in this true story, we must fear God and keep His commandments. The reverence and awe we feel for the Lord should not be overshadowed by the conveniences of life or the busyness of our daily activities. God should not get lost in the shuffle of the hustle and bustle of hectic days. If we fear God, we will make time for Him, and we will keep His commandments.

Give some examples of blessings you have received from obedience to God and His Word.

The fear of the Lord should go beyond respect for God; we should be motivated to foster a love for our Creator in our hearts. While we started out walking with the Lord and felt a strong connection to Him when we first received the Holy Spirit, we must recognize that every relationship requires consistent nurturing. We cultivate our walk with God and show love for Him by keeping His commandments.

INTERNALIZING THE MESSAGE

The Christian woman found herself in a difficult situation at work. A couple of her coworkers were engaged in suspicious activity. Her boss frequently left the office, leaving her in charge. Although she was capable of handing the extra workload, more than once she wondered about the situation. Was he sick? Were there family problems she did not know about? Was something sinister afoot? He looked healthy, but his dealings seemed shady.

At the same time, she found herself carefully watching another coworker in charge of financial matters. The woman had recently gotten involved with a new love interest who seemed to show up more at her work than he should. Since they all worked for a community center, people came and went on a regular basis, but something seemed "off."

The God-fearing woman prayed that the Lord would help her with each situation. Maybe I am being paranoid, she thought. But the Holy Spirit confirmed that she should exercise wisdom and caution even though she lacked any evidence against either person. She trusted in the Lord because she knew she served the almighty God, who saw and knew things she did not.

Her concerns about her boss were confirmed when she got word that another man had threatened to shoot the boss for sleeping with his wife. The Christian woman realized the consistent absences were likely explained by adultery. Worse yet, she knew that the offended husband was likely to make good on his vow of violence because he had shot another man in the past. Fearing for her boss's safety, she told him that his personal life was none of her business, but she felt she should warn him. Although we can never truly know for sure, her intervention might have saved his life.

The Christian woman continued to exercise wisdom with the other coworker, being very careful not to engage in any of the center's financial dealings. Eventually, the coworker's dark deeds came to light. She had begun dating an ex-convict who had not truly repented and changed his ways. The two of them worked together to steal money from the company. The Christian woman thanked the Lord that she had avoided being implicated because even an innocent person can sometimes fall into the snare of the wicked.

In our daily lives, we must trust the Lord to see the things we cannot see. Although the woman felt unsure if she could trust her own judgment, she knew she could trust the wisdom of the God who judges perfectly. Because her coworkers did not fear the Lord, they broke the commandments prohibiting adultery and stealing. Because the woman feared the Lord, she was not in danger of being shot or going to prison for theft. The fear of the Lord is the beginning of wisdom, but it also helps us write good endings to stories in our lives that could turn out very differently if we fail to trust in the judgment of God.

Prayer Focus
Lead the group in prayer and consider the following topics of focus:
- Examine your life to see if you are following God and keeping His commandments
- For God to reveal to you what He would have you do in your lifetime

GOD'S WORD

FOR LIFE

ADULT LESSON GUIDE
WINTER 2022-2023

TABLE OF CONTENTS

*CS** indicates Christmas Sunday.

1.1

THE NECESSITY OF THE SPIRIT

FOCUS VERSE
John 3:5
Jesus answered, Verily, verily, I say unto thee, Except a man be born of water and of the Spirit, he cannot enter into the kingdom of God.

LESSON TEXT
John 3:1–8;
Acts 19:1–6

TRUTH ABOUT GOD
The Holy Spirit gives us new life and hope for eternal life.

TRUTH FOR MY LIFE
I will receive the gift of the Holy Spirit.

Series Overview:

This series, "The Work of the Spirit," will highlight the role of the Holy Spirit in our lives. These lessons will explore the necessity of the Spirit, what it means to be led by the Spirit and empowered by the Spirit, and how we can receive victory through the Spirit. Though we as Apostolics recognize the importance of being filled with the Holy Ghost, this series will challenge each of us to daily surrender to the work of the Spirit in our lives.

SG TEACHING OUTLINE

Icebreaker: If you had to make major income adjustments, what is the first budget item you would cut?

Lesson Connection: Share the Lesson Connection. (I)

I. JESUS STRESSED THE NECESSITY OF RECEIVING THE SPIRIT

    » *Why do you believe Jesus chose the image of new birth to describe what happens when we are saved?*

    A. Receiving the Spirit Requires Faith and Involves a Sign (V)

    » *Do you remember the first time you heard someone speak in other tongues? What did you think? How did it make you feel compared to when you experienced Him for yourself?*

    B. I Must Receive the Spirit to Be Born Again

II. PAUL STRESSED THE NECESSITY OF RECEIVING THE HOLY SPIRIT

    A. True Faith Should Be Followed by the Baptism of the Spirit

    » *Do you believe it is difficult or easy for the average person to believe God for the gift of the Holy Ghost? How can we help someone who has unbelief?*

    B. I Must Tell Others about the Necessity of Receiving the Holy Spirit

    » *Can you think of someone with whom you would like to share your testimony of being filled with the Holy Spirit? Purpose to connect with that person this week.*

III. YOU MUST BE BORN AGAIN

    A. Essential for Salvation, Sanctification, Ministry, and Resurrection

    » *Describe how the hope of the resurrection has comforted you during a time of loss.*

    B. I Will Receive the Gift of the Holy Ghost

Internalizing the Message

Prayer Focus
Lead the group in prayer and consider the following topics of focus:
• For the Holy Ghost to be poured out on those who desire to be filled
• For God to use us to share this good news with someone this week

LESSON CONNECTION

A supplemental image is available in the Resource Kit. (I)

I t was crushing. George had worked at the plant for nearly twenty years when rumors of an impending downsizing began to circulate. Once the personnel cuts started, he knew his seniority would be a factor in whether he would keep his job. But there he sat in his truck in the company parking lot, holding the letter informing him that his position had been eliminated.

What would they do? He and his wife, Lisa, had grown accustomed to a comfortable lifestyle. Suddenly, money would be tight. They would be forced to evaluate every purchase and expenditure much more carefully. They would need to discern better between needs and wants.

After the kids were in bed, George and Lisa sat down that night to discuss their situation. They held hands across the dining room table and asked God to give them wisdom to make right decisions while they waited on Him to provide the needed employment for their future. After an amen, which led to that unique peace only prayer provides, they turned their attention to their household budget. They would have to make some obvious, temporary adjustments. The vacation they had planned for that summer would have to be delayed. The funds they had been saving for a swimming pool in the backyard might have to pay bills. More meals in, fewer meals out—they would make it work. Gratefully, God quickly opened another employment door in response to George and Lisa's faithfulness and diligent prayer. Still, that season refined their perspective regarding what fiscally mattered.

In economics, some of these needs are called "necessity goods." Necessity goods are the last things customers stop buying when their income declines. And conversely, these are things to which they devote a lower percentage of their spending as their income rises. Generally, necessity goods are divided into eight categories: food, utilities, communications, housing, transportation, medicine, education, and services (such as daycare, dry cleaning, and so on).

There are some spiritual necessity goods as well. Spiritual necessity goods are those relational commodities we simply must have if we are to be in right fellowship with God. The list contains significant items such as prayer, repentance, faith, obedience, the Word of God, submission, water baptism, a pastor, and a church family, among other things.

One gift we cannot purchase but must have is the gift of the Holy Spirit. Without this living dynamic of God in our lives, we may have religion, but we do not have relationship that leads to eternal life. Being filled with His Spirit is an absolute must to live a victorious life here and be ready for the dawning of our new eternal life there.

BIBLE LESSON

I. JESUS STRESSED THE NECESSITY OF RECEIVING THE SPIRIT

Jesus chose very early in His public ministry to have an off-the-record conversation with Nicodemus about new birth in John 3. As a member of the Sanhedrin, the highest ruling body among the Jewish culture, he had significant influence and means. He had taken note of Jesus' teaching and miracles and desired to speak with Him to learn more. However, Nicodemus felt it best to do so under the cloak of darkness lest he jeopardize his social standing.

Nicodemus came to Jesus by night and acknowledged Jesus' heavenly origin. "No man," he said, "can do these miracles that thou doest, except God be with him" (John 3:2). Jesus seized upon Nicodemus's limited expression of faith to introduce a critical topic to the human lexicon. Jesus replied, "Except a man be born again, he cannot see the kingdom of God" (John 3:3). While the phrase "born again" is common to us, consider how confusing this term must have been to Nicodemus. Born again? That is not physically possible. "How can a man be born again when he is old? can he enter the second time into his mother's womb, and be born?" (John 3:4).

Why do you believe Jesus chose the image of new birth to describe what happens when we are saved?

Jesus' answer is one of the foundational planks of the New Testament church. "Verily, verily, I say unto thee, Except a man be born of water and of the Spirit, he cannot enter into the kingdom of God" (John 3:5). While being born again of the water—defined as water baptism in the New Testament—is a worthy and wonderful subject, this lesson is centered on the second half of Jesus' instruction—being born again of the Spirit. When the Holy Ghost was poured out in Acts 2, the experience Jesus promised Nicodemus became a reality on the earth.

Jesus did not say that a believer would be well served by receiving the Spirit. Nor did He say that we can be a better Christian if we do so. Nor did He merely recommend it. He commanded it in the stark clarity of His words. You must be born again.

A. Receiving the Spirit Requires Faith and Involves a Sign

Teacher Option: A supplemental video is available in the Resource Kit. **V**

Of course, today we have a great advantage over Nicodemus. He had never heard of someone being baptized with the Spirit. We, on the other hand, have the testimony of collective millions of believers who have experienced this wonder themselves. And we know they have because, as Jesus instructed, we have heard the sound. There is a sound associated with this infilling of the Spirit that is unique to it and completely confirms it. By examining the various times in the Book of Acts when someone was born again of the Spirit, we can observe the consistent sign given from Heaven of the Spirit's infilling. Just as they did in Acts 2, every individual will speak in an unknown tongue when they are first filled with the Holy Spirit.

Do you remember the first time you heard someone speak in other tongues? What did you think? How did it make you feel compared to when you experienced Him for yourself?

B. I Must Receive the Spirit to Be Born Again

What was true for Nicodemus is true for each of us as well. There is only one way to be born again: we must be filled with the Spirit of God through this miraculous Spirit baptism. Anything less does not bring us into obedience to the teaching of Jesus. The imperative remains.

This is why it is incumbent on each of us to make this desire personal. More than merely accepting this in a collective sense concerning our church or even the entire world, salvation is personal. I will not automatically be filled with the Spirit simply because I attend a church that believes this way. I do not receive the Spirit baptism just by being part of a family that has this heritage. I must desire and pursue this experience for myself. You must desire and pursue this experience for yourself.

II. PAUL STRESSED THE NECESSITY OF RECEIVING THE HOLY SPIRIT

Since Jesus taught the necessity of being born again, it makes sense that we would find record of those who followed Him declaring the same truth. And indeed we do. The apostle Paul is recorded as heralding the same message. In Acts 19, Paul arrived in Ephesus and met a group of disciples who had been impacted by John the Baptist's preaching. These men were not evil; they were believers in the coming Messiah. They desired to follow and serve Him, but they were limited by their lack of knowledge of His identity, what He taught, and what they should do.

Seeing their hunger, Paul posed a most significant question to them: "Have ye received the Holy Ghost since ye believed?" (Acts 19:2). Paul did not accept their sincerity as an adequate spiritual résumé. Rather, as soon as he realized these men sincerely loved the Lord, he prompted them to take the next necessary step of obedience and be born again of the Spirit. This is the logical and proper theological result of faith in Christ.

A. True Faith Should Be Followed by the Baptism of the Spirit

The same truth confronts us. Faith in Christ should lead to us experiencing the baptism of the Spirit. It is the natural outflow of faith in Him. When the disciples of John responded with confusion that they had not even heard of the Holy Ghost, Paul knew something was amiss. Paul was so taken aback by their response that he inquired about their water baptism. Upon learning that they had never been baptized in the name of Jesus, Paul remedied that immediately (Acts 19:5).

The very next verse records, "And when Paul had laid his hands upon them, the Holy Ghost came on them; and they spake with tongues, and prophesied" (Acts 19:6). As soon as they understood that Jesus was the Messiah, and as soon as they were baptized in Jesus' name, these men were immediately born again of the Spirit when Paul prayed for them. Their faith was not enough. Their water baptism was not enough. They had to proceed beyond mere mental assent to truth and demonstrate obedient faith to the truth. Faith is always demonstrated in obedience, and obedience will always lead to new birth for the hungry heart.

B. I Must Tell Others about the Necessity of Receiving the Holy Spirit

Do you believe it is difficult or easy for the average person to believe God for the gift of the Holy Ghost? How can we help someone who has unbelief?

While speaking with tongues is the initial sign of the infilling of the Spirit, there must be other ongoing signs that God's Spirit resides in us. This list is not exhaustive, but God's Spirit should produce fruit in us. (See Galatians 5:22–23.) His Spirit should convict us. (See John 16:8.) His Spirit should pray through us in intercession. (See Romans 8:26–27.) Since the baptism of the Holy Spirit is such a wonderful experience, we should desire everyone we know to share this same gift. Each of us who has been filled with His Spirit is commissioned to tell others. This is not the calling of preachers only; this is the commission of every believer.

III. YOU MUST BE BORN AGAIN

Can you think of someone with whom you would like to share your testimony of being filled with the Holy Spirit? Purpose to connect with that person this week.

The imperative nature of Christ's command regarding new birth in undeniable. He left no room for discussion or private opinion on the matter. Being born again is not a choice that is right for some but not for others. It is not an option that can be exercised at one's pleasure. It is a universal mandate of the church age.

A. Essential for Salvation, Sanctification, Ministry, and Resurrection

Being filled with the Spirit is an irreplaceable component of the gospel's work in our lives. According to I Corinthians 15:2–4, the gospel is defined as the death, the burial, and the resurrection of Jesus Christ. We obey the gospel by associating with Jesus' death in repentance, His burial in water baptism, and His resurrection by Spirit baptism. Only through the life-giving power of the Spirit's infilling do we have the life of Christ resident within us. These words from the Book of Romans make the Spirit's essentiality quite clear: "But ye are not in the flesh, but in the Spirit, if so be that the Spirit of God dwell in you. Now if any man have not the Spirit of Christ, he is none of his" (Romans 8:9).

Sanctification is the process of being set apart in two aspects. We are set apart from sin, and we are set apart to God. Either one without the other is incomplete. If we seek to be set apart from sin without being set apart to God, we become like the Pharisees who confused religion with relationship. If we seek to be set apart to God without being set apart from sin, we will dwell in the carnal waters of moral and ethical compromises.

The only way to be effectively sanctified is through the ongoing work of God's indwelling Spirit in our lives. Multiple verses speak to the Spirit's sanctifying work. (See Romans 15:16; I Corinthians 6:11; II Thessalonians 2:13.) God gives us the Spirit to help us resist the persistent downward pull of our flesh. "This I say then, Walk in the Spirit, and ye shall not fulfil the lust of the flesh. For the flesh lusteth against the Spirit, and the Spirit against the flesh: and these are contrary the one to the other: so that ye cannot do the things that ye would. But if ye be led of the Spirit, ye are not under the law" (Galatians 5:16–18).

The Spirit empowers us for ministry. Not every child of God is called to be a preacher, but every one of us is called to be a minister, or servant. That is how Scripture defines the word minister. We are all called to faithfully serve God, our fellow church members, and the greater kingdom. But we cannot do a spiritual work with fleshly power. We can only accomplish something of eternal value by the strength of something higher than ourselves. That strength comes by God's Spirit.

Because of God's Spirit, we have a blessed hope that the end of life here is not the end of life. Paul wrote, "But if the Spirit of him that raised up Jesus from the dead dwell in you, he that raised up Christ from the dead shall also quicken your mortal bodies by his Spirit that dwelleth in you" (Romans 8:11). Ephesians 1:14 teaches that the Spirit we have received is the down payment, or the earnest, of our eternal inheritance. At the coming of the Lord, all those who are dead in Christ will be gathered up first, and then those Spirit-filled believers who are living will be caught up to join them.

Describe how the hope of the resurrection has comforted you during a time of loss.

B. I Will Receive the Gift of the Holy Ghost

One man wisely said that a revelation without a response will only leave you with an education without an experience. When we know what we must do, it only remains for us to do it. On a very personal level, you must choose to open your heart to the New Testament experience of spiritual new birth. It is a decision you will never regret.

INTERNALIZING THE MESSAGE

The old man was a worshiper. He had walked with God for decades, and his love for the Lord had only gotten richer and deeper. While his physical strength might have been waning a bit, that did not keep him from stepping out of his pew and exercising his remaining strength in "enjoying the Holy Ghost," as he was wont to say.

A visitor to the church one night was somewhat taken aback by the elder's shouts of praise, his shuffling dance, and especially his expressions in other tongues. Having come from a religious background that denied the validity of the baptism of the Holy Ghost, the visitor was somewhat disapproving of the man's conduct.

After service, the visitor boldly made her way up to the simple, country gentleman, and with an expression on her face that could sour milk, she derisively stated, "You know, you don't have to do all that." His reply was golden. "Ma'am, you don't have to take a bath either, but it sure feels good, and it makes you more pleasant to be around."

In reality, we do have to have the Spirit. It is a necessity, but gratefully it is not an unpleasant one. His Spirit is not something we endure; He is someone we enjoy. Romans 14:17 promises us righteousness, peace, and joy in the Holy Ghost. In a world of corruption, chaos, and calamity, who would not want to experience protective righteousness, pervasive peace, and persistent joy? These promises and so much more are available to every believer who will simply obey the gospel.

A sign by an electrical panel in a workplace was meant to keep people from touching it. It read, "Warning, this will hurt while it kills you!" Perhaps we should post a sign at the altar that reads, "Attention, this will please while it saves you!" Every testimony of every Spirit-filled believer who lives full of the Spirit would agree that the gift of the Holy Ghost was the richest blessing ever received in this life. And even more, it prepares you for the life to come.

Prayer Focus
Lead the group in prayer and consider the following topics of focus:
• For the Holy Ghost to be poured out on those who desire to be filled
• For God to use us to share this good news with someone this week

1.2

LED BY THE SPIRIT

FOCUS VERSE
Romans 8:14
For as many as are
led by the Spirit of
God, they are the
sons of God.

LESSON TEXT
Exodus 13:17–22;
Acts 3:1–10;
Romans 8:12–17

TRUTH ABOUT GOD
God wants to lead
His people.

TRUTH FOR MY LIFE
I will be led by the
Spirit in all I do.

Thinking about Last Week:

Have students refer to their Daily Devotional Guide
to answer the following questions:
1. What most affected you as you read through
   the Lesson Text and the Biblical Insights?
2. How did it shape your prayers and thoughts
   throughout the week?
3. Do you feel you grew closer to the Lord this
   past week? Why or why not?

SG TEACHING OUTLINE

Icebreaker: Where is the scariest place you have gotten lost while on a trip?

Lesson Connection: Share the Lesson Connection.

I.   GOD HAS ALWAYS DESIRED TO LEAD HIS PEOPLE
» *Why do you believe God is so committed to leading His people? Why do we need to be so committed to following His leading?*

   A.   Israel Was Led by the Spirit in the Wilderness Ⓘ
» *In what ways is the Holy Spirit fire that leads us from within better than the pillar of fire that went before Israel?*

   B.   The Shepherd Desires to Lead His Sheep Ⓥ
» *Do you believe more people are comfortable being led or being driven? Why do you believe God chose the former for influencing us?*

   C.   I Will Be Led by the Spirit in All I Do

II. ACTS 3 SHOWS WHAT HAPPENS WHEN BELIEVERS ARE SPIRIT-LED
» *Think of a time over the last few weeks when you believe God led you to a hurting person. Can you look back and see His hand at work in orchestrating the interaction? How?*

   A.   The Spirit Led Peter and John to Minister

   B.   I Will Be Sensitive to the Spirit and to the Needs of Others

III. BEING LED BY THE SPIRIT, PETER ACTED IN FAITH

   A.   The People Were Amazed at the Power of God

   B.   I Will Act in Faith So Others See the Power of God
» *Relate a time when you acted in faith and God came through. What were the consequences of that moment?*

Internalizing the Message

Prayer Focus
Lead the group in prayer and consider the following topics of focus:
• For God to lead us to do what He wants us to do
• For God to help us listen for His voice and for the needs of hurting humanity

LESSON CONNECTION

The following scenario is not hard to imagine because most of us have been in similar circumstances at one time or another. Tim and his father had driven a little over an hour from their farm to the nearby large city to secure a couple of needed parts for their tractor. Since this was before the days our phones could dictate our every turn via GPS, Tim and his dad were trying to decipher an outdated and rather inaccurate map to find their way. This method simply was not working. They were lost in the maze of big city streets. They desperately looked for a familiar landmark, a helpful street sign, or anything that would point them in the right direction.

Each of them had his ideas of what to do. First, Tim suggested a left turn, but when that proved inaccurate, his dad suggested a turn to the right. "I think it's right over here." "No, I'm pretty sure it's somewhere back there." "Maybe we should ask someone?" "No, we'll figure it out." The minute hand advanced while the gas gauge receded, but they were no closer to their intended destination. The tension in the truck was palpable.

Would they get the parts they needed? Fear whispered that they might wander into a dangerous part of town. Finally, desperation won over testosterone, and the weary and frustrated travelers flagged down a man in a car stopped beside them. "Sir, can you help us? We're trying to find the ABC Widget Factory." Taking pity on the two men obviously out of their element, the urbanite replied, "You're in luck. I'm headed right by there. Just follow me, and I'll get you there in a couple of minutes." Suddenly the tension melted. Their fears faded away. Peace took over.

Why? What had changed? They still did not know where they were or where to go. They still did not have their needed tractor parts. They were no closer to what they had set out for.

But there was a difference. Now someone was leading them who did know where they were and did know where they should go. His knowledge and expertise made all the difference for them. Having someone with greater resources than you possess leading you on a confusing journey is of incredible value.

As we journey through this life, many times we are uncertain about our pathway. Questions haunt us from every side. What should I do? What choice should I make? How do I know this will get me to my destination? What if I go the wrong way? Thankfully, we have one who knows all and will direct us if we will submit to His leading. The Holy Ghost is meant to guide us through life and into glory.

BIBLE LESSON

I. GOD HAS ALWAYS DESIRED TO LEAD HIS PEOPLE

God knows we do not know our own way. We are actually rather helpless as we seek to traverse an uncertain world with only our flawed, human perceptions to guide us. The Lord inspired Jeremiah to record these words, which make this fact clear: "It is not in man that walketh to direct his steps" (Jeremiah 10:23). Left to our own direction, we will most surely make choices that lead to heartache, hurt, and chaos. All who have lived any significant length of time have seen this truth demonstrated in their own lives and in others'.

Gratefully, God does not leave us in that hopeless dilemma. We have the sweet assurance that He Himself will be our guide through life if we will trust in Him. His guidance is perfect. We never need to fear or question the direction He points us because God is infinite in wisdom. When the voice of the Lord comes in a direct word, through the pages of the Bible, or from the lips of our spiritual leaders, we can be sure it will never steer us wrong.

Why do you believe God is so committed to leading His people? Why do we need to be so committed to following His leading?

A. Israel Was Led by the Spirit in the Wilderness

One clear example of God's willingness to lead His children can be seen during the Exodus. After four hundred years in Egyptian slavery, Israel was delivered by the mighty hand of God. While God was mighty, the Israelites were undoubtedly a somewhat broken people. They had endured the deprivations and violence of their captors. It was never God's intention to bring them out of Egypt only for them to wander in circles in the wilderness. Yes, they did suffer that fate for forty years as the result of their disbelief, but God did not set them free simply to turn them loose. He planned from the outset to guide them from Egypt to Canaan, and He did so in a most spectacular fashion. "And the Lord went before them by day in a pillar of a cloud, to lead them the way; and by night in a pillar of fire, to give them light; to go by day and night: He took not away the pillar of the cloud by day, nor the pillar of fire by night, from before the people" (Exodus 13:21–22).

Teacher Option: A supplemental image is available in the Resource Kit. **I**

God's desire to guide us will require us to trust. Often we will not understand His direction. Because His ways are so far above ours, He sometimes steers us in paths we cannot understand because He knows they are best for us. He did this very thing for Israel. "And it came to pass, when Pharaoh had let the people go, that God led them not through the way of the land of the Philistines, although that was near; for God said, Lest peradventure the people repent when they see war, and they return to Egypt: but God led the people about, through the way of the wilderness of the Red sea" (Exodus 13:17–18).

In what ways is the Holy Spirit fire that leads us from within better than the pillar of fire that went before Israel?

127

B. The Shepherd Desires to Lead His Sheep

We see this inherent nature of God to lead us by His Spirit in the image of God as our Shepherd. Sheep are not driven; they are led. Any caring shepherd would carefully choose the route his flock would take. He would select it, not for his own comfort, but based on what was best for the sheep. Which route would have the best water? Which would provide abundant grazing? Which would be most secure from predators? Which would offer the fewest dangerous passages? These questions and others like them dictate the route over which a shepherd will lead his sheep.

Teacher Option:
A supplemental video is available in the Resource Kit. **V**

Do you believe more people are comfortable being led or being driven? Why do you believe God chose the former for influencing us?

In the twenty-third psalm, the writer depicted our relationship with God within the shepherd and sheep motif. The Shepherd leads us beside still waters. He leads us in paths of righteousness. He is with us even in shadowy valleys. He goes before us to prepare a table where we may dine. And the result of our following His leading is found in what follows us. "Surely goodness and mercy shall follow me all the days of my life" (Psalm 23:6). If we follow His Spirit as it leads, blessings follow us.

C. I Will Be Led by the Spirit in All I Do

Undoubtedly God will lead us by His Spirit just as He led Israel. Some might argue that we do not enjoy the same dynamic of a pillar of cloud and a pillar of fire, but we have something even better. We have the fire of God's Spirit inside of us by the baptism of the Holy Ghost. We do not have to depend on some external sign. Instead, we enjoy the daily communion of the Spirit, which directs our steps.

Leading is what God does; following is what we as His children do. "For as many as are led by the Spirit of God, they are the sons of God" (Romans 8:14). Being willing to follow God is a mark that distinguishes His children from those who are not. The sobering conclusion is that anyone not following His leading is not living as His child must live.

II. ACTS 3 SHOWS WHAT HAPPENS WHEN BELIEVERS ARE SPIRIT-LED

Following the Spirit of God will have valuable, practical benefits in the lives of His children. If we follow Him, we will not encounter unnecessary temptation. (See Matthew 6:13.) We will be safely led around the traps Satan lays for us. (See Psalm 91:3.) We will enjoy spiritual safety. (See Psalm 78:53.)

While there can be no debate that God leads us in paths for our own good, we must also recognize that He leads us in paths where we can best serve His kingdom. According to Psalm 23:3, we are led in paths of righteousness for His name's sake, not ours. He will direct us into conversations so we can testify to one who does not know Him. He will lead us to encounter a hurting soul for whom we can pray. He will even order our steps about a job transfer based on what is best for His church before what is best for us. God will lead us so hurting people can be helped.

A. The Spirit Led Peter and John to Minister

The day could have easily been just like any other. Peter and John were familiar with the sights and sounds attendant with a trip to the Temple to pray. They had made this trip more times than they could count. It was about 3:00 PM, and the area around the Temple was enjoying its usual buzz of energy and activity.

Think of a time over the last few weeks when you believe God led you to a hurting person. Can you look back and see His hand at work in orchestrating the interaction? How?

As they approached the gate called Beautiful, one sight seemed to be elevated above the others. A moment of striking clarity came to Peter as his eyes locked on a lame beggar seated beside the gate. There was no particular reason this one man arrested Peter's progress because the city was full of such scenes. With no social safety net, begging was the common plight of those unable to work. Yet for some reason Peter would have been hard pressed to explain, the whole world seemed to stop when his eyes were fastened on this needy man.

Peter was experiencing something new, the leading of the Holy Ghost. God had ordained that the lame man would be healed on that day. He simply led Peter and John to that place at that time and then turned Peter's attention toward the beggar. As Peter stood looking at the man, the voice of the Lord directed him to speak to the man and to his condition in the now famous words, "Silver and gold have I none; but such as I have give I thee: In the name of Jesus Christ of Nazareth rise up and walk" (Acts 3:6). Because Peter and John were both sensitive to and submitted to the leading of God's Spirit, the beggar's life clearly was forever changed.

B. I Will Be Sensitive to the Spirit and to the Needs of Others

God desires to accomplish ministry through the hands and voices of His children today as well. His purpose of adding to the church remains, and He will use us to accomplish that mission. As we journey through life, God will orchestrate our steps to place us in a position full of spiritual potential. We must be quick to hear and respond to His voice in such situations, living with an awareness of God's leading. When our lane at the grocery store seems to be going slower than all the others, rather than being frustrated, we should be mindful of ministry opportunities around us. Maybe the lady in front of us cannot find her coupons so we end up walking to our car at the same time as a man or woman God has been drawing. Maybe the traffic was slow so we are at the right place at the right time to pray with someone who has suffered loss. Maybe God has a plan for us to minister today if we will follow His leading.

III. BEING LED BY THE SPIRIT, PETER ACTED IN FAITH

In this biblical account, Peter did not simply become aware of the lame man's condition; he allowed God's Spirit to lead him to act in faith. Why would God have arrested Peter's attention if He were not about to unveil His power to heal? Peter did not believe he was merely to observe. Peter knew he was to act.

A. The People Were Amazed at the Power of God

Those gathered there that day had known about this man and his condition. He was over forty years of age and a daily sight at the Temple, but he had never been seen as he was on that day. But God does not operate a sideshow. He does not perform to entertain. The reason He led Peter and James to that place to perform that miracle was so multitudes would hear the message of salvation. While the people wondered at what had been done, Peter went on to declare what he needed to say. He explained how they had crucified the Messiah, and then he called on them to repent. Peter preached the gospel, and thousands believed because two men were led by God's Spirit to stop and act.

B. I Will Act in Faith So Others See the Power of God

Do not hesitate to pray for someone in the aisle of a department store. Do not be intimidated by the climate of our day from sharing your testimony of God's healing with someone in the hospital. Do not be timid or bashful when interacting with the server at a restaurant. You never know what God might have already been doing in their lives and what He is now willing to do for those He has led you to.

Relate a time when you acted in faith and God came through. What were the consequences of that moment?

If God trusts you enough to lead you to a hungry heart, you must trust Him enough to put your faith into action. He was leading you in the first place to use you effectively in His kingdom for His glory.

INTERNALIZING THE MESSAGE

Franklin Roosevelt, like every world leader, had a duty that taxed his patience. He was frequently forced to endure long receiving lines at the White House as person after person waited for the special moment to shake his hand. He felt the pressure to speak to each of them, but he complained that no one really paid any attention to what was said.

It is reported that he decided to try an experiment one day during a reception. As each person passed through the line and grasped his hand, he murmured, "I murdered my grandmother this morning." The guests responded with phrases like, "Marvelous! Keep up the good work. We are proud of you. God bless you, sir." Each was totally oblivious to what he had just said. No one appeared to actually hear his words until the guests reached the end of the line. While Roosevelt was greeting the ambassador from Bolivia, the ambassador was surprised. He composed himself, leaned over, and whispered, "I'm sure she had it coming."

One must wonder how often we treat the voice of God and His guidance in the same way. We know God is speaking and providing direction, but we blindly continue on our own way without giving attention to the directions He has provided. If we do hear His words, we find some way to explain away what they call us to.

To succeed in the Christian walk, each child of God must commit daily to being a follower of our God who leads. To be a follower, we must listen faithfully to the voice of God as He directs our way. When we do, we will be perfectly positioned for a safe passage to a secure destination and empowered to be effective servants of our King along the way.

The voice of His Spirit will speak to us regularly to ensure we are walking acceptable paths. Jesus promised this before the New Covenant had even been enacted. "Howbeit when he, the Spirit of truth, is come, he will guide you into all truth" (John 16:13). The Spirit of truth now lives inside each born-again believer. He will guide us. Will we listen?

Prayer Focus
Lead the group in prayer and consider the following topics of focus:
- For God to lead us to do what He wants us to do
- For God to help us listen for His voice and for the needs of hurting humanity

SERIES 1: THE WORK OF THE SPIRIT

1.3

EMPOWERED BY THE SPIRIT

FOCUS VERSE
Acts 1:8
But ye shall receive power, after that the Holy Ghost is come upon you: and ye shall be witnesses unto me both in Jerusalem, and in all Judaea, and in Samaria, and unto the uttermost part of the earth.

LESSON TEXT
Acts 1:1–8; 4:29–31; 9:32–43

TRUTH ABOUT GOD
God empowers His people.

TRUTH FOR MY LIFE
I will seek to be empowered by the Spirit.

Thinking about Last Week:

Have students refer to their Daily Devotional Guide to answer the following questions:
1. What most affected you as you read through the Lesson Text and the Biblical Insights?
2. How did it shape your prayers and thoughts throughout the week?
3. Do you feel you grew closer to the Lord this past week? Why or why not?

[SG] TEACHING OUTLINE

Icebreaker: What is your dream car?

Lesson Connection: Share the Lesson Connection. [I]

I. JESUS PROMISED POWER THROUGH THE SPIRIT [V]

    A. That Power Would Enable Us to Be His Witnesses
   » *How do you believe the Spirit's empowerment enables us to be witnesses more effectively?*

    B. I Will Rely on the Spirit's Power to Enable Me to Be God's Witness

II. GOD'S POWER WAS DEMONSTRATED THROUGH THE EARLY CHURCH

    A. The First Believers Asked God to Perform Miracles
   » *How often do you pray for God to perform miracles, signs, and wonders in your church or in your life?*

    B. Stephen Worked Miracles Because He Was Empowered by the Spirit
   » *Have you ever felt intimidated to believe God could perform miracles through your prayers because you thought yourself unimportant in the church? If so, what does Stephen's ministry say to you?*

    C. Peter's Ministry Was Marked by Miraculous Confirmation

    D. We Can Expect God's Power to Be Demonstrated in Our Lives
   » *Do you believe miraculous demonstrations are more or less vital to the church's mission today than in the Book of Acts?*

III. THE SPIRIT STILL EMPOWERS BELIEVERS TODAY

    A. Jesus Said Miraculous Signs Would Follow Believers
   » *How do we balance not following signs with sincerely and earnestly desiring them to follow us? Discuss how to keep this in balance.*

    B. When I Step Out in Faith, God Will Confirm His Message

Internalizing the Message

Prayer Focus
Lead the group in prayer and consider the following topics of focus:
• For God to send miracles, signs, and wonders to confirm His Word
• For God to give us boldness to declare the gospel

LESSON CONNECTION

A supplemental image is available in the Resource Kit. (I)

It all started in 1890. The members of the prestigious Valley Hunt Club in Pasadena, California, desired to spotlight the area they called "The Mediterranean of the West." The inhabitants there decided to hold a festival and invite folks from the snow-covered east for a mid-winter holiday where they could watch games such as chariot races, jousting, foot races, polo, and tug-of-war under the warm California sun. They even staged a race between a camel and an elephant. (In case you are wondering, the elephant won.)

Five years later they held a parade before the games in which the entrants decorated their carriages with flowers and other natural materials. The parade soon included marching bands, equestrian units, and motorized floats.

Today, approximately fifty floats participate in the five-and-a-half mile parade. On average, each float costs well over $250,000. Companies make this investment because nearly seven hundred thousand people watch the parade in person and approximately seventy million watch via broadcasting. For the advertisers, the extensive viewership makes the expense worthwhile through all the advertising and brand recognition. However, in 1938 one company may have regretted their decision.

Their float was making its way down Colorado Avenue with all the others. It was lavishly furnished with tens of thousands of roses. The various colors sparkled in the Southern California sunlight. Children watched wide-eyed. Parents clapped. Everything was going just fine until it was not. Suddenly, the grand vehicle's smooth progression along the parade route was interrupted. The engine coughed and sputtered. Then, much to everyone's amazement, it stopped. It had run out of gas. All the planning, preparation, expense, and execution to be a part of this growing event came to a stop until someone could return with a can of gasoline.

Ironically, the float that stopped the Tournament of Roses Parade in its tracks due to a lack of fuel was sponsored by the Standard Oil Company, the largest oil company in the world at its zenith. While the float itself ran out of fuel, the company behind it had nearly unlimited fuel. Power unrecognized and unutilized is worthless.

As children of God, we are not self-sufficient. We do not operate from a reservoir of human strength or ingenuity. Rather, we are connected to a resource of limitless power on which we draw to succeed in the Christian life. We are empowered by the Spirit. If we stay connected to God, we will never sputter to a stop on our journey.

BIBLE LESSON

I. JESUS PROMISED POWER THROUGH THE SPIRIT

Over the three years the disciples spent with Jesus, they became very accustomed to relying on Jesus' strength and power. Jesus' voice had commanded the wind and waves to be still when they were in stormy jeopardy on the Sea of Galilee. Lame men leaped and ran home because of His power. The deaf heard the voices of their children because of His power. Even death bowed at the power of Jesus' words at Lazarus's tomb, in Jairus's house, and during a funeral procession in Nain.

But Jesus was preparing to leave the disciples. Jesus made them a wonderful promise some time before, if only they would have understood. Jesus promised, "I will not leave you comfortless: I will come to you" (John 14:18). They were anticipating Jesus to come again, and indeed He will. But before His return for His church, Jesus promised that group on the hillside something more immediate. "But ye shall receive power, after that the Holy Ghost is come upon you" (Acts 1:8).

Teacher Option: A supplemental video is available in the Resource Kit. **V**

A. That Power Would Enable Us to Be His Witnesses

Within days of Jesus' declaration, this new spiritual encounter would be unveiled before the world. This was the promise of the Father fulfilled on the Day of Pentecost in Acts 2.

At this final promise of His Spirit's infilling, Jesus drew attention to a different effect of this experience. "But ye shall receive power, after that the Holy Ghost is come upon you: and ye shall be witnesses unto me both in Jerusalem, and in all Judaea, and in Samaria, and unto the uttermost part of the earth" (Acts 1:8). Christ pointed out that the Spirit's empowerment was given so we may do the work of spreading His gospel throughout the earth. This is one of the many wonderful reasons He indwells us.

How do you believe the Spirit's empowerment enables us to be witnesses more effectively?

B. I Will Rely on the Spirit's Power to Enable Me to Be God's Witness

Certainly the new church in Acts needed God's power to evangelize their world, but we do as well. It is likely we need His Spirit even more. The culture around us is godless, and about the only thing assured to generate absolute hatred is a commitment to absolutes. The pond in which we fish for new believers is poisoned with all manner of human philosophy and corruption. Spiritual confusion so permeates our society that even something as basic as gender has been twisted until we are told there are over one hundred different genders beyond male and female.

This is the world we have been commissioned to reach. In witnessing to those so heavily influenced by the godless themes of today, it is vital that we are empowered by the Holy Ghost.

Only His influence and touch can sufficiently pierce the spiritual callouses surrounding the human heart today. The demonstration of spiritual power is vital for us to successfully reach our world. He has promised that the baptism of His Spirit would provide exactly that.

II. GOD'S POWER WAS DEMONSTRATED THROUGH THE EARLY CHURCH

The promise of power to the early church was realized on the Day of Pentecost when the baptism of the Holy Spirit was first given. On that noteworthy day, miraculous fire rested on each of the 120 gathered there, and they began to speak with other tongues as the power of the Spirit filled their lives. As soon as they were filled with the Spirit, the Spirit's power within them began to be evident. Simon Peter, who a few weeks earlier had been so intimidated by being associated with Jesus that he cursed and denied he even knew Jesus, stood before the gathered crowd and boldly declared the gospel. The explanation for this change in behavior is the transformative nature of the Spirit.

A. The First Believers Asked God to Perform Miracles

Immediately after the miracle at the gate, Peter and John were thronged by the multitude. They identified the Spirit as the source of the miraculous power that healed the formerly lame man. Upon doing so, the religious authorities were incensed and had the disciples arrested and held overnight. The next day the religious rulers agreed to threaten them to no longer speak in the name of Jesus to any man. However, the disciples testified that they had to obey the directions of the Spirit, which empowered them.

The disciples quickly recognized what a powerful demonstration of the Spirit produced. According to Acts 4:4, after the lame man was healed and the disciples preached to the gathered multitude, the people responded to the gospel, and God brought the number of believers up to five thousand men. That revelation of the Spirit's power led to the declaration of the gospel through the Holy Ghost. The disciples prayed specifically for God to replicate this powerful pattern again and again.

How often do you pray for God to perform miracles, signs, and wonders in your church or in your life?

B. Stephen Worked Miracles Because He Was Empowered by the Spirit

This pattern of miraculous demonstration leading to public declaration is repeated throughout the Book of Acts. Consider the life of Stephen. As the number of Christians began to grow rapidly, the early church leaders were taxed with the overwhelming temporal needs of many of the members. Elders needed to be cared for. Widows needed provisions. Some felt the Grecian widows were being neglected because they were Grecian, not Jewish. In response, the apostles called the believers together and reminded them that their first and highest calling was to pray, study, and seek God, not to wait on tables. Accordingly, they sought out seven men of good reputation—who were filled with wisdom and the Spirit—to attend to such matters. Among these servant-hearted men was Stephen.

One way the Scriptures describe him is found in Acts 6:8. "And Stephen, full of faith and power, did great wonders and miracles among the people." This faithful servant of God was so full of power that God used him to facilitate great wonders and miracles. The Spirit worked these wonders all while Stephen waited on tables. Each of us should seek for God to likewise use us alongside and within our daily routines.

These works were done "among the people." Once again, the purpose for these miraculous acts was to capture the attention of the people so they would be open to the gospel. The power of God that came on the church equipped them to be witnesses unto Him.

C. Peter's Ministry Was Marked by Miraculous Confirmation

In Acts 9, Peter went to worship with the saints in Lydda. Upon arriving, he was introduced to a man named Aeneas, who had suffered some kind of paralysis for eight years. This palsy left him completely bedfast and unable to care for himself. The power of God in Peter was activated by faith, and he declared the following. "Jesus Christ maketh thee whole: arise, and make thy bed" (Acts 9:34). The man arose immediately. God used this miraculous power to reach the lost. "And all that dwelt at Lydda and Saron saw him, and turned to the Lord" (Acts 9:35). The empowering of the Spirit produced a successful witness.

The next occurrence was in nearby Joppa. A lady there named Tabitha, or Dorcas as she was known in Greek, was much beloved among the family of Christian believers there. She fell ill and died, and since Peter was nearby, they sent for him. When he arrived, "Peter put them all forth, and kneeled down, and prayed; and turning him to the body said, Tabitha, arise. And she opened her eyes: and when she saw Peter, she sat up. And he gave her his hand, and lifted her up, and when he had called the saints and widows, presented her alive" (Acts 9:40–41).

That resurrection was powerful, but what is noted next is powerful as well. "And it was known throughout all Joppa; and many believed in the Lord" (Acts 9:42). When the believers were empowered by the Spirit, the miraculous led to an ingathering of souls. The fame of what God did produced attention to what God said.

D. We Can Expect God's Power to Be Demonstrated in Our Lives

Being used by God in such fashions should not be a surprise to the believer. God's purpose of reaching the lost with the gospel has not changed. What worked then will work now. We can expect miraculous demonstrations of God's power in our own

Have you ever felt intimidated to believe God could perform miracles through your prayers because you thought yourself unimportant in the church? If so, what does Stephen's ministry say to you?

lives. While we cannot conjure up a miracle by any repetition of specific words, fervor, or volume, we can exercise simple faith in the power of God in us. "Now unto him that is able to do exceeding abundantly above all that we ask or think, according to the power that worketh in us, unto him be glory in the church by Christ Jesus throughout all ages, world without end. Amen" (Ephesians 3:20–21).

Do you believe miraculous demonstrations are more or less vital to the church's mission today than in the Book of Acts?

III. THE SPIRIT STILL EMPOWERS BELIEVERS TODAY

Our mission and God's intention to equip us for it have not changed from the days of the apostles until now. We hear the same commission they heard firsthand. "Go ye therefore, and teach all nations, baptizing them in the name of the Father, and of the Son, and of the Holy Ghost: teaching them to observe all things whatsoever I have commanded you" (Matthew 28:19–20). We are compelled to carry the good news of salvation to people next door and to people around the world. And we have the assurance that God is with us as He was with the disciples.

A. Jesus Said Miraculous Signs Would Follow Believers

Our confidence in the Spirit's empowering of our walk with Jesus and work for Him is rooted directly in promises from Him. "And these signs shall follow them that believe; In my name shall they cast out devils; they shall speak with new tongues; they shall take up serpents; and if they drink any deadly thing, it shall not hurt them; they shall lay hands on the sick, and they shall recover" (Mark 16:17–18). These signs follow us, not the other way around. We simply anticipate that God, in His good pleasure, will insert those signs into our lives and ministries to accomplish His will. We are not performers on a stage who conjure up the spectacular to garner attention for ourselves. We are Spirit-filled servants whose Master has assured us that signs and wonders will be attendant to our labors, and only He gets the glory.

How do we balance not following signs with sincerely and earnestly desiring them to follow us? Discuss how to keep this in balance.

B. When I Step Out in Faith, God Will Confirm His Message

We should never seek to be self-aggrandizing, but neither should we cower in fear or intimidation. As a child of God filled with His Spirit, we are ambassadors for Christ in this world. Just as natural ambassadors speak, knowing their home government stands behind them with all its might and authority, so may we. We can speak with delegated authority and a calm assurance that the power of Heaven living in us will be demonstrated in His timing, according to His purpose, and for His glory.

Go. Teach. Baptize. The Spirit will empower you to do so, and miraculous signs will follow you.

INTERNALIZING THE MESSAGE

Tim and Andrea had been saving for years to purchase their new dream car. For most of their married life, they dreamed of driving off the lot as the sun gleamed off the shiny finish and they sat in the luxury of a spotless interior still engulfed in that new-car smell. Each month as they set aside funds, they envisioned that moment. At long last they placed the order, having carefully chosen the color, the style, and each option they wanted on it. Then the wait began for delivery.

Imagine the excitement when Tim called Andrea from work to tell her that the dealership had called and their new car had arrived. They made immediate plans to go there that evening to pick up the keys and realize their long-awaited dream.

When they arrived, there it sat. Glistening in the fading sunlight, it was perfect in every way to them. After they signed the necessary paperwork, Tim settled behind the wheel of his new car for the first time. As he inserted the key, he inhaled deeply the aroma of all the years of saving for this moment. With a loving glance over at Andrea, he turned the key, and . . . nothing happened—not so much as a sound from under the hood.

Tim jumped out of the car and called to the salesperson rather animatedly, "It's dead. The engine is dead."

"No," the salesperson replied. "It's not dead. It just doesn't have an engine. But doesn't it look great?"

Andrea was able to revive Tim after a few minutes. What good is a car that looks spectacular but has no functional source of power? What good is a Christian who might look the part but is similarly powerless? As children of God, we must recognize that we are empowered by the Spirit of God, and we must utilize that power. Tim and Andrea would have been no better off if they had a car with a functioning engine but they never started it. Their car would still have been only for show.

If we never trust in or utilize the powerful infilling of the Spirit we have received, looking the part will not get the job done. Our mission and the desperate condition of our world demand that we insert the key of faith into the ignition and fire up the mighty source of power resident within us.

Start it up. It runs great!

Prayer Focus
Lead the group in prayer and consider the following topics of focus:
- For God to send miracles, signs, and wonders to confirm His Word
- For God to give us boldness to declare the gospel

WORSHIPING WITH SHEPHERDS AND WISE MEN

FOCUS VERSE
Matthew 2:11
And when they were come into the house, they saw the young child with Mary his mother, and fell down, and worshipped him: and when they had opened their treasures, they presented unto him gifts; gold, and frankincense and myrrh.

LESSON TEXT
Matthew 2:11;
Luke 2:15–17

TRUTH ABOUT GOD
God came to be accessible to everyone.

TRUTH FOR MY LIFE
I will worship God no matter my station in life.

Thinking about Last Week:

Have students refer to their Daily Devotional Guide to answer the following questions:
1. What most affected you as you read through the Bible Reading Plan, the Lesson Text, and the Biblical Insights?
2. How did it shape your prayers and thoughts throughout the week?
3. Do you feel you grew closer to the Lord this past week? Why or why not?

SG TEACHING OUTLINE

Icebreaker: What is the most unique nativity scene you have ever seen?

Lesson Connection: Share the Lesson Connection.

I.   WORSHIPING WITH THE SHEPHERDS Ⓥ
>> *What sights and sounds do you often associate with worship?*

A.   The Shepherds Left Their Flocks Behind When They Came to Jesus

B.   I Will Leave Things Behind When I Come to Jesus
>> *Why do you think Jesus asked this rich young man to sell everything and give the money to the poor?*
>> *Can you name other people in the Bible who left things behind to show their love and devotion for Jesus?*

II.   WORSHIPING WITH THE WISE MEN

A.   The Wise Men Brought Gifts When They Came to Jesus Ⓘ
>> *Aside from Jesus, who is your favorite character in the Christmas story?*

B.   I Will Bring My Gifts When I Come to Jesus
>> *What are some other things we can bring to Jesus when we come to worship?*

Internalizing the Message Ⓘ

Prayer Focus
Lead the group in prayer and consider the following topics of focus:
• For God to help us leave behind whatever we need to when we come to Him
• For God to help us bring our gifts to Him when we come to Him

LESSON CONNECTION

I t may have been a silent night for some sleepy families in Bethlehem, but it was a glorious night for the shepherds. While they were watching their flocks, an angel of the Lord appeared to them to announce the birth of Jesus. They may have expected a visit from a wolf, but they certainly didn't plan on a visit from an angel. Their response was decisive and filled with excitement as they said one to another, "Let us now go" (Luke 2:15). Because of their elation at the announcement of the birth of Jesus, they left their flocks behind so they could go to worship the Christ child.

After the birth of Jesus, a star appeared in the heavens and settled over the home where Jesus and His family lived. This bright star was noticed by some wise men, possibly astrologers who lived in the East. Although we sing about three kings, we do not know how many wise men joined forces to make the long journey to discover the meaning of the star. We do know they came a long way and it took them a long time to find their way to Jesus. But thankfully, they found Jesus. After their tiring journey, they arrived at the house of Mary and Joseph, not the stable as some stories portray. In fact, it is believed that Jesus was about two years old when the wise men found Him. We know this because the Book of Matthew records King Herod ordering all male children two years and younger, living in Bethlehem and the immediate vicinity, to be killed, hoping Jesus would be among them.

When the wise men arrived, they had brought treasures with them: gold, frankincense, and myrrh. They presented these gifts to Jesus as an act of worship. They may not have known everything about the Christ, but they knew enough to bring Him gifts of worship.

So, while the shepherds left their flocks behind to go worship Jesus, the wise men traveled a long way bringing treasures with them when they came to worship Jesus. At times worship involves us leaving some things behind, like the shepherds did; at other times worship involves bringing some things with us to present to the Lord, like the wise men did.

BIBLE LESSON

I. WORSHIPING WITH THE SHEPHERDS

Merriam-Webster tells us that *worship* is "to regard with great or extravagant respect, honor, or devotion." Worship can mean showing adoration, having a feeling of profound love and admiration, and loving without question or even to excess. Our love for God should be manifested in our worship of Him. Not only does our worship honor God, but nothing is more fulfilling as a human than being in the presence of God, worshiping Him with all of our heart.

Worship must begin with a knowledge or revelation of whom we worship. To be pleasing to God, this knowledge and revelation must come from God's Word. The night the angel of the Lord appeared to the shepherds was a night of revelation and understanding for them. No doubt what they learned about God prior to that night was eclipsed by the glory of the Lord shining around them. Tradition and past experience must yield to biblical truths and greater revelation.

True biblical worship will satisfy completely, so we do not have to shop around for man-made substitutes. William Temple made this clear in his masterful definition of worship, shared by Warren Wiersbe in his book *The Integrity Crisis.* "For worship is the submission of all our nature to God. It is the quickening of conscience by His holiness; the nourishment of mind with His truth; the purifying of imagination by His beauty; the opening of the heart to His love; the surrender of will to His purpose—and all of this gathered up in adoration, the most selfless emotion of which our nature is capable and therefore the chief remedy for that self-centeredness which is our original sin and the source of all actual sin."

Teacher Option: *A supplemental video is available in the Resource Kit.* **V**

What sights and sounds do you often associate with worship?

A. The Shepherds Left Their Flocks Behind When They Came to Jesus

The shepherds were being summoned to a higher place of worship and adoration than ever before. They were so impacted by the multitude of heavenly host that they all agreed to leave their flocks to go worship. If we want to come to Jesus and become all He wants us to be, we may have to leave some things behind.

We are not the first to leave things behind to follow our God. This principle is introduced to us in the Old Testament. When a man desires to marry, he must "leave his father and his mother, and shall cleave unto his wife" (Genesis 2:24). If a woman wants to marry, she must leave her home and be joined to her husband.

Another instance in the Old Testament tells us Abraham had to leave his home country to obey the call of God on his life (Genesis 12:1-3). Sometimes God will call on us to leave some things behind as a form of worship to show our love and devotion to Him. One of the Ten Commandments tells us, "Thou shalt have no other gods before me" (Exodus 20:3). God should always be first in our lives. Other gods in our lives can be jobs, success, beauty, or money, just to name a few.

B. I Will Leave Things Behind When I Come to Jesus

In Matthew 19:16–22, a story is told of one who came to Jesus. He was young and he was rich. He referred to Jesus as "Good Master" in an attempt to show Jesus he knew Him and had learned of Him. This rich young man then asked, "What must I do to inherit eternal life?" After Jesus responded, this young man made it clear he had obeyed the commandments. When Jesus asked him to sell everything he owned and follow Him, the young man could not do it. There were some things he could not leave behind, and it cost the young man the relationship with Jesus he sought after.

Why do you think Jesus asked this rich young man to sell everything and give the money to the poor?

In contrast to the wise men, the shepherds—being poor and lowly—had nothing to bring with them. However, there were some things they could leave behind. Like many of the Jews during Jesus' lifetime, the shepherds realized the path they were on was not leading them to growth and fulfillment in their relationship with God. That night everything changed, and it changed with fresh and new revelation. Jesus had been born and the shepherds were willing to leave everything behind to worship Him.

Can you name other people in the Bible who left things behind to show their love and devotion for Jesus?

As Jews, these shepherds had been instructed by the Law—our Old Testament—to love and worship God. The Book of Deuteronomy contains the *Shema*, the heart of Old Testament worship, "And thou shalt love the LORD thy God with all thine heart, and with all thy soul, and with all thy might" (Deuteronomy 6:5).

The Jews had been tempted on many occasions to worship idols and sin against God. Scripture reveals several times they turned their backs on God and left Him behind. But when God extended mercy and called them back to Himself, they were often too poor to bring treasures. Instead, they were asked to leave some things behind. Leaving their old lives was in itself an act of worship.

What would it have been like to have received an angelic invitation, to be the first of humanity to visit God manifest in the flesh and have nothing to bring? If you have ever gone to a birthday party or wedding reception and realized you forgot to bring a gift, it can be somewhat embarrassing. The shepherds were the first people to arrive, according to Luke, but they arrived empty-handed. Perhaps they did not know what to bring. Or perhaps the excitement of the angelic announcement so stunned them that they decided to go where Jesus was before even thinking about an appropriate gift. The shepherds show us the importance of presenting our own selves as gifts of worship to the King of kings.

II. WORSHIPING WITH THE WISE MEN

A. The Wise Men Brought Gifts When They Came to Jesus

In contrast, Gentile worshipers were on their way to see this Messiah. These wise men were not coming empty-handed. Their gifts tell us a lot about what we ought to think when we approach the Lord to worship. When we come to worship, we ought to bring gifts that tell Jesus we recognize who He is and desire to give Him worship He is worthy of.

Aside from Jesus, who is your favorite character in the Christmas story?

Matthew is the only writer who mentioned wise men. Mark and John made no comment about the birth of Christ, while Luke, who wrote the most about the events surrounding Jesus' birth, left this scene out. Matthew's single, brief passage has not only sparked a great deal of imaginative speculation over the centuries but has also raised a lot of questions. Although Matthew mentioned three types of gifts the wise men presented, there may have been two, three, or more men in this band of travelers. Some have even suggested there might have been as many as twelve.

Teacher Option: *Show image to either take the place of the question or to help illustrate it.* **I**

One of the most familiar images from any nativity scene may be the wise men attending Jesus' birth and the star hovering over the stable where He was born. But few people actually know what the Bible really says about this event, or what it actually means for us today.

In Matthew 2:1, we read, "Now when Jesus was born in Bethlehem of Judaea in the days of Herod the king, behold, there came wise men from the east to Jerusalem." It would appear from Matthew 2:2, 7, that the star, which the wise men had seen, had first appeared the night of Jesus' birth. Matthew says the Magi came to Jerusalem seeking the Messiah, having seen the star that had been in the sky since His birth. King Herod summoned these Magi and wanted to know the exact time the star had appeared, presumably so he could pinpoint the precise moment of Jesus' birth. We are not sure what these wise men told him, but knowing that Herod issued a decree to kill all baby boys two years old and under may indicate Jesus had been born up to two years earlier. The wise men did not arrive at the same time as the shepherds, who arrived the same day as Jesus' birth. Indeed, Jesus' family was no longer in a stable; they were living in a house at the time of the wise men's arrival.

"And when they were come into the house, they saw the young child with Mary his mother, and fell down, and worshipped him: and when they had opened their treasures, they presented unto him gifts; gold, and frankincense, and myrrh" (Matthew 2:11).

Whether these wise men understood what their gifts may have represented, the gifts they gave held great significance. These gifts truly reflected the character of Jesus. They were also prophetic as they represented who Jesus was and what He would ultimately suffer. The wise men's worship and adoration of Him were in large part represented in what they brought to Him.

The gold may have represented His royalty. Jesus was the King of the Jews. He was and is the King of kings. The wise men may have recognized this. They completely bypassed King Herod—bringing Herod nothing—and gave their complete allegiance to Jesus. They brought Jesus frankincense, which was an aromatic incense. This gift may have represented His divinity. He truly was God in flesh, thereby making Him qualified to offer Himself as a sacrifice. Among their treasures was myrrh. Myrrh was a perfume used during the embalming process. This gift may have represented—in a prophetic manner—the future death and burial of Jesus. Myrrh may have represented His suffering and humanity.

B. I Will Bring My Gifts When I Come to Jesus

The wise men worshiped based on their God-given revelation of Him. They worshiped the one who was King, Priest, and would sacrifice Himself for their redemption. Today, we may not bring literal gifts to Him, but we can bring Him the rest of our lives, making Him the true King of our lives. We can bring Him our desires, showing Him our lives are not going to be based on things that make us happy but things that make Him happy. We can bring our love: our love for Him, our love for ourselves, and our love for others. We can bring Him our faith, our lives, our families, and our finances. We can bring Him our faith in the future, which may involve retirement, traveling, hobbies, health, and even the Rapture or death. We can bring Him our faith in Heaven itself.

What are some other things we can bring to Jesus when we come to worship?

When we come to Jesus, we leave sin and worldliness behind. We bid farewell to sinful habits and addictions. These actions show us and Jesus that we love Him and desire to please Him. This is worship. We worship with the shepherds when we leave our sinful past behind us and submit to His will for our lives. We worship with the wise men when we bring Him gifts of faith and obedience, showing we trust Him and submit our lives to Him. All our desires, hopes, and dreams are now in His hands. We choose to serve and worship Him, not just on Christmas Day as we celebrate His birth, but every day of our lives.

INTERNALIZING THE MESSAGE

A supplemental image is available in the Resource Kit. Ⓘ

Robertson McQuilkin, former president of Columbia International University of Columbia, South Carolina, shared his testimony.

"Life was heavy on me. My dearest friend and intimate companion, my delightful wife Muriel, was slipping away, one painful loss at a time, as Alzheimer's disease ravaged her brain. Just as the full impact of what was happening to us hit home, the life of Bob, our eldest son, was snuffed out in a diving accident. Two years later, to care for Muriel, I left my life work at its peak. I was numb. Not bitter, let alone angry. Why should I be? That's the way life is, life in a broken world. But the passion in my love for God had evaporated, leaving a residue of resignation where once had been vibrant faith.

"I knew that I was in deep trouble, and I did the only thing I knew to do—I went away to a mountain hideaway for prayer and fasting. It took about twenty-four hours to shake free of preoccupation with my own wounds and to focus on the excellencies of God. As I did, slowly love began to be rekindled. And with love came joy. I wrote God a love letter, naming forty-one of His marvelous gifts to me, spotlighting eleven of His grandest acts in history, and exulting in ten of His characteristics that exceed my imagination. Surely He enjoyed my gratitude—who doesn't appreciate gratitude?

"But I discovered something else. Something happened to me. I call it the reflex action of thanksgiving. My love flamed up from the dying embers, and my spirit soared. I discovered that ingratitude impoverishes—but that a heavy heart lifts on the wings of praise."

Sometimes we are like the wise men who bring something magnificent to Jesus; sometimes we are like the shepherds who leave behind something to come to Jesus. Either way, let us choose to come to Him every day and worship Him with all our heart.

Prayer Focus
Lead the group in prayer and consider the following topics of focus:
- For God to help us leave behind whatever we need to when we come to Him
- For God to help us bring our gifts to Him when we come to Him

SERIES 1: THE WORK OF THE SPIRIT

1.4

VICTORY THROUGH THE SPIRIT

FOCUS VERSE
Romans 8:6
For to be carnally minded is death; but to be spiritually minded is life and peace.

LESSON TEXT
Romans 7:14–8:8

TRUTH ABOUT GOD
Only God's Spirit can produce lasting victory in our lives.

TRUTH FOR MY LIFE
I will live in victory through the power of the Spirit.

Thinking about Last Week:

Have students refer to their Daily Devotional Guide to answer the following questions:
1. What most affected you as you read through the Lesson Text and the Biblical Insights?
2. How did it shape your prayers and thoughts throughout the week?
3. Do you feel you grew closer to the Lord this past week? Why or why not?

SG TEACHING OUTLINE

Icebreaker: How many steps do you get in each day?

Lesson Connection: Share the Lesson Connection.

I. SUBMITTING TO THE SPIRIT IS THE ONLY WAY TO OVERCOME THE FLESH
    » *Why do you believe it is so difficult for us to overcome our flesh?*

    A. Jesus' Humanity Submitted to God's Plan in Gethsemane
        » *Can you think of a time when you prayed this prayer of Jesus regarding your will and His? Share the story and the outcome with the group.*

    B. I Will Submit to the Spirit through Prayer

II. I HAVE VICTORY THROUGH THE SPIRIT

    A. Free from Condemnation and the Law of Sin and Death
        » *How can we keep this law of sin in our members from becoming an excuse for giving in to temptation?*
        » *What do you see as the primary differences between conviction and condemnation?*

    B. I Will Live in the Freedom Granted by the Spirit

III. WALKING IN THE SPIRIT V
        » *What is your definition of walking in the Spirit? How should walking with Him affect our daily lives?*

    A. Experiencing Life and Peace through the Spirit

    B. I Will Live in Victory through the Power of the Spirit

Internalizing the Message I

Prayer Focus
Lead the group in prayer and consider the following topics of focus:
• Committing to God to walk daily with Him
• For God to give us the power we need to overcome temptation

LESSON CONNECTION

I t was the least likely day for an attack, which is probably why the coalition of Arab nations chose it. October 6, 1973, was the Jewish Day of Atonement (or Yom Kippur), the holiest day on Israel's calendar. Since this was also during Ramadan, a holy month in Islam, there was no reason for the nation of Israel to expect any military action against them.

Certainly, in the twenty-five years since Israel became a formal state in 1948, there had been a few seasons of armed conflict just to maintain their existence. Israel had already survived the Suez Crisis, the Six-Day War, and what was commonly called the War of Attrition. The idea of defending herself against her enemies was regrettably familiar, but no one expected it on that October morning in 1973. But it came anyway.

Forces from Syria, Egypt, Jordan, Iraq, Saudi Arabia, Libya, Tunisia, Algeria, and Morocco descended on Israel in the early morning hours. They were even supplemented by forces from Fidel Castro's Cuba. Their primary targets were the Sinai Peninsula in the south near Egypt and the Golan Heights in the north near Syria.

Collectively, the attacking forces outnumbered the Israeli Defense Force (IDF) by three to one. Plus, Israel's enemies were armed with the latest in Soviet military equipment, including double the tanks and artillery pieces. The outcome seemed to be a foregone conclusion to the aggressors and to the rest of the world watching with grave concern. But God had other plans for His special people.

The IDF launched counterattacks, and just seven days later, they had pushed the enemy forces in the north back far enough that the Israelis were lobbing artillery shells into the Syrian capital of Damascus. By the time the United Nations brokered a ceasefire on October 25, just nineteen days after the surprise attack, the IDF was within approximately sixty miles of the Egyptian capital of Cairo. Many consider this to be one of the top five most surprising military victories in history.

There can be very little question that God intervened on behalf of His people in that 1973 conflict, and this should come as no surprise. Every child of God who has lived for Him for any significant length of time has seen Him do the same. By the power of His Spirit that lives within us, we have seen Him snatch victory from the jaws of defeat time after time. Just when a situation looks hopeless, a victorious outcome is affected by the moving of His Spirit.

Born-again believers have a resident powerful source of victory producing miracles more spectacular than the Yom Kippur War. Humanity is able to triumph over flesh, sin, and death by the might of the Holy Spirit.

BIBLE LESSON

I. SUBMITTING TO THE SPIRIT IS THE ONLY WAY TO OVERCOME THE FLESH

We are held hostage by our flesh (our carnal selfish instinct). The truth of that shocking statement is self-evident with even a cursory examination of our lives. Our spiritual nature brought to life by new birth exists in a vehicle of temporal existence, which consistently gravitates away from obedience to God. It is not just that our flesh struggles in pleasing God; it cannot do so. "So then they that are in the flesh cannot please God" (Romans 8:8).

Even after we are born again and receive the Spirit of God, our flesh is still not able to be in harmony with our spirit "For the flesh lusteth against the Spirit, and the Spirit against the flesh: and these are contrary the one to the other: so that ye cannot do the things that ye would" (Galatians 5:17). This condition seems dire. Since the carnal mind cannot be subject to God and the flesh is completely contrary to the Spirit, and since our earthly existence is constrained to flesh, how are we supposed to succeed in living for God? The answer is found in Romans 8:9: "But ye are not in the flesh, but in the Spirit, if so be that the Spirit of God dwell in you." Those who have been born again by Spirit baptism have power whereby we live a new life. Our old nature dies in repentance, is buried in baptism, and we rise to enjoy a new life. (See Romans 6:4.)

Nothing else empowers us to overcome the flesh except the Spirit of God. We cannot rely on willpower, resolutions, good ideas, or self-help books. We can mortify our flesh and live after the Spirit only when we submit to God's influence and leadership in our lives. Absent that, our flesh will consistently overcome our best intentions and rule over our lives.

Why do you believe it is so difficult for us to overcome our flesh?

A. Jesus' Humanity Submitted to God's Plan in Gethsemane

Jesus is the perfect example of this principle. He had already warned His disciples that He was about to be executed. "From that time forth began Jesus to shew unto his disciples, how that he must go unto Jerusalem, and suffer many things of the elders and chief priests and scribes, and be killed, and be raised again the third day" (Matthew 16:21).

Because Jesus knew what was ahead of Him, it is reasonable that His flesh would recoil from the terrors He was soon to face. The scourge, thorns, and nails all deposited their agony on Him just as they would on any other human. He was exempt neither from the pain nor the fear that its impending arrival produced. His flesh passionately desired to be delivered from this suffering. If Jesus had chosen to yield to His flesh and reject the will of God, redemption would never have occurred.

151

We are allowed to see the moment when this submission occurred in the Gospels as they record His nighttime journey to an olive grove known as Gethsemane. In that quiet place, Jesus waged the war between flesh and Spirit. "And he was withdrawn from them about a stone's cast, and kneeled down, and prayed, saying, Father, if thou be willing, remove this cup from me: nevertheless not my will, but thine, be done" (Luke 22:41–42).

Can you think of a time when you prayed this prayer of Jesus regarding your will and His? Share the story and the outcome with the group.

B. I Will Submit to the Spirit through Prayer

Within the final words of Luke 22:42 we find the answer for our daily struggle with our flesh: "Not my will, but thine, be done." That prayer is the key. We can live a life of victory over our flesh by the power of the Spirit if we consciously and soberly choose to follow God's will, not our own.

The will of God is not only concerned with major life choices that might come along every couple of years; God's will is invested in the hundreds of small choices we make each day that affect our spiritual direction. Years ago, WWJD was a growing trend. People were asking, "What would Jesus do?" The focus on WWJD of recent years is good, but it may not be the best question. Perhaps we would be better to ask, "WWJHMD?" Instead of what would Jesus do, perhaps we should ask, "What would Jesus have me do?" The answer to that question should guide our decisions.

II. I HAVE VICTORY THROUGH THE SPIRIT

The spiritual battle in which we are engaged is fierce. The enemy of our souls does not play by any set of rules. There is no Geneva Convention that governs the conduct of the warriors in this battle. Since we know this, we should take this matter seriously. We should not cross over the threshold to new life through the salvation message with any false expectation that there is only tranquility on the other side. Instead, we enter into a war. Paul said, "But I see another law in my members, warring against the law of my mind, and bringing me into captivity to the law of sin which is in my members" (Romans 7:23). From the first moment of our new life as a born-again Christian, there will be a conflict raging in us and around us.

Living full of the Holy Ghost and under His direction and lordship are the keys to experiencing ongoing victory as we journey through this world. Every foe, whether demonic or fleshly, must bow to the power of the Spirit. In myself, I am destined to be conquered; in the power of the Spirit, I am assured of abundant victory. "If ye through the Spirit do mortify the deeds of the body, ye shall live" (Romans 8:13).

A. Free from Condemnation and the Law of Sin and Death

Paul expressed his solidarity with every Christian of all ages when he identified with our common struggle. The things we know we should do seem to be a struggle to actually do. Things we know we should not do are very easy to do. The apostle expressed it this way, "For to will is present with me; but how to perform that which is good I find not. For the good that I would I do not: but the evil which I would not, that I do" (Romans 7:18-19).

Consider the enemy's playbook. He tempts a believer to sin, the believer gives in to temptation, and Satan points his finger in the believer's face. The enemy of our soul declares the believer guilty, dirty, and worthless, hoping for punishment against the believer for the very action Satan suggested in the first place. As children of God, if we embrace these lies, we can quickly feel isolated from the Savior who only longs for repentance so He may forgive and restore us to pure fellowship.

This inclination toward sin found in our flesh and the resulting condemnation it can produce are not weak foes. They may only be overcome by the power of the Holy Ghost, but they can be overcome. Consider the testimony of the Scriptures. "O wretched man that I am! who shall deliver me from the body of this death? I thank God through Jesus Christ our Lord. So then with the mind I myself serve the law of God; but with the flesh the law of sin" (Romans 7:24-25). Jesus Christ delivers us from the death waiting in our flesh when we disobey God's Word. His Spirit gives us victory over the practice, the power, and the penalty of sin.

"There is therefore now no condemnation to them which are in Christ Jesus, who walk not after the flesh, but after the Spirit" (Romans 8:1). When we walk after the Spirit, condemnation is not our spiritual heritage. God's Spirit leads us to repentance and the resultant communion with God. We are convicted of our sin so we may repent, but we are not judged worthless or dirty when we repent. John wrote, "If we confess our sins, he is faithful and just to forgive us our sins, and to cleanse us from all unrighteousness" (I John 1:9).

B. I Will Live in the Freedom Granted by the Spirit

In many ways, how we live is a choice. We can accept the devil's lies and live in continued bondage to sin and the condemnation that comes from sin, or we can believe the Word of God and live in victory over sin with the freedom that comes from obedience. The devil will lie to us, but God will call to us. We must decide to which voice we will submit.

Victory is not something we must win; victory is a reality of our spiritual inheritance. The apostle Paul triumphantly wrote, "Nay, in all these things we are more than conquerors through him that loved us" (Romans 8:37). Victory is part of our kingdom identity woven into our spiritual DNA. It is who we are, not merely something we do. Therefore, we will overcome if we stay submitted to God's Spirit. At times we may feel weak, condemned, and defeated, but in Christ, we are strong, free, and victorious. What we feel does not dictate what is true. As a

How can we keep this law of sin in our members from becoming an excuse for giving in to temptation?

What do you see as the primary differences between conviction and condemnation?

noted political commentator often says, "Facts don't care about your feelings."

III. WALKING IN THE SPIRIT

Our life in the Spirit is not an intermittent encounter with Him; it is a moment-by-moment existence in Him. Walking speaks of our daily connection with Jesus Christ by His Spirit. For every person who does not have some type of impairment that prevents it, walking is second nature. It is just a natural function of living life. No one marvels or cheers when we walk. Walking is normal for a human.

Walking in the Spirit should be normal for a Christian. There is no fanfare or expectation that we will be recognized for our efforts. A child of God simply walks. We yield to the leading of God's Spirit as we conduct the journey from here to Heaven with a consistent, patient walk in Christ.

What is your definition of walking in the Spirit? How should walking with Him affect our daily lives?

A. Experiencing Life and Peace through the Spirit

Living such a life not only guarantees our safe passage to eternal life but also provides rich blessings and benefits here. The world through which we walk is one of confusion and chaos. An ever-growing percentage of the populace depends on pharmaceuticals to find calmness and stillness in their lives. Certainly there are cases where these are medically necessary, but many others are unknowingly trying to remedy a spiritual void with a chemical solution.

God has offered us a better way. When the Holy Spirit is the guiding force in our thinking, the result is life and peace. Victory over depression, discouragement, and anxiety is available to us through the baptism of the Spirit. "For the kingdom of God is not meat and drink; but righteousness, and peace, and joy in the Holy Ghost" (Romans 14:17).

B. I Will Live in Victory through the Power of the Spirit

The choice is ours. We can live in defeat, or we can decide to live in victory. Since we are "heirs of God, and joint-heirs with Christ" (Romans 8:17), we get to partake in the inheritance of our heavenly Father. He has promised us life and peace by His Spirit. No child of God must live in persistent darkness. We have victory over darkness by the power of the indwelling Spirit of God.

INTERNALIZING THE MESSAGE

A supplemental image is available in the Resource Kit. ⓘ

On a cool evening in the spring of 1909, two heavyweight boxers entered the ring in Paris, France, to fight for the World Heavyweight Championship. On one side stood Joe Jennette at 185 pounds. Across the ring was Sam McVey at 205 pounds. Not only was the championship on the line, but so was a purse of $6,000—roughly $175,000 today.

Such events in that era were often billed as a fight to the finish. In other words, these were not ten- or fifteen-round affairs. There would be no judges' decision if both men were still standing at a predefined end. No, these two combatants would continue until one of them simply could not go on. On that night in Paris, this fight proved to be quite the contest of wills and stamina.

Ultimately, Jennette won the fight when McVey refused to come out from his corner—for the forty-ninth round. Beyond the sheer length of the match and the physical stamina required to endure it, spectators were amazed at the outcome because Jennette had been knocked down twenty-seven times prior to winning the victory.

We, too, are in a conflict. It is obviously a spiritual one, not physical. Still the parameters are the same: the one who endures to the end will be the one crowned. (See Matthew 10:22.) We will be knocked down by the blows that Hell and life bring. But if we are willing to continue fighting, the outcome is foreordained. We will win.

Jennette had only his own willpower to rely on to rise each time he was leveled, but we have the strength of the Lord to help us back to our feet to try again. God's Holy Spirit will enable us to continue far beyond where our own power can carry us. As we look around the church, we will see scores of people whose lives have been fiercely and mercilessly battered, but they still populate the pews because they have gotten back up again and again.

You can make it. If you keep walking with Jesus, keep fighting the good fight of faith, you will win. You may suffer blows, but you can get up again. God's Spirit living in you is the ultimate source of victory. No matter how long it takes, and no matter how many bruises you may bear, look up from the mat and say with firm resolve, "Rejoice not against me, O mine enemy: when I fall, I shall arise; when I sit in darkness, the LORD shall be a light unto me" (Micah 7:8).

Prayer Focus
Lead the group in prayer and consider the following topics of focus:
• Committing to God to walk daily with Him
• For God to give us the power we need to overcome temptation

SERIES 2: VICTORY THROUGH FAITH

2.1

THE TWELVE SPIES

FOCUS VERSE
Numbers 13:30
And Caleb stilled the people before Moses, and said, Let us go up at once, and possess it; for we are well able to overcome it.

LESSON TEXT
Numbers 13:1-3, 17-33

TRUTH ABOUT GOD
God desires to reveal His promises to us.

TRUTH FOR MY LIFE
I will seize God's promises in faith.

Series Overview:

This series, "Victory through Faith," follows the Israelites as they learn to believe God's promises and ultimately conquer the Promised Land. These lessons focus on the report of the twelve spies, the crossing of Jordan, the battle of Jericho, and Joshua's final address to the Israelites. God declared special promises to Israel through Moses and Joshua and has made unfailing promises to each of us through His Word. This series will help us step into promised victory through exercising our faith.

(SG) TEACHING OUTLINE

Icebreaker: If you remember the dress that went viral online, did you see it as black and blue or gold and white?

Lesson Connection: Share the Lesson Connection.

I. ISRAEL SELECTED TWELVE SPIES

   A. God Wanted to Show His People the Blessings that Awaited Them
      » *Why are many people excited and also anxious about the future?*

   B. God Desires to Reveals His Promises to Us
      » *How does the way our heavenly Father prepares us for opportunities and promises compare to the way our earthly parents do? What is similar and what is different?*

II. UNFAITHFUL SPIES

   A. Ten Unfaithful Spies Expressed Disbelief (I)
      » *Why do you think different people have widely differing perspectives of the same situation?*

   B. We Must See through God's Eyes
      » *What are some reasons people of faith fail to pursue and embrace the promises of God?*

III. FAITHFUL SPIES

   A. Two Faithful Spies Expressed Complete Confidence in God

   B. When God Makes Promises to Us, We Must Seize Them with Faith
      » *What are some other examples of conditional promises of God?*

Internalizing the Message (V)

Prayer Focus
Lead the group in prayer and consider the following topics of focus:
• For God to forgive us if we allow doubt or fear to paralyze us
• For God to help us see life through eyes of faith

LESSON CONNECTION

The heat of the July sun beat mercilessly on her back as she stood trembling at the edge of the swimming pool. Her toes functioned more like fingers as they gripped the rounded edge of the concrete deck. A voice from the pool beckoned again, "Jump!" Fear gripped little Emilee's pounding heart as possibility was held captive by uncertainty. She could clearly see that the swimming pool was a place for fun and refreshment, but she could also see the danger of the depths of the billowing water that awaited her. "I can't!" she shrieked.

"I'll catch you," assured her father. In that moment, her mind was flooded with "what ifs." *What if he drops me? What if he makes me try to swim on my own? What if I try to swim and I sink?* "Please, Daddy, don't make me," she begged.

With calm assurance, her dad promised he would not drop her. He promised to teach her how to swim. He assured her she would be so glad she took the leap. The cool, refreshing waters were far better than the scorching sun radiating down on her fair skin. Cautiously, she leaned forward as her arms reached for her daddy. Courage swelled as her tiny heart pounded rapidly. In an instant, trust overcame her fear and she took her father at his word. Splash!

Fear is a powerful emotion. It has crippled the mighty and limited the capable. It is mighty enough to keep us from achieving our goals and living our best. It feeds stagnation and keeps us from taking advantage of opportunities. Many people are living in the self-made prison of their own fears.

However, a life lived by overcoming fear is not only something we all deserve, but it is something for which God commanded us to strive. That means it is completely possible. Without overcoming our fears, we can never experience some of God's greatest promises. We do not want to simply tolerate our fears—we must eliminate them.

BIBLE LESSON

I. ISRAEL SELECTED TWELVE SPIES

The dramatic story of Moses leading the Israelites out of Egyptian captivity and miraculously crossing the Red Sea is one of Scripture's most notable narratives. Great steps of faith were required to walk along a seabed with massive walls of water standing as sentries on each side. Mere weeks after this act of faith and experiencing God's divine intervention, Israel was poised to experience the fulfillment of a promise centuries in the making. Twelve men eagerly assembled, representing the twelve tribes of a great nation God had promised Abraham. In Numbers 13, God commissioned them, "Send thou men, that they may search the land of Canaan, which I give unto the children of Israel" (Numbers 13:2).

A. God Wanted to Show His People the Blessings that Awaited Them

The energy level must have been through the roof as the joyful masses from each tribe assembled their leaders. Hundreds of years earlier, God had challenged Abraham to trust Him, forsake the comforts of his homeland and family, and set out for a land God would show him. Imagine the excitement and anticipation of Abraham's descendants on this day. Tears of joy likely flowed as each tribe of this budding nation sent their representative to spy out the land.

Why are many people excited and also anxious about the future?

Imagine God's desire for His chosen people. He had watched the faith of Abraham grow over time. Abraham had witnessed the ups and downs in the life of his son Isaac. The painful feud between Isaac's sons, Jacob and Esau, had positioned Jacob to father the twelve sons who would lead the tribes of Israel. God desired the twelve spies from these tribes to finally witness and report on the promised blessings.

It had taken a long time for God to build the foundation of the nation He promised Abraham, but the time had come for God to position them to receive His promise. The process was hard and confusing at times. The children of promise experienced many struggles along the way—most recently, four hundred years of Egyptian captivity. But God's timing and plan for them was perfect. Over the many years, even in the trying times, God was preparing His people to experience the beauty of His promise.

B. God Desires to Reveal His Promises to Us

Every loving parent hopes their children will experience the best in life. Mature relationships, spiritual discipline, healthy independence, and financial security tend to top the list of priorities. Along the way, a parent will share promises of blessings or benefits to come. Part of a parent's job is to prepare children to receive and manage these blessings and benefits.

This may include needed discipline, development of patience, or lessons in gratitude.

A father and mother understand the blessings and curses that promised rewards can bring. A car can provide much desired independence and mobility to a teen, but it also presents the potential for great danger. Dating relationships, if maturely approached, can aid a teen or young adult in wisely deciding on a life partner when the time is right. The same can also provide great pitfalls if approached unwisely or without safe boundaries. Life is full of opportunities and promises. The preparation to embrace them is usually as important as receiving them.

How does the way our heavenly Father prepares us for opportunities and promises compare to the way our earthly parents do? What is similar and what is different?

Similarly, God has many promises for His children. Knowing our nature, God will do His best to strengthen our character, mature our faith, and position our lives to receive His best. This often takes time, testing, and experience. We must be ready and willing to claim God's promises when He prompts us to proceed. Fear can paralyze progress even in a godly person. Just ask ten of Israel's twelve spies.

II. UNFAITHFUL SPIES

A. Ten Unfaithful Spies Expressed Disbelief

"Burn the boats!" This familiar phrase often evokes courage. When Hernan Cortez and his men arrived in Veracruz, Mexico, in 1519, they had one goal: conquest. The story is told that upon his arrival, Cortez ordered his men to burn all their ships. He did not want to lead his men into the challenges ahead while they thought they had any option but victory. He understood human nature's tendency to lose courage in the face of adversity. When retreat is not an option, courage must overcome the fear to press forward.

Teacher Option: A supplemental image is available in the Resource Kit. [I]

Before they left on their journey, Israel's twelve spies were commissioned to be of good courage. What they witnessed during their forty-day journey was amazing. The land they glimpsed was everything God had promised. They brought back a testimony of a land that flowed with milk and honey. They came toting grapes, figs, and pomegranates. However, ten of the twelve spies returned after forty days of spying out Canaan, and they were looking for the boats. Although they had witnessed the Promised Land and God had poised them to seize it, their hopes were drowning in the sea of fear and disbelief. They were looking for a boat—actually a trail—back to Egypt. They were blinded by the challenges rather than motivated by the promises. As with courage, fear and disbelief can be contagious. The negative report and fear soon began to trickle through the once excited and motivated multitude. Promise was quickly eclipsed by fear.

Why do you think different people have widely differing perspectives of the same situation?

B. We Must See through God's Eyes

Perspective is powerful. Some people have a knack for seeing a problem in every possibility. To them, the glass is never half full;

it is always half empty. The loveable fictional character Winnie the Pooh had a friend who always had this mindset. Perhaps you have heard of Eeyore, the donkey. No matter how positive the situation, Eeyore found something negative to say. One of his classic lines is: "I wish I could say yes, but I can't."

In the middle of challenges, many people lose their perspective. People who get so distracted by challenges that they cannot see the magnitude of the possibilities are said to be "missing the forest for the trees." They become so blinded that they wish they could say yes, but they cannot. In Israel's case, ten of the spies failed to view the Promised Land through the lens of God's miraculous power to fulfill His promises. When they should have said yes, they could not.

Throughout history the people of God have experienced some of God's greatest blessings because they refused to be blinded by the magnitude of the obstacles. David said yes to Goliath when everyone else said no because David was convinced of the cause. (See I Samuel 17.) Noah tackled the daunting task of building an ark, which saved his family, because he trusted God's Word. (See Genesis 6.) The prophet Elisha prayed that his servant would see through different eyes. All the servant could see was the army surrounding the city, but Elisha could see the provision of God—far more were fighting for them than against them. (See II Kings 6.) When we trust God, we are able to see through eyes of faith.

The battle cry of the apostle Paul sums up the necessary stance of a child of God: "If God be for us, who can be against us?" (Romans 8:31). God loves His children and although difficulties and challenges come, He wants us to see the big picture. He keeps His promises. Our task is simply to be of good courage and say yes.

What are some reasons people of faith fail to pursue and embrace the promises of God?

III. FAITHFUL SPIES

A. Two Faithful Spies Expressed Complete Confidence in God

Have you ever heard of Shammua? How about Shaphat? Perhaps you have heard the story of Igal, son of Joseph or Palti, son of Raphu. Surely you have heard of the great exploits of Gaddiel, Gaddi, and Ammiel and the great faith and feats of Sethur, Nahbi, and Geuel? No? Well, what about Joshua and Caleb? Most of us have heard of Joshua and Caleb, but the other ten names, not so much. They were the ten faithless spies who lacked courage and were overcome by fear. Fearful and inactive people are rarely ever noteworthy. The courageous inspire and motivate others to great things.

Joshua and Caleb were not distracted by the obstacles. Rather, they were motivated by the promises of God. God described Caleb as having "another spirit" that led him to follow God fully. (See Numbers 14:24.) This spirit prompted Caleb to declare that Israel was fully capable to take the land God promised.

Faith will always prompt action. Doubt cripples; faith mobilizes. Fear paralyzes; faith marches forward into the promises of God. Obedience is always the action when we believe God is fully capable of fulfilling His promises.

B. When God Makes Promises to Us, We Must Seize Them with Faith

Forty years! A trip that should have taken eleven days lasted forty years—forty years of wasted time, shattered dreams, and unnecessary loss. Israel's disobedience, fear, and rebellion led to lost promises for those who were twenty years old and older. It meant lost time, opportunities, and blessings to those who were younger. A fifteen-year-old would have been fifty-five years old before moving into the Promised Land.

How many times have God's people missed out on God's best because we are limited by our own fear or disobedience? God's Word is full of promises for those who will overcome their fears and surrender their will to His. At the very basic level, God wants everyone to experience salvation. Second Peter 3:9 reminds us that the Lord is "not willing that any should perish, but that all should come to repentance." The promise of salvation is predicated on each individual stepping out in faith, overcoming fear and self-will, and finding a place of repentance.

Beyond the new-birth experience, God has many promises for His people, but most of God's promises are conditional. They require action in response to the Word of God. God responds to active faith by providing divine promises. When we as His children believe His Word, humble ourselves, and show our faith and trust through obedience, we will receive His promises. God cannot lie.

God promised that the devil will flee from us if we first submit ourselves to God and resist the devil (James 4:7). We are promised our basic needs will be met if we seek first the kingdom of God and His righteousness (Matthew 6:33). We can receive wisdom from God if we will ask Him (James 1:5). We can do all things, but not in our own strength—only through Christ who strengthens us (Philippians 4:13). The list is long. Many blessed promises of God apply to us today, but they require us to seize them through active faith.

What are some other examples of conditional promises of God?

By staying the course with God's plan and ways, Israel would have arrived in the Promised Land in about eleven days. Instead, an eleven-day trip stretched into an arduous, forty-year sojourn. How many of us have done something similar or become victims of someone else's offenses? How many times could we have gotten through things much quicker, but because of our obstinance and failings, we end up prolonging our situation? Perhaps we ask for forgiveness for a transgression but maintain our pride and become further estranged in a relationship. In this way, we forfeit the "promised land" of reconciliation.

INTERNALIZING THE MESSAGE

A supplemental video is available in the Resource Kit. **V**

On September 17, 1935, at 10:00 AM, a child was stillborn. After being revived, he was rushed to the hospital with severe brain damage. The doctor's prognosis was not hopeful, and he predicted the child would not survive twenty-four hours. The doctor advised the family to pray for the child to experience a merciful death because he would never walk, talk, or see if he somehow survived.

The child survived but faced daunting odds. The story of his life is riveting. He was always seemingly a step behind. While other children were learning to walk, he was learning to crawl. While others were running, he was stumbling. His parents spent countless hours working with him, determined to give him as normal of a life as possible.

After his first day of riding a bike, he was scraped, bruised, black, blue, and green. He leaned the bike up and declared, "You had your day; tomorrow is mine. I'll break you tomorrow. I'll ride you. If I die, right before I die, I'm going to ride you."

His name was Allan C. Oggs, Sr., and he did learn to ride that bike. In spite of limited physical abilities, he went on to marry, have children, and become a successful evangelist in the United Pentecostal Church International. He chronicled his life story in his inspirational autobiography, *You Gotta Have the Want To.*

What many would have seen as a life of obstacles and roadblocks, Brother Oggs saw as challenges to overcome. He often used his disabilities and challenges to his advantage. He traveled the world preaching and challenging people to be overcomers. He compared his physical challenges and mindset of overcoming them to how all of us must tackle life's obstacles. He declared his life's motto, "You gotta have the want to!"

Whatever we face in our lives, we must never forget the promises and possibilities we have in Christ. It does not matter what obstacles life or the devil throws our way, we must strive to see through God's eyes. We must believe what God has promised is possible through His strength. God's power coupled with our "want to" can usher us into a life pursuit where we claim the amazing promises in God's Word.

Prayer Focus
Lead the group in prayer and consider the following topics of focus:
- For God to forgive us if we allow doubt or fear to paralyze us
- For God to help us see life through eyes of faith

2.2

CROSSING THE JORDAN

FOCUS VERSES
Joshua 3:11–13
[11] Behold, the ark of the covenant of the Lord of all the earth passeth over before you into Jordan.
[12] Now therefore take you twelve men out of the tribes of Israel, out of every tribe a man.
[13] And it shall come to pass, as soon as the soles of the feet of the priests that bear the ark of the LORD, the Lord of all the earth, shall rest in the waters of Jordan, that the waters of Jordan shall be cut off from the waters that come down from above; and they shall stand upon an heap.

LESSON TEXT
Joshua 3:1–17

TRUTH ABOUT GOD
God goes before us and removes obstacles from our path.

TRUTH FOR MY LIFE
I will step out by faith and trust the Spirit to lead me.

Thinking about Last Week:

Have students refer to their Daily Devotional Guide to answer the following questions:
1. What most affected you as you read through the Lesson Text and the Biblical Insights?
2. How did it shape your prayers and thoughts throughout the week?
3. Do you feel you grew closer to the Lord this past week? Why or why not?

SG TEACHING OUTLINE

Icebreaker: Which of Jesus' miracles amazes you most?

Lesson Connection: Share the Lesson Connection.

I. THE ISRAELITES PREPARED TO ENTER THE PROMISED LAND
    » *How can our past failures and lack of faith prepare us for future challenges and opportunities?*

    A. They Consecrated Themselves
        » *What are some areas of spiritual consecration where the "pay now and benefit later" principle can be applied? What about the opposite?* **V**

    B. God Showed He Was with Joshua and the Israelites and He Promised Victory
        » *Think of a person you know who has great faith. What are some of this person's characteristics?*

    C. To Live Victoriously, We Must Follow the Leading of the Spirit

II. THE ISRAELITES CROSSED THE JORDAN RIVER

    A. By the Power of the Spirit, the Ministry Stepped into the Jordan and God's People Followed
        » *In what area has God positioned you to lead? How?*

    B. God Parted the Waters of Jordan

    C. We Must Step Out by Faith and Trust the Spirit to Lead Us, Believing God Will Make a Way for Us
        » *What obstacle is currently deterring you from taking a new step of faith?*

Internalizing the Message **I**

Prayer Focus
Lead the group in prayer and consider the following topics of focus:
• For God to help us trust Him and take Him at His word
• For God to help us step out in faith and obey Him

LESSON CONNECTION

I t was the most festive of occasions: a wedding day. The invitations had been sent long ago, the guest list completed, and the big day had finally arrived. The crowd was buzzing as the bridal party put the final touches on their wedding garments. The bride was radiant yet anxious, her heart palpitating with anticipation. Not to be outdone, the groom's heart was leaping in his chest as the bride walked through the doors. Emotions swelled. They exchanged vows, sealed their union with a kiss, and the reception began.

Merriment abounded. As the band played, the servers served the meal. Everyone was elated—except for the parents of the bride and groom. They were feeling humiliated. They had overlooked one important detail.

Soon some of their guests overheard this oversight. One of these guests quickly realized she had a solution for their embarrassing situation. One of her children had the ability to remedy the situation and get the festivities back on track.

She motioned to her son and pulled Him to the side. She whispered something in His ear. He was reluctant to act, but she was His mom. Without hesitation, His mother called to the waitstaff and made a direct, emphatic statement, "Whatever He says to do, do it." In one short statement, Mary, the mother of Jesus, summed up the key to supernatural provision. To borrow from Nike, when Jesus speaks, just do it.

Jesus gave the instructions to the waitstaff. These orders would have been silly to most, but they were strangely specific. Jesus told them to haul water from the waterpots to the master of the feast so he could taste it. These may have been the handwashing waterpots. Somewhat surprised, the servants obeyed exactly what He directed. Miraculously, by the time anyone tasted the water, Jesus had turned it into wine. He met the guests' need, saved the bridal party from embarrassment, and gave us a glimpse that this Jesus of Nazareth was not just a man. The guests were thoroughly impressed, and the celebration was a huge success. The master of the reception even commended the groom for serving the best to his guests.

This was the beginning of Jesus' miracles, and it all started with a wise directive by the one on earth who knew Jesus best: His mother. She knew Him well enough to know His ability. This led her to declare, "Whatever He says to do, do it." It was great advice then, and it is still great advice today.

BIBLE LESSON

I. THE ISRAELITES PREPARED TO ENTER THE PROMISED LAND

Forty long, painful years had slowly passed since Israel's ten faithless spies declared their inability to possess what God had promised. Despite Joshua and Caleb's courageous and impassioned proclamation, the multitude balked at the promise of God. The ensuing decades were a continual reminder of what disobedience to God's Word can produce. One by one, grandfathers and grandmothers succumbed to age, disease, and the elements. Fathers marched into unnecessary battles against the likes of the Amalekites and Midianites. Mothers watched their children and grandchildren grow up as vagabonds. They moved and changed locations forty-two times after their Exodus from Egypt. A generation died, never having experienced the Promised Land that had been one step of faith away.

Once again God's people of purpose stood on the precipice of their Promised Land. Their leader, the faithful and faith-filled Joshua, assembled a new generation of Israelites. Their time had come, but their faith would once again be tested. Their response to the vision and command of God's faithful leader would be pivotal to their success.

How can our past failures and lack of faith prepare us for future challenges and opportunities?

A. They Consecrated Themselves

An old saying declares, "Some lessons are only learned the hard way." It is the frustration and sometimes grief of parents to watch their children ignore good advice. So many people waste time and opportunities in their youth due to ignoring good advice. It has been said, "You can pay now and play later, or you can play now and pay later. But if you pay later, the price is always greater."

Israel had taken the supposedly safe route. It was the route of least resistance, at least initially. The price they paid was the buried remains of past opportunities. Now, Joshua, their new leader, had received a renewed call from God. It was time to advance into the Promised Land. They had fought many battles. They had lost four decades. Graves reminding them of squandered opportunities littered the landscape. It was hard, but God was presenting them a new direction that would take wholehearted consecration.

Teacher Option: A supplemental video is available in the Resource Kit. V

Joshua's first words to the Israelites before they entered were: "Sanctify yourselves: for to morrow the LORD will do wonders among you" (Joshua 3:5). Consecration and sanctification are vital to connect with God's promises. This is especially true when entering territory we have never experienced before.

What are some areas of spiritual consecration where the "pay now and benefit later" principle can be applied? What about the opposite?

When God leads His people into territory they have never experienced, it requires sanctification. It was true then; it is true now. Throughout biblical history, God's nature is revealed. The greatest revivals and victories resulted from sanctification unto

God. From young leaders such as Joseph, Esther, and Josiah to aging ones such as Noah, Deborah, and Joshua, holiness unto God results in favor with God.

Joshua realized God's nature, so his first call to the people before proceeding toward the promise was "sanctify yourselves." When children of God sanctify themselves, two things happen. First, they gain God's attention. Second, they have a spiritual mindset of faith to take territory and possess promises they have never seized.

B. God Showed He Was with Joshua and the Israelites and He Promised Victory

Noted leadership expert John Maxwell emphatically asserts, "Everything rises or falls on leadership." Ten of the twelve original spies were viewed as leaders in their tribes. Their faithlessness and fear significantly influenced those who trusted them. Leaders who are crippled by fear will infect their followers with the same.

God told Joshua He was going to magnify Joshua in the sight of Israel so they would know God was with him. One way God clearly demonstrated He was with Joshua was in Joshua's demonstration of faith in casting vision. "And Joshua said, Hereby ye shall know that the living God is among you, and that he will without fail drive out from before you the Canaanites" (Joshua 3:10).

When a God-called leader steps out in faith to declare the promises of God, it builds faith in those who follow. Joshua's vision could see the promise beyond the obstacles. He began to declare what he saw as though it was already theirs. The late evangelist Billy Cole was known to declare with his booming voice of faith, "Say what you see until you see what you say." When a person is sanctified unto God for His purpose, God will instill faith to believe for promises that seem to be impossible.

God promised to be with Joshua as God was with Moses. As followers of Jesus today, Christians often opine about old-time religion and the stories of how God moved in their parents' and grandparents' generations. But just as God was with Joshua as He was with Moses, He will be with us as He was with previous generations. It starts with sanctification. God will reveal His promises in miraculous ways when we consecrate as they did. The promises of God are still real. He is looking for a faith-filled generation to ready themselves.

Think of a person you know who has great faith. What are some of this person's characteristics?

C. To Live Victoriously, We Must Follow the Leading of the Spirit

"Behold!" This word is one we no longer routinely use, but *behold* was frequently used in Scripture. It would be similar to a child eagerly attempting to gain her parent's attention. "Look, Dad!" This was Joshua's intent when he tried to focus the attention of Israel. "Behold, the ark of the covenant of the Lord of all the earth passeth over before you into Jordan" (Joshua 3:11).

Casual affirmation of God's presence never leads us out of the mediocrity of just wandering. Israel was not lost. They knew where they were, and they knew where God intended them to be. Their faithlessness had simply led them to a new kind of bondage: life outside of God's intended purpose. Such is the case for many followers of God. They wander through life as children of promise but are simply unprepared to receive it.

God has many promises for His people. Like Israel on the brink of the Jordan River, God is still seeking people who will quit wandering and begin to follow the leading of His Spirit into promises He has for us. After hearing these precious promises, the children of Israel "removed from their tents, to pass over Jordan" (Joshua 3:14). They did what a previous generation was unwilling to do. They took God at His word. Their wandering was over, and their faith prompted movement toward the presence and promise of God. This step set the supernatural in motion.

II. THE ISRAELITES CROSSED THE JORDAN RIVER

A. By the Power of the Spirit, the Ministry Stepped into the Jordan and God's People Followed

God empowers us for God-sized challenges and achievements. We can accomplish many things on our own, but the promises of God are only obtained by the power of the Spirit. God often uses leaders as catalysts in pursuing the promises of God. Although the kingdom of God definitely has spiritual leadership and authority structures, we are all called to be leaders in some fashion. You may not be a pastor or ministry leader in the church, but God has called us all to some area of leadership. Husbands are to lead their wives humbly and spiritually. Fathers and mothers are commanded to raise and lead their children to worship the one true God. Youth are urged to be examples of the believers in all areas of their lives. All believers are empowered to be witnesses who share the gospel and lead people to discipleship in Christ.

To effectively achieve leadership or influence, we must be submitted to the Spirit of God. The apostle Paul declared, "For as many as are led by the Spirit of God, they are the sons of God" (Romans 8:14-17). To be a healthy and productive child of God, we must strive to be led of the Spirit. The Spirit will always lead in agreement with and direction of the Word of God.

In what areas has God positioned you to lead? How?

Israel had heard the Word of God. God was with their leader, leading them in a way they had not passed before. God was with them and going before them. The spiritual leaders, the priests, did what leaders are supposed to do: they led by example. They stepped first into the Jordan River, which went against everything they knew to be safe. The Jordan was flooding her banks. Apart from a miracle, they may be swept away or pulled under the mighty muddy Jordan. But they obeyed God's command and responded in faith. God's promises will come to pass to those who step out in faith under the power of God's presence.

B. God Parted the Waters of Jordan

The chilly water of the Jordan River licked the soles of the priests' feet. Forty years earlier God's leader had stretched a staff over the face of another body of water, the Red Sea. The waters had parted, and God's people crossed on dry ground. This day was different. Moses was gone. An entire generation was gone. Today's miracle would require more than one man raising a rod; it would demand many men of God stepping into the river and trusting God to part it.

Before the chill of the water could surround the priests' feet, the priests felt the swift retreat of the once overflowing river. God had just parted the Jordan River. God removed the first barrier to the Promised Land in a moment of obedient faith.

God showed He was with Joshua at the Jordan River as He was with Moses at the Red Sea. God did the work when His leaders and His people moved in faith. God's leaders stood in the middle of the river on firm ground. What others would have seen as unsafe and unwise, the people of God viewed as the safest place to be.

C. We Must Step Out by Faith and Trust the Spirit to Lead Us, Believing God Will Make a Way for Us

Every born-again follower of Jesus has heard His voice calling. Often, it is to a place of deeper consecration. Generally, this is the first call we hear. We hear Him call us to repentance and right relationship with Him. From a place of sanctification and consecration, God is able to lead us into His supernatural promises and purposes. Beyond consecration, however, we have likely heard Him call in other areas, perhaps a call to engage in a particular ministry in the church or community. You may have heard Him calling you to work in particular spiritual gifts. Others may have heard the voice of God to launch a ministry, start a church, or be a missionary. The call of God is usually daunting and seemingly impossible. If it were easy or possible for us on our own, our faith and the Spirit of God would be unnecessary.

What obstacle is currently deterring you from taking a new step of faith?

In all cases of pursuing God's call, following spiritual leadership and authority is critical. Speak with your pastor, share your burden, and humbly follow the one God has placed in your life to lead you. Do follow, regardless of the obstacles. You may see your pastor's direction or requirements as an obstacle; God may see them as a test of your faith to obediently and sacrificially step forward. God's methods and His leader's direction may appear to be leading you into deep waters, but your trust and obedience will likely result in God opening the door for you to cross into places you have never been before.

INTERNALIZING THE MESSAGE

A supplemental image is available in the Resource Kit. ⓘ

In the spring of 2021, a young couple stood nervously before the Global Missions Board of the United Pentecostal Church International. They had traveled to St. Louis, Missouri, seeking approval to be full-time missionaries. The voice of the Lord had spoken to the young mother of five children when she was just a child herself. When she was in middle school, God had called her to be a missionary and confirmed where He wanted her to minister. She met her husband at Bible college, and he felt the same calling. God was calling them to the nation of Chad.

When people hear the name of that nation, many quizzically respond, "Where?" Chad is not a most notable place. Likely, those who know it have heard of it because of its extreme danger due to the risk of terrorism, kidnapping, unrest, and violent crime. In other words, Chad is not a place most would visit, much less live.

As Rodney and Kimberly Sims shared their burden, Kimberly voiced one of her greatest frustrations of traveling in North America to raise funds for their mission to Chad. She repeatedly had to field questions from other parents about why she would take her five children to such a dangerous place. Her answer brought many on the Global Missions Board to tears. She tearfully but boldly proclaimed, "I would rather be in the most dangerous place on earth in the will of God than in the safest place on earth outside the will of God." Her words brought conviction to the hearts of many. The safest place to be is in the will of God.

God has a place for all of us to go. He has a spiritual destination He wants us to experience. We have wandered far too long in familiar territory, and it is time to launch into new spiritual frontiers. For others, God has specific callings and locations He wants us to pursue. The challenges will always be plenty. Self-will, financial challenges, and personal sanctification often present seemingly insurmountable obstacles.

Others may question our resolve, and we may sometimes question our abilities, but we must answer the question the children of Israel answered on the banks of the Jordan River. When God calls and leadership leads, will we remove our tents of comfort and follow God's Spirit? God has given unto us exceeding great and precious promises. (See II Peter 1:4.)

Let us never forget the wise words of a God-called missionary: the safest place to be is in the will of God.

Prayer Focus

Lead the group in prayer and consider the following topics of focus:
- For God to help us trust Him and take Him at His word
- For God to help us step out in faith and obey Him

2.3

JERICHO

FOCUS VERSE
Joshua 6:20
So the people shouted when the priests blew with the trumpets: and it came to pass, when the people heard the sound of the trumpet, and the people shouted with a great shout, that the wall fell down flat, so that the people went up into the city, every man straight before him, and they took the city.

LESSON TEXT
Joshua 6:1–25

TRUTH ABOUT GOD
God can provide victory through unconventional means.

TRUTH FOR MY LIFE
I will follow God and trust Him for victory.

Thinking about Last Week:

Have students refer to their Daily Devotional Guide to answer the following questions:
1. What most affected you as you read through the Lesson Text and the Biblical Insights?
2. How did it shape your prayers and thoughts throughout the week?
3. Do you feel you grew closer to the Lord this past week? Why or why not?

SG TEACHING OUTLINE

Icebreaker: If you could get one photo at any major tourist attraction in the world, where would it be?

Lesson Connection: Share the Lesson Connection. [I]

I. THE CHALLENGE AT JERICHO

    A. God Gave Joshua an Unconventional Battle Plan

        » *What are some mysterious ways you have seen God lead a person into greater arenas of faith?*

    B. Israel's Obedience

    C. I Will Choose to Obey Even When I Do Not Understand God's Plan

        » *What are other songs we find easy to sing but harder to live?*

II. MARCHING TO VICTORY

    A. The Israelites Followed God's Plan to the Letter [V]

        » *Why is it important to obey God's commands even when they do not make sense to us?*

    B. God Gave Israel Total Victory over Jericho

        » *What commandments in Scripture require great faith but are worth the payoff?*

    C. When We Obey God, He Will Respond and Tear Down Walls in Our Lives

        » *Why does God respond so favorably to complete obedience?*

Internalizing the Message

Prayer Focus

Lead the group in prayer and consider the following topics of focus:
- For God to help us trust His Word, no matter how many are skeptical of His Word
- For God to help us share His Word, no matter how many are skeptical of His Word

LESSON CONNECTION

A supplemental image is available in the Resource Kit. I

n AD 1368, Zhu Yuanzhang founded the Ming dynasty in China. Within one hundred years, construction commenced on what would become known as the Great Wall of China. For the next three centuries, the wall expanded to 13,000 miles, including more than 25,000 towers, each protected by a permanent garrison. What was this wall's main purpose? It was built to prevent a large-scale Mongolian invasion.

The Great Wall of China is a grand example of the numerous walls that have been constructed throughout human history. The first massive wall-building project was thanks to the Roman Empire. The Romans developed sophisticated engineering techniques, allowing many of their structures to remain largely intact. Some of them may last even beyond the twenty-first century. At first the Romans built the walls primarily for defense. Those walls protected the city for centuries, allowing its inhabitants to huddle behind them during invasions and hostile occupation. In 216 BC, the Carthaginian commander, Hannibal, was turned away from an attack on the city of Rome after he destroyed the Roman army at Cannae. The large, imposing walls proved too much for him and his army to overcome.

Not all walls are defensive in nature. Some are designed to keep people in. A case in point was the infamous Berlin Wall. The Berlin Wall separated East Germany and West Germany for nearly three decades. It became a symbol of the Iron Curtain that separated Western Europe and the Eastern Bloc during the Cold War. It was ultimately a barrier to progress and the unification of a nation. At a critical point during the Cold War, then President Ronald Reagan uttered these words that have echoed through the following decades: "Mr. Gorbachev, tear down this wall!" Over the next few years, the shockwaves of Reagan's words reverberated, became a rallying call, and the wall indeed fell. Its fall ultimately led to German reunification on October 3, 1990. As important as walls can be, history has shown some walls simply need to fall. Often, all it takes is for someone courageous enough to make some noise.

BIBLE LESSON

I. THE CHALLENGE AT JERICHO

A. God Gave Joshua an Unconventional Battle Plan

Picture the excitement and amazement the Israelites felt after passing through the Jordan River on dry ground. Many of them had not been born when their parents crossed through the Red Sea after leaving Egypt. Some were small children with only a vague memory of the Red Sea crossing. But the story was legendary. Imagine a grandfather gathering his grandchildren around to tell them how the walls of water stood on each side as he, their grandmother, and the children's parents walked through the sea—on dry ground. His voice may have growled as he mimicked the rumble of the waters crashing down on the Egyptian army who was hot on their trail.

This new generation of Israelites had experienced their own dry ground miracle. God had performed the miraculous and removed a great obstacle between them and their promise. Twelves stones from the dry bed in the Jordan River, one from every tribe, would serve as a memorial to future generations of God's miraculous intervention.

As exciting as this moment was, these energized people of promise were soon to discover two key principles of advancement into God's promises. First, there are always battles along the journey into the promise. In the New Testament, the apostle Paul would describe how the righteousness of God is revealed: from faith to faith. The just will live by faith (Romans 1:17). A person of faith will be led from one situation to another that requires faithful obedience to God and His righteous ways.

The second key principle of advancement into God's promises is that God's methods and paths to victory are usually different from our preferences. Some have remarked, "If you want to make God laugh, share with Him your plans." If you would have asked Israel their ideal plan for breaching the walls of Jericho, it would have likely included ladders, fire, and battering rams. Yes, they would have to fight, but it would be an unconventional, God-designed battle plan that would lead them to victory, a plan that would require great faith and unmistakably prove God was in control.

B. Israel's Obedience

Between the Jordan River and Jericho, Israel received signs that God was in control and was blessing their faith and sanctification. Word of Israel's successful crossing of the Jordan River on dry ground spread throughout Canaan. The kings of the cities were frightened and lost courage because of the miracle. Israel continued their sanctification in the fifth chapter of Joshua by reinstituting the covenantal sign of circumcision, which had

What are some mysterious ways you have seen God lead a person into greater arenas of faith?

ceased during their wilderness wandering. Additionally, they were now in the Promised Land, although they had not fully obtained the promise. But the blessing of obedience was becoming clear. They began to eat the fruit of that land. Forty years of manna as their daily diet had finally ended.

Obedience tends to beget obedience. Even though God's next plan on their journey into promise seemed strange, they obeyed. They were learning to walk by faith. There would be setbacks and failures along the way, but that day would be one more God-sized step of faith.

C. I Will Choose to Obey Even When I Do Not Understand God's Plan

A variety of lifeless promises are buried on many Christians' walks of life. These lifeless promises are casualties of doubt. People doubted and hesitated to obey God's plan. Many followers of Jesus live frustrated and unfulfilled because they have never learned to fully trust and fully obey. They are often looking for loopholes to submission. Excuses abound for why they cannot submit: it is too costly, too hard, or too unreasonable. And they question, "Hath God really said?"

Every Sunday Christians gather in churches to sing songs of praise and worship. Many melodious anthems of praise flow from the lips of believers. Sadly, the songs are often sung dishonestly, but most likely not intentionally. Jesus Himself once quoted the prophet Isaiah when he declared, "This people draweth nigh unto me with their mouth, and honoureth me with their lips; but their heart is far from me" (Matthew 15:8). "How does this relate to songs of worship?" you may ask. What about the beautiful chorus "I Surrender All"? It is so easy to sing, but do we really mean it? All? Honestly, for many, it is really just "I surrender some." Or consider the song "Lead Me Lord, I Will Follow." Do we wholeheartedly mean that? What if He leads where we do not want to go? Until we really purpose in our hearts to live what we say and sing with our mouths, we are destined to experience far less of the Kingdom promises in God's Word.

What are other songs we find easy to sing but harder to live?

Jesus said the meek shall inherit the earth, those who hunger for righteousness shall be filled, the merciful shall obtain mercy, the pure in heart shall see God, and the peacemakers shall be called the children of God (Matthew 5:5–10). This requires heartfelt and purposeful obedience. The correlation between integrity, honesty, purity, prayer, fasting, forgiveness, and receiving specific promises of God are clear in His Word. All of them are difficult. They require Job-like trust in God—even if it feels like it will kill us.

But the promises are worth the struggle. Influence with God and man is worth the struggle to maintain our integrity. Battling to stay pure in an impure world is worth seeing and experiencing God's fullness. Our generation desperately needs the miraculous precipitated by prayer and fasting. Similarly, the forgiveness and liberation that only come from being forgiving are priceless.

So, the next time you sing "I Surrender All," or some song like it, examine your heart and decide to surrender all. Surrender all in honesty when it does not seem profitable to your business dealings. Surrender all in the passions of your dating or marriage relationship to be and remain pure. Surrender all when someone wounds you and you want vengeance, but you choose to live clear of bitterness. Complete obedience, even when we do not understand, brings the fullness of God's promise to direct our paths. As Proverbs 3:5–6 states, "Trust in the LORD with all thine heart; and lean not unto thine own understanding. In all thy ways acknowledge him, and he shall direct thy paths."

II. MARCHING TO VICTORY

A. The Israelites Followed God's Plan to the Letter

God's plan was clear. The priests were to carry the Ark of the Covenant around the city walls of Jericho one time per day for six days. Seven additional priests were to walk before the Ark blowing seven rams' horns while the rest of the people were to remain utterly silent. Then, on the seventh day, they were to encompass the city seven times. On the seventh time, the people were supposed to shout as the priests blew the rams' horns.

But why? Why not just walk around one time for one day? They would have had more energy for the battle that awaited them on the other side of the walls, right? Why must they walk around the wall at all? Surely God could just knock down the walls and spare them the effort. Are we sure God even said to do this? The children of Israel could have asked numerous questions. The human propensity to question God goes all the way back to the beginning when the tempter posited the question, "Hath God said?" (Genesis 3:1).

This new generation of Israelites was learning to trust God's ways even if they did not understand them. Through the passing of the Jordan River on dry ground, they were discovering that obedience to God pays off even in the face of challenges. Another unspoken miracle happened at Jericho. There is no record of murmuring or questioning. A people whose history was rife with questioning, murmuring, and complaining simply did what God commanded them to do. They marched, they stayed silent, and they shouted exactly when instructed. Their act of complete obedience yielded miraculous access to and momentum in the first major battle in the Promised Land. The wall fell down flat.

B. God Gave Israel Total Victory over Jericho

Husbands and wives, sons and daughters marched with their lips clenched tightly to keep from making a sound. The urge to converse with each other was real. Through those many days,

Teacher Option: A supplemental video is available in the Resource Kit. **V**

Why is it important to obey God's commands even when they do not make sense to us?

they were doubtless tempted to just chat a bit. "Why?" probably nagged the thoughts of some, but they strictly observed God's command to be silent and march. Then, on the seventh day and on the seventh trip around the wall, the shouts erupted. The rumble of the stones blended with the chorus of the crowd as the stones cascaded one on top of the other. Shouts of obedience quickly transitioned into shouts of praise and then to war cries. Once again, obedience yielded God's favor and divine intervention as God did as He had promised and toppled the walls. The people went straight up into the city and fought a victorious battle.

There have been skeptics of the Jericho story for many years. In the 1950s, archaeologist Kathleen Kenyan concluded Jericho was destroyed 150 years before Israel's invasion in 1400 BC. Consequently, many assumed the biblical account was merely folklore or a convenient religious story. Many decades later, however, another archaeologist reviewed Ms. Kenyan's research. Bryant Wood of the University of Toronto revealed his finding in the March/April issue of the scholarly journal *Biblical Archaeology Review*. He shared his findings of extensive ceramic remnants and carbon-14 dating, which contradicted Kenyan's dating of the destruction of the city. Additionally, large amounts of stored grain were found in the remains, which indicated a relatively short siege of the city. Most significantly, he also noted collapsed mud bricks were found inside a lower retaining wall. The collapsed bricks had apparently served as a ramp for the Israelites to go straight up into the city as described in the biblical narrative. Wood concluded, "Here is impressive evidence that the walls of Jericho did indeed topple as the Bible records."

God gave Israel the victory He had promised. Did they have to fight? Yes. But once again, God provided the miracle by removing the obstacles that blocked the promise. Their complete obedience led to God's complete provision. This divine principle of submission and obedience is still at work in God's kingdom today.

What commandments in Scripture require great faith but are worth the payoff?

C. When We Obey God, He Will Respond and Tear Down Walls in Our Lives

When God's children will trust Him enough to obey Him fully, He will do the miraculous. Walls that seem insurmountable can be leveled. Barricades blocking spiritual progress can be removed. Addictions and habits that have bound and sentenced God's children to be wilderness wanderers for years can lose their grip. Demonic oppression and possession must disappear when a heart is fully submitted to God. James, the brother of Jesus, provided a clear picture of this reality of spiritual victory in James 4. "Submit yourselves therefore to God. Resist the devil, and he will flee from you. Draw nigh to God, and he will draw nigh to you. Cleanse your hands, ye sinners; and purify your hearts, ye double minded" (James 4:7-8). Israel discovered this at the wall of Jericho; we must discover it at the walls that separate us from God's promises.

Why does God respond so favorably to complete obedience?

INTERNALIZING THE MESSAGE

Once upon a time, a peasant farmer owned an ox. The ox was valuable to him and key to his farm's success. On a fateful day, the ox fell into an empty, old well whose water had dried up. The ox began moaning distressed cries for help. Responding to the ox's plaintive cries, the peasant discovered the helpless ox and tried to rescue it. He attempted hoisting the ox with ropes and chains, but the beast's size and weight were too much. He lowered a ladder thinking the ox could climb out, but the ox could not navigate the rungs of the ladder. His many attempts to aid his farm friend were futile. Finally, with great sorrow, he gave up on the ox. He decided to mercifully put the ox out of its misery. He purposed to bury the ox by shoveling dirt into the well.

As the farmer regrettably heaved each pile of dirt into the well, the ox demonstrated its will to survive. As each lump of earth landed on its back, the ox defiantly shook it off. With the debris that was meant to bury the ox now under its feet, the ox began to climb up, pile by pile, step by step.

As the ox began to rise higher, the peasant farmer noticed the ox's determination. He feverishly continued to pile more and more dirt into the well. It was a messy endeavor that left them both in need of a good bath, but eventually the ox was able to rise up and climb out. What was used as an attempt to bury it, the ox transformed into a pathway to an improbable way of escape.

At different points in life, we can each find ourselves in seemingly overwhelming circumstances. We are in the pit of despair. Sometimes we find ourselves there by random chance; other times the pit is dug of our own poor choices. The walls of the pit may seem to be closing in, and even those who love us may lose hope. In such times, we must remind ourselves of our God who is for us and never leaves us. As the messiness of circumstances piles on, do not lose hope. Be dedicated and determined to emerge victorious.

We serve a God who works in unconventional ways to turn our trials into our testimonies. He can transform our pain in life into His purpose for our life. Whether He helps us bring the walls down or helps us rise above them, we must be faithful and trust in Him. If He says, "Shout," shout. If He says, "Be silent," be silent. If He says, "Go up," go up. Like Israel entering the Promised Land, faith and obedience to God will bring us to the other side of the walls and into His promises.

Prayer Focus
Lead the group in prayer and consider the following topics of focus:
- For God to help us trust His Word, no matter how many are skeptical of His Word
- For God to help us share His Word, no matter how many are skeptical of His Word

2.4

AS FOR ME AND MY HOUSE

FOCUS VERSE
Joshua 24:15
And if it seem evil unto you to serve the LORD, choose you this day whom ye will serve; whether the gods which your fathers served that were on the other side of the flood, or the gods of the Amorites, in whose land ye dwell: but as for me and my house, we will serve the LORD.

LESSON TEXT
Joshua 24:1–24

TRUTH ABOUT GOD
God wants us to remain firmly committed to Him.

TRUTH FOR MY LIFE
Despite past victories, I must continually commit myself to the Lord.

Thinking about Last Week:

Have students refer to their Daily Devotional Guide to answer the following questions:

1. What most affected you as you read through the Lesson Text and the Biblical Insights?
2. How did it shape your prayers and thoughts throughout the week?
3. Do you feel you grew closer to the Lord this past week? Why or why not?

SG TEACHING OUTLINE

Icebreaker: Have you ever lost a competition you just knew you were going to win?

Lesson Connection: Share the Lesson Connection. **I**

I. JOSHUA SUMMONED THE ISRAELITES

    A. Joshua Told of God's Blessings to Abraham, Isaac, and Jacob

      » *Why is it important to remember and share our testimony of God's faithfulness?*

    B. Joshua Recounted the Miracle of the Exodus and Reminded the People of Their Victories

      » *What are some dangers for people who have not experienced struggles and challenges in life?*

    C. We Must Always Hold On to the Testimony God Has Given Us

II. JOSHUA OFFERED A NEW CHALLENGE

    A. Joshua Commanded the Israelites to Get Rid of Their Idols

      » *What are some present-day idols that hinder people from completely serving God?*

    B. Joshua Challenged the People to Serve the Lord

      » *Is it easier to choose God when the rest of the group is choosing Him?*

    C. Joshua Made a Commitment That He and His Family Would Serve the Lord

    D. Despite Past Victories, We Must Continually Commit Ourselves to the Lord

      » *How can we balance the celebration of past victories with maintaining a laser focus on future battles?*

Internalizing the Message **V**

Prayer Focus

Lead the group in prayer and consider the following topics of focus:
- For God to forgive us if we have any idols in our lives
- For God to help us finish strong in our faith

LESSON CONNECTION

A supplemental image is available in the Resource Kit. **I**

" I never took the fight seriously." Those somber words of former heavyweight boxing champion "Iron" Mike Tyson came several weeks after arguably the greatest upset in the history of professional boxing. Around thirty thousand fans crammed into the Tokyo Dome. The bell clanged and two hulking men began to pummel each other. The crowd anticipated Tyson to fight to a resounding defeat of a relatively unknown boxer named James "Buster" Douglas.

As the rounds added up, the crowd and critics realized something was wrong. In the tenth round, a relatively unknown Buster Douglas defeated a battered and staggering "Iron Mike" by knockout after he knocked Tyson to the canvas for the first time in Tyson's storied career. The boxing world was stunned, but the defeated heavyweight champion realized it was his own fault. "I was out of shape, more or less," Tyson said in a *New York Times* article in March 1990. "I let myself get too heavy before the fight. I lost twenty-five pounds in Japan in the last month before the fight. It was too much. . . . I fell into sloppy habits. . . . [Douglas] beat an out-of-shape guy who didn't prepare properly."

Mike Tyson's defeat teaches us a little about human nature. Over time we tend to stop doing the things that led to our success. We may get sloppy in maintaining what led to our success. Dieters often find this to be true. Through hard work, willpower, and discipline, people lose weight. Then little allowances are made that lead to reduced discipline. Gradually, the weight begins to creep back onto their frame. Dieting is an ongoing battle. Similarly, consider how many marriage relationships fail due to spouses who fall into sloppy habits. The selfless, loving attitudes and behaviors they exhibited early in the relationship give way to criticism, apathy, and selfishness.

It is the same with our relationship with God. Samson found out the hard way what happens when you forget the fundamentals of living in the favor of God. Like "Iron Mike," Samson was a heavyweight champion in his own right. He was mightily used of God to lead and defend against the enemies of God. But over time he too fell into sloppy habits. Sloppy habits, a lack of self-discipline, and ignoring key fundamentals always lead to failure.

BIBLE LESSON

I. JOSHUA SUMMONED THE ISRAELITES

A. Joshua Told of God's Blessings to Abraham, Isaac, and Jacob

As Israel left the wilderness behind, they were tasked with the responsibility of possessing a prosperous future. Joshua realized prosperity is a difficult test to pass. God spoke through the 110-year-old leader with sobering caution. God reminded Israel they were inheriting a land for which they did not work. They would be residing in cities they had not toiled to build. The fruit on their lips and in their bellies came from vineyards they neither planted nor nurtured.

We learn lessons as we look back at Israel's history and our own. Routinely revisiting one's legacy and the unfolding of God's promises is important to our future. It helps us realize God's promises are rarely immediate. We serve a God of process. Israel needed to understand God desired to raise up a people who would serve Him and no other gods. Second, God chose a man who would follow by faith. Third, faith is obedience and loyalty to God while He is preparing us for the right time to receive the promise.

Israel needed this reminder. So do we.

B. Joshua Recounted the Miracle of the Exodus and Reminded the People of Their Victories

Why is it important to remember and share our testimony of God's faithfulness?

Once Joshua highlighted the faith and perseverance it took for Abraham to initiate the promise, he began to highlight God's faithful hand in their national history. Of course, any Israelite living under Joshua's leadership had heard the stories of the Exodus and the miracle at the Red Sea. Yet God deemed it important to highlight the miraculous favor and provision He had extended to them. God not only delivered their forefathers from their Egyptian enemies, but He fought for them as well and delivered their Canaanite enemies into their hand (Joshua 24:11).

Imagine Joshua's aged voice cracking with emotion as he recounted this treasured history. Most of the people he was addressing had not lived through much of it. They had not known Egyptian bondage. Neither had they felt the grip of fear at the Red Sea nor heard the crashing waves as God buried the army of their enemies in a watery grave. This generation of Israelites were not at Mount Sinai to see and hear the Ten Commandments God etched in stone by His own finger and gave to Moses. Most of the people Joshua was addressing were in the latter stages of the fulfillment of God's promise. Even at that, God demonstrated His powerful provision and presence as they miraculously crossed the Jordan River and began to possess the Promised Land. They were a people with a rich legacy. Their forefathers had a tremendous testimony. Similarly, God had given each of

What are some dangers for people who have not experienced struggles and challenges in life?

them a personal testimony to share with the world and with the next generation.

C. We Must Always Hold On to the Testimony God Has Given Us

As Christians, the chosen people of the New Covenant, God has given us exceeding great and precious promises (II Peter 1:4). Whether you have been a child of God for six months or six decades, you have a testimony. For some, this testimony is deliverance from drug or alcohol addiction. For others, God delivered them from depression or despair. Still others have testimonies of healed bodies or mended relationships. We each have our testimony of what God has brought us from and carried us through.

Like Joshua, as we journey toward the promises of God, we amass victories and grow through our failures. As we continue walking by faith, we see the promises of God gradually begin to unfold in our lives. For many, this includes relational health. A life lived according to the principles of God invariably produces mature and rewarding interpersonal relationships. Many children of God experience financial stability as they learn—even from their mistakes—to develop stewardship habits that honor God. The promises of peace and joy result in mental wellness as we learn not to fear and to cast our cares on Jesus (I Peter 5:7).

For most Christians, our testimonies have come through battles. We have experienced many challenges. We may have lost some battles. We may even bear some scars. But if we are living by faith, we keep moving forward and fighting. The result is a testimony of God's provision and faithfulness. Heed the warning words God spoke through Joshua to Israel, and let us never forget what it took to get where we are.

Consider not only our own struggles and sacrifices but also those of the children of God who have come before us. Elders of the faith helped lay the groundwork to get us where we are today. These testimonies are meant to be shared and guarded.

II. JOSHUA OFFERED A NEW CHALLENGE

A. Joshua Commanded the Israelites to Get Rid of Their Idols

Just as Joshua echoed God's voice to a blessed and prosperous Israelite nation, we must remember to heed the voice of God in our blessed and prosperous lives. Joshua urged Israel, "Now therefore fear the LORD, and serve him in sincerity and in truth: and put away the gods which your fathers served on the other side of the flood, and in Egypt; and serve ye the LORD" (Joshua 24:14).

Although the children of Israel were benefactors of God's great grace, Israel still had idols from their past. The gods Abraham's father may have worshiped continued to plague the lives of the children of promise. Hundreds of years after God called Abraham, his family was still struggling to surrender those idols from their past. And they may have even embraced the worship of some of the Egyptian gods while Israel was in bondage. Remember when Aaron fashioned a golden calf at the foot of Mount Sinai?

As people of the New Covenant, we must guard against the danger of embracing gods of our culture and our past. While God is leading us into His promises, we must never become divided in our loyalty or devotion. We must hear and heed the first words God spoke to Moses, "I am the LORD thy God, which have brought thee out of the land of Egypt, out of the house of bondage. Thou shalt have no other gods before me" (Exodus 20:2–3). Our parents may have dealt with some of these same idols. The love of money, entertainment, and sensual pleasures are often secretly carried along with us toward the promises of God.

As Joshua urged those of the Old Covenant to serve God with sincerity, or completeness, and turn aside from their false gods, God's voice echoes into the twenty-first century. "Serve Me with completeness and turn aside from false gods that distract and hinder you." (See Joshua 24:14.)

What are some present-day idols that hinder people from completely serving God?

B. Joshua Challenged the People to Serve the Lord

As Joshua concluded his impassioned plea, he came to a resolute conclusion. He challenged those he addressed as he drew the proverbial line in the sand. He demanded they make a choice. He listed for them three choices: the God of Abraham, the false gods of Abraham's ancestors, or the gods of the land in which they now lived. Joshua's point was abundantly clear: it was time to decide.

For many years Israel had made decisions based on groupthink that allowed them to escape individual responsibility. They murmured together, worshiped a golden calf together, doubted together, and even experienced victories together. Joshua declared this day was going to be much different. "Choose you this day whom ye will serve" (Joshua 24:15).

No matter what others do, we must make a personal commitment to lead ourselves and our homes in the ways of God. Attending church together and doing ministry together are important. But over the course of time, others may compromise and accept idols that weigh them down. They may begin embracing gods of selfishness, criticism, and even bitterness. Gods of carnal entertainment and conformity to worldly values may creep in. We must not allow the gods others embrace cause us to lay down our own convictions and commitments to God. Every individual Christian must decide "whom ye will serve."

Is it easier to choose God when the rest of the group is choosing Him?

C. Joshua Made a Commitment That He and His Family Would Serve the Lord

Joshua's challenge was bold and direct. So was his answer to his own challenge. He had seen Israel stagger between loyalties for years. He had witnessed the idolatry of God's people in Egypt. He saw firsthand their propensity to gravitate toward false gods throughout their journey toward the Promised Land. Joshua sensed the urgency of the hour. He saw the double-mindedness still present in some Israelites, so he challenged them to choose.

But before giving them a chance to answer for themselves, Joshua boldly declared, "As for me and my house, we will serve the LORD" (Joshua 24:15). The line drawn, the dye cast, Joshua's decision preceded the answer or declaration of any other Israelite. He and his family would wholeheartedly serve the Lord. Joshua's question still hangs in the air for you to answer: whom will you serve? The time for wavering is over. When that day dawns, what will your answer be? Will it be demonstrated in your walk? in your talk? Our choice will always be followed by our actions. Our actions truly testify what choice we made.

D. Despite Past Victories, We Must Continually Commit Ourselves to the Lord

We battle different adversaries than those Israel battled. We are tempted by different gods than they were. Our weapons are not carnal. We do not fight with flesh and blood. We do not fight against nations or clans. Neither do we advance on and conquer physical territories. The gods that grab our hearts are not carved of wood or fashioned of brass, but our temptations and battles are just as real as theirs were.

As the redeemed children of the New Covenant, we are fighting the good fight of faith. As we continue in this war, we will fight many hard-fought battles. We must conquer enemies of bitterness and unforgiveness. We will fight against carnal appetites of lust, greed, and worldliness. Idols of entertainment and materialism will present themselves as alternatives to seeking first the kingdom of God.

God calls us to walk by faith (II Corinthians 5:7). Faith distilled to its simplest form is simply complete trust in and obedience to God and His Word no matter the outlook. Paul wrote to the church in Rome and declared, "For therein is the righteousness of God revealed from faith to faith: as it is written, The just shall live by faith" (Romans 1:17). God's righteousness is ultimately revealed when we who have been justified by faith proceed to live by faith. We live from faith to faith.

How can we balance the celebration of past victories with maintaining a laser focus on future battles?

Unlike Israel entering into the promises of God, we must never become complacent. Although the Israelites could boast of their past victories, Joshua issued a present challenge: choose this day. We must always be grateful for and celebrate our past victories achieved through faith. God's promises achieved through faith are worthy of celebration, but we must keep the finish line in sight. We are not there yet. Our race is not completely run. The final bell of the fight of faith has yet to ring. We must take the fight seriously until the very end.

INTERNALIZING THE MESSAGE

A supplemental video is available in the Resource Kit. **V**

On April 11, 2015, at the Hayward Field in Eugene, Oregon, hopeful athletes met to run in the Pepsi Team Invitational track meet. The crowd of over three thousand roared as the contestants in the three-thousand-meter steeplechase raced toward the finish line. The steeplechase combines different skills into one race: distance running, hurdling, and long jumping. Runners must clear twenty-eight hurdles and seven water jumps along the nearly two-mile-long course. Interestingly, the steeplechase originated in England when people raced from one church's steeple to the next. The steeples were used as markers due to their high visibility. Runners encountered streams and stone walls when running between towns, which is why the hurdles and water jumps are now included.

During the steeplechase on April 11, 2015, Oregon's Tanguy Pepiot, a senior from France, had a commanding lead as he approached the final one hundred meters. In his mind, victory was sealed. He was so confident that he began waving his arm for the crowd to cheer louder. Unfortunately for Pepiot, no one informed the University of Washington's Meron Simon that the race was over. As Pepiot urged the crowd to cheer louder for his sure victory, he smiled as he heard them respond. It was only fitting. Pepiot was a student athlete at the University of Oregon, and this race was being held on his home track. But he did not realize that the crowd's heightened cheers were not celebrating him. They were urging him to stay focused as Simon rapidly closed in on the outside. By the time Pepiot realized what was happening, Simon crossed the finish line and won by a foot with a time of 8:57.86 compared to 8:57.96 for Pepiot.

Pepiot lost the race after he broke one of the key rules in sports by celebrating before he won. A look of shock and dismay broke across his face as Simon passed him at the finish line by ten one-hundredths of a second.

"I heard some noise," Pepiot explained. "I was very surprised. Then I checked the screen, and I was like, 'Whoa, somebody's coming!'"

Simon explained, "I thought he had me. . . . I thought he was just so far ahead. Then I heard the crowd get crazy, and he started throwing his hands up. I was like, 'I don't think he knows I'm coming.' I just went to the line and just raced."

Our race of faith also begins at a steeple: a local church. Our race is filled with many obstacles and pitfalls to overcome. It is long and tiring, but we have in sight another steeple, or pinnacle. It is the eternal city of New Jerusalem. As we near the finish line of this race, we must stay engaged and focused on finishing well. We cannot afford to be distracted so near the end of our race.

Prayer Focus
Lead the group in prayer and consider the following topics of focus:
- For God to forgive us if we have any idols in our lives
- For God to help us finish strong in our faith

SERIES 3: PUTTING OTHERS FIRST

3.1

WHO BELONGS?

FOCUS VERSE
Mark 10:45
For even the Son of man came not to be ministered unto, but to minister, and to give his life a ransom for many.

LESSON TEXT
Mark 10:13–22, 41–52

TRUTH ABOUT GOD
God loves and cares for those whom the world overlooks.

TRUTH FOR MY LIFE
I will look for ways to lovingly serve those who are hurting.

Series Overview:

This series, "Putting Others First," will take a look at Jesus' love for the oft overlooked. Jesus welcomed children the world rejected, and He healed a blind man the world ignored. He even ministered to a rich young ruler who had everything but the gospel. While others esteemed riches and authority, Jesus valued service and ministry to one another. Everyone, those with little or much, is welcome in the kingdom of God.

SG TEACHING OUTLINE

Icebreaker: If you could only speak one last word to your family or friends, what would it be?

Lesson Connection: Share the Lesson Connection. Ⓘ

I. JESUS' MINISTRY SHOWED THAT HE CARED FOR EVERYONE

A. The Young, the Rich, and the Blind
   » *In what ways can we show love and care for children, particularly those who are not part of our own family?*
   » *Do you feel jealous or insecure when other people excel in areas where you struggle? How can you change those feelings?*

B. I Will Show God's Love to Everyone I Meet Ⓥ
   » *How can we increase our sensitivity to the needs of others, including their spiritual needs?*

II. JESUS' MINISTRY SHOWED THAT HIS HEART WAS SET ON SERVING OTHERS

A. Jesus Ministered Out of Love

B. Some People Rejected Jesus' Love

C. Jesus Called His Disciples to Show Love through Service
   » *If you stood before Jesus today, would He consider you a sheep or a goat? If you feel more like a goat than a sheep, what can you do to change that?*

D. I Will Look for Ways to Lovingly Serve Those Who Are Hurting
   » *What resources or skills can you use to minister to someone in need this week?*

Internalizing the Message

Prayer Focus
Lead the group in prayer and consider the following topics of focus:
• For God to help us see the needs of others even above our own
• For God to use us to meet others' needs

LESSON CONNECTION

A supplemental image is available in the Resource Kit. (I)

William Booth, the founder of the Salvation Army, was known for his passionate commitment to loving and serving people, particularly the poorest residents of the poorest sections of London. Many inspiring quotes about evangelism and Christian service have been attributed to Booth, but one of the most insightful quotes attributed to him is also the shortest.

In 1910 the leaders of the Salvation Army invited the aged Booth to address their annual convention scheduled to convene during the Christmas season. Booth's health had deteriorated so much he was not able to attend. He died less than two years later. Since he could not be present, the meeting's organizers asked him to send a telegram to be read to those in attendance.

Sending messages via telegram was a costly method of communication, so Booth's remarks would have to be brief. Telegraph operators charged by the word, and the ministry's funds were limited. William Booth would have to find some way to inspire his fellow workers using as few words as possible. According to the story, Booth pondered what he could say that would communicate the feelings that had inspired him to devote his life to ministering to those in need. He wanted to say something to motivate Salvation Army personnel who had been selflessly giving their time and energy during the coldest and darkest months of the year to serve their poorest and most vulnerable neighbors.

When the day of the convention arrived, the meeting hall filled with delegates eager to hear from their founder. When it was announced that Booth was not able to be present, the disappointment was palpable. But spirits lifted when someone opened the telegram from Booth and the moderator prepared to read the founder's brief remarks.

On the telegram, Booth shared a single word—a word that succinctly summarized his life's work and the vision he had for the organization he founded.

The message simply read, "Others."

BIBLE LESSON

Others. That single word also summarizes what motivated the ministry of Jesus Christ. Jesus outlined His ministry and mission in a simple statement to His disciples in Mark 10:45. "For even the Son of man came not to be ministered unto, but to minister, and to give his life a ransom for many."

I. JESUS' MINISTRY SHOWED THAT HE CARED FOR EVERYONE

Who belongs? In God's kingdom, everyone belongs. God's grace is not limited to a select few. The Bible closes with an invitation to whosoever will (Revelation 22:17). Everyone can freely drink from the living water Jesus offers regardless of gender, national origin, ethnic identity, or social status.

Jesus went out of His way to minister to outsiders who had been rejected by the religious and cultural establishment. He stopped by a well in Samaria to minister to a Samaritan woman living in adultery. Jesus traveled to the Gentile lands of Tyre and Sidon where He cast the devil out of a Syrophenician woman's daughter (Mark 7:24–30). He called the tax collector Zacchaeus out of a sycamore tree and went home for dinner with him, causing the whole community to question Jesus' choice of company. Jesus never apologized for loving people, especially the people everyone else seemed to find distasteful.

A. The Young, the Rich, and the Blind

In a single chapter, the Gospel of Mark makes it clear that Jesus loved and cared for everyone, no matter the person's status or station in life. In Mark 10, Jesus ministered to individuals from three distinct walks of life: children, a rich young ruler, and a blind beggar named Bartimaeus.

Parents seemed to be excited for their children to meet Jesus. They brought them to Him. In our culture, we expect politicians and preachers to kiss babies and give candy to children, but this was not the case in the first century. Children in Jesus' day were considered unimportant. In Greek and Roman culture, infanticide was common and culturally acceptable. Wicked King Herod murdered baby boys in Bethlehem seemingly without a second thought (Matthew 2:16–18). Despite what some may argue, today's widespread acceptance of abortion reveals that twenty-first century North American attitudes toward children are not much different.

Jesus' disciples adopted the prevailing attitude of their culture because they responded to this intrusion on Jesus' time with a rebuke for the children and their parents. Imagine their surprise when Jesus offered His own rebuke, responding, "Suffer the little children to come unto me, and forbid them not: for of such is the kingdom of God" (Mark 10:14). In the same verse, Mark records that Jesus was much displeased with His disciples' lack of love and compassion for children.

Jesus is still not pleased with those who neglect the well-being of children. Sadly, the mental, physical, emotional, and spiritual needs of the youngest members of our society are often sacrificed on the altar of career advancement, money, and other temporal distractions. Our God loves and cares for every child, including the fatherless, the orphan, the abused, and the unborn baby in the womb. How we treat the youngest and most vulnerable members of society is a direct reflection of our attitude toward Jesus.

In what ways can we show love and care for children, particularly those who are not part of our own family?

Not long after this story, Jesus encountered the man who has come to be known as the rich young ruler. This man seemed to have everything going for him. He was rich and was in some area of authority. Luke 18:18 described him as a ruler. He did not fit the same demographic profile as Jesus' disciples who were mostly common men without much wealth or power. The disciples may have been impressed by this man's prestigious standing in society and by his money, much like most people today are awed by wealth and celebrity. The disciples also may have felt a twinge of insecurity at the prospect of this man becoming one of them. If someone with this rich ruler's credentials decided to follow Jesus, how would it affect the disciples' place in the spiritual pecking order?

Do you feel jealous or insecure when other people excel in areas where you struggle? How can you change those feelings?

Jesus was not awed by the rich young ruler's wealth, power, or perceived righteousness. Neither was Jesus intimated by his social standing. Jesus simply loved him. "Then Jesus beholding him loved him" (Mark 10:21).

As Jesus continued His journey to Jerusalem and the cross, Mark records one more overlooked person Jesus cared for. As Jesus was leaving Jericho, He was interrupted again, this time by the cries of a blind beggar named Bartimaeus. The crowd accompanying Jesus tried to shame the blind man into silence, but Bartimaeus would not be denied in his effort to get Jesus' attention. As Mark wrote, "He cried the more a great deal, Thou Son of David, have mercy on me" (Mark 10:48).

The desperation in Bartimaeus's voice arrested Jesus' attention. The noise of the crowd and bustle of the nearby city could not drown it out. The love Jesus had for hurting people caused Him to momentarily place His other plans on hold. He stopped and commanded the crowd to call Bartimaeus.

Perhaps Bartimaeus was surprised that Jesus actually noticed his cries. As a blind beggar, he was likely used to being ignored. Most people tried to hurry by him as quickly as possible, hoping he would not notice their presence and ask them for money. Their typical response was akin to what most of us do when we see a roadside panhandler: we sometimes pretend not to notice. In our day, people keep the car windows rolled up, avoid eye contact, and pray the red light turns green quickly.

But not Jesus. He cares about those society neglects and rejects. He welcomes the homeless and the handicapped. He was on His way to save the world from sin, but He made time for a blind beggar everyone else tried to silence. Jesus did not overlook the one while on His way to save the many, even when the one was considered to be from the bottom rung of the social ladder. Jesus transformed Bartimaeus from a highway-side blind beggar into a walking testimony that still teaches us two millennia later about the love Jesus has for all people, even those the world neglects and rejects.

B. I Will Show God's Love to Everyone I Meet

As Spirit-led believers, we must be sensitive to the needs of everyone we encounter, even the rich young rulers of our time. They may drive a luxury import and live in a gated community, but it does not mean they have no needs. Like Jesus, we must be perceptive to their true condition and be prepared to minister to them in any way possible. Of course, the kindest, most compassionate thing we can do for others is to share the gospel with them. People need to hear about the God who loves them so much He came to earth and went to the cross for them. If we are looking for a way to help others, we should begin by sharing the message of eternal salvation.

II. JESUS' MINISTRY SHOWED THAT HIS HEART WAS SET ON SERVING OTHERS

Jesus did not just have kind feelings in His heart toward others; His actions demonstrated His love. He summed up His intentions in Mark 10:45 when he said, "For even the Son of man came not to be ministered unto, but to minister, and to give his life a ransom for many." Jesus was willing to give everything, even His life, just to minister to others.

A. Jesus Ministered Out of Love

Jesus' love and compassion were not limited to His family, friends, and followers. The writers of the Gospels made it clear that Jesus loved everyone. Love motivated everything Jesus did.

Matthew summed up Jesus' itinerary by saying, "Jesus went about all the cities and villages, teaching in their synagogues, and preaching the gospel of the kingdom, and healing every sickness and every disease among the people" (Matthew 9:35). He did not stay on the road preaching because He wanted to build His brand or because He was expecting a financial payoff. Rather, as Matthew wrote in the following verse, "When he saw the multitudes, he was moved with compassion on them" (Matthew 9:36). Compassion moved Jesus. His love was more than a feeling; He expressed it through His actions.

B. Some People Rejected Jesus' Love

Sadly, Jesus' love was not always reciprocated. Jesus' love did not make everyone happy. The end of the rich young ruler's story

Teacher Option: *A supplemental video is available in the Resource Kit.* **V**

How can we increase our sensitivity to the needs of others, including their spiritual needs?

is found in a melancholy verse in Mark 10. "And he was sad at that saying, and went away grieved: for he had great possessions" (Mark 10:22). Real love does not always lead to rosy outcomes. Jesus loved people enough to tell them the truth. In the end, He was crucified by those who did not want to hear the truth.

C. Jesus Called His Disciples to Show Love through Service

Although Jesus knew what was coming, He bravely continued His journey to Jerusalem and the cross. While His disciples did not understand the full weight of what was happening, Jesus' teaching and selfless example would serve as the inspiration for their future lives of sacrificial love.

Throughout Jesus' ministry, He repeatedly called His followers to show love through acts of service. At one point He told them, "Whosoever shall give to drink unto one of these little ones a cup of cold water only in the name of a disciple, verily I say unto you, he shall in no wise lose his reward" (Matthew 10:42). Jesus promised the smallest acts of service would not go unnoticed. Later in the same Gospel, Jesus told a story of sheep and goats. Sheep were those who did His will; goats were those who did not. He concluded Matthew 25 by saying, "Inasmuch as ye have done it unto one of the least of these my brethren, ye have done it unto me" (Matthew 25:40). When we serve others, we are serving Jesus.

If you stood before Jesus today, would He consider you a sheep or a goat? If you feel more like a goat than a sheep, how can you change that?

D. I Will Look for Ways to Lovingly Serve Those Who Are Hurting

Have you ever regretted a missed opportunity to do good? Sometimes we overlook opportunities to show love to others because we are consumed with our own problems. Sometimes life's challenges leave us without the time, energy, or resources to help others. It happens to everyone. But God did not intend for these challenges to be our norm. If we are always so overwhelmed by our own problems that we cannot help others, we should rethink how we are living.

What resources or skills can you use to minister to someone in need this week?

Perhaps our first step should be dedicating some of our resources to serving others. Can we set aside a few dollars a month to give to someone who has an unexpected need? Can we block off one afternoon each month to serve others in our community? Do we have a special skill or talent we can use to minister to others?

Our imagination and willingness to act are the only constraints on our opportunities to do good. Jesus promised if we will seek, we will find (Matthew 7:7; Luke 11:9). This can apply to service as well as to prayer. If we look for opportunities to do good, God will provide. Let us be like Jesus. Let us pray for God to lead us to find someone to serve.

INTERNALIZING THE MESSAGE

One parable in the Gospel of Luke still serves as one of the greatest stories of care and compassion for others. This story has inspired countless acts of love and kindness since the day Jesus first shared it with His followers.

A religious scholar stepped forward to ask Jesus a question, but Jesus answered with a question of His own. The scholar quoted from Leviticus 19:18 where God commanded the people of Israel to "love thy neighbour as thyself." (See Luke 10:27.) Then the scholar asked, "Who is my neighbour?" (Luke 10:29). Jesus responded by telling the Parable of the Good Samaritan.

Jesus began. A man was traveling from Jerusalem to Jericho when he was attacked by a vicious band of thieves. They beat him half to death and left him lying alongside the road to die of his wounds. Soon a priest and a Levite traveled down the same road. Both of these men were so preoccupied with their religious duties that they failed to notice the bleeding man lying by the side of the road. That was the best-case scenario. Worst case, they callously ignored him. They passed by without even asking if he was all right.

Thankfully, another traveler came along, but this man was a Samaritan. The mere mention of Samaritan caused Jesus' audience to wince. Jews hated Samaritans. Thankfully for the wounded man, the Samaritan was not as cold-hearted as the Jewish priest and the Levite. When the Samaritan saw the wounded man, he had compassion on him. This surprised Jesus' Jewish audience. The Samaritan provided emergency medical treatment to stabilize the man's condition before transporting him to safety where he could receive additional care. Since health insurance and government-funded medical care were not part of daily life, paying for the cost of treatment fell to the Samaritan. He willingly shouldered this burden.

Who is our neighbor? According to Jesus, our neighbor is anyone we meet along the road of life, regardless of identity or present condition. Being a neighbor means more than just sending up an occasional emergency prayer to God to remind Him of how bad things are on earth while we silently hope someone else will come along and help. Jesus calls us to get personally involved. He reminds us, "For even the Son of man came not to be ministered unto, but to minister, and to give his life a ransom for many" (Mark 10:45). Being like Jesus means ministering to others, no matter who they are or where they are from, no matter what it costs.

Prayer Focus
Lead the group in prayer and consider the following topics of focus:
- For God to help us see the needs of others even above our own
- For God to use us to meet others' needs

3.2

KINGDOM VALUES

FOCUS VERSES
Mark 10:21–22
²¹ Then Jesus beholding him loved him, and said unto him, One thing thou lackest: go thy way, sell whatsoever thou hast, and give to the poor, and thou shalt have treasure in heaven: and come, take up the cross, and follow me. ²² And he was sad at that saying, and went away grieved: for he had great possessions.

LESSON TEXT
Mark 10:17–31

TRUTH ABOUT GOD
God's kingdom is about giving and serving, not buying and having.

TRUTH FOR MY LIFE
I will put God first in my life.

Thinking about Last Week:

Have students refer to their Daily Devotional Guide to answer the following questions:
1. What most affected you as you read through the Lesson Text and the Biblical Insights?
2. How did it shape your prayers and thoughts throughout the week?
3. Do you feel you grew closer to the Lord this past week? Why or why not?

(SG) TEACHING OUTLINE

Icebreaker: What is your most prized possession?

Lesson Connection: Share the Lesson Connection. (V)

I. THE RICH YOUNG RULER

    A. Eternal Life and the One Thing You Lack
   » *How is understanding Jesus' identity connected to obeying His commands?*

    B. The Young Man Rejected Jesus' Directions
   » *Why do you think the lure of wealth is such a powerful temptation? In what ways does material wealth serve as an idol?*

    C. I Must Heed Jesus' Call to Total Surrender
   » *What gifts do you think God wants to give you? Is anything keeping you from receiving what He wants to give?*

II. JESUS' CALL TO RADICAL SELFLESSNESS

    A. The Danger of Trust in Riches and Our Need of the Spirit (I)
   » *In what ways can material wealth blind us to our need for God?*

    B. Importance of the Kingdom and Its Rewards

    C. I Will Put God First in My Life
   » *What does putting Jesus first in your life look like?*

Internalizing the Message

Prayer Focus
Lead the group in prayer and consider the following topics of focus:
• That God's Word would point out the areas we need to fully surrender to the Lord
• That our words and desires would please the Lord

LESSON CONNECTION

A supplemental video is available in the Resource Kit. **V**

As a young girl, Helen Anderson Cole dreamed of being a famous singer. She took walks through a park near her family's home in St. Louis, Missouri, as she sang at the top of her lungs. She naïvely hoped a Hollywood talent scout might hear her. Her family was impoverished and often lacked basic necessities of life, but Helen dreamed her singing talent would someday rescue them from their desperate situation.

Helen's voice never did attract the attention of a Hollywood agent, but it did earn praise from Pastor Harry Branding. Helen met Pastor Branding when her family attended Pentecostal revival services at a mission hall located at 11th and Hickory Streets in St. Louis. When Helen received the baptism of the Holy Spirit, she could not speak a word of English for three days afterward. Pastor Branding recognized God's hand on this young lady's life and told her, "Helen, I saw you singing in front of thousands of people all around the world."

Despite a life-changing spiritual experience and her pastor's encouragement to pursue God's call, Helen still felt the pull of earthly fame. When a friend told Helen that the Municipal Opera was holding auditions, she auditioned. She saw the cameras and the flashbulbs brighten the room and thought, *At last, I've been discovered.* Helen was elated to be chosen as one of three finalists.

At church the following evening, Helen was surprised when someone approached her and warned, "Be sure your sins will find you out." She soon discovered that her photo had appeared on the front page of the St. Louis Globe-Democrat newspaper as one of the three finalists. That night Helen repented of her ambition for worldly fame and glory and decided to consecrate her talents to the Lord.

Helen eventually became a singing evangelist. She traveled around the world, sharing the gospel through preaching and song. She saw thousands receive the precious gift of the Holy Spirit. Pastor Harry Branding's prophecy was fulfilled repeatedly throughout her life. In addition, Helen was frequently invited to sing at the annual General Conference of the United Pentecostal Church International. Her children later recalled, "We never saw our mother ever come to the platform to sing without the congregation coming to their feet in worship."

Like many believers past and present, Helen Anderson Cole discovered that the rewards of serving Jesus are greater than anything this world offers.

BIBLE LESSON

I. THE RICH YOUNG RULER

We know this man as the rich, young ruler. While we cannot specify how rich or young he was or how much authority he wielded, he seemed to have everything going for him. He addressed Jesus as "Good Master." Both his words and posture communicated respect. He then asked Jesus a question that should be on everyone's lips: "What shall I do that I may inherit eternal life?" Despite the distractions of youth, wealth, and power, this young man appeared to have intense interest in spiritual matters. He also recognized that Jesus had the answer to his question.

Sadly, the rich young ruler's entrance was marked with far more excitement than his exit. He arrived in a rush, eager for an answer to his question, but Mark 10:22 records he "went away grieved." His encounter with Jesus did not turn out as expected. Even Jesus' disciples were shocked by the Master's response. Two millennia later, Jesus' words still challenge those who live in cultures where affluence is widespread. Jesus cut right to the heart of the matter; God's kingdom is about giving and serving, not buying and having.

A. Eternal Life and the One Thing You Lack

Jesus responded to the rich young ruler's question with a question of His own. "Why callest thou me good? there is none good but one, that is, God" (Mark 10:18). Jesus challenged the young man to consider what he really believed about the one he was addressing. If we do not comprehend who Jesus really is, we will be unable to fully commit everything in our lives to Him. The rich ruler's reaction revealed he really did not know.

How is understanding Jesus' identity connected to obeying His commands?

Jesus told the young man he needed to keep the commandments. A smile broke across his young face when he told Jesus he had kept them since he was much younger. He no doubt expected to earn Jesus' commendation for his faithfulness and obedience, but Matthew offered a hint that the rich young ruler still felt a void in his life. After noting that he had kept the commands Jesus listed, the young man had one more question: "What lack I yet?" (Matthew 19:20). Despite a lifetime of commandment-keeping, the rich ruler recognized something was missing. Youth, wealth, and power had not filled the emptiness inside of him. He came to Jesus looking for more.

Jesus' reaction is encouraging to everyone who has ever felt that emptiness. "Then Jesus beholding him loved him," Mark wrote in verse 21. Jesus loved the rich young ruler, even though He knew the young man was not going to respond favorably to what Jesus was about to say. This highlights the deity of Jesus. John wrote of Jesus, He "needed not that any should testify of man: for he knew what was in man" (John 2:25). Jesus knows what is in us—our greed, selfishness, and self-centeredness—yet He loves us anyway.

B. The Young Man Rejected Jesus' Directions

Love is not afraid to speak the truth. Jesus loved this young man enough to tell him what he was missing. "One thing thou lackest," Jesus said. "Go thy way, sell whatsoever thou hast, and give to the poor, and thou shalt have treasure in heaven: and come, take up the cross, and follow me" (Mark 10:21).

The rich young ruler was not ready to accept this level of commitment. His life was so full of material abundance that he had no margin left for serving others. Maintaining his stuff and growing his wealth consumed his life. Although the rich young ruler did not realize it, Jesus was offering him freedom from the tyranny of too much. But the young man could not bring himself to throw off his golden chains and embrace the eternal life he claimed to seek. Instead, Mark 10:22 records, "He was sad at that saying, and went away grieved: for he had great possessions." He could not fathom exchanging all he had for the life Jesus offered.

Paul wrote, "For the love of money is the root of all evil: which while some coveted after, they have erred from the faith, and pierced themselves through with many sorrows" (I Timothy 6:10). Money is not the root of all evil as many have claimed while misquoting Paul's words. But an inordinate affection for money and material gain has certainly led to countless sorrows, ruined lives, and lost souls. The problem with riches is that they often possess us instead of us possessing them.

Why do you think the lure of wealth is such a powerful temptation? In what ways does material wealth serve as an idol?

C. I Must Heed Jesus' Call to Total Surrender

Jesus offered the antidote to the affliction of affluence. His words undoubtedly sounded contradictory to the rich young ruler, and they still turn modern conventions of success on their head. "Sell whatsoever thou hast," Jesus challenged him, "and thou shalt have" (Mark 10:21). This made no sense. How will he have if he sells everything?

The rich ruler's life was overflowing with possessions, so he had no room to receive the eternal blessings he claimed to seek. Many people in today's materialistic world face the same problem. We work overtime and pursue side jobs so we can afford more stuff or make payments on what we already have. This often leaves us too exhausted to pray or spend time studying God's Word. We pack our children's schedules with games, tournaments, and recitals, hoping it will one day earn them a coveted college scholarship so they can enjoy a great-paying career. If all those extracurricular activities happen to squeeze out Sunday worship, midweek Bible study, or family devotions, many dismiss it as collateral damage.

No, Jesus does not call every believer to post a for sale sign in the front lawn or sell all worldly goods in a massive garage sale. But He does call us to clear the clutter that keeps us from Him. For some, that may include parting with a few material possessions. If bass boats, motorcycles, golf clubs, or other possessions consistently keep us from doing the will of God, it may be time to reconsider our relationship with those items.

What gifts do you think God wants to give you? Is anything keeping you from receiving what He wants to give?

II. JESUS' CALL TO RADICAL SELFLESSNESS

Jesus did not ask the rich young ruler to do something He Himself was unwilling to do. Indeed, Jesus had already laid aside the glory of Heaven, which was worth far more than everything the young man owned, and embraced the suffering of earth. Paul explained this sacrifice in greater detail in Philippians 2:5-8. Jesus "made himself of no reputation, and took upon him the form of a servant, and was made in the likeness of men: and being found in fashion as a man, he humbled himself, and became obedient unto death, even the death of the cross." Jesus willingly surrendered His life so we might have eternal life.

The call to follow Jesus is a call to radical selflessness. It is a call to put others first, to seek God's kingdom above all else, even if it means abandoning what we previously held dear.

A. The Danger of Trust in Riches and Our Need of the Spirit

As the rich young ruler sulked away, Jesus turned to His disciples and shocked them with His next statement. "How hardly shall they that have riches enter into the kingdom of God!" To drive home the point, He repeated Himself, "Children, how hard is it for them that trust in riches to enter into the kingdom of God! It is easier for a camel to go through the eye of a needle, than for a rich man to enter into the kingdom of God" (Mark 10:23-25). In *The Words and Works of Jesus Christ,* J. Dwight Pentecost points out, "The popular explanation that the eye of a needle referred to a small gate within the large city gate has no historical basis. Christ was not showing that it is difficult for one who trusts in riches to enter the kingdom. He was showing that it was utterly impossible." It is impossible for anyone to earn salvation.

Teacher Option:
A supplemental image is available in the Resource Kit. 🔲

The disciples were astonished by Jesus' words. In their minds, wealth and power were sure signs of God's favor and blessing. If someone like the rich young ruler, a wealthy man who faithfully kept the law of Moses could not earn heaven, what hope did these poor Galilean fishermen have?

Jesus quickly reassured them, "With God all things are possible" (Mark 10:27). We know God can save sinners from drug addiction, alcoholism, or immoral lifestyles, but He can also save sinners who are ensnared by financial abundance and material wealth. We may not think of ourselves as wealthy, but the average resident of North America has far more than most of our global neighbors. Many North American believers can say with the

Laodiceans, "I am rich, and increased with goods, and have need of nothing." There certainly are many believers in North America who struggle financially and even lack basic necessities. But may Jesus' response to those Christians who have prospered financially not be, "Knowest not that thou art wretched, and miserable, and poor, and blind, and naked" (Revelation 3:17).

In what ways can material wealth blind us to our need for God?

B. Importance of the Kingdom and Its Rewards

If God has blessed us with material wealth, we should be grateful for His provisions. We do not need to apologize for what we have or feel guilty because we have more than someone else. But we must also be careful not to cling so tightly to our blessings that they become a curse. Jesus assured Peter and the rest of His disciples that every sacrifice they made would be rewarded. What was true for those first disciples is also true for us. God sees every sacrifice we make on behalf of His kingdom, and He will reward a hundredfold. (See Mark 10:30.) The blessings God gives in return will always be far greater than our original sacrifice. Best of all, Jesus promised that His followers would experience eternal life in the world to come. (See Mark 10:31.)

C. I Will Put God First in My Life

Just as Jesus called the rich young ruler to follow Him, Jesus calls us to come, take up the cross, and follow Him. Carrying a cross may require us to abandon other pursuits. It will mean reshuffling our priorities. We cannot carry a cross for Jesus and carry the baggage of this world at the same time; we must abandon one for the other.

Carrying a cross requires self-denial. Jesus previously told His followers, "Whosoever will come after me, let him deny himself, and take up his cross, and follow me" (Mark 8:34). In words that foreshadowed His encounter with the rich young ruler, Jesus asked, "For what shall it profit a man, if he shall gain the whole world, and lose his own soul?" (Mark 8:36). The rich young ruler seemed to have everything, but in the end, he was destined to lose everything of real value.

For those who have decided to put God first and pick up a cross, Jesus promised, "Many that are first shall be last; and the last first" (Mark 10:31). God sees every sacrifice you have made; not one has been overlooked or forgotten. You can expect that He will reward a hundredfold in this life and in the one to come.

What does putting Jesus first in your life look like?

INTERNALIZING THE MESSAGE

The past two thousand years of Christian history are filled with stories of individuals who were willing to do what the rich young ruler was not—give up seemingly everything for the sake of the gospel. From Jesus' first disciples to present-day missionaries, many have been willing to even lay down their lives so the message of Jesus could be preached.

Not every story of heroic sacrifice happened in a faraway land. Many have played out in our local church and in churches near ours. Many of the strongest Apostolic Pentecostal congregations were founded by men and women who worked long hours by day to support their families and then spent evenings and weekends preaching, teaching, and reaching for lost people in their communities. As a result, families were saved, lives were changed, and spiritual legacies were established.

Other believers gave up what seemed to be great opportunities because they feared it would compromise their commitment to Jesus Christ. John quit school after completing eighth grade because his older brother told him he could not go to high school and be a Christian. While that is obviously not the case, John believed his brother and decided serving Jesus was more important than gett. ing an education. He never attended high school, but he did live a rich and fulfilling life and died in the faith. His brother, on the other hand, died at a young age from lung cancer brought on by a cigarette addiction.

The writer of Hebrews summed up the stories of the unsung and mostly unknown heroes of the faith by noting that the world was not worthy of them. Furthermore, he added that they all "obtained a good report through faith" (Hebrews 11:38–39). They may not have had wealth or worldly fame, but they will receive the commendation of the King of kings who will one day say, "Well done, good and faithful servant" (Matthew 25:23).

May that be the epitaph of our lives as well.

Prayer Focus
Lead the group in prayer and consider the following topics of focus:
- That God's Word would point out the areas we need to fully surrender to the Lord
- That our words and desires would please the Lord

3.3

KINGDOM PRINCIPLES

FOCUS VERSES
Mark 10:43–44
43 But so shall it not be among you: but whosoever will be great among you, shall be your minister:
44 And whosoever of you will be the chiefest, shall be servant of all.

LESSON TEXT
Mark 9:33–37; 10:35–45

TRUTH ABOUT GOD
God promotes those who do not promote themselves.

TRUTH FOR MY LIFE
I will follow Jesus' example and serve others.

Thinking about Last Week:

Have students refer to their Daily Devotional Guide to answer the following questions:
1. What most affected you as you read through the Lesson Text and the Biblical Insights?
2. How did it shape your prayers and thoughts throughout the week?
3. Do you feel you grew closer to the Lord this past week? Why or why not?

(SG) TEACHING OUTLINE

Icebreaker: What talent do you secretly wish you had?

Lesson Connection: Share the Lesson Connection.

I. WHO WANTS TO BE THE GREATEST? (I)
    » *What does popular culture teach us about greatness? Do those lessons confirm or conflict with the teachings of Jesus?*

    A. Jesus Asked His Disciples about Their Argument
        » *What talents or possessions have you envied in others? Why do you think you have wanted those particular gifts or blessings?*

    B. This Is How You Receive Me

    C. I Will Show Kindness to Others with Humility
        » *How do you feel when others treat you like a servant?*

II. WHO WANTS TO BE SERVANT OF ALL?

    A. The Desire for Position (V)
        » *How have you felt when others were being given opportunities while you were overlooked? Did you gain a different perspective with time?*

    B. The Greatest Will Be Servant of All
        » *In situations where a leader abused power, how could this style of servant leadership have made a difference in the outcome?*

    C. I Will Follow Jesus' Example and Serve Others
        » *How can you serve someone else today?*

Internalizing the Message

Prayer Focus
Lead the group in prayer and consider the following topics of focus:
• For God to give us a heart like His, the heart of a servant
• For God to use us to serve others, especially those who cannot give back to us

LESSON CONNECTION

I f you want to be the president of the United States, be prepared to open your wallet. And while you are at it, you will need to convince a bunch of your friends to open their wallets too. Running for the office of the president of the United States is astonishingly expensive. It helps if you have lots of friends with deep pockets.

According to OpenSecrets.org, candidates for the office of the president of the United States spent a cumulative $5.7 billion on the 2020 election campaign. That amount is more than double what presidential candidates spent in 2016. Then Senator Joe Biden set a record by raising more than $1 billion in campaign contributions. The incumbent President Donald Trump raised $774 million, which would have been a record had it not been surpassed by his opponent.

Spending millions of dollars in an effort to take up residence at 1600 Pennsylvania Avenue seems to be a losing proposition, at least fiscally. Yes, the president earns a nice annual salary—$400,000 plus benefits—but spending nearly a billion dollars to land a job that pays far less does not make financial sense. Certainly, when presidents leave office, they are usually able to parlay their experience into lucrative speaking and book deals, but that does not make up the financial difference. It takes a lot of speaking engagements for even the highest-paid orators to earn a billion dollars.

Why do candidates spend so much money trying to become president? The answer can sometimes be summed up in a single word: power. The president of the United States is widely regarded as the most powerful person in the world. The chief executive's influence extends around the globe. The president's policy decisions impact the lives of millions of US residents. Presidents can cause financial markets to fluctuate with an offhand remark. They can send American troops to fight on foreign battlefields with the stroke of a pen. They may determine the fate of industries and enterprises with a single executive order. If you are the president, your name is a daily fixture in the headlines, and historians will vie for the privilege of telling your story when your time in office comes to an end.

That level of power, influence, and prestige comes with a steep price tag. If you want to be the most prominent political figure in the world, it seems you need to be willing to do nearly anything to earn that privilege.

BIBLE LESSON

I. WHO WANTS TO BE THE GREATEST?

Teacher Option: A supplemental image is available in the Resource Kit. **I**

Historians argue endlessly about which US presidents should be considered the greatest, but four have been immortalized in a fashion none of the other forty plus presidents can claim. Sculptor Gutzon Borglum blasted the likenesses of George Washington, Thomas Jefferson, Abraham Lincoln, and Theodore Roosevelt into the granite face of Mount Rushmore, creating an iconic monument that draws more than two million visitors to South Dakota's Black Hills every year.

Most of us will never see our likeness carved in the side of a mountain, but most of us would like to think our influence and legacy will live on even after we leave this world—that we will not be forgotten. Jesus addressed this basic human desire when He told His disciples, "Whoever desires to become great among you shall be your servant" (Mark 10:43, NKJV). Jesus explained the road to true greatness does not run along the path of self-promotion or the exercise of unfettered authority. Greatness is not about commissioning a sculpture in your honor or gaining a million followers on social media. True greatness comes when one person humbly serves another, even when no one else notices. In case Jesus' disciples did not fully understand His words, Jesus added, "And whoever of you desires to be first shall be slave of all" (Mark 10:44, NKJV).

What does popular culture teach us about greatness? Do those lessons confirm or conflict with the teachings of Jesus?

A. Jesus Asked His Disciples about Their Argument

Imagine the disciples' humiliation when Jesus asked them what they were arguing about. The disciples had good reason to be embarrassed. "They had disputed among themselves, who should be the greatest," Mark 9:34 reads. They probably blushed as they shared this with Jesus, realizing just how silly their argument must have sounded to the Lord. Sometimes the best way to gain perspective on a disagreement is to take it to Jesus and confess it audibly to Him in prayer.

Concern about social standing is an inborn human trait. We want to be known for making the best grades, being the most athletic, or being the most physically attractive. Even in adulthood, we do not shake this obsession. We want to drive the nicest car, live in the biggest house, or make the most money, and we are willing to exhaust ourselves to attain these status symbols. It has been widely observed that we will spend money we do not have to impress people we do not even like.

What talents or possessions have you envied in others? Why do you think you have wanted those particular gifts or blessings?

Even people of faith are not immune to this sort of social posturing. We debate among ourselves about the most gifted preacher, singer, or musician, or which church or conference is at the top of the list. We work hard so our church or ministry will be highly regarded by our peers. Like the disciples, we want to be in the conversation when people are discussing greatness.

B. This Is How You Receive Me

The disciples may have been a little surprised when Jesus did not immediately launch into a full-fledged rebuke. Instead, the Lord used that moment to teach a lesson that still applies today. Jesus began by saying, "If any man desire to be first, the same shall be last of all, and servant of all" (Mark 9:35). To illustrate His point, Jesus took a child in His arms and said to His disciples, "Whosoever shall receive one of such children in my name, receiveth me" (Mark 9:37).

Children usually do not worry about most things adults obsess over. Children probably will not commend you on your well-crafted lesson. Neither do they lie awake at night fretting about who was not at church last Sunday. They usually do not notice if our clothes reflect the latest fashions. They do notice whether we show them genuine love and concern. Children have an uncanny ability to spot a phony. They can tell who really cares and who does not, and they respond accordingly.

Children usually cannot repay the love we show them either. Our church's largest offerings are probably not pouring in from the toddler class. They typically do not give their Sunday school teachers birthday cards stuffed with cash. Ministering to children who require so much and return so little usually does not bring earthly recognition or reward. But Jesus assured us, when we humbly receive the weakest and lowliest in His name, we are receiving Him. Jesus also promised that we have a heavenly Father who openly rewards the good that is done in secret (Matthew 6:4, 6, 18).

C. I Will Show Kindness to Others with Humility

According to Jesus, true greatness is showing kindness to others in a spirit of humility. He said, "If any man desire to be first, the same shall be last of all, and servant of all" (Mark 9:35). Greatness is volunteering to teach the Sunday school class no one else wants to teach. Greatness is changing dirty diapers and wiping runny noses in the church nursery without complaining. It is blisters and callouses at the all-church workday. It is showing up for prayer meeting after a long day at work when you really just want to go home. It is driving out of your way to pick someone up for church. It is faithfully serving on the job even when your boss does not seem to notice. It is remaining faithful to a struggling marriage with an unsaved spouse. It is responding to hate with kindness and choosing reconciliation over retaliation.

Greatness is having a servant's heart. Noted evangelical pastor Erwin Lutzer is quoted as saying, "How do you know you have a servant's heart? Look at your reaction when you are treated like a servant." None of us appreciates being treated inferior to anyone else. Yet Jesus said, "If the world hate you, ye know that it hated me before it hated you" (John 15:18). Jesus' contemporaries did not recognize His greatness until after they crucified Him. Like our Master, we are more likely to carry a cross than to wear a medal.

How do you feel when others treat you like a servant?

II. WHO WANTS TO BE SERVANT OF ALL?

What did you want to be when you were young? Most of us dreamed of one day holding jobs that come with prestige and a large paycheck, like a doctor, a lawyer, or a professional athlete. As we grew older, we may have abandoned those dreams for various reasons. For some, it was because they discovered joy and fulfillment in another line of work that more closely matched their gifts. Many successful individuals have found that serving others and financial reward are not mutually exclusive.

Ultimately, we serve others by serving God. As we follow Him and submit to His Word, He will direct us into the areas of service that most closely match our talents and temperament. He created us to serve with joy, not to spend our days just chasing a paycheck or fulfilling someone else's dream for our life. He loves us, and He has prepared a place for us in His kingdom—a place of service.

A. The Desire for Position

We get into trouble when we prioritize position above service. In Matthew 19:28, Jesus promised the twelve disciples that they would sit upon twelve thrones, judging the twelve tribes of Israel. In Mark 10:35, James and John came to Jesus with a follow-up request. Matthew records that they drafted their mother into presenting their petition. When Jesus asked what they wanted, the two brothers responded, "Grant unto us that we may sit, one on thy right hand, and the other on thy left hand, in thy glory" (Mark 10:37). Jesus responded by essentially saying, "You don't know what you're asking for."

Many people are guilty of seeing only the perks of certain positions while conveniently overlooking the sacrifices and struggles that happen behind the scenes. People want to be the leader until a crisis arises. In those moments, we are content to sit back and second-guess the person in charge while breathing a sigh of relief that it is not us.

Teacher Option: A supplemental video is available in the Resource Kit. V

It is easy to become frustrated when it seems God is overlooking us while promoting others. But He knows what we can handle, and He loves us too much to give us everything we think we want when we want it. God knows whether we are ready for the pressure that will come at the next level of service. It is better to bloom where He plants us than to be destroyed by being promoted too quickly. He knows when we are ready, and when the time is right, the right door will open. In the meantime, let us serve the Kingdom by serving others. God will call our number, and we will experience success because we trusted His timing.

How have you felt when others were being given opportunities while you were overlooked? Did you gain a different perspective with time?

B. The Greatest Will Be Servant of All

Unfortunately for James and John, the other ten disciples overheard their conversation with Jesus, and they were not happy about it. Interestingly, their response seems to have been, "I should have thought to ask Jesus for that." They wanted their résumés to be at the top of the stack. They were upset because they thought James and John beat them to the head of the line.

This presented Jesus with a prime opportunity to share an important Kingdom principle with His closest followers. They were imitating Gentile rulers by seeking after power and position. Jesus said, "They which are accounted to rule over the Gentiles exercise lordship over them; and their great ones exercise authority upon them" (Mark 10:42). But in God's kingdom, the path to power is not flexing your muscles and stomping on anyone who gets in your way. Jesus corrected them, "But so shall it not be among you" (Mark 10:43).

Just as in Mark 9, Jesus once again turned the accepted leadership principles of His day on their head. "Whosoever will be great among you, shall be your minister," He told them, "and whosoever of you will be the chiefest, shall be servant of all" (Mark 10:43-44). Jesus then used His own life as an example of true Kingdom service. "The Son of man came not to be ministered unto, but to minister, and to give his life a ransom for many" (Mark 10:45).

In situations where a leader abused power, how could this style of servant leadership have made a difference in the outcome?

To see the shining example of servant leadership, simply look at Jesus Christ. He turned twelve ordinary men into a movement that claimed more than 2.5 billion followers in 2020. He did not commission His followers to make converts by the sword or some other display of power but rather by putting God first and loving their neighbors as themselves (Matthew 22:37-39). In so doing, His church has become a global force for good and has thrived in the face of persecution.

C. I Will Follow Jesus' Example and Serve Others

Serving others means telling them about Jesus. Like the Book of Acts believers, we are also called to turn our world upside down. That can seem like an overwhelming challenge at first. The world is in a terrible mess, but we must remember that God does not hold us accountable for what we cannot control. He simply calls us to take responsibility for what happens within our sphere of influence. Making a difference for the masses begins with being a difference for an individual. It begins with serving a friend or neighbor in need.

How can you serve someone else today?

INTERNALIZING THE MESSAGE

One of the greatest illustrations of servanthood is found in John 13 at what Christians usually call the Last Supper. After sharing a meal with His twelve disciples, Jesus surprised them all by taking off His outer garments and wrapping a towel—the attire of a common household servant—around His waist. He then poured water into a basin, stooped down, and began to wash His disciples' grime-covered feet.

The disciples were shocked at this role reversal. Washing feet was considered a menial task, far beneath the dignity of an esteemed teacher like Jesus. Peter was especially indignant. "Thou shalt never wash my feet," he insisted (John 13:8). But Peter did not understand why Jesus was doing what He was doing. This was about much more than just cleaning feet. Jesus was preparing to shed His blood on the cross for the spiritual cleansing that Peter and the rest of the disciples so desperately needed.

When Jesus finished making His way around the table, He put His outer robe back on and once again took His seat. Then He asked, "Know ye what I have done to you?" (John 13:12).

John did not record the disciples' reaction to Jesus' question. Perhaps their only response was a blank stare, shock evident in their eyes. Maybe they were already beginning to grasp the uncomfortable implications of Jesus' actions. If the Son of God was willing to assume the role of the lowest household servant, what did that mean for them? How far should they be willing to stoop?

Then Jesus broke the silence by answering His own question. "If I then, your Lord and Master, have washed your feet; ye also ought to wash one another's feet" (John 13:14).

As they heard Jesus' words, perhaps James and John thought back to their earlier request to be seated at the Lord's left and right hand. Maybe they flushed with embarrassment, realizing how silly their ambitions must have seemed to Jesus. Or maybe this realization came after Jesus resurrected from the dead, and they had time to process everything that had happened.

One thing is certain: the disciples eventually did grasp the message Jesus wanted to convey. They spent their lives serving others and establishing the church Jesus envisioned. Eventually, they even gave their lives as martyrs for the sake of the gospel.

In both life and death, the disciples illustrated the words of the apostle Paul in Philippians 2:5-7. "Let this mind be in you, which was also in Christ Jesus: who . . . made himself of no reputation, and took upon him the form of a servant."

May we be willing to go and do the same.

Prayer Focus
Lead the group in prayer and consider the following topics of focus:
- For God to give us a heart like His, the heart of a servant
- For God to use us to serve others, especially those who cannot give back to us

3.4

A GOD OF JUSTICE

FOCUS VERSE
Micah 6:8
He hath shewed thee, O man, what is good; and what doth the LORD require of thee, but to do justly, and to love mercy, and to walk humbly with thy God?

LESSON TEXT
Psalm 146:7–9;
Micah 6:6–12;
Mark 11:15–19

TRUTH ABOUT GOD
Jesus cares about the abused, particularly those who have been abused in His name.

TRUTH FOR MY LIFE
I will love and support those who have been wronged.

Thinking about Last Week:

Have students refer to their Daily Devotional Guide to answer the following questions:
1. What most affected you as you read through the Lesson Text and the Biblical Insights?
2. How did it shape your prayers and thoughts throughout the week?
3. Do you feel you grew closer to the Lord this past week? Why or why not?

SG TEACHING OUTLINE

Icebreaker: Is God more merciful or just?

Lesson Connection: Share the Lesson Connection.

I. JUSTICE IS A BIBLICAL PRINCIPLE

    A. God Is Just

        » *Why do you think Jesus focused so much of His ministry on the poor and needy? What implications does that have for the church today?*

    B. As God's People, We Are to Be Just

        » *W hat does justice look like at your workplace?*

II. WHAT DOES GOD REQUIRE OF US?

    A. Sacrifices Alone Are Not Sufficient

    B. Do Justly, Love Mercy, Walk Humbly with God **V**

    C. I Will Offer to God What He Requires of Me

        » *Make a list of blessings you have received because of someone else's sacrifices. How can you sustain that cycle of blessing?*

III. CLEANING OF THE TEMPLE

    A. Jesus Discovered Corruption in the Temple and Fiercely Defended the Temple and the Innocent

    B. Jesus' Call to Prayer Ensures Our Perspective about Justice Is Right

        » *Why is prayer so important to the work of true justice?*

    C. I Will Love and Support Those Who Have Been Wronged

        » *How does remembering our past help ensure a proper perspective of God's love for others?*

Internalizing the Message **I**

Prayer Focus
Lead the group in prayer and consider the following topics of focus:
* For God to help us do justly, love mercy, and walk humbly with Him
* For God to give us the courage to help relieve others' suffering when we are able

LESSON CONNECTION

On that unforgettable day, Jesus seemed to be everywhere at once. He was flipping tables and benches, leaving a trail of chaos in His wake. Men shouted in surprise and anger as they clawed at the air, desperately trying to recapture doves Jesus freed from their cages. Moneychangers crawled and grasped at coins scattered across the floor, trying to keep their profits from rolling out of sight. Jesus' disciples scrambled for cover and ducked as doves fluttered past. No one wanted to be in Jesus' way as He rushed furiously about the court of the Gentiles.

All eyes were focused on Him. The indignation in His eyes mirrored the outrage in His heart at what was happening in the Temple precincts. He took this personally.

The disciples had witnessed something similar three years earlier when Jesus chased merchants and moneychangers out of the Temple with a whip (John 2:13–17). But this call to repentance had not lasted. The religious profiteers returned, and so had Jesus. His passion for protecting the sanctity of the Temple grounds had not lessened.

Temple life had not always been this way. At one time, sacrifices were sold and money exchanged at markets on the Mount of Olives. But the high priest Caiaphas, responding to pressure from other Jewish leaders, granted permission for these markets to be relocated to the court of the Gentiles on the Temple campus. Overnight, a place that had been dedicated to prayer and worship was transformed into a shopping center. Gentile worshipers were crowded out by greedy merchants. The Jewish leaders seemed to be all right with this devolution. In their eyes, these Gentile interlopers were unfit to set foot on the Temple precincts anyway.

But Jesus was incensed. "My house shall be called of all nations the house of prayer," He fumed, quoting Isaiah 56:7. He looked around, eyeing the moneychangers and merchants who were glaring at Him with malicious expressions. "Ye have made it a den of thieves," He roared (Mark 11:17).

The disciples discovered that nothing seemed to make Jesus angrier than abuse and injustice in the name of religion. They did not realize that their Master would soon suffer even worse abuse at the hands of men who believed they were doing God's will. Reverence for holy things would soon become the pretense for the most horrible crime in history— the crucifixion of the Son of God. Jesus turned on His heel and strode out of the Temple as His disciples followed closely behind.

BIBLE LESSON

I. JUSTICE IS A BIBLICAL PRINCIPLE

A. God Is Just

Even a cursory review of the Bible reveals how much God cares about justice. The Hebrew word for justice, *mishpat*, appears 421 times in the Old Testament and is frequently translated as *judgment* in the King James Version. Believers should care about justice because God cares about justice. Deuteronomy 32:4 describes the Almighty by saying, "All his ways are judgment [*mishpat*]: a God of truth and without iniquity, just and right is he." Psalm 146:7–9 elaborates on God's justice by declaring He upholds the cause of the oppressed.

God's justice is demonstrated in His actions. Jesus performed many miracles for the benefit of the poor and oppressed, including widows, those who were sick, and societal outcasts such as lepers. The first miracle performed in the Book of Acts was the healing of a lame beggar. (See Acts 3:1–10.) Jesus and His followers believed in and practiced justice.

Why do you think Jesus focused so much of His ministry on the poor and needy? What implications does that have for the church today?

B. As God's People, We Are to Be Just

As Spirit-filled believers, we must also be just, which includes giving people "what they are due, whether punishment or protection or care," to quote from Timothy Keller. The Book of Proverbs promotes the pursuit of justice in daily life, including in the marketplace. Proverbs 11:1 reads, "A false balance is abomination to the LORD: but a just weight is his delight." While most of us no longer use weights and balances on the job, there is a timeless call for honesty in business. Christians should not participate in any business transaction that knowingly takes advantage of others, especially the poor and needy. Some careers should be off-limits to believers for this reason.

Christians who serve in positions of leadership or authority must treat their employees, coworkers, and customers fairly and with respect, regardless of the circumstances or any personal disagreements or differences that may exist. We cannot mistreat and abuse others and expect to disciple them to Jesus.

What does justice look like at your workplace?

II. WHAT DOES GOD REQUIRE OF US?

A. Sacrifices Alone Are Not Sufficient

The prophet Micah asked a question many of us may have asked. "Wherewith shall I come before the LORD, and bow myself before the high God?" (Micah 6:6). Micah then launched into a list of extravagant offerings and sacrifices, including thousands of rams and ten thousand rivers of oil. Micah asked if God requires us to sacrifice everything, including our firstborn child.

These questions were rhetorical because God does not ask us to give what we do not have. None of us have access to ten thousand rivers of oil. And God is not impressed with an outward show of worship and sacrifice that tries to mask the stench of a disobedient heart. Jesus quoted the prophet Isaiah when He said of the religious leaders of His day, "This people draweth nigh unto me with their mouth, and honoureth me with their lips; but their heart is far from me. But in vain they do worship me" (Matthew 15:8–9).

Later in the same Gospel, Jesus again confronted the Pharisees about their practice of tithing on the herbs they grew in their gardens. Their fastidious approach to giving may have been commendable, but they were ignoring what Jesus called "the weightier matters of the law, judgment, mercy, and faith" (Matthew 23:23). Personal holiness and morality are important, but they do not excuse a lack of care and concern for others. Sacrifice in one area does not make up for disobedience in other areas.

B. Do Justly, Love Mercy, Walk Humbly with God

God has shown us what is good and what He requires, Micah said. "To do justly, and to love mercy, and to walk humbly with thy God" (Micah 6:8). God is looking for a pure heart that serves God and serves others.

In today's Western culture, it has become popular to express good thoughts to others, often via social media. This has become the current substitute for "I'm praying for you." But good thoughts only benefit the person who thinks them; good words are not much more effective. Even prayer is not a valid substitute when we could take reasonable action to help. God requires us to do justly, not just think, talk, or even pray justly.

The New Testament writer James pointed out that if we meet someone who lacks food and clothing, it is not helpful to say, "Depart in peace, be ye warmed and filled" (James 2:16). "I'm praying for you" does not lessen hunger pangs. There is only one solution for an empty stomach—food. If we have the power to meet a need but refuse, our faith is dead, James concluded (James 2:17). If a person is capable of meeting his or her own needs but refuses to do so due to laziness, that is another matter. (See II Thessalonians 3:10.)

Teacher Option:
A supplemental video is available in the Resource Kit. (V)

Justice is an act, not a feeling. Justice involves rolling up our sleeves and getting personally involved in relieving the suffering of the world. Lisa Sharon Harper, cofounder and executive director of New York Faith and Justice, said, "Justice is a way of showing the world what heaven looks like." If we want to bring Heaven to earth, we must start by pursuing justice.

C. I Will Offer to God What He Requires of Me

When we recognize how merciful God has been to us personally, it will produce the proper attitude we need to do the work of true justice. A true understanding of mercy will keep us from arrogantly dismissing the downtrodden and hurting as "losers" who just need to work harder or make better choices. Those who do justly know that, if it were not for God's grace and mercy, our story could be much different. The just person knows that God loves hurting people, regardless of how they look, talk, smell, or act. Just people express genuine sympathy and concern for others, including taking action to meet their needs and relieve suffering.

As Micah noted, humility is necessary. Most of us cannot claim responsibility for many of the blessings we enjoy. Our parents, grandparents, and even great grandparents worked hard to give us the life we now enjoy. We have been afforded many opportunities others may not have been given. Even if we have made good choices in life, they were often a result of biblical teaching we received during our formative years, not from our innate personal goodness. We should remember the words of Jesus in Luke 12:48, "Unto whomsoever much is given, of him shall be much required." One of those requirements is showing mercy, grace, and compassion to those who have not enjoyed the same blessings we have enjoyed.

Make a list of blessings you have received because of someone else's sacrifices. How can you sustain that cycle of blessing?

III. CLEANSING OF THE TEMPLE

A. Jesus Discovered Corruption in the Temple and Fiercely Defended the Temple and the Innocent

This brings us back full circle to the Temple in Jerusalem. When Jesus entered the Temple precincts and confronted the merchants and moneychangers, He directly assailed the most powerful religious family in Jerusalem. According to the Jewish historian Josephus, Annas the son of Sethi had been appointed high priest by the Roman governor Cyrenius in AD 6 or 7, and he served until being deposed in AD 15. Annas used his time in office to build a thriving business that came to be known as the booths or bazaars of the sons of Annas. All Annas' five sons followed their father in the office of high priest. The booths of Annas had a monopoly on the sale of sacrificial animals, and they conducted their lucrative trade in the court of the Gentiles. When Jesus cleansed the Temple of this corruption, Annas felt the sting mainly in his wallet.

Annas, Caiaphas, and the rest of their cartel were wicked men who did not mind exploiting worshipers for personal gain. But Jesus did not share that attitude. In quoting Isaiah 56:7, Jesus reaffirmed that God intended His house to be a place for all nations (Mark 11:17). Jesus did not abuse anyone, but neither was He afraid to confront those who refused to repent or whose actions kept others from God. Jesus fought on behalf of the excluded and marginalized to make sure they had access to God.

B. Jesus' Call to Prayer Ensures Our Perspective about Justice Is Right

Jesus' insistence that His house be called a house of prayer illustrates there can be no true justice without prayer. We cannot even know what justice is until we have first sought God. Without prayer, humanity's pursuit of justice will be corrupted. Even today, some demands for justice are little more than a thinly veiled desire for revenge. True justice is not making someone else suffer payback for our own hardships. Our parents and grandparents have often taught us that two wrongs do not make a right. But if we are not Spirit-led, human passions will pervert even the best intentions.

We need to pray if we are to have God's perspective on and passion for justice. If we do not pray, we will be tempted to sweep injustices under the rug, especially if they have not impacted us directly. Pursuing true justice can be difficult and painful. It often seems easier to ignore problems than to deal with them. Pursuing justice is rarely convenient. It makes people uncomfortable. It can cause misunderstandings. Only through prayer does the Holy Spirit give us the desire to deal with injustices and the wisdom to resolve them in a godly manner.

Why is prayer so important to the work of true justice?

C. I Will Love and Support Those Who Have Been Wronged

How should the church respond to injustice in our world? The answer begins with an acknowledgement of our past. God warned Israel that they would enjoy blessings He had prepared for them when they finally entered the Promised Land, but they would need to routinely remember where they came from. The purpose of this exercise was to continually remind the people of Israel to show compassion to and administer justice on behalf of foreigners and the less fortunate. Sadly, Israel soon forgot this critical lesson.

We Oneness Pentecostals are only a few generations removed from worshiping under brush arbors while being pelted with rotten fruit. Pentecostals were mocked as holy rollers and accused of being devil-possessed and insane. Many early Pentecostals were poor, uneducated, and lacked social standing. But God's power more than compensated for their lack of prestige. Entire families were forever changed by the Pentecostal experience.

As the years passed, brush arbors were replaced by state-of-the-art church facilities featuring the latest innovations. The people on the pews went to college and landed better-paying jobs. Many achieved respectability in the community. But while we should celebrate advancement, we must never forget who we once were. We cannot turn our backs on the persecuted and the disadvantaged. That was us in the not-so-distant past.

How does remembering our past help ensure a proper perspective of God's love for others?

With God's help, we will stay humble and grounded. Our churches will be places where everyone can find love and compassion, regardless of race, ethnicity, social status, or economic resources. God does not show favoritism, and neither can we. He is a God of justice, and we must imitate Him by giving the people who have been wronged the love and support they are due.

INTERNALIZING THE MESSAGE

A supplemental image is available in the Resource Kit. ⬛

Church history includes many examples of men and women who dedicated their lives to ministering to the less fortunate, the hurting, and the abused. A. B. Simpson, a Canadian-born Presbyterian pastor and theologian, is one such person. Simpson's story is an inspiration to anyone who takes Jesus' command to minister to "the least of these" seriously.

After graduating from Knox College in Toronto, Ontario, Simpson began serving in a series of pastorates. He served first in Hamilton, Ontario, and then in Louisville, Kentucky. Finally, in 1880, he was called to serve as pastor of Thirteenth Street Presbyterian Church in New York City. This was a prestigious post with an annual salary of $5,000. When adjusted for inflation, that would equate to a six-figure salary today.

Immigrants were flooding into New York City in the early 1880s, and Simpson had a burden to minister to these new arrivals. Most of these newcomers were poor and had not yet adopted American customs. As an immigrant himself, Simpson undoubtedly felt sympathy for their situation. But when he tried to add approximately one hundred Italian immigrants to the rolls at Thirteenth Street Presbyterian Church, affluent church leaders refused to let them join. They worried that allowing poor immigrants to become part of their congregation would discourage their rich friends and neighbors from joining their church.

Simpson was so disgusted by these leaders' attitudes that he quit his pastorate. He then founded Gospel Tabernacle, "a church in the heart of the city, where all— the poor, homeless, sick, and displaced—would be welcome" (cmalliance.org). His passion for reaching the world only continued to grow. Simpson dreamed of serving as a missionary in China, but when that did not work out, he turned his attention to other evangelistic pursuits. He published a missions magazine and opened a college to train missions workers. In 1887, he founded what would become known as the Christian and Missionary Alliance, a missions organization that still operates today.

Is the church a comfortable place where only people just like us are welcome? Or do we have room for the hurting and the outcasts, the people no one else wants? Are we willing to love and serve those who have faced injustice and abuse at the hands of this world and even at the hands of other churches? To what lengths are we willing to go to make it happen?

How we answer that question may determine how much we really want to be like Jesus.

Prayer Focus

Lead the group in prayer and consider the following topics of focus:
- For God to help us do justly, love mercy, and walk humbly with Him
- For God to give us the courage to help relieve others' suffering when we are able

GOD'S WORD

FOR LIFE

ADULT LESSON GUIDE

SPRING 2023

TABLE OF CONTENTS

*ES indicates Easter Sunday.

1.1

THE TWO DEBTORS

FOCUS VERSE
Luke 7:47
Wherefore I say unto thee, Her sins, which are many, are forgiven; for she loved much: but to whom little is forgiven, the same loveth little.

LESSON TEXT
Luke 7:36–50

TRUTH ABOUT GOD
God forgives our sins.

TRUTH FOR MY LIFE
I will express my love for Jesus because He forgives my sins.

Series Overview:

Jesus taught some of His best lessons through parables, or stories with a spiritual application. This series will take a close look at four of those parables: the Two Debtors, the Talents, the Prodigal Son, and the Rich Man and Lazarus. As we look into these sacred stories, we will see the amazing love of God coupled with His unblemished holiness.

(SG) TEACHING OUTLINE

Icebreaker: What is your most prized possession?

Lesson Connection: Share the Lesson Connection. (I)

I. JESUS TAUGHT IN PARABLES

    A. The Woman with the Alabaster Box

    B. The Parable of the Debtors

    C. Simon's Response

    D. Gratitude for God's Forgiveness

      » *Why do you think Simon was more focused on the woman's heinous sin rather than his own?*

      » *What does extravagant worship look like in our day? Would a simple raised hand and song have been enough for the woman to show her gratitude to God?* (V)

II. THE POWER OF LOVE AND FORGIVENESS

    A. The Woman's Act of Love

    B. All Have Sinned

      » *How would we view sin differently if we saw it through God's eyes?*

    C. No Sin Is Too Big for God to Forgive

    D. I Will Express My Love for Jesus Because He Forgives My Sins

      » *How do you express your love for Jesus for His forgiveness?*

Internalizing the Message

      » *Do you think the lady kept the alabaster box that once held the perfume? If so, why?*

Prayer Focus

Lead the group in prayer and consider the following topics of focus:
- For God to forgive us of our sins and give us humility
- For God to help us worship Him with a thankful heart for all He has done for us

LESSON CONNECTION

A supplemental image is available in the Resource Kit. Ⓘ

This is a story about two Lloyds. One was an executive; one was a poor college student. While Lloyd the executive worked to better his organization, Lloyd the college student worked to pass freshman finals. After a couple starter jobs, our college student began working at the same organization as our executive. One day Lloyd Shirley called on Lloyd (LJ) Harry to help him with a computer issue. Lloyd Shirley took a liking to Lloyd Harry.

The executive called the student into his office for help with his computer. While there, the student happened to see a little laptop called a Libretto. It was practically pocket size in the late 90s. It made a MacBook look like a chalkboard.

LJ remarked, "That is the coolest laptop I've ever seen."

Brother Shirley asked, "Would you like it?"

Would I like it? That's like asking if someone would like a cheeseburger after a seven-day fast. LJ would have loved that laptop. His handwriting in class had begun to look more like hieroglyphics than class notes. God bless the teachers who tried to read it. If LJ could have afforded a laptop, he would have bought one, but they were pricey. Being a full-time student and part-time bank teller did not bode well for financial independence.

Suddenly Lloyd Shirley gathered the Libretto, the cord, the drives, and said, "You can do some work for me to work it off." LJ was stunned speechless. He fixed the computer issue he came for, thanked the benevolent Lloyd for his kindness, and went back to his desk. Right there on his desk was his very own Libretto laptop. Suddenly, the joy of what he had just been given was quickly overshadowed by the weighty reality of how little he made and how much this laptop cost. It would take hours and hours and hours outside of school, church, homework, and work just to pay for it.

But Brother Shirley was kind. He never reminded LJ that he owed him for it. The executive just let the student use it all the way through college. And he did. He typed up all his class notes through his final senior final. Then the beautiful spring day dawned when LJ was ready to graduate. Right around graduation day, the two Lloyds met up again and Lloyd the college student, now graduate, realized he had never worked one hour to pay for the Libretto. That is the day Brother Shirley reminded him of the laptop. He said with a smile, "Remember that laptop?"

Gulp. LJ thought, *It's too late to work it off now. I leave for Florida in just days.*

Before he could fret any further, Brother Shirley spoke again, "It's all yours." Lloyd the exec forgave Lloyd the student of his debt. To this day the two Lloyds are friends, and LJ is still thankful for Brother Shirley's kindness in giving him a laptop to get him through college and forgiving him of the debt when he graduated.

BIBLE LESSON

I. JESUS TAUGHT IN PARABLES

Once Jesus hung up His carpenter's apron, He walked into a ministry of teaching the world around Him about the kingdom of God. Jesus chose to teach many of His lessons as stories, or parables. Parables were stories about people or things most people would understand. They were the lenses Jesus gave to the people He taught to give them a glimpse of the glory of the kingdom of God. He shared one such parable with a holy man named Simon.

A. The Woman with the Alabaster Box

As the setting sun tossed long shadows on the streets, Simon came bursting through the door. His servants had seen that look before. That look meant overtime. Right after Simon burst through the door, another man followed him, followed by a crowd who had been following Him. The servants scurried back into the kitchen and dipped out more soup for all of Simon's guests.

Simon was called a Pharisee. He was one of the holy men in Israel who kept the Law to its fullest extent. He was conscious to dot every i and careful to cross every t. He was especially curious about this man Jesus, who grew up in Nazareth and had just raised a widow's dead son back to life. Simon had been taught that only God can work those wonders. How did Jesus? Simon wanted to know if everything everyone was saying about Jesus was true. Was He really the Messiah, or was He just another man trying to be God? While they sipped their soup and talked, one more guest made her way in. She quietly wound through the crowd and stopped at Jesus' filthy feet. Tears flooded her flushed face. Simon's servants looked at each other, wondering which one of them would have to be the bouncer.

As she wept, her tears fell on Jesus' feet, washing off some of the dust from the dusty city streets. She knelt down and let her long, dark hair down as she began to wipe her tears with her hair. She cracked open a beautiful alabaster box she brought with her and poured her sweet perfume on Jesus' feet. This worshiping woman kept weeping and pouring perfume and kissing Jesus' feet. The whole time, she had not whispered a word, but her worship screamed of her love for Jesus and thankfulness for what He had done for her. No one else in that room really knew what He had done for her, but they all knew what she had done. She was a notorious sinner. A holy and even uncomfortable hush fell as everyone heard only the soft weeping of this wicked woman.

Simon the Pharisee was appalled. He wanted to stand and yell, "Sinner!" But he just sat there and pulled his religious robes tight against his chest. There was no way Jesus could be a prophet, else He would have known how filthy and unworthy this woman was. Simon began devising a way to toss Jesus and His wicked worshiper out of his holy house. Jesus knew exactly what Simon was thinking, so Jesus broke the uncomfortable silence and weaved this parable.

B. The Parable of the Debtors

A man loaned money to two people—five hundred pieces of silver to one, fifty pieces of silver to another. Unfortunately, when it came time to pay their creditor back, neither one of them could. The creditor knew what that meant. The debtors knew what that meant. Unpaid debt carried the threat of dark days in debtors' prison, slaving away for masters they neither knew nor loved until they had paid back the last denarius. They gulped, knowing they were helpless to help themselves, but their creditor freely forgave them both and canceled their debts. They were free to go. Their debts were forgiven. This was too good to be true.

Then Jesus looked into Simon's dark brown eyes and asked him, "Now Simon, which of the debtors do you think loved him more after that?"

C. Simon's Response

Simon was savvy. Jesus was good at asking questions to which He already knew the answers. Simon swallowed hard and answered weakly, "I suppose the one whose larger debt was forgiven." Jesus smiled. Simon relaxed a little, and Jesus nodded, "You're right, Simon." Then Jesus turned to look at the weeping woman who was still pouring perfume on Him and kissing His feet. Jesus then asked Simon, "Do you see this woman? Simon, when I came in your house this afternoon, my feet were dusty from walking the streets. You rushed me past the basin and towel and into the dining room. You motioned for me to sit down as you announced who I am and why I'm here, but you never once offered to wash the dust off my feet."

Jesus continued, "But look at this woman. She has flooded my feet with her tears and dried them with her hair. And Simon, you didn't greet me with a kiss (a simple, standard sign of hospitality), but since she came in here, she has not stopped kissing my feet. And you didn't even offer to anoint my head with oil, but she broke a beautiful alabaster box of more beautiful and expensive perfume, and she poured the perfume all over my feet."

The room was silent as Jesus paused for seconds. It felt like hours.

"You are right about one thing, though. She is a sinner."

Hearing Jesus call her a sinner made her shudder. She knew she was not worthy to wash His feet, but she hoped Jesus did not know her past or her present. But He clearly did. How would He respond? Would Jesus judge her like the others judged her? Perhaps like Simon had?

D. Gratitude for God's Forgiveness

Simon was not as wicked as this woman, but he was not as thankful as her either. Perhaps our testimony is the same as Simon's. Maybe we have been blessed to be part of a godly family all our lives. Perhaps our testimony is God has kept us from scars He does not have to heal us from. If so, we should be abundantly thankful because we have been abundantly blessed. Thankfully, God loves and forgives sinners like Simon and sinners like us. Thankfully, we have the opportunity to show God gratitude for His forgiveness through our worship.

Why do you think Simon was more focused on the woman's heinous sin rather than his own?

But what if our story is more like her story? Perhaps we have a past we are not proud of but cannot erase, piling up one sin upon another until we cannot bear to wake in the morning because of the crushing weight of our guilt. But along came Jesus, and He forgave us of our sins—all our sins. If her story is our story, we should be abundantly thankful because we too are abundantly blessed. That is why we should follow her lead and fall at Jesus' feet in extravagant worship.

What does extravagant worship look like in our day? Would a simple raised hand and song have been enough for the woman to show her gratitude to God?

II. THE POWER OF LOVE AND FORGIVENESS

A. The Woman's Act of Love

Jesus answered Simon's question before Simon had a chance to ask it. "That's why she has shown me such love. But Simon, a person who has been forgiven of a little will only love a little." (See Luke 7:47.) This act of worship was no act; this was love. Washing Jesus' feet with her tears, drying them with her hair, anointing His feet with precious perfume, and even kissing His feet were all ways of showing Jesus how much she loved Him.

Teacher Option: *A supplemental video is available in the Resource Kit.* **V**

Jesus said, "Your sins are forgiven. Your faith has saved you. Go in peace." (See Luke 7:48–50.) Peace. It had been years since she really felt peace, but just hearing Him say the word gave her peace her soul craved. She never felt better. Simon never felt worse.

Simon saw sinner; Jesus saw forgiven. That stirred up a firestorm. Simon's religious colleagues nearly choked on a bullock bone. No one could forgive sins, especially hers, but God. How dare He purport to be equal with God. This was blasphemy. Moses would roll over in his grave if we could find it. While they steamed over proper theology, they forgot one simple theological truth: all have sinned.

B. All Have Sinned

Romans 3:23 says it as succinctly as possible, "For all have sinned, and come short of the glory of God." All of us, even the best of us, have sinned. Truth be told, all of us still sin (I John 1). That is never a license to sin, but it is a sobering reminder that we have no share in self-righteousness. Without the atoning sacrifice of Jesus Christ, we are no better than the worst sinner our sanctified minds may think of. All our sins forged the same hammer that nailed Jesus to the cross. While the human consequences of sin may be different, only the imputed righteousness of Jesus takes care of the eternal consequences of sin.

Some sin seems to be harmless. A husband clicks where he ought not while on a business trip. A student takes a little pill to take the edge off. We shout out a few unkind, unclean words in traffic. Surely God does not care about those. Our society certainly does not. Society even divides crime into two categories: misdemeanor and felony. But what about to God? Does God care about a little lie like He does about first-degree murder? Does He see all sin the same?

The consequences in the courtroom may be different, but the consequences in our souls are not. All have sinned, and sin separates us from God. All our sins nailed Jesus to a cross. Whether we are Simon or this worshiping woman before she was a worshiper, we all need to repent and get right with God. It is being born again, regenerated by the transforming work of the Spirit, that brings us into covenant with God (Ephesians 2). That is our only hope for forgiveness.

How would we view sin differently if we saw it through God's eyes?

C. No Sin Is Too Big for God to Forgive

The good news is God still forgives. That was music to her ears. It should be music to ours. If you wrecked your life and others', God still wants to forgive you. And He will freely forgive you if you will repent. We do not need to beg God because God wants to forgive us and free us from guilt. That is one of the main reasons He came from Heaven to Earth to give His life on Calvary. He came to freely forgive.

D. I Will Express My Love for Jesus Because He Forgives My Sins

When we realize how much we have been forgiven, it will show up in how we worship Jesus and love Him. When we realize the depth of the pit from which we were dug, it will show in the depth of our devotion to Him. Sometimes our worship calls us to jump for joy in red-hot Sunday services. Other times that worship calls us to bury our faces in the carpet at the altar and weep when we realize just how merciful Jesus is and how sinful we have been.

If we could ask this woman from Luke 7, she would tell us that wholehearted worship is rarely, if ever, prescribed or pretty. But it is worship. And worship is the only right response to Jesus for the forgiveness He has showed to us.

How do you express your love for Jesus for His forgiveness?

INTERNALIZING THE MESSAGE

It has been over twenty years since LJ walked into Brother Shirley's office to work on his computer and Brother Shirley gave him the Libretto. LJ used it all the way through college and a few years after college, but as time passed, it grew more difficult to find parts for it, and it ran on Windows 95. That is a few operating systems ago. But that laptop is still remarkably valuable, not just because it helped him take class notes. It is remarkably valuable because it reminds him of the undeserved kindness Brother Shirley showed him when LJ was a poor, needy college student. To this day he keeps that Libretto as a reminder of someone who loved him and showed him grace.

We should remember the same. Maybe no one gave you a laptop or even a toy top, but Jesus has given all of us the greatest gift any of us could ever receive. He has given us the gift of forgiveness, even the gift of salvation. A simple thank you card does not seem sufficient. Neither does an hour on Sunday to sing a few songs and listen to a sermon. We will reflect the depth of our gratitude to God for His love through our worship. Let us give God wholehearted worship and thanks for all He has done for us. Let us live our lives to love the one who gave His life to love us.

When we worship greatly, we remember that we have been forgiven greatly. When we worship little, perhaps we think we have only been forgiven little. But we have been forgiven of much more and given much more than we truly know. May this parable of these two debtors and the stark contrast between self-righteous Simon and the once sinful, now worshiping woman teach us that all of us have sinned, all of us have been forgiven, and all of us should live all our lives to love and worship Jesus.

Do you think the lady kept the alabaster box that once held the perfume? If so, why?

Prayer Focus

Lead the group in prayer and consider the following topics of focus:
- For God to forgive us of our sins and give us humility
- For God to help us worship Him with a thankful heart for all He has done for us

1.2

MY PART IN THE KINGDOM OF GOD

FOCUS VERSES
Matthew 25:14–15
¹⁴ For the kingdom of heaven is as a man travelling into a far country, who called his own servants, and delivered unto them his goods. ¹⁵ And unto one he gave five talents, to another two, and to another one; to every man according to his several ability; and straightway took his journey.

LESSON TEXT
Matthew 25:14–30

TRUTH ABOUT GOD
God gives all believers responsibility in His kingdom.

TRUTH FOR MY LIFE
I will do my part to advance the kingdom of God.

Thinking about Last Week:

Have students refer to their Daily Devotional Guide to answer the following questions:

1. What most affected you as you read through the Lesson Text and the Biblical Insights?
2. How did it shape your prayers and thoughts throughout the week?
3. Do you feel you grew closer to the Lord this past week? Why or why not?

(SG) TEACHING OUTLINE

Icebreaker: What is the largest amount of money you have ever seen at one time?

Lesson Connection: Share the Lesson Connection.

I. THE PARABLE OF THE TALENTS (I)

    A. All the Talents Belonged to the Master

      » *How would you feel if your boss came to you tomorrow, opened up a briefcase, counted off ten thousand crisp one-hundred-dollar bills, handed them to you, and rode off to the airport? What would you do with the money?*

    B. The Three Servants

      » *Why do we often battle resentment when someone else is promoted or blessed more than us? How do we stave off resentment?*

    C. I Will Faithfully Invest My Talents in the Kingdom of God (V)

      » *What would you say is your most skillful God-given gift? How are you using it for the glory of God?*

II. INVESTING MYSELF IN THE KINGDOM

    A. The Joy of Serving

    B. Self-Reliance, the Enemy of Obedience

      » *In addition to skills and talents, what other gifts from God might we use for the glory of God? What about our finances, our friendships, our influence?*

    C. I Will Do My Part to Advance the Kingdom of God

Internalizing the Message (I)

      » *What will you do today to use the gifts God has given you to glorify Him and bless His kingdom?*

Prayer Focus
Lead the group in prayer and consider the following topics of focus:
- For God to show us the gifts and talents He has given us
- For God to help us use those gifts and talents for His glory and to bless His kingdom

LESSON CONNECTION

There is a flurry around the office. The boss has come in early and left late nearly every day this week. It's not unusual for him to get a jump start on the day, but he has never come in this early this many days in a row, at least not in the last four years. But he is clearly on a mission. He has come out of his office more this week to talk with the frontline staff than he has in the last month. And he has been fielding calls at work from his wife more and more. When he steps out of the office with his phone glued to his ear, he looks worried. What is happening?

Is he worried? Should we be worried? Is the boss leaving? Is the company closing? Are we all losing our jobs? How will I feed my three dogs, two cats, and one parakeet? For the last few weeks, there has been a cloud over the office. But one Wednesday, the cloud cleared. The boss's administrative assistant came rushing in the door with an overnight package. I overheard her say, "Your passport arrived just in time." He stepped into the main workspace and announced he was heading out of the country on a long-awaited, long-overdue overseas vacation.

All the worry and flurry of phone calls had been firming up vacation plans, especially plans to leave the country. We all breathed a little easier when we left that Wednesday because we knew we would still have our jobs when we came in on Thursday. I felt bad for jumping to the worst possible scenario in my mind, but I had never seen him so flustered. He was usually so calm. The last day before he left for vacation, his desk was as clean and clear as the day he moved in. The worry on his face transferred to his assistant as she realized his work would be her work for the next two weeks. Unless she could find a satellite phone that reached the center of the Caribbean, she would not be able to call him when she didn't know what to do.

From company to company, corporation to corporation, even church to church, this scene is nearly the same when the boss is about to go on vacation or a business trip, especially if the boss is leaving the country.

BIBLE LESSON

I. THE PARABLE OF THE TALENTS

Teacher Option: *A supplemental image is available in the Resource Kit.* **I**

In Jesus' Parable of the Talents from Matthew 25, the master of the house came out of the house to search for his three most loyal employees. When the master found them, he asked one of them to load one bag onto the wagon while he opened another. They had never seen so much money. One talent alone was valued at twenty years of salary. Eight talents were just an arm's length away.

A. All the Talents Belonged to the Master

The boss lifted out five talents and handed his first servant all five talents. This money would take care of him for one hundred years. The boss reached in again, lifted up two talents, and gave them to the second servant. Finally, the boss reached into the bag a third time, picked up the one remaining talent (still worth twenty years of salary), and gave it to the last servant. Jesus intentionally said the master of the servants left immediately and left his servants holding the money in their hands. But before they quit their jobs and went on a spending spree, they understood the money was not theirs; it belonged to their boss. He earned it, and he was free to do with it what he wanted, but they were not.

Clearly in this parable, the master represents our Lord, and the talents represent the gifts He gives. We do not deserve more than we have and should not bemoan anyone for having more than we have. All of the gifts God gives—gifts to sing, preach, teach, administer, easily make friends, easily make money, work with our hands, work with our minds—belong to God. And all of the gifts God gives—our houses, our vehicles, our clothes, our food—belonged to God before He ever gave them to us. We should use these gifts for God's glory.

How would you feel if your boss came to you tomorrow, opened up a briefcase, counted off ten thousand crisp one-hundred-dollar bills, handed them to you, and rode off to the airport? What would you do with the money?

B. The Three Servants

The name tags Jesus slapped on these men read, "Servants." Although this message is for all humanity, Jesus only spoke it to His disciples. There was nary a hardened sinner to be found in the whole congregation when He preached this parable. Jesus hinted that just spending time in the Master's house is not enough. We are called to invest the gifts God gave us because He expects a return on His investment when He returns.

When the dust cleared, the Bible reads, "He that had received the five talents went and traded with the same, and made them other five talents" (Matthew 25:16). The first servant was savvier than most. He wore expensive suits and sipped coffee with brokers and bankers. Many bosses may have worried handing over so much money to one servant, but this servant was promising. The servant traded, bartered, bought, sold, and he earned five more talents. When his master returned, the servant would hand over ten talents—nearly two hundred years' worth of wages.

Why do we often battle resentment when someone else is promoted or blessed more than us? How do we stave off resentment?

The second servant was different. While his stockbroker servant friend had smooth hands and wore expensive suits, this servant had calloused hands and wore work boots. He knew what seeds to plant and when to plant them. He carried his two talents into town, bought as many seeds as two talents could buy, and then he went home and planted them when the time was right. His work was different from the first servant, but just as valuable. Although he was given less and gained less, Jesus did not paint him as bitter or resentful but as grateful for the opportunity to invest his master's money and give him a return on that investment.

The third servant stood and watched his two friends run into the marketplace to make more money for their master. Surely he could do something to invest his master's money, but he was no risk-taker. He carried around an umbrella on cloudless days. Jesus drew this servant in greater detail than the first. Maybe Jesus spent more time on him because most identify with him—just ordinary people doing ordinary jobs. Abraham Lincoln said, "God must love the common people because He made so many of them."

Rather than run into town, he walked to the shed, found a shovel, and dug a hole deep enough to bury the talent. He may not have gained, but he did not lose either. Surely his master would be satisfied to get back what he gave. Some may read this story and deduce that the master loved the five-talent servant more than the one-talent servant, but that is not true. He knew them, and he knew what they could do. He knew they were different, and they came with their own gifts. He did not underestimate the first servant by giving him too little; neither did he overwhelm the second servant by giving him too much. That is why he gave them differing gifts according to their differing abilities to be a blessing with what they were given.

C. I Will Faithfully Invest My Talents in the Kingdom of God

Do not be jealous or resentful. Jesus knows what we can handle, so He will not underestimate our ability by giving us too little or overwhelm our ability by giving us too much. It may be honesty, it may be humility, it may be a little bit of both, but few of us would profess to be a five-talent servant. Those are the people who can crochet, ride a unicycle, play the kazoo, drop a transmission, and make a key lime pie that would make your lips pucker and eyes water. They are gifted.

Teacher Option: A supplemental video is available in the Resource Kit. V

More of us would profess to be a two-talent servant. God has given us a few gifts and talents. Yet more of us might profess to be a one-talent servant. God has given us the ability to do one thing and do it well. Whatever gifts God gave you, use the gifts to give glory to Him. This parable points out there is room for five-talent servants in the kingdom of God. And for two-talent servants. And for one-talent servants.

James was right to write, "Every good gift and every perfect gift is from above, and cometh down from the Father of lights, with whom is no variableness, neither shadow of turning" (James 1:17). James summed up the principle of this parable: every gift we have comes from God and should be used to glorify God and to bless His kingdom. If God gave you the gift to work on vehicles, ask your pastor if you can help keep the vans serviced or even provide a service to people in the church who cannot afford routine maintenance. If God gave you the gift to cook, offer to cook for funerals or fellowships. Perhaps God gifted you with creativity; invest that into your church's website or social media or print promotions. The gifts God has given us are more than just for making money; they are to glorify God and help us make disciples.

What would you say is your most skillful God-given gift? How are you using it for the glory of God?

II. INVESTING MYSELF IN THE KINGDOM

Their master was away a while, but one day without warning, he returned. The chauffeur pulled past the front door, parked between the pillars, and the servants came out to greet their boss.

A. The Joy of Serving

It would have been easier to keep the sun from shining than to keep the first servant from smiling. It brought him joy to see his master so pleased. His master put his hand on the servant's shoulder, smiled, and said, "Well done, good and faithful servant. You've been faithful over a few things; I'll make you ruler over many. Enter into the joy of your Lord." (See Matthew 25:21.)

The second servant stepped up with his dirt-covered hands full—two talents in one hand, two in the other. And just like he did for the first servant, the master put his hand on this servant's shoulder and said, "Well done, good and faithful servant. You've been faithful over a few things; I'll make you ruler over many. Enter into the joy of your Lord." (See Matthew 25:22–23.)

The master did not scold the second servant for doing less than the first because he doubled what he was given just like the first servant. When our Lord returns, He will not ask you why you did not preach on Sundays if He did not gift you to preach on Sundays. And He certainly will not ask you why you did not repair the vans if you struggle to start a leaf blower. We find abundant joy when we use the gifts God gave us to glorify Him and make disciples for Him.

B. Self-Reliance, the Enemy of Obedience

Our third friend trusted in himself and himself alone. Because he was not overly gifted, he buried his talent and did nothing to bless his boss. His boss was livid. He reminded the servant of his own words. "You know I'm not the easiest guy in the world to work for. Why didn't you take this talent to the bank so it would draw some interest? That would give me a little more when I came back than I had when I went away." Then the master acted in a way many of us would deem unfair. He commanded, "Take that one talent away from him and give it to the one who has ten" (See Matthew 25:28)

Before we have a chance to ask why, Jesus gave us the because: "For unto every one that hath shall be given, and he shall have abundance: but from him that hath not shall be taken away even that which he hath. And cast ye the unprofitable servant into outer darkness: there shall be weeping and gnashing of teeth" (Matthew 25:29–30).

These sentences sound cruel to our sensitivities. It does not sound fair. The ten-talent servant had enough. At least let the one-talent servant keep what little he had. But Jesus was letting us know what matters to Him. It is not what we have or how much we have; it is what we do with what we have.

In addition to skills and talents, what other gifts from God might we use for the glory of God? What about our finances, our friendships, our influence?

C. I Will Do My Part to Advance the Kingdom of God

If God only gave you one talent, He does not expect you to bring back five. He expects you to take the one talent He gave you and invest it to glorify Him and bless His kingdom. If He gave you two talents, He expects you to use both of them for His glory and to bless His kingdom. If he gave you five talents, be thankful and use those talents to point people to Jesus, not just to you. As Jesus said in Luke 12, "To whom much is given, much is required." (See Luke 12:48.) Use those gifts as a means to bring glory to God. There is great joy in glorifying God and using His gifts to make disciples for Him.

INTERNALIZING THE MESSAGE

Teacher's note: Hand out the worksheet available in the Resource Kit and have students fill it out.

Before we pray, we will complete this worksheet. Think carefully about the gifts God has given you. Think about the skills you have—the things you love to do and are able to do. These skills do not have to be pulpit or even platform gifts. They can be baking, building, repairing, typing, knitting, designing, writing. Think about your God-given gifts and write them down on your worksheet.

Then think about ways you could use those God-given gifts to glorify God and bless His kingdom. Maybe you can help bake for guests who come on Sundays. Maybe you can help keep the church campus clean or in good repair. If God uses you to design at work, how could you use those design gifts to glorify God and bless His kingdom?

Ask yourself what you are doing with your God-given gifts. God is not impressed if you can fill out the entire sheet. From what we have learned from this parable, He is more interested in how we are using the many or few gifts we have for the glory of God. If you find yourself checking "no" more times than "yes," this lesson may be the Spirit calling you to dig up the gift God gave you and invest it somewhere to glorify Him and grow His kingdom.

What will you do today to use the gifts God has given you to glorify Him and bless His kingdom?

Prayer Focus
Lead the group in prayer and consider the following topics of focus:
- For God to show us the gifts and talents He has given us
- For God to help us use those gifts and talents for His glory and to bless His kingdom

1.3

THE FATHER IS WAITING

FOCUS VERSE
Luke 15:32
It was meet that we should make merry, and be glad: for this thy brother was dead, and is alive again; and was lost, and is found.

LESSON TEXT
Luke 15:11–32

TRUTH ABOUT GOD
God loves the prodigals and waits patiently for their return.

TRUTH FOR MY LIFE
All who wander can return to their loving, heavenly Father.

Thinking about Last Week:

Have students refer to their Daily Devotional Guide to answer the following questions:
1. What most affected you as you read through the Lesson Text and the Biblical Insights?
2. How did it shape your prayers and thoughts throughout the week?
3. Do you feel you grew closer to the Lord this past week? Why or why not?

SG TEACHING OUTLINE

Icebreaker: What is the farthest you have ever traveled away from home?

Lesson Connection: Share the Lesson Connection. [I]

I. THE YOUNGER SON

    A. He Pursued a Life of Self-Determination

       » *Why do you think the young man wanted to leave home so badly?*

    B. I Will Yield to God's Authority in My Life

II. THE OLDER SON

    A. He Lived a Life of Self-Righteousness

    B. He Did Not Acknowledge His Inheritance or His Brother's Restoration

       » *Do we have a difficult time rejoicing when someone is restored? If so, why?*

    C. I Will Reject Self-Righteousness and Rejoice in the Restoration of Others [V]

       » *What are practical ways we can rejoice with someone who is restored?*

III. THE LOVING, FORGIVING FATHER

    A. He Allowed His Sons to Make Their Own Decisions

       » *Why do you think our heavenly Father allows us to make decisions that may harm us?*

    B. He Desired to Restore Both Sons to a Wholesome Relationship with Him

    C. All Who Wander Can Return to Their Loving, Heavenly Father

       » *Do you struggle more with outward sins everyone can see or inward sins only God can see?*

Internalizing the Message

Prayer Focus
Lead the group in prayer and consider the following topics of focus:
• For God to help us be content and thankful to be close to Him
• For God to help us welcome people back to right relationship with Him

LESSON CONNECTION

A supplemental image is available in the Resource Kit. (I)

Alex and his older sister were tired of all the unreasonable demands their parents made of them. The Founding Fathers of the United States promised Alex and Alicia life, liberty, and the pursuit of happiness, but their parents demanded clean rooms, clean plates, and a curfew. The children were tired of tyranny, so one bright sunny day, they woke up early, packed their backpacks, and walked out of the house into freedom. They were pretty proud of themselves.

When they reached the railroad tracks—less than a half mile away—they turned right onto the tracks and kept walking. This life would be the one they dreamed of—no parents telling them to do their chores, no teachers assigning homework. They were finally free to go anywhere, meet anyone, do anything, except for one minor detail: they had little food and even less money. Alex was ten years old; Alicia was twelve. Aside from that, the world was theirs. They had not yet figured out how to get around truancy or child labor laws. They would worry about that when they needed to.

While they walked, they heard an ATV start up in the distance. The distant whir of the motor came closer. Someone was heading their way. They couldn't afford to be spotted. The runaways ran from the tracks, down the hill, and into a little cornfield. As the neighbor on the four-wheeler came closer, they tried to hide behind the cornstalks, but neither Alex nor Alicia was that thin. The neighbor stopped on the tracks above them and bellowed, "You kids better get out of that cornfield!"

Maybe he saw them, maybe he was just trying to roust them out, but they were rookie runaways. They didn't know what to do. They just knew they had been caught, so they sheepishly walked out of the cornfield and trudged back toward the tracks. They walked slower than a turtle climbing a down escalator. If they took their time, they would have more time to think of an excuse, but their neighbor was not so thoughtful. He revved up his Honda and chased them as fast as their wobbly preteen legs would carry them. It is a wonder they did not trip and end up with train tracks on their faces and tire tracks on their backs. Their neighbor chased them all the way from the cornfield to their house to two waiting, worrying parents.

BIBLE LESSON

I. THE YOUNGER SON

Jesus told a story about a young man who did not want to live at home anymore. He was the younger of two sons, and one day he approached his father with a request that almost made his dad spill his bowl of Granola Flakes. "Dad, I want my inheritance—now." The young man expected a lecture or a twinge of disappointment in his father's eyes. Instead, his father headed out of the room and came back with bags full of money. When the young man saw that much money as his inheritance, his eyes grew as big as silver shekels.

A. He Pursued a Life of Self-Determination

After breakfast, the young man went to his room, gathered his things, gave his father a firm handshake, gave his older brother a nod, and he walked out the door. As he made his way down the drive, the servants working in the field bowed out of respect, but he did not even glance their way. He was so proud.

He crisscrossed the country for days and nights, staying in the plushest hotels and eating in the finest restaurants. When there were enough miles between him and home, he walked into the first bar he found in his new hometown. He reached into his pockets, pulled out a wad of cash, laid it on the bar, and bought everyone a drink. He had more money than he could ever spend. Before long the locals realized the move-in was rich. It didn't take him long to make friends.

He had more money and more friends than he could count. How could his dad have kept him hemmed in all those years behind that iron gate? The rich young runaway treated his new friends to steak one night, lobster the next, and drinks for everyone. But one night after several of these spending sprees, he ran out of cash, and he ran out of friends. They turned on him as fast as they had turned to him. From that night forward, it would appear his life took a turn for the worse. Actually, his life took its first turn toward home.

Why do you think the young man wanted to leave home so badly?

B. I Will Yield to God's Authority in My Life

If only this young man would have realized his father was not trying to keep him hemmed in; he was trying to keep danger out. God has also blessed us with authority figures to keep us safe and to keep danger out. From the beginning of Scripture, God established parents to be the authority figures for their children. (See Deuteronomy 6:4–8.) A cursory study of the Bible reveals some parents who abused or neglected that authority role, but there are also shining examples of parents who loved their children enough to provide for them and protect them from danger.

Pastors and ministers are another God-given authority for our spiritual well-being. According to Ephesians 4:11–12, "And he gave some, apostles; and some, prophets; and some, evangelists; and some, pastors and teachers; for the perfecting of the saints, for the work of the ministry, for the edifying of the body of Christ." We are blessed to have a man or woman of God in our lives to help us live for the glory of God and help make disciples as we walk from here to Heaven. Living in submission to God-given authority is a blessing, especially when that authority is living in submission to God.

II. THE OLDER SON

The younger son had an older brother who stayed at home. He appeared to be everything his younger brother was not. While Junior ran away to spend his entire inheritance, his older brother remained at home to help his dad tend the farm. He appeared to be faithful, content, and loyal. This firstborn son appears to be the character in the story we should example, but he is not.

A. He Lived a Life of Self-Righteousness

After a while, a mud-caked prodigal with slumped shoulders finally arrived back home. He had suffered the effects of living life on his own terms, outside the protection and provision of his father. As he and his thankful, tearful dad made their way back toward the house together, his dad called out to the servants to kill the fatted calf.

Some of the more rhythmic servants grabbed tambourines while some of the non-rhythmic servants just tried clapping on the right beat. This was the first time in a very long time they heard music in this house. But one family member was missing from the celebration. The older brother was still out in the field faithfully doing his chores when he heard the music.

Soon he discovered the calf, the music, and the celebration were all to honor his baby brother who ran away but returned home. Verse by verse, Jesus revealed the hideous chink in the older brother's armor: self-righteousness. "And he was angry, and would not go in: therefore came his father out, and intreated him" (Luke 15:28).

B. He Did Not Acknowledge His Inheritance or His Brother's Restoration

The older brother was enraged. He was ready to fight, but he was not ready to feast. He would sleep under the cornstalks if he needed to; he was not going inside to celebrate his prodigal brother who misspent his inheritance on sin. In Luke 15 Jesus was talking to Pharisees, the religious elite, who felt like their self-righteousness earned them favor with God. They were not dissimilar to this older brother. He kept a record of all he did right, and he let his father hear it.

The older son's whole relationship was built on work, not love. He served all those years. He worked his fingers to the bone, his hands to callouses. From sunup to sundown, he broke his back to make the farm all his dad wanted it to be. And on top of that, he never broke one of his father's commandments at any time. That's probably not true, but that is how he felt.

This was wrong. He was right. Why didn't his father give him a party for just being faithful? While he stewed on his right to be bitter and angry, his dad put his arm around his shoulders, looked him in the eye, and answered, "Son, thou art ever with me, and all that I have is thine. It was meet that we should make merry, and be glad: for this thy brother was dead, and is alive again; and was lost, and is found" (Luke 15:31–32).

The older son had not spent one shiny shekel of his inheritance. His reward would come later, after his father died; then his faithfulness and loyalty would be rewarded. Perhaps he thought celebrating his younger brother's return home would be the same as celebrating his sin, but it was not. It was celebrating the father's mercy.

Do we have a difficult time rejoicing when someone is restored? If so, why?

C. I Will Reject Self-Righteousness and Rejoice in the Restoration of Others

Only five short verses from the end of the story, we see the older brother seething. Surely the story would end as he, his baby brother, and his thankful father lived happily ever after, but it did not. We still wade through self-righteousness in this story and possibly in our own. But we do not have to. When God restores people who walked away from Him, do not be jealous of them; rejoice with them. Even if them returning to worship with you on Sundays costs you a closer parking space, rejoice with them. God does.

Teacher Option: A supplemental video is available in the Resource Kit. **V**

In this selfsame chapter, Luke wrote, "I say unto you, that likewise joy shall be in heaven over one sinner that repenteth, more than over ninety and nine just persons, which need no repentance" (Luke 15:7). If there is joy in Heaven over one sinner who repents, there certainly should be joy on earth. God is holy. His celebration does not diminish His holiness or celebrate our sin; His celebration celebrates His mercy and our forgiveness.

III. THE LOVING, FORGIVING FATHER

A. He Allowed His Sons to Make Their Own Decisions

What are practical ways we can rejoice with someone who is restored?

We do not want to model our lives after the younger son. He left home with everything and came home with nothing. Neither do we want to live like the older son. He stayed home, but his heart was far from his father. He was seething with self-righteousness. But the father loved his younger son despite his selfishness and his older son despite his self-righteousness, and he allowed both young men to make their own decisions.

Sometimes God allows things He does not approve of. When we pray, we need to be sure we are praying according to God's will, not ours. It is very simple to know the will of God from this story: if the answer to your prayer draws you closer to God, it is God's will. If it will push you further from God, it is not. Likewise, the father allowed his older son to make his own decision to remain at home and keep working on the family farm. Because the son stayed, the father gladly promised everything he owned to the son. That is amazing grace. God will not pressure us to stay close to Him or push us away from Him. We make our own decisions, but as this story perfectly illustrates, we also live with those decisions.

Why do you think our heavenly Father allows us to make decisions that may harm us?

B. He Desired to Restore Both Sons to a Wholesome Relationship with Him

The father desired to restore both sons to right relationship with him. His younger son's sins were outward; everyone could see them. But the father wanted to restore his son by giving him a fresh change of clothes, new shoes, a ring for his finger, and a homecoming celebration the neighbors would talk about for years. His older son's sins were inward; only the father could really see them. But the father wanted to restore this son by promising he would one day reward his faithfulness. The older son just needed to trust the heart of his father that he would be gracious to him, just as he was to his brother.

C. All Who Wander Can Return to Their Loving, Heavenly Father

At the risk of oversimplifying, there are two groups of Jesus followers: those who have walked away from God and those who have not. Charles Dickens called the Parable of the Prodigal Son "the greatest short story ever written." It is not only a great story because the father worked to restore his sons; it is a great story because our Father continually works to restore us. If you walked away from God, you can come home. You can return to God and receive the same grace-filled reception the prodigal son received. You have not done too much or gone too far or been away too long. All who wander can return.

If you have remained faithful and loyal to your walk with God, remain. If your heart has strayed, and you serve God more out of duty than devotion, you can return to right relationship with Jesus. God wants to restore you and remind you that your reward may come later, but your reward will surely come. One day we will kneel before Him and hear Him say, "Well done, thou good and faithful servant." There was room in the father's house, and there is room in our Father's house for all His sons and daughters.

Do you struggle more with outward sins everyone can see or inward sins only God can see?

INTERNALIZING THE MESSAGE

Alex and Alicia made it home quicker than they hoped. They were home before they had time to build a believable excuse for running away from home. Their mom and dad were happy to have them home, but they were not willing to overlook this dangerous decision. And rightfully so. These children were not even teenagers yet, and they were wandering by themselves into the world. That afternoon, hugs gave way to a lecture and deserved discipline.

When we return to the Father, we know He will run to meet us. He will hold us and welcome us home. But do not let the mercy of God be the license you hold to run away from God. Before you run off intending to return, remember, the prodigal son never regained what he gave away. He still carried the memories of his misspent inheritance. He bore scars in his mind and on his body that he lived with the rest of his days. Although the older brother remained at home, he still bore the memory of the day he told his dad how he really felt.

Thankfully our Father forgives our sins and will not remember them against us anymore, but our families and friends may have a difficult time forgetting what we have done or said to them out of self-righteousness. Let us live in a way to be closer to our Father and serve Him out of wholehearted devotion for who He is and what He has done.

Prayer Focus
Lead the group in prayer and consider the following topics of focus:
- For God to help us be content and thankful to be close to Him
- For God to help us welcome people back to right relationship with Him

1.4

FOR A SEASON

FOCUS VERSE
Luke 16:31
And he said unto him, If they hear not Moses and the prophets, neither will they be persuaded, though one rose from the dead.

LESSON TEXT
Luke 16:19–31

TRUTH ABOUT GOD
God gives us a season to accept Him.

TRUTH FOR MY LIFE
I will choose to live for God today.

Thinking about Last Week:

Have students refer to their Daily Devotional Guide to answer the following questions:

1. What most affected you as you read through the Lesson Text and the Biblical Insights?
2. How did it shape your prayers and thoughts throughout the week?
3. Do you feel you grew closer to the Lord this past week? Why or why not?

SG TEACHING OUTLINE

Icebreaker: Share the most remarkable rags-to-riches story you have heard.

Lesson Connection: Share the Lesson Connection. Ⓘ

I. PRESENT CIRCUMSTANCES ARE NOT ALWAYS INDICATIVE OF FUTURE REALITY
  » *If you were just looking at the station in life of the rich man and of Lazarus, whom do you think was more blessed? Explain.*

  A. The Great Reversal Ⓥ
  » *What are you most looking forward to in Heaven?*
  » *What resources can you use today to help make disciples for God's glory?*

  B. I Will Not Judge My Spiritual Position Based on My Temporal Reality
  » *Since many of God's people in the Bible were persecuted and poor, where does the prosperity gospel stem from?*

II. TODAY IS THE DAY OF SALVATION

  A. The Rich Man's Request
  » *What do you think is the most tormenting part of Hell?*

  B. Abraham's Response

Internalizing the Message

Prayer Focus
Lead the group in prayer and consider the following topics of focus:
• For God to help us be ready for the day we will meet Him
• For God to help us notice people who may need our kindness

LESSON CONNECTION

A supplemental image is available in the Resource Kit. (I)

Clara was an accountant, and Paul was a mechanic. They fell deeply in love and married. For nine years they longed to grow their family of two into a family of three, but could not. When they realized they would not have children biologically, they adopted a baby boy they named Steven Paul.

Steven grew up, graduated from high school, and enrolled in college, but his dreams of a career right out of college would have to wait. He did not have enough money to pay his tuition. Regretfully, he withdrew from college after just one semester.

While Steve was growing up, his mechanic father taught him how to work on cars. Steve wasn't very interested in the cars themselves, but he was intrigued by the electronics that made them work. Every weekend Paul took his son to the junkyard where they rummaged for spare parts. Steve's interest in electronics continued to grow as the days turned into weeks, into months, into years. As Steve's interest grew, Paul opened his garage to his son to give him a space to experiment on electronics.

Seven houses down, an engineer for Hewlett Packard (HP) heard about Steve's interest and acumen in electronics. The neighbor brought Steve gadgets and gizmos to play with. His fourth-grade teacher did the same. They were amazed at this young boy's interest in all things tech. Eventually, their engineer neighbor invited Steve to join the Hewlett-Packard Explorers Club, a group of students who met weekly in the HP cafeteria. There Steve saw his first desktop computer. It weighed around forty pounds, but in Steve's words, "It was a beauty of a thing." Once when the group needed parts they did not have, Steve thumbed through the phone book and called the CEO of HP to ask for them. They talked for twenty minutes. By the end of that call, the CEO offered Steve an internship.

By the time he turned twenty-three years old, Steve Jobs was worth $1 million. In 1984, he designed the first Macintosh computer. When he died at the age of fifty-six, his net worth totaled over $10 billion. Steve Jobs began working with his blue-collar father in a garage and built an empire worth billions of dollars. Rags-to-riches stories like these inspire us to continue working hard and dreaming harder to see our dreams blossom into reality. These stories are not limited to modern times. They happened all throughout history, even in the Bible. Sometimes these stories do not have a happy ending until after the story has been told.

BIBLE LESSON

I. PRESENT CIRCUMSTANCES ARE NOT ALWAYS INDICATIVE OF FUTURE REALITY

A. The Early Existence of the Rich Man and Lazarus

Let's leave the high-tech headquarters of Apple to stroll down a first-century cobblestone street. Soon we come to the end of the block and the envy of the block. The sprawling palatial mansion takes up both sides of the street—a mansion supported by pillars and surrounded by gates. Emblazoned on the side of the mailbox in gold stencil is simply, "A rich man." The sight of this mansion with its fountains and flower gardens takes our breath away. But there is one feature that does not fit. It is the rogue brushstroke in this painting the artist brushed. Lying outside the iron gate is a frail beggar named Lazarus.

Lazarus was a common name in the first-century world. The name Lazarus means "God will help," but it does not appear God is helping this Lazarus much. His body is ravaged with a disease that has sapped his strength and left sores in its wake. Everything he owns can easily be stuffed into a duffel bag with plenty of room to spare.

Lazarus is dirt poor; the rich man is filthy rich. But Lazarus has more than money could buy. He may not have two shekels to buy his own bread, but at some point, he lifted his eyes higher than this world and realized he needed to get right with God and ready for eternity. Lazarus cried out to God, and God saved Lazarus.

B. The Great Reversal

If you were just looking at the station in life of the rich man and of Lazarus, whom do you think was more blessed? Explain.

Scripture records that Lazarus died, but there is no mention of him being buried. There was likely no funeral or preacher to eulogize what a good man he was. In fact, a song was often sung for beggars: "Rattle his bones over the stones. He's but a pauper whom nobody owns." Likely, Lazarus was loaded onto a cart, hauled to the outskirts of town, and thrown into Gehenna with all the trash and bones of other beggars.

But Lazarus was right with God and ready for eternity. Since Jesus told this story before He went to Calvary, He told of Lazarus being carried by the angels into Abraham's bosom. The Jews had precious few heroes they admired more than Abraham, the father of the faithful. Lazarus was able to rest close to the heart of the one he knew as a father.

When we repent, are baptized in Jesus' name and filled with His Holy Spirit, we have Heaven to gain. Heaven, where the street is pure gold as transparent glass, the gates are made of precious pearl, and the walls are made of jasper. That heavenly city is big enough for billions of believers to call Heaven home. Lazarus could testify that all the problems that plague us in this life will not even be a memory in Heaven.

Teacher Option:
A supplemental video is available in the Resource Kit. **V**

What are you most looking forward to in Heaven?

Heaven will be Heaven because of who will be there. Jesus, the one who created us and died for us, is preparing a place for us. And He is coming back for us to take us there. We will rest from all of our labors, and with unveiled faces, we will finally see Jesus. The one we sing to here, we will see there. We will cast our crowns at His feet and join the song of the sainted millions: "Worthy is the Lamb that was slain to receive power, and riches, and wisdom, and strength, and honour, and glory, and blessing" (Revelation 5:12).

Although Lazarus was plagued by sickness and poverty on earth, he was beyond blessed in Heaven. But there was another character in this parable whose story must be told. The rich man was clothed in purple and fine linen, the finest fabrics of his day—akin to $5,000 Italian suits and $3,000 alligator shoes today.

But his fortune could not fend off the determined hand of death. The entire community came out to pay their respects. His funeral was teeming with his employees, family, and friends. Some were hoping to get their hands on his money. The preacher assigned to eulogize the rich man could write pages to testify of his business savvy and salesmanship, but he could not write two sentences to truthfully tell of his walk with God.

While it is true we can have nothing on earth and still have everything in Heaven, it is equally true we can have everything on earth and completely miss Heaven. Being wealthy does not automatically mean we will not be saved, but Jesus was clear that "it is easier for a camel to go through the eye of a needle, than for a rich man to enter into the kingdom of God" (Matthew 19:24). If God has blessed you with riches, do not trust in them. Trust in God who gave you the riches to glorify Him and make disciples for Him. Lazarus's rags-to-riches story and the rich man's riches-to-rags story are known as the "great reversal."

What resources can you use today to help make disciples for God's glory?

C. I Will Not Judge My Spiritual Position Based on My Temporary Reality

Lazarus's life tells a different story than the one we often hear from radio or TV preachers. God's will is to bless us with what we need on earth, but God is much more interested in us being right with Him and ready for Heaven. Health and wealth do not always mark God's approval, just as poverty and sickness do not necessarily signal God's disapproval. Even if we or the ones we love battle sickness or cannot seem to pay the bills, that does not automatically mean God is displeased. God wants us to be ready for Heaven, not just healthy and wealthy on earth.

Since many of God's people in the Bible were persecuted and poor, where does the prosperity gospel stem from?

Many of us could testify of people who were good stewards in life—of their bodies and their finances—and still lived paycheck to paycheck or died after a long battle with disease. A glance at their lives may infer God was displeased with them; therefore, He did not bless them. The most blessed life cannot be measured by dollars or social media followers; the most blessed life is measured by our obedience to the will of God. When we have been born again and are living to honor and glorify God, we are abundantly blessed no matter how much or how little we own.

II. TODAY IS THE DAY OF SALVATION

A "Why Worry" poster hung in a small-town barber shop. It read, "There are only two reasons to worry. Either you are well, or you are sick. If you are well, then there's no need to worry. But if you are sick, there are two reasons to worry. Either you will get well, or you will die. If you get well, then there's no need to worry. If you die, then there are two reasons to worry. Either you will go to Heaven, or you will go to Hell. If you go to Heaven, then there's no need to worry, but if you go to Hell, you'll be so busy shaking hands with friends that you won't have to worry."

That is not the picture Jesus painted of Hell in Luke 16. Neither is it how the apostles and prophets described Hell. We see a much more grisly picture of Hell in this parable and in other passages.

A. The Rich Man's Request

When the rich man closed his eyes in death, he opened his eyes in Hell. If his money could have bought him access into the presence of God, he would have paid any price. But he made his decision in life to live apart from God, and that decision sentenced him to eternity apart from God. When he looked up, he saw a somewhat familiar man. He knew him from life, but the man did not look the same. He was that sick, homeless man the servants called Lazarus, the weakened beggar from outside the iron gate, but Lazarus was healed and at rest.

However, the rich man was in torment. He called out from the belly of Hell, "Father Abraham, have mercy on me, and send Lazarus, that he may dip the tip of his finger in water, and cool my tongue; for I am tormented in this flame" (Luke 16:24). Without stretching the imagination too far, it would appear from this story that people in Hell may be able to see people who have gone to Heaven. We know this story was told before Jesus died on Calvary and rose from the grave, so perhaps the setting is different now. But if this much is true, part of the torment of eternity in Hell will be seeing people for eternity in Heaven, knowing you will never step foot there.

And then there is your memory. The rich man did not need name tags to know who Lazarus and Abraham were; he called them both by name. He even called Abraham, "Father Abraham," indicating he was a Jew and had likely heard a sermon or two in a service or two. For all eternity, he would remember the chances he had to get right with God. All the altar calls when he could have prayed but did not, all the messages he heard preached but never responded to—he wished he had valued his soul more than his portfolio.

What do you think is the most tormenting part of Hell?

B. Abraham's Response

The rich man's soul was so tormented in the flames of Hell that he begged for a drop of water to ease a second of the pain. But Abraham replied, "Son, remember that thou in thy lifetime receivedst thy good things, and likewise Lazarus evil things: but now he is comforted, and thou art tormented" (Luke 16:25). To be sure, there will be people in Heaven who were wealthy on earth and people in Hell who were poor on earth. In the New Testament, men and women of means who were born again used the riches God gave them to help disciple others to be born again.

The rich man winced at the memory of his life, which is why he ended up in Hell. The Bible does not even hint to us that this man was evil. He may have been a philanthropist, giving millions to children's hospitals and leprosy research. But eternity was based more on what he did not do than what he did do: he did not repent of his sins and get his soul right with God.

Abraham broke the sobering news for him to hear and for us to eavesdrop, "And beside all this, between us and you there is a great gulf fixed: so that they which would pass from hence to you cannot; neither can they pass to us" (Luke 16:26). Separation from God is what truly makes Hell torment. It will not just be Hell's unquenchable flames or the memory of messages preached and altars ignored. What truly makes Hell torment is eternal separation from God because between Heaven and Hell is a great gulf fixed, and there is no bridging or crossing that gulf.

INTERNALIZING THE MESSAGE

The rich man may have lived and died in extravagance, but his unsurrendered soul would spend eternity in Hell simply because he did not choose to live for God. Many people ask the probing question, "Why would a loving God send anyone to Hell?" But they may not consider that God does not send anyone to Hell; our sin does. The more appropriate question should be, "Why would a just and holy God allow any of us into Heaven?" The answer to that question is God's amazing grace.

This rich man's story has already been told, but ours has not. The rich man cannot make Heaven his home, but we may because we still have today to choose to live for God. The most important decision we will make in our lives has nothing to do with the neighborhood we move into, the college we enroll in, the car we choose to drive, or even the man or woman we choose to marry. The most important, lasting decision we will make is to live for God. That decision brings the promise of abundant life here and eternal life there. There is no greater choice than to choose to live for God.

Let us choose today, "I will live for God."

Prayer Focus
Lead the group in prayer and consider the following topics of focus:
- For God to help us be ready for the day we will meet Him
- For God to help us notice people who may need our kindness

SERIES 2: PORTRAITS OF SALVATION

2.1

ONCE LOST . . . NOW FOUND

FOCUS VERSE
Luke 19:10
For the Son of man is come to seek and to save that which was lost.

LESSON TEXT
Luke 15:1–10; 19:1–10

TRUTH ABOUT GOD
The Messiah's mission is to seek and to save the lost.

TRUTH FOR MY LIFE
I will celebrate that Jesus sought me and saved me.

Series Overview:

This series, "Portraits of Salvation," gives us snapshots of ways the Scriptures portray salvation. Luke 15 highlights the lost sheep, lost coin, and lost son, while Luke 19 celebrates Zacchaeus's salvation. The Passover points to the blood of Jesus, and John 3 tells the story of Jesus' sacred conversation with Nicodemus. The series closes with the grace-filled adoption story of Mephibosheth.

SG TEACHING OUTLINE

Icebreaker: What is the longest you have ever been lost?

Lesson Connection: Share the Lesson Connection.

I.   JESUS LOVES THE SINNER
   » *How does it make you feel to know that Jesus died for you while you were lost?*

   A.   He Will Seek for Those Who Are Lost
      » *Can you recall a time you felt the overwhelming relief of finding something or someone lost?*

   B.   He Will Rejoice Over Finding a Sinner V
      » *How often do you see the value in people like Jesus does?*

   C.   I Will Rejoice When the Lost Are Found
      » *Think about the last person you recall being born again. Did you feel overwhelming joy?*

II.   JESUS FOUND ZACCHAEUS

   A.   Zacchaeus Was Lost

   B.   Jesus Sought for and Changed Zacchaeus
      » *Have you ever considered the miracle that Jesus found you where He did and saved you?*

   C.   I Celebrate That Jesus Sought for Me and Changed Me

Internalizing the Message I

> **Prayer Focus**
> Lead the group in prayer and consider the following topics of focus:
> • For God to seek and save those who are lost
> • For God to help us rejoice when He seeks and saves the lost

LESSON CONNECTION

Imagine hiking through the woods on a beautiful summer day. You are following the clearly defined trail and enjoying the scenery. Like most walks in the woods, sights and sounds off the trail draw your attention. You decide to venture just a few feet away to look at a unique rock formation that caught your eye. Before you know it, you have wandered a little farther from the trail while looking at other things.

Suddenly the trail is nowhere in sight. You have wandered so far that you are officially lost. Frantically you look in all directions for some familiar landmark. Seeing none, a sense of hopelessness settles over you. It will take a miracle for someone to find you.

Being lost means we have become disconnected from what makes us feel secure. It takes away our sense of balance in life and leaves us looking for something. Lost means that what was once clearly seen and visible is now hidden from sight. Being lost can also bring about the greatest feeling of aloneness a human being can experience.

Whatever causes us to become lost—whether it is because we were preoccupied or merely forgetful—can cause us to spiral into despair. Our minds begin to reel with thoughts of what life will be like if we are never found. The heart-gripping fear that a mother experiences when she realizes her child has been lost is indescribable. She will go to any extreme and will lose all sense of respectability and decorum to find her child.

Far beyond any danger of being physically lost is being spiritually lost. The Word of God is a clear path for anyone wanting to be saved. Becoming distracted by the things of this world can cause us to leave the well-worn path and become lost. One distraction after another leads us farther from God.

But when we are spiritually lost, all is not hopeless. Luke 19:10 tells us, "For the Son of man is come to seek and to save that which was lost." Take heart. While we are looking to be saved, God is looking to save us. Like the mother with a lost child, the Lord will go to great extremes to find each lost soul.

BIBLE LESSON

I. JESUS LOVES THE SINNER

The love of a parent for a child is almost indescribable. Words spoken, cards written, even gifts given all fall far short of expressing the depth of love from a parent to a child. Regardless of what wrong a child may commit, Mom and Dad are still going to love the child. How much greater is the love of Jesus for people, no matter their sin. Although sin has consequences now and in eternity, no sin will ever cause God to stop loving us.

John 3:16 reads, "For God so loved the world, that he gave his only begotten Son." His love was so deep for lost humanity that He was willing to die as a sacrifice for our sins.

While we were lost a million miles away from Jesus spiritually, He died for us so we could be in close relationship with Him. Think about that for a moment. Jesus loved you enough that He died for you before you were even born. John 15:13-14 gives us amazing insight into His love, for it reads, "Greater love hath no man than this, that a man lay down his life for his friends. Ye are my friends, if ye do whatsoever I command you."

We all have close friends we say we would be willing to do anything for. But if really put to the test, we may not be willing to die for them. Jesus had no such reservation. When a sacrificial death was required for our sin, He willingly laid down His life for us—even people who have no relationship with Him.

How does it make you feel to know that Jesus died for you while you were lost?

Since the beginning of time, the Lord has been reaching for people. Imperfect, weak, discouraged, disillusioned, disappointed, or defeated—He loves us all. There has never been a sinner whom God has not loved.

A. He Will Seek for Those Who Are Lost

In Luke 15, Jesus began a trio of parables by telling of the shepherd who counted his sheep only to realize one was missing. Although ninety-nine sheep were accounted for, the shepherd set out to find the one lost sheep. Some people may feel that losing one is not a big deal. Why go to the trouble of finding one lost sheep?

While it may not have mattered to others, it mattered to the shepherd. He knew the sheep would die if left separated from the flock. At that moment, the one lost sheep was as valuable to him as the ninety-nine that were safe. At peril to his own life, the shepherd went out to find the lost sheep. Imagine the relief the shepherd felt when he laid eyes on the one that was lost. The lost sheep was safe because the shepherd found it. The shepherd carefully lifted the sheep onto his shoulders and carried it back to the fold.

Can you recall a time you felt the wonderful relief of finding something or someone lost?

The second parable is of the woman who lost a silver coin. It may have been a drachma, which was equal to a day's wages. She frantically turned her home upside down in a desperate search for the coin. Because the light was so poor, she lit a lamp to help in her search. Frantically, she looked in every corner and under every piece of furniture. She even swept the floors in case it was covered with dirt. Suddenly, there it was. She had ransacked her own house, but she found the coin.

B. He Will Rejoice Over Finding a Sinner

The joy of the shepherd finding the lost sheep and the woman finding the lost coin pale in comparison to Jesus finding a lost sinner. Luke 15:10 tells us, "Likewise, I say unto you, there is joy in the presence of the angels of God over one sinner that repenteth."

If human beings rejoice over temporal things being found, can you imagine how much the Lord rejoices over an eternal soul being found? People place great value on money and possessions, but the Lord places greater value on people.

How often do you see the value in people like Jesus does?

Hebrews 12:2 expresses the joy Jesus felt in saving the lost. "Looking unto Jesus the author and finisher of our faith; who for the joy that was set before him endured the cross, despising the shame, and is set down at the right hand of the throne of God." Amazing. Jesus endured the pain and agony of the Cross because of the joy that lay before Him. For Jesus, the joy of saving the lost was greater than any pain He would have to suffer.

Isaiah 61:10 gives us instruction as to how we should respond toward the Lord for purchasing our salvation. "I will greatly rejoice in the LORD, my soul shall be joyful in my God; for he hath clothed me with the garments of salvation." We should rejoice because of the joy that is set before us in our salvation.

Teacher Option:
A supplemental video is available in the Resource Kit. **V**

C. I Will Rejoice When the Lost Are Found

When the disciples asked Jesus to teach them to pray, Jesus responded by saying, "After this manner therefore pray ye: Our Father which art in heaven, Hallowed be thy name. Thy kingdom come. Thy will be done in earth, as it is in heaven" (Matthew 6:9–10).

That prayer was a sincere request for the will of God to be done on the earth. God is not willing that any should perish (John 3:17; II Peter 3:9). It is God's will for all the world to be saved. We understand not everyone will accept salvation, but all of Heaven rejoices when people are born again. When you repented of your sins, Heaven rejoiced. It only makes sense that we should rejoice when others are born again. We should all be like the father of the prodigal son who proclaimed, "This my son . . . was lost, and is found" (Luke 15:24).

Think about the last person you recall being born again. Did you feel overwhelming joy?

II. JESUS FOUND ZACCHAEUS

A. Zacchaeus Was Lost

In Luke 19, we meet Zacchaeus, a rich tax collector. As a rule, the Jews hated tax collectors. They were agents of the hated Roman empire who collected taxes. They had the power to increase the actual fees due as long as they sent back the required amount to Rome. They could pocket the excess. Many of them became wealthy at the Jews' expense. Evidently Zacchaeus followed this practice and was despised for it, but Jesus showed us that even a man like him can be saved.

B. Jesus Sought for and Changed Zacchaeus

Zacchaeus sought to see Jesus, but he knew it was not going to be easy. As the children's song goes, Zacchaeus was a wee little man. If he were going to see Jesus, he would have to do something out of the ordinary. His desperate desire drove him up a tree. Literally. He ran ahead of the crowd and found a sycamore tree in the direct path where Jesus was walking. As quickly as he could, he climbed it to make sure he was above the rest of the crowd so he could see Jesus.

Here the story takes an interesting twist. Zacchaeus climbed the tree because he wanted to see Jesus, but within just a few moments, Jesus was looking for him. Luke 19:5 reads, "And when Jesus came to the place, he looked up, and saw him, and said unto him, Zacchaeus, make haste, and come down; for to day I must abide at thy house."

It would be easy to assume Jesus was passing through Jericho with nothing else on His mind but finding Zacchaeus. Perhaps this was the case or perhaps He was heading somewhere to teach or work a miracle. Whatever the motivation, the short, despised tax collector came down out of the tree quicker than he went up it. Zacchaeus received Jesus joyfully.

Imagine the scene. Zacchaeus was joyful to have seen Jesus, and Jesus was joyful to have found Zacchaeus. However, the rest of the crowd was not joyful, and they made it known. The whispers and murmurs soon started. "Can you believe Jesus is going to the house of a sinner? Can you believe Jesus would spend any time at all with the man who got rich off our taxes?"

Zacchaeus felt the sting of their words and quickly defended himself to the Lord. "Half of my goods I give to the poor; and if I have taken any thing from any man by false accusation, I restore him fourfold" (Luke 19:8). Jesus quickly responded and let Zacchaeus and the crowd know why He had come to Jericho. "This day is salvation come to this house, forasmuch as he also is a son of Abraham. For the Son of man is come to seek and to save that which was lost" (Luke 19:9-10).

Have you ever considered the miracle that Jesus found you where He did and saved you?

C. I Celebrate That Jesus Sought for Me and Changed Me

People love a good party or celebration. There is something about getting together with people you love and celebrating a milestone or accomplishment. The laughter, the fun, the memories we make are some of life's best treasures. However, out of all the holidays, birthdays, anniversaries, and other celebrations of life, none deserve more rejoicing than the day of our salvation. There is no greater day in our lives than the day Jesus found us and saved us. That day is far greater than all the other celebrations in life combined.

Remember, just as Heaven rejoiced at the day of our salvation, we should also rejoice. We should celebrate the deliverance and spiritual freedom God has given us. Make every day a reason to recall what the Lord has done and rejoice in His presence.

It had to be a strange feeling for Zacchaeus to realize Jesus knew where he was and that Jesus also knew Zacchaeus was lost. But he would not be lost for long. Pardon the pun, but like Zacchaeus, we were a little "short" when it came to being saved. One day we went looking for Jesus. We knew where we were, but we also knew we were lost. Just like Zacchaeus, it was a startling realization that Jesus was already seeking for us.

Think back to the moment you realized you were lost and needed God to save you. Then think about when you were born again of the water and the Spirit. There is no feeling on earth quite like it. Once we realize we have been saved, God gives wonderful joy. Every day we should seek to recapture that same joy. The words of the hymn "Amazing Grace" need to become our testimony, "I once was lost, but now I'm found."

INTERNALIZING THE MESSAGE

A supplemental image is available in the Resource Kit. ⓘ

Six-year-old Cody Sheehy made headlines when he vanished into the freezing wilderness of northeast Oregon. Thankfully, he made it out safely after eighteen hours of determined slogging. When he retraced his steps thirty-two years later, Sheehy said getting lost was one of the best life lessons he ever had.

He had weighed about forty pounds and stood three-and-a-half feet tall. His family was living in a remote area of Wallowa County, Oregon, and one day Cody got lost in those woods while playing with his older sister during a picnic. Within a short time, a search party began looking for him. They went back and forth across the Blue Mountains on horseback all night. Rain started to fall, and the temperature was barely above freezing. They never found Cody.

However, he did not stay lost. Some would say he found himself. He simply began walking. He walked between fourteen and twenty miles over the next eighteen hours. He eventually walked out of the mountains and into the Wallowa Valley. His walk was quite eventful as he fell into a river and climbed a tree to escape two terrifying coyotes. He was cold and exhausted. His experience caused him to develop acute tendonitis in his ankles that put him on crutches for a week. But he literally saved himself from being lost.

Like Cody, we were all lost. However, there are two major differences between his story and ours. First, we cannot find ourselves spiritually. We do not have the power within ourselves to save ourselves from sin. No matter how hard we try, we will still be lost.

Secondly, Jesus never stopped looking for us. While the elements and time worked against those looking for Cody, Jesus never lets anything stand in the way of Him finding a lost person. The parables of the lost coin and the lost sheep are evidence of that. The story of Jesus going out of His way to find Zacchaeus shows us just how much He loves the lost.

Whether you were lost in the house, separated from the sheepfold, or Jesus found you up a tree somewhere, He was looking for you and did not stop looking until He found you.

Prayer Focus
Lead the group in prayer and consider the following topics of focus:
- For God to seek and save those who are lost
- For God to help us rejoice when He seeks and saves the lost

ES

WITNESSES OF THE RESURRECTION

FOCUS VERSES
Luke 24:46-48
[46] And said unto them, Thus it is written, and thus it behooved Christ to suffer, and to rise from the dead the third day: [47] And that repentance and remission of sins should be preached in his name among all nations, beginning at Jerusalem. [48] And ye are witnesses of these things.

LESSON TEXT
Luke 24:1-9, 13-16, 25-38, 44-48

TRUTH ABOUT GOD
The resurrection of Jesus Christ inspires believers to share the good news of the gospel.

TRUTH FOR MY LIFE
We must be witnesses of the Resurrection to those who have not yet heard.

Thinking about Last Week:

Have students refer to their Daily Devotional Guide to answer the following questions:
1. What most affected you as you read through the Lesson Text and the Biblical Insights?
2. How did it shape your prayers and thoughts throughout the week?
3. Do you feel you grew closer to the Lord this past week? Why or why not?

SG TEACHING OUTLINE

Icebreaker: Have you ever been around a celebrity and didn't know it?

Lesson Connection: Share the Lesson Connection.

I.   WOMEN WERE THE FIRST WITNESSES TO THE RESURRECTION

A.   They Remembered Jesus' Words and Told the Disciples about the Resurrection

B.   We Must Remember His Promises
   » *How did you feel immediately following your experience of receiving the Holy Ghost? Does that change as we age?*

II. THE TWO MEN FROM EMMAUS WITNESSED THE RESURRECTION I
   » *How would you have felt if you were one of those two disciples? Do we sometimes doubt who Jesus is because we are disappointed?*

A.   When They Realized Jesus Had Been with Them, They Left to Tell the Disciples about the Resurrection

B.   We Must Not Allow Disappointment to Blind Us from Recognizing Jesus Is with Us
   » *Have you ever experienced disappointment so severe you could not think straight? Can you share how God helped you survive that experience?*

III. THE DISCIPLES WITNESSED THE RESURRECTION

A.   Jesus Appeared and Told Them to Tell Others about the Resurrection
   » *Since Jesus commanded His disciples to preach repentance and remission of sins, how important is it for us to share the gospel with others?*

B.   We Must Believe in the Reality of the Resurrection

IV. THE WITNESS OF THE RESURRECTION IS ALL AROUND US TODAY

A.   We Witness the Resurrection by Experiencing the Gospel

B.   We Must Be Witnesses of the Resurrection to Those Who Have Not Yet Heard
   » *Have you received the Holy Ghost? How will you share that experience with others?*

Internalizing the Message V

Prayer Focus
Lead the group in prayer and consider the following topics of focus:
• For God to give us faith to believe the gospel
• For God to give us courage to share the gospel

LESSON CONNECTION

A trained salesman did his best to sell shoes, but he was unsuccessful, no matter how hard he tried. He went back to the factory and complained to the supervisor. "There must be something wrong with the shoes," he declared confidently. He was sure his low sales numbers were not his fault.

As they were talking, an older gentleman entered the office. The supervisor introduced the gentleman to the salesman as the company's highly respected owner. The supervisor shared the salesman's complaints with the owner and asked for his help to solve the problem the salesman was having selling the company's shoes. The owner remarked he never had any trouble selling the shoes, and then he continued to elaborate on the excellence of the product. He was confident in their quality because he had made the first pair of shoes and knew firsthand the value of the leather chosen for his brand of shoes, boots, and sandals. He knew the highest quality of thread and adhesives were used to hold them together. Their premium quality guaranteed they would last a long time and provide many years of comfort and protection.

The young salesman was amazed at the story behind the shoes and the quality care put into making them. With this information, he went back to work with a new admiration for the products he sold. And for many years he was the company's number one salesperson, earning multiple awards and bonuses. Knowing the value of the product was a game-changer for the salesman, who used to look with disdain at the pair of shoes he wore from the factory where he worked.

Those who meet the Creator and experience the life-changing gospel will be the most effective in representing Him in the world. To best share the gospel with others, we must first experience it for ourselves.

BIBLE LESSON

I. WOMEN WERE THE FIRST WITNESSES TO THE RESURRECTION

Mary Magdalene carried some of the spices required for burial. When her friends finally arrived, she could hardly hold herself back. She was walking so fast that her friend Joanna tried to slow her down.

"Mary, what's your hurry? He's not going anywhere."

Mary couldn't put her finger on why she was running, but an urgency rose in her heart. As they got closer to the tomb, they were astonished to find the large stone that covered the opening already had been removed. To her surprise, Jesus' body was missing. The group of women just stood there shocked. The tomb was empty.

A. They Remembered Jesus' Words and Told the Disciples about the Resurrection

Suddenly two men appeared in shining, white apparel. Fear gripped the women's hearts, and they immediately dropped to their knees with their faces toward the ground. The men asked, "Why seek ye the living among the dead? He is not here, but is risen" (Luke 24:5-6). As the angels spoke, the women were astonished. As hope rose in their hearts, they ran to excitedly tell the disciples what they had seen and heard. It is not clear why the disciples didn't believe the women at first. Peter and John bolted from the group and ran to find everything just as the women had reported. John stooped down and peered inside, but Peter ran past John and into the empty tomb.

B. We Must Remember His Promises

Jesus promised He would be with us always and never leave us (Hebrews 13:5). Yet we trudge along, groaning about how hard it is to get through life alone. Just as Jesus promised He would rise on the third day, He also promised new life through the Holy Ghost. (See John 14:16-17.) Jesus promised power through His name when we receive the Holy Ghost (Luke 24:49). As Christians, we live far below our privilege when we forget God's promises.

The promises of God are sure (II Corinthians 1:20). We can count on them. When Jesus prophesied that He would rise from the grave on the third day after His death, the disciples should have expected it to happen. Unfortunately, because of their lack of faith, they almost missed one of the most important parts of the plan of Christ. Jesus planned to be alive and working among us after He died and rose again. The fact that Jesus is alive is central to God's plan of salvation.

How did you feel immediately following your experience of receiving the Holy Ghost? Does that change as we age?

267

II. THE TWO MEN FROM EMMAUS WITNESSED THE RESURRECTION

Cleopas and his friend were walking from Jerusalem to Emmaus, deeply engaged in conversation about Jesus. Then out of nowhere, a stranger joined them. We know it was Jesus, but they did not. The Bible says they saw Him, but they did not recognize Him as Jesus (Luke 24:16). When Jesus asked why they were so downcast, they were astonished that someone in the vicinity had not heard about Jesus and His crucifixion.

How would you have felt if you were one of those two disciples? Do we sometimes doubt who Jesus is because we are disappointed?

Finally Jesus responded to their doubt-filled discussion. He explained that all that had happened was documented in the ancient, inspired writings. He expounded on the prophets' words, but the two disciples still did not recognize Him. He went with them to eat in the village, and as He broke bread, their eyes were opened. What a surprise to realize this was the resurrected Jesus. Within seconds, He vanished.

A. When They Realized Jesus Had Been with Them, They Left to Tell the Disciples about the Resurrection

What a beautiful moment when Cleopas and his companion realized they had been talking with the resurrected Christ. Immediately they rushed back to Jerusalem to seek out the other disciples. Knowing the validity of truth inspires us to share it more readily with others. According to Acts 1:3, the time span between Jesus' resurrection and ascension was forty days. During this time, numerous passages of Scripture testify that Jesus appeared to many people, eating and walking and talking with them. People had multiple opportunities to discover that Jesus rose from the dead and was alive again.

B. We Must Not Allow Disappointment to Blind Us from Recognizing Jesus Is with Us

Have you ever experienced disappointment so severe you could not think straight? Can you share how God helped you survive that experience?

It would be easy to allow disappointment and dismay to become our focus when we are going through difficulties. As we see in this passage, many followers of Jesus only focused on Jesus' crucifixion. We must be careful to turn our attention to the one who will never leave us or forsake us, especially during harsh trials that try to crush our faith. We must look beyond our present circumstances and hold onto the promise that Jesus is right here with us. We must allow His presence to be our focus.

III. THE DISCIPLES WITNESSED THE RESURRECTION

A. Jesus Appeared and Told Them to Tell Others about the Resurrection

As the two men who walked to Emmaus ate with the disciples, Jesus appeared in their presence. He spoke to them saying, "Peace be unto you." Still, when He appeared, they were terrified. They thought He was a ghost. Jesus assured them He was not a ghost because He had flesh and bones. He then allowed them to see His hands and His feet, but they were still having trouble realizing the impact of that signal moment. Then Jesus asked for something to eat as He ate with them and expounded on the Scriptures.

What a revelation it was to hear Jesus teaching once again. Jesus used that moment to confirm who He was and that His work would continue. These disciples would carry on His mission after He ascended. He was indeed the Messiah but not in the way they originally thought. Jesus' kingdom was going to be heavenly, not earthly. Jesus spent time teaching His followers and reminding them that the promise of the Father would live on.

In Luke 24:47–49 Jesus commissioned His disciples to preach repentance and remission of sins in His name. As Christ's eyewitnesses they would bear the responsibility of sharing the good news. Jesus instructed them to wait in Jerusalem until the promise of the Father endued them with power from on high. This was a prophecy of the promise of the Holy Ghost, which came to those waiting in an upper room on the Day of Pentecost. (See Acts 2.)

Since Jesus commanded His disciples to preach repentance and remission of sins, how important is it for us to share the gospel with others?

B. We Must Believe in the Reality of the Resurrection

As twenty-first century believers, we are generations removed from the people who witnessed the resurrection of Christ in real time. However, as we read, hear, and believe the account of the Resurrection, we have firsthand experience because we feel and know that God lives in our hearts. We experience the reality of the Resurrection. We must have faith and believe that Jesus lived, died, and rose again the third day. The disciples fulfilled Jesus' commandments. On the Day of Pentecost, they instructed those who gathered on how they could experience the promise Jesus spoke of through the gospel.

> *"Then Peter said unto them, Repent, and be baptized every one of you in the name of Jesus Christ for the remission of sins, and ye shall receive the gift of the Holy Ghost. For the promise is unto you, and to your children, and to all that are afar off, even as many as the Lord our God shall call" (Acts 2:38–39).*

IV. THE WITNESS OF THE RESURRECTION IS ALL AROUND US TODAY

Jesus was the most obvious witness of the Resurrection to His followers. They may have questioned what they saw, but they could not deny that He talked to them, ate with them, and allowed them to see and feel His hands and feet. Just as Jesus took the time to walk among humanity for forty days before returning to glory, we can witness the resurrection of Christ all around us today.

A. We Witness the Resurrection by Experiencing the Gospel

Believing is the first part of the journey. Our faith calls us to act upon our belief. When we believe that Jesus lived, died, and rose again, we agree that He did what He promised to do. Although we were not there nearly two thousand years ago, we can witness the Resurrection by experiencing all God has for us. God plans for us to be resurrected from death to life. He made the way for us to be saved from sin, delivered from death, and raised up to new life. The gospel—the death, burial, and Resurrection—is an illustration of our salvation.

> *"Therefore we are buried with him by baptism into death: that like as Christ was raised up from the dead by the glory of the Father, even so we also should walk in newness of life" (Romans 6:4).*

Secondly, we identify with Christ through His death, burial, and resurrection. Death is dying out to sin. We die out to sin through repentance, or turning from sin. Repentance calls us to walk away from all the things that separate us from Christ. When we repent, we ask God to forgive our sins so we can walk closely with Him. He is faithful to forgive us when we repent.

We identify with Christ's burial and take on His name when we are baptized in Jesus' name. Just as Jesus was buried in a tomb, we are buried in a watery grave of baptism. This is one reason baptism must be by immersion. According to Romans 6:4, we identify with Jesus' death when we are buried in baptism.

We experience the power of His resurrection through the infilling of the Holy Ghost. Peter spoke of the Resurrection when he preached on the Day of Pentecost only a few days after Christ ascended into Heaven. Jesus' words were still fresh in his mind. He stood up and declared that the people who were hungry for the promise of the Father should repent, be baptized in the name of Jesus, and they would experience resurrection through the baptism of the Holy Ghost. (See Acts 2:38.)

B. We Must Be Witnesses of the Resurrection to Those Who Have Not Yet Heard

It is crucial that we experience the full process of the Resurrection and that we share our experience with those who have not heard. We are experiencing the power of the gospel when we identify with Christ through His death, burial, and resurrection. Jesus told those who witnessed His resurrection to preach about it, proclaiming this glorious experience to all nations, beginning at Jerusalem (Luke 24:47).

Have you received the Holy Ghost? How will you share that experience with others?

Today we can mirror the mission by preaching salvation through the death, burial, and resurrection of Christ. It is still applicable today just as it was when Peter preached in Jerusalem. It is critical to Christ's mission that we follow His blueprint for salvation.

INTERNALIZING THE MESSAGE

A supplemental video is available in the Resource Kit. (V)

In the late 1940s, Brownie Wise first saw Tupperware, a new polyethylene product for food storage, which was being sold with limited success at department stores. Wise was a successful branch manager for a well-known home party company. With her zeal and philosophy of sales, she convinced several other managers that Tupperware should be sold at home parties because users needed to learn how to "burp" the airtight seal correctly. Wise switched over to this new product, recruited dealers and managers, and thrived by selling Tupperware at home parties. Wise started a company she called Tupperware Patio Parties and sold far more Tupperware than the stores. Her success caught the attention of the chemist Earl Tupper, who created the lightweight, non-breakable plastic containers in 1946. Tupper saw an opportunity to make home parties successful, and he asked Wise to become the vice president of his company. Earl Tupper took Tupperware out of the hardware and department stores to sell it exclusively through the home party plan.

It is much easier to sell something you believe in. A young believer, who loved God but was extremely shy, struggled sharing Him with others because she was so afraid to talk. In time, she had the opportunity to use and sell Tupperware. The experience changed her life as she excitedly shared her enthusiasm for this product. One day after a party, while she was driving home, the Lord spoke to her, "If you can sell Tupperware, you can share the gospel." She truly believed that the gospel was a lifeboat to those drowning in the sea of sin. This otherwise shy young woman found the boldness to begin sharing Christ with her friends and coworkers.

If we have experienced the saving power of Jesus Christ, we can share it with others. We don't have to be theologians or scholars to share our testimony with others. Experiencing the death, burial, and Resurrection through the gospel of Jesus Christ is enough to begin sharing our story. Proclaim it. We have witnessed firsthand what His gospel can do for us. We can fulfill His mission because we are true witnesses of the Resurrection.

Prayer Focus
Lead the group in prayer and consider the following topics of focus:
- For God to give us faith to believe the gospel
- For God to give us courage to share the gospel

2.2

COVERED BY THE BLOOD

FOCUS VERSE
Exodus 12:23
For the LORD will pass through to smite the Egyptians; and when he seeth the blood upon the lintel, and on the two side posts, the LORD will pass over the door, and will not suffer the destroyer to come in unto your houses to smite you.

LESSON TEXT
Exodus 12:21–27;
Matthew 27:33–54

TRUTH ABOUT GOD
Jesus Christ's shed blood delivers us from sin.

TRUTH FOR MY LIFE
I will live above the power of sin in my life.

Thinking about Last Week:

Have students refer to their Daily Devotional Guide to answer the following questions:
1. What most affected you as you read through the Lesson Text and the Biblical Insights?
2. How did it shape your prayers and thoughts throughout the week?
3. Do you feel you grew closer to the Lord this past week? Why or why not?

[SG] TEACHING OUTLINE

Icebreaker: What are some funny phrases Christians say that others may not understand?

Lesson Connection: Share the Lesson Connection.

I. THE PRACTICE OF PASSOVER

    A. Though Israel Was Captive in Slavery, God Brought About Their Deliverance

        » *Have you realized that some of the things that happen in your life might be God trying to get your attention?*

        » *Have you ever considered the physical actions the people had to perform to offer sacrifices to God?*

    B. I Will Have Peace Because Jesus' Blood Protects My Life

II. JESUS DIED AT PASSOVER

        » *How can you show Jesus your gratitude for being our ultimate sacrifice?*

    A. Though Humanity was Captive in Slavery to Sin, Jesus Brought Deliverance [V]

    B. I Will Actively Thank Him for the Forgiveness of Sin

        » *Do you view every day as a way to actively express your thanks to God?*

III. HIS BLOOD PRODUCES FREEDOM IN MY LIFE

    A. Freedom from the Penalty, Power, and Practice of Sin

        » *Have you ever compared the struggle in Romans 7 to the freedom in Romans 8?*

    B. I Will Live above the Power of Sin in My Life

Internalizing the Message [I]

Prayer Focus
Lead the group in prayer and consider the following topics of focus:
- For God to help us be grateful for the price He paid for us
- For God to help us live above the power of sin

LESSON CONNECTION

When California gold fever broke out, a man traveled west to strike it rich. He left his wife in New England with their son. As soon as he arrived and found gold, he was planning to send for them. A long time passed and he still had not struck gold, but he made enough money to send for them. His wife's heart leaped for joy. She took their son to New York, boarded a Pacific steamer, and sailed away to San Francisco.

They had not been long at sea before the cry rang through the ship, "Fire! Fire!" Gunpowder was on board, and the captain knew the moment the fire reached the powder, every man, woman, and child would perish. The ship crew broke out the lifeboats, but the boats were too small. In a minute the lifeboats were overcrowded. The last boat was just pushing away when the mother pled with them to take her and her boy. They replied, "No, we have as many as we can hold."

She begged them so much until they finally agreed to take one more passenger. She held her son in her arms, gave him one last hug, kissed him, and dropped him over the burning ship into the lifeboat. She cried out, "My boy, if you live to see your father, tell him that I died in your place."

As the preacher D. L. Moody shared that story, he gave the following altar call. "That is a faint type of what Christ has done for us. He laid down His life for us. He died that we might live. Now will you not love Him? What would you say of that young man if he should speak contemptuously of such a mother? She went down to a watery grave to save her son. Well, shall we speak contemptuously of such a Saviour? May God make us loyal to Christ! My friends, you will need Him one day. You will need Him when you come to cross the swellings of Jordan. You will need Him when you stand at the bar of God. May God forbid that when death draws nigh it should find you making light of the precious blood of Christ!" (D. L. Moody, *Anecdotes and Illustrations of D.L. Moody*).

BIBLE LESSON

I. THE PRACTICE OF PASSOVER

As we age, we tend to think more about dying. Ecclesiastes 8:8 reads, "There is no man that hath power over the spirit to retain the spirit; neither hath he power in the day of death: and there is no discharge in that war." We all will face death one day; that reality cannot be avoided.

We can only imagine how prisoners on death row feel when facing an execution date. The utter hopelessness would be beyond comprehension. But imagine the overwhelming exhilaration if they were told someone else had volunteered to die in their place. The prisoners know they are guilty and will die for their crimes, yet some stranger has stepped in and assumed their crimes and the penalty that goes with them. That means the actual guilty one will go free. Through a substitutionary death, the guilty is now declared not guilty.

The children of Israel may have experienced a piece of this feeling every Passover celebration. They knew that sin had broken their relationship with God. They realized they were guilty and deserved to die. Without a payment for their sin, they could only look forward to death. Hebrews 9:22 declares, "And almost all things are by the law purged with blood; and without shedding of blood is no remission." If no blood was offered as a sacrifice for sin, their sins would not be remitted.

A. Though Israel Was Captive in Slavery, God Brought About Their Deliverance

Israel lived under bondage to the Egyptians. They spent 430 years in captivity, far removed from their homeland. Each passing day brought a greater sense of hopelessness. Most likely, there were days they wondered if God had forsaken them and left them to die in Egypt. But they were God's chosen people. He was not about to leave them or forsake them.

To affect their release, God sent Moses and Aaron to the house of Pharoah to demand he let God's people go. Time after time Pharoah refused. With each refusal God sent a new plague to convince Pharoah to free the Jewish people.

At the first Passover, God instructed the man of each Jewish household to kill a young lamb or goat that had no defects. Each family was to roast and eat the sacrifice. Any leftover meat was to be burned. They were to eat fully dressed, with their sandals on and their walking sticks in their hands.

Some of the lamb's blood was to be taken and smeared on the top and sides of the door-posts of each home. The marking of that blood brought the true meaning of Passover into their lives.

Have you realized that some of the things that happen in your life might be God trying to get your attention?

Have you ever considered the physical actions the people had to perform to offer sacrifices to God?

275

To deliver His people, God went throughout the land of Egypt. (See Exodus 12:12.) If the blood was not applied to the home, the firstborn of every household would die. God promised Moses, "When I see the blood, I will pass over you" (Exodus 12:13); hence the term *Passover*. God passed over the lives of those marked by the blood of the sacrifice, thus sparing them from death. Israel understood there was no deliverance without the covering of blood. The morning after that first Passover, Israel experienced a peace they had not felt in years. They were no longer captives; they were free.

B. I Will Have Peace Because Jesus' Blood Protects My Life

We can experience that same peace and freedom today through Jesus Christ. While sin has wreaked havoc in our lives and kept us bound, Jesus shed His own blood to bring us peace.

Isaiah 9:6 promises that the coming Messiah will be the Prince of Peace. Jesus is indeed our peace. To better understand how He is the Prince of Peace, let's look at another Old Testament feast, the Day of Atonement. It is the highest holy day on the Jewish calendar, during which the high priest offered a sacrifice for the sins of the people. That sacrifice reconciled the people to God. Then the high priest released a goat into the wilderness, symbolizing the carrying away of the sins of the people. This scapegoat would never return to the camp of Israel.

One could say the sacrifice of atonement restored the broken relationship between man and God. It also brought peace to the relationship. The Hebrew word for peace is shalom. It means wholeness, completeness, and a sense of permanence. Jesus took that which was broken and put it back together again.

Atonement is taking that which was broken and bringing it back together—to one again. That is exactly what Jesus did. Through His death, burial, and resurrection, He set our broken relationship with Him at one again. It is comforting to know we have the Prince of Peace no matter what circumstances life might bring our way.

Jesus' shed blood brings peace to the turmoil in our minds and spirits. Because Jesus was our atonement, His sacrificial blood paid the penalty for our sins, and we live with a peace far greater than anything else in life could ever bring.

II. JESUS DIED AT PASSOVER

For Israel, Passover was not to be a one-time event. The Lord commanded Passover to be observed on an annual basis. Exodus 12:3–6 was the beginning of the instructions for Passover. "Speak ye unto all the congregation of Israel, saying, In the tenth day of this month they shall take to them every man a lamb, according to the house of their fathers, a lamb for an house: and if the household be too little for the lamb, let him and his neighbour next unto his house take it according to the number of the souls; every man according to his eating shall make your count for the lamb. Your lamb shall be without blemish, a male of the first year: ye shall take it out from the sheep, or from the goats: and ye shall keep it up until the fourteenth day of the same month: and the whole assembly of the congregation of Israel shall kill it in the evening."

God never intended for Israel to only celebrate Passover during their deliverance from Egypt. Exodus 12:25–27 lets us know they were to observe Passover in the Promised Land. Every sacrificial animal pointed to the ultimate sacrifice, Jesus Christ. He would be God manifested in the flesh to redeem all humanity. Jesus would carry all the sins of the world and pay the payment to bring remission.

In the year Jesus died, the Jews again celebrated Passover by killing a lamb for the Temple sacrifice. During their normal celebration and offering, they missed the fact that Jesus died as the final sacrifice of atonement. When He cried from the cross, "It is finished," He was declaring an end to offering blood sacrifices for the sin of the people.

How can you show Jesus your gratitude for being our ultimate sacrifice?

A. Though Humanity Was Captive in Slavery to Sin, Jesus Brought Deliverance

Year after year sacrificial lambs were offered at Passover. Year after year the sins of the people were rolled ahead in anticipation of the arrival of the Messiah. When John the Baptist saw Jesus, John declared, "Behold the Lamb of God, which taketh away the sin of the world" (John 1:29). Paul wrote to the church in Ephesus, "In whom we have redemption through his blood, the forgiveness of sins, according to the riches of his grace" (Ephesians 1:7).

These verses of Scripture and a myriad of others all point to the fact that Jesus Christ was our atonement. We no longer bring a sacrificial lamb or goat to present to God. Instead, we point to Jesus Christ, the Lamb that took away the sin of the world. By His death He delivered the world from the bondage of sin. His death, burial, and resurrection allow people to find a way through the new-birth experience to truly be free from sin.

Teacher Option: *A supplemental video is available in the Resource Kit.* **V**

B. I Will Actively Thank Him for the Forgiveness of Sin

Although Passover had somber overtones, it was a time of rejoicing for the people. They expressed their gratitude to God for forgiving their sins and allowing them to move forward in their relationship with Him. The incredible sense of thanksgiving filled them. By living a life pleasing to God, they were actively expressing thanks to Him. Our lives should be the same. When we understand the incredible price Jesus paid to forgive our sin, we should be filled with gratitude. Every day we live should be a day we thank Him for the gift of forgiveness.

Do you view every day as a way to actively express your thanks to God?

277

III.   HIS BLOOD PRODUCES FREEDOM IN MY LIFE

The result of the atonement was twofold. First, the sins of the people were rolled ahead through the innocent blood of a sacrifice. Secondly, the people walked into their tomorrow without the weight of those sins. They experienced freedom that could only be produced by the sacrifice of atonement.

When Jesus died at Calvary, forgiveness was provided for all the sins of humanity. Secondly, when we have had Jesus' blood applied to our lives through the new-birth experience, God grants us freedom we have never felt before.

A. Freedom from the Penalty, Power, and Practice of Sin

From the beginning God told us the penalty of sin is death. "The soul that sinneth, it shall die" (Ezekiel 18:20). However, because Jesus Christ willingly suffered the punishment for our sin, the penalty of our sin is forever removed from our lives when we are born again. The apostle Paul let us know that the blood of Christ has destroyed the power of sin in our lives. He spent the entire seventh chapter of the Book of Romans detailing the power of sin in our lives. He was quick to tell us that neither the law of God nor our conscience can deliver us from the power of sin.

Have you ever compared the struggle in Romans 7 to the freedom in Romans 8?

The struggle is real, and the battle is intense. The only real victory and power over sin is through the blood of Jesus Christ.

B. I Will Live above the Power of Sin in My Life

Ultimately, how we live our lives is our choice. Every day we will make choices throughout the day that will be a testimony of how we have decided to live our lives. Paul began the eighth chapter of Romans with these words, "There is therefore now no condemnation to them which are in Christ Jesus, who walk not after the flesh, but after the Spirit" (Romans 8:1).

The power of the Spirit becomes the source of our strength. As we live for Him and walk in the Spirit, the desire for sin will fade away. The closing verses of Romans 8 are so powerful. They testify that nothing has the power to separate us from the love of God.

INTERNALIZING THE MESSAGE

A supplemental image is available in the Resource Kit. [I]

One of the most hopeless places on earth would be death row. The cells might only be eight by ten feet. Crammed into that small cell is a bed, toilet, and sink. A few inmates also have a desk and chair shoved into their limited space. Their cell is about the size of the average bathroom in your house. Imagine having a bed, toilet, sink, desk, and chair all shoved into a room approximately the size of your bathroom. And you're locked in there for twenty-three hours per day.

Physical activity is limited to sleeping, showering, and perhaps an occasional visitor. Some prisons allow an hour or so for exercise in the prison yard. The average length of time a prisoner lives on death row awaiting execution is more than fifteen years. Shockingly, forty percent of these inmates have been there over twenty years. It has become common for prisoners to die on death row from sickness or other natural causes.

While the physical routine would be maddening enough, we can only imagine how terrifying the mental anguish is, living every day knowing you are condemned to die for a crime you committed. What would your thoughts be with each passing day? Would you hold out hope for a last-minute stay of execution? Would you dream about the governor of your state issuing an 11:59 PM pardon?

We all have been living our lives on a spiritual death row. We are guilty as charged. Like all others who have sinned, we are condemned to die for our sin. But from time to time, we dream about finally being set free. We long to break out of the prison of sin. Yet, no matter how much we dream about it, there seems to be no way out. There is no last-minute reprieve or pardon. It seems we are destined to die in our sin.

Until now. According to II Corinthians 6:2, "Now is the day of salvation." Jesus Christ has stepped into the prison of sin in our lives and offered to take our place. He has already died so we can live. He became bound to the cross so we could be spiritually free.

His atoning sacrifice at Calvary covered our sin. We can find our way to freedom through repentance and having our sins washed away by being baptized in the name of Jesus Christ. Then we can become new creatures in Him by receiving His Spirit. Jesus removes the condemnation of sin by allowing us to walk in the Spirit. This results in us never being separated from the love He has for us. What amazing love. He died for us so we can live.

Prayer Focus
Lead the group in prayer and consider the following topics of focus:
- For God to help us be grateful for the price He paid for us
- For God to help us live above the power of sin

2.3

YOU MUST BE BORN AGAIN

FOCUS VERSE
John 3:3
Jesus answered and said unto him, Verily, verily, I say unto thee, Except a man be born again, he cannot see the kingdom of God.

LESSON TEXT
John 3:1–21

TRUTH ABOUT GOD
God's method of salvation remains unchanged since the Passion.

TRUTH FOR MY LIFE
I will firmly establish my faith on the Apostolic message of new birth.

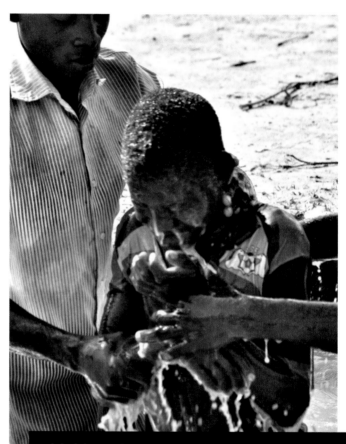

Thinking about Last Week:

Have students refer to their Daily Devotional Guide to answer the following questions:

1. What most affected you as you read through the Lesson Text and the Biblical Insights?
2. How did it shape your prayers and thoughts throughout the week?
3. Do you feel you grew closer to the Lord this past week? Why or why not?

SG TEACHING OUTLINE

Icebreaker: Which of Jesus' twelve disciples do you most identify with?

Lesson Connection: Share the Lesson Connection.
> » *Why do you think it is hard for some people to leave behind their old lives to follow Jesus?*

I.   JESUS MEETS NICODEMUS

    A.   Nicodemus Had Some Questions about Jesus
> » *Why do you think God delights in giving us second chances?*

    B.   The Answer Is to Be Born Again
> » *Do you understand the message of new birth in a way that you could explain to others?*

    C.   I Must Be Willing to Share this Message with a "Nicodemus"

II.   JESUS MEETS EACH OF US Ⓘ
> » *Do you recall where you were and the feelings you experienced when Jesus met you?*

    A.   People Wrestle with Spiritual Questions

    B.   The Commandment Is to Be Born Again
> » *Have you been born again?*

    C.   I Will Remain Committed to the Apostolic Message of New Birth

Internalizing the Message Ⓥ

Prayer Focus
Lead the group in prayer and consider the following topics of focus:
- For God to help us live as born-again believers
- For God to help us share the gospel so other people can be born again

LESSON CONNECTION

In 1954, first-time parents John and Angelena bought their infant daughter a miniature toy piano. A third-generation piano teacher, Angelena was determined her daughter would carry on the family legacy of pianists. At three years old, their little girl began taking piano lessons from Grandmother and quickly mastered the art of reading music before she could yet read English.

The plan seemed perfect and progressed splendidly. At age fifteen, the young pianist entered the University of Denver as a music major. At seventeen she was accepted into a highly competitive summer music program in Aspen that plunged her already intensive studies into even stricter focus.

Yet somehow, the gifted student began to feel something was amiss. As she worked with piano prodigies and genius instructors, slowly she realized with acute pain that her feet were headed down the wrong path. In the most difficult conversation of her young life, the college student sat down with her proud parents and broke the traumatic news that she could no longer be a music major.

The family reeled, her parents shattered by the wrecked plans and their daughter overwhelmed by a lost sense of identity and grappling with the new sentiment of purposelessness. Amid this sea of uncertainty, the former pianist entered a class in international politics. Immediately she was captured by a sense of belonging—this world felt like home!

The professor took an interest and began the mentoring journey. So it was that in abandoning one life, Condoleezza Rice began a new one. Through one change of life direction, the would-be piano teacher became a world leader who helped navigate the fall of the Berlin Wall and the collapse of the Twin Towers. Her decision that seemed at the time an abandonment of one life gave way to a new life that had ripple effects around the entire globe.

Sadly many people miss their purpose and cope with lifelong regrets because they refuse to abandon their old life and embrace a new one. While such regrets are disappointing in the natural, reluctance to release the old and embrace new life in Jesus Christ is of eternal significance we must address. The resounding message of Scripture is that surrender to God erases the past as He gives us new life rich with hope and promise.

Why do you think it is hard for some people to leave behind their old lives to follow Jesus?

BIBLE LESSON

I. JESUS MEETS NICODEMUS

Nicodemus sought a private meeting with Jesus at night (John 3:2). Hours earlier the sun splashed the western sky with bright orange and pink. Just minutes later, the sun disappeared as darkness settled in. Perhaps Nicodemus chose to meet Jesus at night so no one else would see him spending time with the controversial figure. After all, Nicodemus was a Pharisee and a ruler of the Jews. Such a meeting with such a man could endanger Nicodemus's standing and position in the community.

A. Nicodemus Had Some Questions about Jesus

No matter why they met at night, Nicodemus had some questions only Jesus could answer. These questions went far beyond basic theology, otherwise Nicodemus could have answered them himself or asked some of his many educated colleagues.

Nicodemus opened the conversation with Jesus by calling Him Rabbi. He even acknowledged Jesus was sent from God. Nicodemus opened by showing respect and quickly recognized the miracles Jesus had performed, "No man can do these miracles that thou doest, except God be with him" (John 3:2).

Nicodemus appeared to be asking Jesus two questions: who are You really, and what do these miracles mean that You are performing? Jesus' response is both compelling and captivating. He did not respond to the compliments Nicodemus lobbed His way. Neither did Jesus answer the somewhat obscure questions hidden within them. Rather, Jesus went to the heart of the issue and answered the real question Nicodemus had not yet voiced. Jesus told him all about new birth (John 3:3–5). Perhaps this was Jesus' way of telling this curious Pharisee that He is the God of second chances.

Why do you think God delights in giving us second chances?

B. The Answer Is to Be Born Again

Jesus then introduced a concept foreign to Nicodemus's thinking and training. Jesus answered, "Verily, verily, I say unto thee, Except a man be born again, he cannot see the kingdom of God" (John 3:3). Jesus was answering Nicodemus's unasked question by telling him: you must be born again.

Nicodemus understood religion well. He was aware of the promise that the Messiah would come and bring salvation humanity so desperately needed. Yet Jesus told Nicodemus he needed to be born again if he wanted to see the kingdom of God he thought he knew so much about.

Instantly, Nicodemus began to wrestle with what he had just heard. More questions arose (John 3:4). How can a man be born when he is old? Is it even possible to enter his mother's womb a second time and be born? Can a grown man really be born again?

Nicodemus was attempting to answer a spiritual question with a physical explanation. He failed to realize Jesus was not speaking of the natural birth at all. It was a foregone conclusion that a person only has one natural birth. Therefore, the key to the answer was in the word again (John 3:3).

Jesus was not telling Nicodemus he had to do what he had already done or that he had to do something impossible. Jesus was quick to clarify what He meant after Nicodemus pressed Him with questions. Nicodemus was confused, so Jesus declared plainly, "Verily, verily, I say unto thee, Except a man be born of water and of the Spirit, he cannot enter into the kingdom of God. That which is born of the flesh is flesh; and that which is born of the Spirit is spirit" (John 3:5–6).

Jesus was not teaching about natural birth at all; He was teaching about spiritual birth. New birth is not the physical birth of a person but a rebirth of a person's spiritual life. It is a spiritual second chance—a do-over.

Jesus wanted everyone to know we must be born of water and of the Spirit to see and enter the kingdom of Heaven. Perhaps Nicodemus cocked his head at the thought of being born twice. The Lord knew what Nicodemus was thinking and asking in his own mind. Jesus calmly continued, "Marvel not that I said unto thee, Ye must be born again" (John 3:7). This message is not meant to be confusing at all. This hope and promise of a second chance is why the Messiah came. He came to make it possible for people to be born again of water and the Spirit. He came to transform our lives through a new-birth experience.

Do you understand the message of new birth in a way that you could explain to others?

C. I Must Be Willing to Share this Message with a "Nicodemus"

Chances are we know very few people named Nicodemus. In our world they are named Manuel, Meghan, Randall, Monique, David, and so on. No matter their name, we must be willing to share this new-birth message with them, like Jesus shared it with Nicodemus. People are looking for more out of life, and the answer is found in the new life Jesus offers.

Teacher Option: A supplemental image is available in the Resource Kit.

II. JESUS MEETS EACH OF US

In Acts chapter 10, a Gentile soldier named Cornelius hungered for more of God. An angel of God instructed Cornelius to send men to Joppa to the house of Simon the tanner because Simon Peter was staying there. Simon Peter would tell Cornelius how to be saved and get right with God. When the preacher arrived at the soldier's house, Peter made a powerful, bold declaration of faith: "Of a truth I perceive that God is no respecter of persons: but in every nation he that feareth him, and worketh righteousness, is accepted with him" (Acts 10:34–35).

Ask anyone whose life the Lord has transformed, and you will find that God meets each of us where we are. He knows the condition of our lives better than we do. Regardless of what is happening in our world or the mistakes we have made, God always extends an invitation to transform our lives through being born again.

Do you recall where you were and the feelings you experienced when Jesus met you?

A. People Wrestle with Spiritual Questions

Part of our maturing only happens through questioning. As we learn to speak, we begin asking questions, often centered around the words what and why. We want to know why things exist, what makes them work as they do, and why things are the way they are. The list of questions we will ask in our lifetime is endless.

Naturally, we also wrestle with spiritual questions. Since we know we were created for the purpose of relationship with God, we may sometimes ask, "Why does God want a relationship with me?" We might even ask, "What does that relationship look like?"

At some point we will all ask the question, "What does it really take to be saved and have this relationship with God?" This is the most important question any person will ever ask. This question drove Nicodemus to meet Jesus in the middle of the night.

B. The Commandment Is to Be Born Again

When we look again at the answer Jesus gave Nicodemus, we see how Scripture further explains it. The gospel, or the good news, saves us. The gospel message declares Jesus was born, He died at Calvary, and He resurrected from the grave on the third day to bring the opportunity for salvation to all humanity. The gospel shows us the hope of a new life. As we respond to the gospel through the new-birth experience, we find the abundant life Jesus promised us. (See John 10:10.)

The death, burial, and resurrection of Jesus is symbolized in our lives through the act of repentance, baptism, and receiving the Holy Ghost. When we repent of our sins, we recognize we must die out to sin. Romans 6:6–7 reads, "Knowing this, that our old man is crucified with him, that the body of sin might be destroyed, that henceforth we should not serve sin. For he that is dead is freed from sin."

We identify with His burial through water baptism in the name of Jesus Christ. Our baptism leads to our new life in the Spirit: "Know ye not, that so many of us as were baptized into Jesus Christ were baptized into his death? Therefore we are buried with him by baptism into death: that like as Christ was raised up from the dead by the glory of the Father, even so we also should walk in newness of life" (Romans 6:3–4).

Just as Jesus rose from the grave to new life, we rise from the waters of baptism to new life in Christ. Paul continued in Romans 6, "Therefore we are buried with him by baptism into death: that like as Christ was raised up from the dead by the glory of the Father, even so we also should walk in newness of life. For if we have been planted together in the likeness of his death, we shall be also in the likeness of his resurrection" (Romans 6:4–5).

Identifying with Jesus' death, burial, and resurrection is what Jesus referred to as new life during His discussion with Nicodemus. Being born of the water happens at water baptism. Just as being born of water means water baptism, being born of the Spirit means Spirit baptism.

Have you been born again?

C. I Will Remain Committed to the Apostolic Message of New Birth

Being born again is merely the beginning of our new life. Philippians 2:12 commands us, "Work out your own salvation with fear and trembling." We must commit every day to living for God. Numerous warnings in Scripture alert us to the dangers of falling away from our relationship with God. Being sure that our personal devotional life is a priority will help us remain committed to the new-birth message of hope and eternal life.

Paul told the church in Galatians 1:9, "If any man preach any other gospel unto you than that ye have received, let him be accursed." There is no other gospel than the death, burial, and resurrection of Jesus Christ. No other way fulfills our right response to the gospel than repentance, water baptism in Jesus' name, and the infilling of the Holy Spirit.

INTERNALIZING THE MESSAGE

A supplemental video is available in the Resource Kit. **V**

He was brash. Most every time he would start to speak, some of those around him would cringe. His impulsiveness had been on display several times in their short time together. Knowing the type of man he had been, it is miraculous to see the man he became.

His name was Simon Peter. He was quite the character during the three and a half years he spent with Jesus and the other disciples. One minute he could be sociable and engaging; the next he was almost repulsive in his mannerisms and speech. He vowed to follow Jesus to the death, only to deny Him three times within a few hours. In a moment of angry frustration, Peter drew a sword and cut off the ear of one of the men who came to arrest Jesus.

How does a man like Peter become the dynamic, anointed preacher who preached the greatest message of all time on the Day of Pentecost? It's quite simple. Peter was born again. He was given a do-over in life.

Peter's life story is a testimony to us of how radically new birth can change our lives. His story shows us the incredible power of transformation the Spirit brings to everyone who is sincerely hungry for a relationship with God.

If you are needing another chance at life, you are in the right place at the right time. You can be born again and find abundant life as Jesus intended for us to live. The moment we are born again, we begin to live a more abundant life. That first breath of the Spirit of God will undeniably prove what Paul said in II Corinthians 5:17, "Therefore if any man be in Christ, he is a new creature: old things are passed away; behold, all things are become new."

Prayer Focus

Lead the group in prayer and consider the following topics of focus:
- For God to help us live as born-again believers
- For God to help us share the gospel so other people can be born again

2.4

WELCOME TO THE FAMILY

FOCUS VERSE
Romans 8:15
For ye have not received the spirit of bondage again to fear; but ye have received the Spirit of adoption, whereby we cry, Abba, Father.

LESSON TEXT
II Samuel 9:1-13;
Romans 8:12-15

TRUTH ABOUT GOD
God gives each person the opportunity to live a new and better life.

TRUTH FOR MY LIFE
I will not live my life below my standing as God's child.

Thinking about Last Week:

Have students refer to their Daily Devotional Guide to answer the following questions:

1. What most affected you as you read through the Lesson Text and the Biblical Insights?
2. How did it shape your prayers and thoughts throughout the week?
3. Do you feel you grew closer to the Lord this past week? Why or why not?

SG TEACHING OUTLINE

Icebreaker: Who is your favorite lesser-known Bible character?

Lesson Connection: Share the Lesson Connection. Ⓘ

I. MEPHIBOSHETH'S ADOPTION

   A. Mephibosheth was Lame in His Feet

   B. The King Sought Out Mephibosheth and Adopted Him
      » *Can you recall the feeling when you realized God really does love you?*

   C. I Should Actively Seek for the Hurting

II. SPIRITUAL ADOPTION IN THE NEW TESTAMENT

   A. Every Person is Spiritually Lame
      » *Do you realize that you were born as a sinner?*

   B. The King of Kings Has Sought Us Out and Adopted Us into God's Family
      » *How should our lives be different once we realize God as a loving Father adopted us into His family?*

   C. We Have Rights and Privileges as Children of God
      » *Can you honestly say you see yourself as God sees you, as His son or daughter?*

   D. I Will No Longer Live My Life Below My Standing as His Child
      » *Are you living in the full hope of the promises God has made to you in His Word?*

Internalizing the Message Ⓥ

Prayer Focus
Lead the group in prayer and consider the following topics of focus:
• For God to help us be thankful He adopted us
• For God to help us care for others who still need to be spiritually adopted

LESSON CONNECTION

A supplemental image is available in the Resource Kit. ⓘ

Within every human being is the basic need of belonging. We desire family and community. The bond from one person to another is essential to our physical, mental, and emotional health. Even more important, it is critical to our spiritual health.

Merriam-Webster defines an *orphan* as a "child deprived by death of one or usually both parents." *Webster* defines *adopted* as "legally made the son or daughter of someone other than a biological parent." Orphans hope and need to be adopted.

When children lose their parents, they lose an essential connection to family that is necessary to be happy, healthy, and productive. Unless they are adopted into a loving and nurturing family, that connection may never be regained.

The World Orphans organization reports there are approximately 140 million orphans in the world. That means 140 million young children need a family to love them and believe in them. They need parents who will take them in regardless of where they come from. Those parents will help them focus on their future and not on their past. Ultimately and ideally, these children will grow up to be healthy, happy, and productive. They in turn will raise children who will do the same.

Just like physical orphans, we were all spiritual orphans. We needed a spiritual family to take us in and nurture us. We needed a Father to love us, protect us, and provide for us. The Bible lets us know that God has adopted us into His family. When we are born again, we are part of the largest adopted family on the face of the earth.

BIBLE LESSON

I. MEPHIBOSHETH'S ADOPTION

Meet Mephibosheth. He was just a child when we first see him in Scripture. He had quite the lineage. His father was Jonathan and his grandfather was Saul, the first king of Israel. Mephibosheth grew up as royalty with all the attendant privileges that go with being in the lineage of the king.

However, after he lost his father and his grandfather in one battle, he was left with no immediate family to take care of him. He became an orphan in a short span of time and no longer enjoyed any of the luxuries of his previous life.

A. Mephibosheth Was Lame in His Feet

Life turned difficult when Mephibosheth was only five years old (II Samuel 4:4). A man came running through the gates of the city with an urgent message. He was weary and bloodied from the battle he was fleeing. As he ran into the city, he cried out, "King Saul and his sons are dead! They have been killed in the battle!"

Pandemonium erupted in the palace. Everyone knew the enemy would not be far behind this beleaguered messenger. Quickly, Mephibosheth's nurse told him to run as fast as he could, but his five-year-old legs could only move so quickly. His nurse scooped him up in her arms and kept running. In her haste to get to safety, something caused her to stumble and lose her grasp on the little boy. She fell to the ground and watched in horror as he fell out of her arms. He cried out in extreme pain.

Quickly she discovered the fall had paralyzed him. On that tragic day, his life changed completely. His nurse gently lifted him back into her arms and carried him to Lo Debar, a small town a long way from the capital city. From there the young boy would learn to live with a disability he never chose.

B. The King Sought Out Mephibosheth and Adopted Him

For years Mephibosheth lived removed from the rest of the world until one day an unexpected knock came on the door. A messenger stood with orders from King David to bring Mephibosheth to the palace. The newly crowned king wanted to see him (II Samuel 9).

One can only imagine the thoughts that raced through Mephibosheth's mind. *What does David want with me? Does he want to take my life so I am not a threat to him? Perhaps he then thought, Me, a threat? I can't run or fight. I'm no threat to the king. Let me be.*

As Mephibosheth entered the palace, he bowed humbly in the presence of the king. But he was surprised at King David's tone of voice. Mephibosheth did not hear anger or animosity. David

Can you recall the feeling when you realized God really does love you?

called his name tenderly, kindly. There was a hint of compassion in David's voice.

David's next words overwhelmed Mephibosheth. Second Samuel 9:7 reads, "And David said unto him, Fear not: for I will surely shew thee kindness for Jonathan thy father's sake, and will restore thee all the land of Saul thy father; and thou shalt eat bread at my table continually."

Mephibosheth could not believe what he was hearing. He lifted his head, looked at David, and answered, "What is thy servant, that thou shouldest look upon such a dead dog as I am?" (II Samuel 9:8). He felt he had nothing to offer. He couldn't imagine why David would show such kindness when he felt so undeserving.

The king turned to his servant Ziba—who had been Saul's servant—and declared, "I have given unto thy master's son all that pertained to Saul and to all his house. Thou therefore, and thy sons, and thy servants, shall till the land for him, and thou shalt bring in the fruits, that thy master's son may have food to eat: but Mephibosheth thy master's son shall eat bread alway at my table" (II Samuel 9:9–10).

In one remarkable act of compassion, David adopted Mephibosheth into his family. His royalty restored, he would now live with the attendant privileges of being a king's son.

C. I Should Actively Seek for the Hurting

We never really know people's stories just by looking at them. However, we know many people we encounter are hurting, and several are suffering as spiritual orphans. We need a compassionate heart like David that causes us to seek out those who have been injured by life. Each of us needs a desire to give people a seat at our table.

II. SPIRITUAL ADOPTION IN THE NEW TESTAMENT

Just as Mephibosheth was adopted by David in the Old Testament, there is a New Testament method of adoption. This method goes beyond physical adoption and focuses on spiritual adoption. The Pauline Epistles address this spiritual adoption to show us how much God loves all humanity.

A. Every Person Is Spiritually Lame

All human beings were born spiritually lame, regardless of how healthy they were physically. According to Psalm 51:5, David understood this when he said, "Behold, I was shapen in iniquity; and in sin did my mother conceive me."

Do you realize you were born as a sinner?

Paul explained this principle in Romans 5: "Wherefore, as by one man sin entered into the world, and death by sin; and so death passed upon all men, for that all have sinned" (Romans 5:12). We were all born with this crippling sin nature in our lives. If it were left to work its debilitating work, we would hide away and live our lives in obscurity.

B. The King of Kings Has Sought Us Out and Adopted Us into God's Family

However, just like David had plans for Mephibosheth, God had other plans for us. God refused to let us live our lives crippled by the effects of sin with no remedy. David sent a messenger to the house of Mephibosheth, but God sent Himself as a messenger in the person of Jesus Christ with a message of restoration for us.

Through the gospel—the good news of the death, burial, and resurrection of Christ—we too can be adopted into the family of God. As we identify with each part of the gospel by repenting of our sins, being immersed in baptism in the name of Jesus Christ, and receiving the baptism of the Holy Ghost with the initial sign of speaking with other tongues, we become sealed in adoption to Him.

God had this planned from the beginning. "Even so we, when we were children, were in bondage under the elements of the world: but when the fulness of the time was come, God sent forth his Son, made of a woman, made under the law, to redeem them that were under the law, that we might receive the adoption of sons" (Galatians 4:3-5).

God planned to provide a way for us to be adopted into His family, the body of Christ. Romans 8:15-16 further explains what happens to us at the point of adoption. "For ye have not received the spirit of bondage again to fear; but ye have received the Spirit of adoption, whereby we cry, Abba, Father. The Spirit itself beareth witness with our spirit, that we are the children of God."

Everything changed once we were born again. We no longer have to live in fear of the consequences of sin. When the Spirit of the Lord entered our lives, we received the Spirit of adoption. We became part of Jesus' royal family, so now we cry out to Him as children cry out to their father. Through the gospel, the lost relationship between Creator and creation has been restored.

C. We Have Rights and Privileges as Children of God

Along with adoption come rights and privileges as children of God. Titus summed up some of these: "But after that the kindness and love of God our Saviour toward man appeared, not by works of righteousness which we have done, but according to his mercy he saved us, by the washing of regeneration, and renewing of the Holy Ghost; which he shed on us abundantly through Jesus Christ our Saviour; that being justified by his grace, we should be made heirs according to the hope of eternal life" (Titus 3:4-7).

This passage teaches that God adopted us and saved us by the gospel that regenerates us. *Regeneration* means to be

How should our lives be different once we realize God as a loving Father adopted us into His family?

"formed or created again." The new-birth adoption makes us a new creature in Christ. We run from our old life of guilt and shame into the arms of God who gives us an eternal place at His table. Along with our seat at Christ's table, we are granted rights and privileges as children of God. Galatians 4:7 reminds us, "Wherefore thou art no more a servant, but a son; and if a son, then an heir of God through Christ." God now sees us as sons and daughters in His kingdom. That is a miracle to consider. We are heirs of God through our relationship with Jesus Christ.

Can you honestly say you see yourself as God sees you, as His son or daughter?

The ultimate privilege of being His child is knowing we will one day spend eternity with Him. Romans 8:16–17 explains this well: "The Spirit itself beareth witness with our spirit, that we are the children of God: and if children, then heirs; heirs of God, and joint-heirs with Christ; if so be that we suffer with him, that we may be also glorified together."

The Spirit of God bears witness that we are His children. As children, we are heirs. In fact we are joint heirs with Christ. Just as Jesus endured living in this world and was one day glorified for all of eternity, we can endure the troubles and trials of this world knowing we will be glorified with Jesus one day.

D. I Will No Longer Live My Life Below My Standing as His Child

Palace life was probably awkward for Mephibosheth at first. As one of the king's sons, he had new clothes and furniture. Chefs prepared him better meals than he could remember. He wanted for nothing. Just a few days earlier, Mephibosheth had been hiding in Lo Debar, scraping out a meager existence.

The day did dawn when Mephibosheth finally accepted what was happening to him. He might have even realized this life was not just what David wanted for him; this life was God's desire for him as well.

Jeremiah 29:11 says it like this, "For I know the thoughts that I think toward you, saith the LORD, thoughts of peace, and not of evil, to give you an expected end." God has great plans and desires for us. However, if we refuse to live as His children, those things will never come our way.

Are you living in the full hope of the promises God has made to you in His Word?

The great experience of being born again of water and the Spirit is only the beginning of the blessings the Lord has in store for us. Ephesians 1:13–14 calls the experience of receiving the Holy Spirit just a down payment toward what God is going to give us.

We should live our lives with confidence that we are loved and accepted by God. We should declare within ourselves that we are blood-bought children of the living God, and as such, all the promises for the church are ours.

INTERNALIZING THE MESSAGE

A supplemental video is available in the Resource Kit. [V].

A young couple visited a boarding house that provided shelter to children awaiting adoption. The caretaker brought out all the children who had recently bathed and were well dressed. These children had been properly schooled in manners. The staff hoped this young couple would spend time with each child and select one for adoption.

As they moved down the line and spoke to each child, they did not find the one they were looking to adopt. Rather sheepishly, they asked the caretaker, "Do you have any more children?" He replied, "Yes, but he has not been cleaned up or dressed. He really isn't ready for anyone to consider him today."

The couple immediately said, "That's all right. Can we see him anyway?" Reluctantly the caretaker agreed. After a few minutes, one of the members of the staff brought out the young boy and stood him alongside the rest of the children. He was dirty, his face unwashed and hair uncombed. His clothes were ragged and torn. He had no shoes on his feet, and his head hung in shame as he stood next to the others. Obviously he was not a prime candidate for adoption.

After a few minutes of serious discussion and wiping tears from their eyes, the couple said to the caretaker, "We want this child." The stunned man immediately replied, "But he is not as nice as the other children. I'm telling you; he is unmannered. Even his own parents couldn't love him." He continued his protestations, "And we have been unable to get him to behave. Why in the world would you want to adopt him?"

The couple paused. After regaining their composure, they replied, "We see in him the blessings of God for our home. We also see that by becoming a part of our family, there is an even better hope in life for him." Feeling a twinge of guilt, the caretaker asked, "Do you at least want us to clean him up and give him some fresh clothes?" The couple lovingly answered, "No, we want the child just as he is right now. We will take care of all of that once he is finally home."

That is exactly how God saw us. When no one else saw any value at all, God said He would take us just as we were. Were we unlovable? Absolutely. Did we need cleaned up? Certainly. Did we have issues? Without a doubt.

Were those reasons for Him to reject us and move on to someone else who had it more together? Not on your life. Jesus loved us too much to leave us where He found us. Instead, He did for us what David did for Mephibosheth. Jesus adopted us and made us His own.

Prayer Focus
Lead the group in prayer and consider the following topics of focus:
• For God to help us be thankful He adopted us
• For God to help us care for others who still need to be spiritually adopted

3.1

GOD BRINGS VICTORY

FOCUS VERSES
Judges 4:22–24
22 And, behold, as Barak pursued Sisera, Jael came out to meet him, and said unto him, Come, and I will shew thee the man whom thou seekest. And when he came into her tent, behold, Sisera lay dead, and the nail was in his temples.
23 So God subdued on that day Jabin the king of Canaan before the children of Israel.
24 And the hand of the children of Israel prospered, and prevailed against Jabin the king of Canaan, until they had destroyed Jabin king of Canaan.

LESSON TEXT
Judges 4:1–24

TRUTH ABOUT GOD
God will bring victory even if He has to choose a new deliverer.

TRUTH FOR MY LIFE
I will experience victory when I accept and follow God's call.

Series Overview:

In this series, "God Our Judge and King," we walk through the Book of Judges to see how God used judges and prophets to lead and speak to His people. We will study Deborah, Gideon, Samson, and finally Samuel and Saul. No matter how little or much we feel we have to offer God, He is able to use us for His glory.

SG TEACHING OUTLINE

Icebreaker: Who is the most heroic woman you have known?

Lesson Connection: Share the Lesson Connection. ⓘ

I. GOD CALLED BARAK
    » *Can we allow God to speak to us through the inspired word of another?*

    A. Israel Faced Oppression at the Hands of the Canaanites

    B. Deborah Prophesied of Barak's Victory
        » *How does knowing that God has the end in view help us face the present circumstances?*

    C. Barak Refused to Fight without Deborah Ⓥ
        » *What other notable women do you recall from biblical history?*

    D. We Must Heed God's Call
        » *What difficult tasks has God asked of you? How has He enabled you to perform them*

II. GOD PROVIDED VICTORY THROUGH JAEL

    A. Deborah and Barak Routed the Canaanite Army

    B. Sisera Fled and Was Subdued by Jael, Who Achieved Complete Victory
        » *What application can we make to spiritual battles and conflicts?*

    C. I Will Experience Victory When I Accept and Follow God's Call

Internalizing the Message

Prayer Focus
Lead the group in prayer and consider the following topics of focus:
• For God to help us hear His call for our lives
• For God to give us faith to answer His call, no matter the cost

LESSON CONNECTION

A supplemental image is available in the Resource Kit. ⬚

In the early 1900s, the leaders in the newborn aviation industry were all men. The Wilbur and Orville Wright brothers and Charles Lindbergh were the big names in flying. But Amelia Earhart changed all that. During World War I, Amelia served as a Red Cross nurse's aid in Toronto, Ontario Canada. During that time she watched pilots in the Royal Flying Corps train at a local airfield in Toronto. That exposure to flying may be what birthed a love for aviation in her.

After the war, she returned to the United States and enrolled at Columbia University in New York as a premed student, but she never lost her love for flight. She took her first airplane ride in California in 1920 with famed World War I pilot Frank Hawks—and was forever hooked. The next month, Amelia started flying lessons with female flight instructor Neta Snook. To help pay for those lessons, Earhart worked as a filing clerk in Los Angeles. She saved up her money and purchased her first airplane, a yellow Kinner Airster she nicknamed "the Canary."

Earhart passed her flight test and earned a National Aeronautics Association license in December of the same year. Two days later, she participated in her first flight exhibition at the Sierra Airdrome in Pasadena, California. From there, she went on to set several aviation records in her short career. She was the first woman to fly solo above 14,000 feet. Ten years later, she was the first woman (and second person after Charles Lindbergh) to fly solo across the Atlantic Ocean. This trans-Atlantic flight is arguably her most notable record.

Congress awarded her the Distinguished Flying Cross—a military decoration awarded for "heroism or extraordinary achievement while participating in an aerial flight." She was also the first woman to receive that honor. Later that year, Earhart was the first woman to complete a solo, nonstop flight across the United States. She took off in Los Angeles and landed nineteen hours later in Newark, New Jersey.

Amelia Earhart worked hard to open the door for women to become aviators. She helped form the Ninety-Nines, an international organization for the advancement of female pilots. Now there are women pilots from countries all around the world. Although men mainly flew at that time, no one could question Amelia's expertise and experience in the cockpit. She was a female hero. She may have been a little like Deborah in Judges 4.

BIBLE LESSON

I. GOD CALLED BARAK

God's calling is individualized. Some have heard God speak in dreams while others have seen Him in visions. Barak received God's call through the prophecy of Deborah, a judge and prophetess in Israel. She sent Barak a direct message as a commandment from God, "Go and draw toward mount Tabor, and take with thee ten thousand men of the children of Naphtali and of the children of Zebulun. . . . I will draw unto thee to the river Kishon Sisera, the captain of Jabin's army, with his chariots and his multitude; and I will deliver him into thine hand" (Judges 4:6–7).

A. Israel Faced Oppression at the Hands of the Canaanites

Can we allow God to speak to us through the inspired word of another?

In the tumultuous times of the judges, Israel's repeated failure to follow the Lord led to oppression by her neighbors. When Israel repented and cried out to God for deliverance, He often brought supernatural restoration, but their gradual backsliding led them into repeated apostasy. God again allowed their adversaries to bring judgment that they might correct their sinful behaviors. God used leaders called judges to lead Israel to victory and back into relationship with God.

Throughout the Book of Judges, this repetitious cycle of rebellion, repression, repentance, and restoration continued. Each time, the tribes of Israel sank lower into immorality and became more depraved in their conduct like the pagan people living around them. God's desire to be in covenant relationship with His people was not realized. However, God revealed His prevailing mercy through His continual love for His people, and that love moved Him to respond to their repentance and bring deliverance from their oppression.

Among the northern tribes, King Jabin served as God's judgment when Deborah became a judge in Ephraim. The commander of Jabin's army, Sisera, had been Jabin's strong arm for two decades and had gained an infamous reputation for cruelty. After twenty years of intense oppression, Israel again cried out in repentance and pled for deliverance. God heard their prayers and initiated His plan for victory. While God prompted the call and command for Barak to take action, He also stirred Sisera to deploy his host of troops and chariots to prepare for battle.

B. Deborah Prophesied of Barak's Victory

When Deborah spoke the prophetic word of God's calling to Barak, she also prophesied the victory that would result from the battle. "I will deliver him [Sisera] into thine hand" (Judges 4:7). When God declares victory, there is no need for doubt or despair. The conclusion has been determined.

God knows every detail of our situation, our calling, our responsibility, and the ultimate outcome beforehand. The omniscient one does not speak prematurely. He already sees the outcome and has anticipated every roadblock and every turn of events along the way. He knows the path we will take and the pitfalls and struggles we will encounter on the journey.

How does knowing that God has the end in view help us face the present circumstances?

C. Barak Refused to Fight without Deborah

God called Barak to lead the military effort against Jabin's army, and He gave Barak the strategy for the battle that would guarantee victory. Despite this assurance of success, Barak resisted God's call and shared his protest with Deborah. Barak was reluctant to accept the leadership role to which he had been called. He even refused to go to battle unless Deborah agreed to go with him.

Some skeptics have accused Barak of cowardice for being dependent on Deborah to accompany him into battle. However, Barak was clearly a competent leader. He was able to rally ten thousand men from the tribes of Naphtali and Zebulun to prepare for war. His reluctance may have been out of admiration for Deborah's spiritual leadership and his desire to have God's presence and prophetess with him in the greatest battle of his generation.

Teacher Option: *A supplemental video is available in the Resource Kit.* **V**

Deborah agreed to accompany Barak, but she warned him that the honor for the victory would be given to a woman. It was typical to see men in military and leadership positions, but it is noteworthy to see Deborah as a judge and prophetess in Israel. She emerged as a heroine who brought an end to the cruel oppression of King Jabin's army commander.

What other notable women do you recall from biblical history?

D. We Must Heed God's Call

When God gives us His word and confirms His calling, our response should be faith and courage rather than doubt and timidity. In humility we may never feel adequate for the task to which we are called. We may feel ill-equipped and underqualified for the responsibilities we have been given. However, God always qualifies the called. He will never task us with an impossible calling, but He will enable us to achieve the goals He gives us and accomplish His call. Paul wrote, "For the gifts and calling of God are without repentance" (Romans 11:29).

What difficult tasks has God asked of you? How has He enabled you to perform them?

God does not make mistakes. He has never called someone and changed His mind because the person lacked ability. The psalmist David wrote, "As a father pitieth his children, so the LORD pitieth them that fear him. For he knoweth our frame; he remembereth that we are dust" (Psalm 103:13–14). God knows our weaknesses and limitations. As our Creator, He knows our ability and inability. God is with us as our qualifier and enabler.

II. GOD PROVIDED VICTORY THROUGH JAEL

God is never nervous about the outcome or worried over surprise obstacles. He sees the end before the beginning and knows every difficulty and problem we will encounter along the way. He already has the solution. Our God will not give us more responsibility than we can carry or require us to carry it alone. Draw courage from the promises of God's Word. "I am with you alway, even unto the end of the world" (Matthew 28:20). "He which hath begun a good work in you will perform it" (Philippians 1:6). "The Lord is not slack concerning his promise" (II Peter 3:9).

Sometimes God chooses the most unlikely participants to work out His plan and the most creative solutions to bring about the victory. God had a surprise ending for the commander of King Jabin's army. Sisera never suspected that his death had been predetermined before he entered the battle. As the moth is drawn to a flame, Sisera was irresistibly drawn into conflict out of arrogant confidence that his forces and chariots of iron could never be defeated.

A. Deborah and Barak Routed the Canaanite Army

As agreed, Deborah accompanied Barak into battle. Barak summoned ten thousand warriors from his native tribe of Naphtali and neighboring tribe of Zebulun. They gathered near Mount Tabor as Sisera rallied his forces and chariots to attack. Deborah assured Barak that this was the battle she predicted and the victorious outcome God had guaranteed. She said, "Up; for this is the day in which the Lord hath delivered Sisera into thine hand: is not the Lord gone out before thee?" (Judges 4:14).

That simple question, "Is not the Lord gone out before thee?" gave Barak courage to prepare for a battle that looked impossible to his experienced eyes. There was no way they could hope to overthrow the Canaanite force by their own strength and limited weaponry. The enemy's horses and chariots would run them down and certainly overcome their defenses. To move forward in faith, Barak needed Deborah's assurance of the Lord's promises. When the Lord goes before us, we have no reason to fear.

God was several steps ahead of them, staging the details for a victory celebration. While the exact portrait of the battle is blurry, we do know that the Lord went before Barak and brought confusion and terror to disorient King Jabin's mighty troops. It was like they were fighting an invisible host. Their confusion frightened even the well-trained warriors. Some scholars have suggested the chariots weren't as effective in the mountains as they were on the level plains. The enemy abandoned their horses and chariots and fled in fear before Barak and his forces. All their chariots were useless before the hand of the Lord God.

Emboldened, those under Barak's leadership pursued the Canaanites as they retreated for their lives. Barak's army pursued them all the way to their homes and slew them with the sword. Victory was so complete, "All the host of Sisera fell upon the edge of the sword; and there was not a man left" (Judges 4:16). The Lord fought for Barak, and Barak and his army destroyed all their enemies.

B. Sisera Fled and Was Subdued by Jael, Who Achieved Complete Victory

In the chaos, Sisera abandoned his chariot and fled on foot. He was intent on escaping capture or death. He could expect no mercy after all the cruelty he had inflicted on their people. Sisera fled and found the camp of Heber the Kenite, with whom King Jabin made an alliance. Sisera felt safe among this tribe, and he desperately needed rest and refreshment. There he met Heber's wife, Jael. She welcomed Sisera into her tent to rest. When he asked for water, she brought him milk. She gave Sisera a blanket and promised to stand guard at the door. Jael patiently waited until his exhaustion caught up with him. As he slept, she stealthily raised a tent peg and mallet, aimed for his temple, and drove the peg through his head and into the ground. Sisera never awakened from his sleep; this cruel oppressor died at the hands of a woman.

After thoroughly routing the armies of Canaan, Barak turned his attention to bringing the commander of their army to justice. Barak tracked the fleeing leader to the camp of the Kenites. That is where Barak met Jael. She invited him in to see Sisera lying dead in her tent. Through this heroic act, Jael became the honored champion of the story as she brought an end to Sisera's cruel regime. King Jabin and his kingdom were destroyed. God indeed gave Barak and the tribes of Israel deliverance from their oppression, thus fulfilling the prophecy of Deborah. And just as Deborah had prophesied, honor was given to a woman, Jael, for the victory over Sisera.

The graphic and sometimes disturbing experiences detailed in the Book of Judges often seem distant and irrelevant for our times. However, every biblical account gives us insight into God's involvement in our lives. Paul wrote concerning the experiences of Israel in the wilderness, "These things happened unto them for ensamples: and they are written for our admonition" (I Corinthians 10:11).

What application can we make to spiritual battles and conflicts?

C. I Will Experience Victory When I Accept and Follow God's Call

While our battles are often more mental, emotional, or spiritual, we can have the same confidence in God's ability to bring us through to victorious deliverance. Jesus Christ fights our battles and pushes back against every effort of the enemy.

Our faith is in God. No power can resist Him. No foe can defeat Him. With the Holy Spirit operating in our lives, we are a powerful force for good. Answering the call of God becomes a natural response, and all things become possible through faith in Him.

INTERNALIZING THE MESSAGE

"How many times have I told you?" Brenda ran through the doorway as she slammed the door behind her. She slid across the freshly mopped hallway and into the decorative hall tree, which toppled and fell against the curio cabinet. Everything rattled and shifted before an antique teacup crashed from the glass shelf to the floor. Her mom rushed into the room, her hand covering her mouth in anxious premonition of what she would find following the catastrophic noise and the complete silence. She saw Brenda sitting on the floor wide-eyed as she viewed the disaster. She exploded, "How many times have I told you to slow down?! Look what you've done!"

Mother and daughter both shed their share of tears as they cleaned up the shattered teacup and scattered pieces. Brenda apologized for not listening, and her mother assigned her extra chores to reinforce the lesson. Brenda dried her tears and promised to do better. Of course, they both knew this was not the last time something would be broken. Mother would have to instruct and correct her daughter again. It is part of the process of growth and maturity for most. Some never seem to learn the lessons and reform their behavior. Some seem destined to repeat offenses perpetually and never learn from their mistakes or remember the lessons taught.

Every parent has probably used that rhetorical question more than a few times: How many times have I told you? Sometimes, it seems children just don't listen, they forget, or they are testing the boundaries again. When things don't work out well and their disobedience catches up with them, their parents find themselves scolding their children again, "How many times have I told you not to throw a ball in the house?" "How many times have I said no cookies before dinner?" "How many times have I told you not to ride your bike in the street?"

Perhaps that is the way God felt about Israel. How many times had He warned them against idolatry? Or cautioned them about participating in pagan practices at the high places? Or reminded them of the commandments and called them to obedience? How many times had Israel resolved to do better but failed? How often had they been lured by the enticements of the Canaanite culture and tempted by their sensual cult? As a loving parent, God sought for those who would embrace His covenant and commit to His commandments. He planned victory and success for all those who simply follow His plan.

Over and over God has assured us of His great love. God has promised victory and an overcoming life to everyone who submits to Him and desires to become His disciple. How many times has He told us, "I love you" and "I will never leave thee, nor forsake thee"? (Hebrews 13:5). We have the assurance of His love and the promise of a victorious outcome.

Prayer Focus
Lead the group in prayer and consider the following topics of focus:
- For God to help us hear His call for our lives
- For God to give us faith to answer His call, no matter the cost

3.2

GIDEON AND THE STRENGTH OF HONESTY

FOCUS VERSES
Judges 6:15–16
[15] And he said unto him, Oh my Lord, wherewith shall I save Israel? behold, my family is poor in Manasseh, and I am the least in my father's house.
[16] And the LORD said unto him, Surely I will be with thee, and thou shalt smite the Midianites as one man.

LESSON TEXT
Judges 6:11–21, 36–40

TRUTH ABOUT GOD
God will not turn us away when we express our doubts in honesty.

TRUTH FOR MY LIFE
I will fight through doubt and trust God.

Thinking about Last Week:

Have students refer to their Daily Devotional Guide to answer the following questions:
1. What most affected you as you read through the Lesson Text and the Biblical Insights?
2. How did it shape your prayers and thoughts throughout the week?
3. Do you feel you grew closer to the Lord this past week? Why or why not?

SG TEACHING OUTLINE

Icebreaker: Were you picked first, in the middle, or last in gym class?

Lesson Connection: Share the Lesson Connection.

I.   GOD CALLED AN UNLIKELY HERO
   » *Have you ever found yourself in a position for which you felt unqualified?*

   A.   The Midianites Had Oppressed the Israelites
      » *Why does it sometimes seem easier to see God's hand of judgment than to recognize the abundance of His blessings?*

   B.   God Called Gideon While Gideon Was Hiding from the Enemy

   C.   Gideon Honestly Expressed His Doubts

   D.   I Can Be Honest with the Lord about My Situation **V**
      » *Why is it so hard to believe that God can use us to fulfill His purpose?*

II. GOD CONTINUALLY CONFIRMED HIS CALL TO GIDEON
   » *When God promises victory for something we have prayed for, how should we respond?*

   A.   Gideon Prepared a Sacrifice

   B.   Gideon's Fleece

   C.   I Will Fight Through Doubt and Trust God **I**
      » *How can honesty bring about stronger faith in our relationship with God?*

Internalizing the Message

Prayer Focus
Lead the group in prayer and consider the following topics of focus:
• For God to help us hear His voice as He calls us
• For God to help us through our doubts to trust His call

305

LESSON CONNECTION

When all the guys got together for some friendly competition, most looked forward to the games with great excitement. They could hardly wait to match their athletic skills with the boys from the nearest village. Sometimes the games got rowdy, tempers flared, and a fight ensued. Those who weren't in the fray gathered around them, egging on their favored one in the scuffle. It was all fun and games until someone became too aggressive and punched to hurt. Then the others grabbed a rock or weapon to even the score. That's when fun and games got serious.

The rivalries between villages, especially those outside their group, were important for establishing a pecking order. Even without an award or a trophy, they all knew who was the toughest, the strongest, and who demanded the most respect. This rite of competition is not much different from the way other species in the animal kingdom assert dominance and identify the most powerful. This contest was a matter of reputation. While some groups carried the banner of having the toughest fighters and the greatest lineage of champions, other groups were known as the perpetual underdogs.

"Losers!" the boys jeered whenever the underdogs showed up. "What a bunch of wimps," they mocked. Who said words don't hurt? Whether in jest, with sarcasm, or outright intention to be demeaning, words can cut to the quick and leave lasting scars. The bullying never stopped. It's really nothing new. Humanity has always seen those who vie for control sometimes bully and intimidate others who can never measure up in strength or agility. Some will never feel the satisfaction of success because they have always been less than the best. They will always believe the voices they have heard confirming they were never good enough.

One particular community had the reputation of losers for sure—Gideon grew up in it. He was a young man whose peers had labeled weak since he was a kid. After all, he was from the clan with the reputation for being the weakest in Manasseh, and he considered himself to be the least capable in his family. It wasn't for lack of trying. He carried more than his share of the work and did his best to help with the harvest. Gideon gathered wheat for the threshing and prepared the crops for the hostile winter season. Gideon was actually as strong as most, but he was called weak so long the label stuck. Growing up with the constant taunts of being a loser affects a person's confidence and self-image.

Beyond the tribal competitions, a greater force loomed beyond the valley. When the enforcers came through the village, no one was safe. The community was powerless against their weapons and sheer dominance. The Midianites oppressed the people of the region, abused anyone who got in their way, and took whatever they wanted. The Midianites repeatedly ravaged Israel's crops, causing hunger and starvation all too often in their struggling community.

BIBLE LESSON

I. GOD CALLED AN UNLIKELY HERO

In times of overwhelming odds, God delights in calling the most unlikely candidates to accomplish His purposes. Moses protested, "I'm not an orator. I can't talk very well." Deborah could have objected, "But there's never been a woman judge in Israel." Amos was an obscure shepherd when God called him. Everyone has an excuse of why they can't, but through God's grace, God knows we can.

Have you ever found yourself in a position for which you felt unqualified?

No one would have picked Gideon to rally the troops against the mighty Midianites. Even when Gideon was in charge, no one expected the total and complete destruction of the Midianite forces. Israel would have been happy to bring in just one crop from the field and into the barns without interference. No one would have chosen Gideon to be a military leader and a national hero, but God saw what he could be and called him anyway. Only God can see beyond the evident limitations and reveal the hidden hero.

A. The Midianites Had Oppressed the Israelites

For seven years the Midianites' attacks were relentless. Every season the thugs from Midian roamed the countryside waiting for the first signs of harvest. They rushed in, took what they wanted, and trampled the rest. They left nothing behind. Israel's surrounding tribes were powerless to stop them. The Israelites hid in caves and behind rocks or trees to escape the Midianites' brutality. Israel had to become creative or die. These crops were their livelihood. If they could not save enough to eat, they would not survive the winter. There was never enough. They lived in survival mode, but their future prospects did not look good.

Then God's people cried out to God for deliverance. An unnamed prophet visited Israel and reminded them of their forefather's deliverance from Egyptian bondage and their gift of the Promised Land. He also revealed their oppression was a result of their rejecting the covenant with the Lord. They had embraced the pagan gods of the land. Their present troubles were a consequence of their disobedience to God's commandments and their failure to exclusively follow Him.

Why does it sometimes seem easier to see God's hand of judgment than to recognize the abundance of His blessings?

In Leviticus, long before the occupation of the Promised Land, God warned the people of the consequences of idolatry and the penalties for disobedience. He also reminded them of His blessings they would enjoy if they kept the covenant and honored the name of the Lord their God. The Lord promised, "If ye walk in my statutes, and keep my commandments, and do them; then I will give you rain in due season, and the land shall yield her increase, and the trees of the field shall yield their fruit. And your threshing shall reach unto the vintage, and the vintage shall reach unto the sowing time: and ye shall eat your bread to the full, and dwell in your land safely" (Leviticus 26:3–5).

B. God Called Gideon While Gideon Was Hiding from the Enemy

Gideon was secretly threshing wheat in a winepress. This device was typically used for crushing grapes to extract their juices, but he was using it to crush the stalks of grain and separate the straw from the chaff. It would have been quicker and more efficient to thresh in the open air, pitching the grain up in the wind to separate the chaff, but that was too risky. The enemy could have been spying and rushed in and taken the grain, robbing it from those who so desperately needed it.

Suddenly a voice spoke and startled Gideon. He didn't expect anyone to be nearby. He had not seen or heard anything, so who was speaking to him? Gideon saw a man sitting under a tree. The man made an unusual statement, "The LORD is with thee, thou mighty man of valour" (Judges 6:12). Gideon realized this visitor was more than just a man; He must be a messenger from the Lord. He must have the wrong man. Gideon was no warrior; he was scared like everyone else. Gideon responded, "If the LORD be with us, why then is all this befallen us?" (Judges 6:13). The angel of the Lord ignored Gideon's question and continued, "Go in this thy might, and thou shalt save Israel from the hand of the Midianites: have not I sent thee?" (Judges 6:14).

C. Gideon Honestly Expressed His Doubts

This must be some mistake. Gideon knew he couldn't be the one to deliver Israel and defeat Midian. He protested, "Oh my Lord, wherewith shall I save Israel? behold, my family is poor in Manasseh, and I am the least in my father's house" (Judges 6:15). His self-assessment was quite different than God's confident calling. All his life he had seen himself as inferior in strength and deficient in courage. However, God called him a mighty warrior and commissioned him to act in the strength he possessed. The Lord promised total victory because God Himself promised, "I will be with thee, and thou shalt smite the Midianites as one man" (Judges 6:16).

Israel had been praying for this promise, but Gideon found it difficult to believe he would be the man God would use to bring it to pass. He was frightened. He was fearful. He could not believe he was the right man for this dangerous and daring job.

D. I Can Be Honest with the Lord about My Situation

Expressing doubts is not a sin. God knows our shortcomings better than we do. He is aware of our inabilities, but He also knows our capabilities. When we honestly confess our concerns to God, He will assure us of His abiding presence and His path to victory in overcoming our inhibitions and fears.

God knows us better than we know ourselves. When we cannot see our own potential, we must trust the one who created us, who knows what we can accomplish. Trusting God is revealed in

Teacher Option:
A supplemental video is available in the Resource Kit. **V**

Why is it so hard to believe that God can use us to fulfill His purpose?

our honesty before Him. We can confess our fears and failures, but we must also believe what our God says about us. God cannot lie, so if He calls us mighty and gives us an impossible task, we should not question His wisdom or His assessment of our ability.

II. GOD CONTINUALLY CONFIRMED HIS CALL TO GIDEON

With every objection God reaffirmed His will that Gideon was the person to lead the nation to victory. The answer to every petition and prayer was already on the way. It became quite clear what God desired Gideon to do. God clearly communicated His call to His man. He patiently waited for Gideon to process this new information and make the mental adjustments necessary to answer God's call.

> *When God promises victory for something we have prayed for, how should we respond?*

A. Gideon Prepared a Sacrifice

Gideon realized he should bring a sacrifice of worship to honor this holy moment. He asked the angel of the Lord to stay while he quickly ran to get something to offer as a sacrifice to God. The angel of the Lord agreed. Gideon returned with the meat of a young goat, broth from cooking it, and loaves of unleavened bread. The angel instructed him to place the bread and meat on a rock and pour the broth over it. Gideon obeyed. Then the angel pointed his staff toward the sacrifice, and the fire of God miraculously consumed it all.

Gideon trembled in the presence of the Lord, but God reassured him and said, "Peace be unto thee; fear not: thou shalt not die" (Judges 6:23). Gideon then built an altar on that site and called it Jehovah-shalom—the Lord is peace.

God again spoke to Gideon that night and called him to offer another sacrifice after destroying idolatrous altars to the god Baal and the goddess Asherah. Gideon's father, Joash, had built the altar, and people from the village went there to worship the idol. Gideon obeyed the Lord, but for fear of the people, he destroyed the altars under the cover of darkness.

The next morning the people found the altar of Baal in shambles and the image of Asherah cut down. In their stead they found a new, proper altar built to the Lord God. The people's response revealed their spiritual depravity. They called for Gideon's death rather than repent. Joash refused to approve the execution of his son and offered, "If he [Baal] be a god, let him plead for himself, because one hath cast down his altar" (Judges 6:31).

Gideon was ready for his next divine assignment. This plan would require great faith from Gideon and would require the people to have faith that God was calling Gideon and would go with him. Gideon blew the trumpet and called volunteers to follow him. Messengers spread the word to the tribes of Manasseh, Asher, Zebulun, Naphtali, and the surrounding tribes.

B. Gideon's Fleece

Even with a large group of 32,000 men ready to fight, Gideon still needed more assurance that God was with him. He prayed for the Lord to confirm His call through a test. Gideon asked God to cause the dew to fall only on the fleece Gideon placed on the threshing floor. This would leave all the surrounding ground dry. Gideon said, "Then shall I know that thou wilt save Israel by mine hand, as thou hast said" (Judges 6:37).

God honored his request. In the morning Gideon filled a bowl with dew as he wrung out the wet fleece. This was undeniable, but he still struggled with his doubts. Could this have happened by coincidence? Gideon pled once more for God to allow one more test. The second time Gideon asked that the fleece remain dry while the surrounding ground was wet with dew. Patiently, God led Gideon through his doubts in God's plan to lead Israel to freedom from the Midianites.

C. I Will Fight Through Doubt and Trust God

So far, God had worked several miraculous signs for Gideon. He sent fire to consume the sacrifice, preserved Gideon's life after he destroyed the false altars, soaked only the fleece with dew, and then soaked only the grass with dew. Gideon was finally ready to accept God's calling and commit to the task before him. These undeniable, supernatural signs gave Gideon confidence that he would be victorious, no matter what came next.

Teacher Option: *Show image to either take the place of the question or to help illustrate it.*

Gideon began with 32,000 warriors, but even that seemed small compared to the multitude of the Midianite forces. Yet God warned Gideon, "That's too many." God instructed him to send home everyone who was fearful. It must have been a shock to watch 22,000 fearful soldiers pack up and return home. He still had 10,000 men, but God warned, "That's still too many." God wanted this victory to be for His glory alone. No one could boast in their own strength or attribute the victory to their strategic planning.

Gideon led the remaining 10,000 volunteers to the brook and gave them a test. He watched as they drank water. Only 300 remained watchful while they drank from the stream. God sent home the 9,700 who knelt on their knees to drink and only kept the 300 vigilant volunteers. Gideon never considered going into battle with a mere 300 men against the mighty Midianites. If he did not know assuredly that God was with him, he himself may have returned home fearful.

How can honesty bring about stronger faith in our relationship with God?

Faith in God is not blindly claiming we know everything God is doing. Rather, our faith is often shrouded in fears of our own inadequacies, timidly asking God for more assurance as we struggle with our honest doubts. Nothing is impossible with God, but we are sometimes unsure He will work through us. As God confirms His leading, we can honestly face our fears and discover new confidence in our dependence on God.

[SG] TEACHING OUTLINE

Icebreaker: If you could be any superhero, who would it be?

Lesson Connection: Share the Lesson Connection.
> *Have you ever bought or sold something that had much more value than you realized?*

I. GOD CALLED SAMSON AND EMPOWERED HIM
> *In a world with quick answers from technology and the ease of online ordering, what can we do to recognize our need for God?*

    A. God Manifested His Power in Samson When He Killed a Lion (I) (V)

    B. God Empowered Samson to Defeat the Philistines

    C. I Will Rely on God's Power to Defeat My Enemies
> *In what situations do you need to call on the Lord for help?*

II. SAMSON STILL NEEDED GOD

    A. Samson Took Revenge on the Philistines and Fought Them at Lehi
> *What is the most unconventional victory you can recall in your life?*

    B. In His Desperation, Samson Cried Out to God

    C. I Will Cry Out to God in My Time of Need
> *What is preventing you from calling on the Lord for what you need?*

Internalizing the Message

Prayer Focus
Lead the group in prayer and consider the following topics of focus:
• For God to help us rely on Him for our strength
• For God to help us never take our relationship with Him for granted

LESSON CONNECTION

Time and time again, we read stories of people possessing wondrous works of art or priceless treasures without even knowing it. Archaeologists have found ancient writings in the land of Israel on stones used to build houses. Those constructing the home failed to realize their cornerstone once served as a part of an artifact, commemorating the victory of a great king. The monarch may have lost his kingdom a long time ago, but the memory still lived on, waiting to be discovered. For generations, the stone failed to fulfill its intended purpose of proclaiming a great victory.

Entire libraries of ancient writings remained hidden until modernization led to the building of a subway or some other project. Construction rather than archaeological excavation led to some of the most important finds in history. Many people trying to advance their civilization have found items of incalculable value hidden beneath their feet. Beachcombers with metal detectors have unearthed ancient coins and weapons. They have also found wedding rings and jewelry once important to the owners but seemingly lost forever. The beautiful beachscape often acts as the sands of time, transporting us to a place long gone—but not forgotten.

We often read stories of people going to garage sales, swap meets, or estate auctions and buying seemingly ordinary paintings that turned out to be priceless works of art. Some people kept these items in their possession for many years without realizing their true value.

We read of important historical letters being found in antique desks. The first issue of Action Comics featuring Superman was found in the wall of a house. We read of an additional painting hidden under the canvas of another painting. These stories all reveal that many people do not know what they truly possess. As a result, they devalue the valuable. They fail to treasure their treasures. What they view as no real prize transforms into a prized possession when they recognize its worth. In thinking about these situations, we must realize our need for the Lord. We have someone to cry out to in our time of need, but often we remain silent. We have Almighty God to help us when we have no might, but we often fail to appreciate our need for Him. In our time of need, we need to lift our voice and call on the Lord.

Have you ever bought or sold something that had much more value than you realized?

BIBLE LESSON

I. GOD CALLED SAMSON AND EMPOWERED HIM

Samson holds a unique distinction among the numerous leaders that populate the Book of Judges. Of all the judges, Samson alone received God's call before his birth. The man of God appeared to Samson's parents and told them of the amazing child who would soon enter their lives. He also gave them instructions for raising their special boy.

God's prenatal call of Samson has yet another layer of uniqueness. Most barren women in the Bible cried out to the Lord when they could not conceive. However, Samson's mother chose not to cry out to God because the Lord had grown tired of the Israelites falling into sin, being delivered into the hands of their enemies, and crying out to God for a deliverer. As a result, God told the Israelites He would no longer save them. He said they should pray vain prayers by crying out to their false deities to help them (Judges 10:13-14).

Samson's parents likely desired a child, but they had heard the mandate of the Almighty, forbidding their prayers. Therefore, the Lord intervened. God called Samson before birth and empowered him. Despite his unique calling and story, Samson failed to always recognize his need for the Lord. Perhaps God put Samson in certain difficulties to teach him this lesson. This strong man with weak resolve needed the Lord—whether he realized it or not.

In a world with quick answers from technology and the ease of online ordering, what can we do to recognize our need for God?

A. God Manifested His Power in Samson When Samson Killed a Lion

Many depictions of Samson show the biblical judge with bulging muscles and a physique achievable only through intense daily workouts and an incredible diet. These imaginings probably veer far from the truth. Rather than being on the cover of a muscle magazine, Samson probably looked like an ordinary man. In appearance, he was more the mild-mannered Clark Kent than the Man of Steel.

Teacher Option:
A supplemental image is available in the Resource Kit. **I**

The Spirit of the Lord made all the difference. Samson discovered his power when a lion sprang on him as he walked near the vineyards of Timnah. The Spirit of the Lord empowered the unsuspecting young man as he tore the lion apart as if it were a young goat (Judges 14:5-6). He accomplished the amazing feat without a weapon—just his bare hands.

Teacher Option:
A supplemental video is available in the Resource Kit. **V**

The account offers us another insight into Samson's uniqueness. Several times in the Book of Judges, the Bible speaks of the Spirit of the Lord being on judges to deliver God's people. However, the Spirit of the Lord came mightily (rushed) on Samson to empower him. This phrase also described how the Spirit of the Lord moved on King Saul and David. All three men felt the rushing mighty wind of God's Spirit.

Given the lion's speed and might, Samson likely had little time to react. The Lord protected him and supercharged him when he needed it most. While this exploit revealed the Spirit coursing through Samson's ordinary-looking muscles, the situation may also explain Samson's mindset as we read of his continuing adventures. Samson's easy access to the Spirit may have caused him to take the Lord for granted. If Samson could defeat a lion without much of a thought, he might become thoughtless and careless in his relationship with God.

B. God Empowered Samson to Defeat the Philistines

Neglecting his relationship with God, Samson focused on his burgeoning relationship with a Philistine woman in Timnah whom he planned to marry. When the days of their wedding feast began, he may have felt the stares of the Philistines who saw him as an interloping Israelite. Samson prepared to one-up his enemies by showing them his mental superiority. Samson challenged the Philistines to a contest of wits and presented a riddle to them: "Out of the eater came forth meat, and out of the strong came forth sweetness" (Judges 14:14). He then gave the Philistines seven days to solve the riddle.

After a week, they still could not solve the enigma. They threatened to burn Samson's fiancé and her father's house if she did not help them solve his riddle. The unhappy bride-to-be accused Samson of hating her because he did not tell her the answer. Samson kept many secrets. While others may have bragged, Samson did not even tell his parents about slaying the lion. He told his fiancé that he had not shared the answer with his own people. Nevertheless, she pleaded, begged, coaxed, and cajoled him into providing the answer. Then she informed on him to save herself from the treacherous Philistines. They solved the riddle just before the deadline: "What is sweeter than honey? and what is stronger than a lion?" (Judges 14:18).

The sweetness of his wedding feast was ruined. Samson owed his enemies the reward for their answer. Once again, the Spirit of the Lord provided Samson with the strength he needed. He killed thirty Philistines to provide the garments for his unfairly lost wager.

C. I Will Rely on God's Power to Defeat My Enemies

In life, we often find ourselves in seemingly unfair situations. We might even feel so angry that we wish we could teach people who hurt us a lesson or two. We must quell these desires for vengeance and instead trust in the Lord. Violence is not the answer—no matter how justified we may feel.

While the Lord does not empower us to defeat our enemies through physical force like Samson did, we still have authority over our foes. Through prayer and fasting, we are empowered by God and emerge victorious from difficult situations. By reading the Word of God, we discover the power of trusting in the Lord—no matter how bleak our situation seems. God has the power to deliver us even when we feel overpowered by those who oppose us. God can provide answers even when we look to the heavens and only see cloud-shaped question marks taunting us with unsolvable riddles. When our enemies threaten us, God can save us. Rather than cry out to God because of our unjust treatment, we must call on the Lord to change our attitude and help us.

Many people in this world use social media to vent and voice their complaints. They complain of injustice and how terrible people in the world behave. They may even be correct many times, but even if they are right, social media has very little power to truly change situations. Prayer is more powerful than any post or tweet. In a world where easy answers seem to be at our fingertips on a phone or computer keyboard, we must recognize our need for the Lord and rely on Him.

In what situations do you need to call on the Lord for help?

II. SAMSON STILL NEEDED GOD

Samson consistently found himself needing God's help. The Philistines lived near Israel's coast and kept encroaching into their land. Samson treated them as friends and foes. The strong man often found himself in conflict with these frenemies. When Samson left his wedding feast, his bride's father gave his daughter to the best man because he thought Samson hated her. When Samson returned, his would-be father-in-law offered his younger, prettier daughter to Samson, but Samson furiously refused her hand in marriage. Samson felt spurned and sought to avenge his hurt on the Philistines for ruining his marriage. Samson caught three hundred foxes, tied their tails together, and set their tails on fire. Then he set the fiery foxes loose in the Philistine wheat fields (Judges 15:1–4).

When the Philistines identified Samson as the one who destroyed their crops, they returned to his former fiancé's house and burned it to the ground, killing the woman he loved and her father (Judges 15:6). Samson's fiancé tried to avoid the Philistines' wrath by giving in to their demands. In the end, they still acted heinously and murdered her and her father.

A. Samson Took Revenge on the Philistines and Fought Them at Lehi

An even more enraged Samson vowed to avenge the fiery deaths of his fiancé and her father. Samson struck the Philistines down hip and thigh with a great slaughter. The phrase "hip and thigh" means he attacked them mercilessly, striking them with great blows. The Philistines showed no mercy to the innocent, and Samson granted them no grace or leniency either.

Feeling like a superhero who had avenged the death of his loved ones, Samson believed he had no reason to continue fighting. He made his way to the cleft of the rock at Etam. His surviving

Philistine enemies eerily knew they were far from danger. They raided Lehi, telling the men of Judah that they had come to bind Samson. Three thousand men of Judah found Samson in the cleft. They told him they came to bind him and hand him over to the Philistines. It was a bold move. Samson could have mockingly asked these three thousand men, "You and what army?" Instead, he agreed to go with them as long as they promised not to kill him themselves (Judges 15:11–13).

When the Philistines approached the bound Samson, the Spirit of the Lord again rushed on him. Samson felt like a human torch as his arms became like flax that caught fire, melting the bonds off his hands. Though Samson usually fought barehanded, this time he found an unconventional weapon: the jawbone of a donkey. This mirrored the unusual fighting strategies of Shamgar who used an ox goad (Judges 3:31) and Gideon who won victory with jars, lights, and trumpets (Judges 7). Samson killed a thousand enemies with a donkey's jawbone.

What is the most unconventional victory you can recall in your life?

B. In His Desperation, Samson Cried Out to God

Despite achieving such a fantastic victory, Samson soon discovered he still needed God. After the battle, he feared he would die of intense thirst. Samson cried out to the Lord, asking the Almighty why He would allow him to die after winning such a great victory (Judges 15:18).

God provided Samson with much needed water from the spring. That refreshing place became known as Enhakkore: the spring of the caller (Judges 15:19). Although Samson's parents did not cry out to the Lord for a child because the Lord had refused to hear the cries of Israel, Samson restored the cry of God to Israel.

C. I Will Cry Out to God in My Time of Need

We must cry out to the Lord in our times of need. Sometimes we achieve a great spiritual victory only to discover how costly it was for us. We may feel burnout or thirst for rest. Like Samson, we must call on the Lord. Samson did not rely on his strength and assume he did not need the Lord. Sometimes we make that mistake, assuming we are stronger than we are. But we are never so mighty that we do not need the Almighty.

At other times, we fail to call on the Lord because we feel weak and lack the faith that God will answer. We feel shame for sin. Knowing we have neglected our God, we believe we have no right to receive His mercy. Even if we have little faith, we must cry out to God. He will strengthen our faith. If we feel shame, we must cry out to God in repentance. Even if we have not served the Lord as we should, we can still come boldly to the throne of grace and obtain mercy and find grace to help in time of need (Hebrews 4:16). No matter our situation, we can always call on the Lord.

What is preventing you from calling on the Lord for what you need?

INTERNALIZING THE MESSAGE

Joe was having lots of difficulties in life. His work situation strained him so much that remaining in his position at work seemed impossible. His relationships with family members felt fractured. No matter how hard he tried, it seemed he just could not bridge the gap. Joe found little time for church. He felt angry, frustrated, and at the end of his rope.

In his desperation, he asked his pastor over for coffee in hope that the man of God had some sage words of advice. Joe greeted his pastor at the door and offered him a seat on the couch as he began to share the details of his difficult situation. When both men eased onto the cushions, the couch shifted.

"Sorry, pastor," Joe said. "This leg on this old couch broke, and I used a book to fix it."

As both men rose, the pastor eyed the broken couch and the book propping it up. The pastor wisely spoke, "Joe, I think I know what your problem is."

Joe felt elated. "Oh, Pastor, that's wonderful! I knew you'd have the answer. What is it?"

The pastor knelt by the couch. Joe thought his pastor wanted to pray and also knelt. Instead, the pastor reached for the book Joe had used to prop up the couch. When the pastor pulled out the book and wiped off the dust, Joe could see the title "Holy Bible" in gold letters jumping off the black leather cover like a warning light.

"Joe, you've been using the Bible to support your couch, but you haven't allowed the Bible to support you. The Word of God is a strong foundation. You're struggling because you have not used the Bible for its intended purpose, and it has cost you dearly."

Suddenly Joe realized the answers to all his problems had been right next to his feet as he sat on the couch. The Word of God stated that Jesus had put all things under his feet. Joe, however, had not trusted in the sovereign power of God. Like Samson, Joe chose to use the promises of God for something less that their intended purpose. While Samson found victory and thirst-quenching salvation in an unconventional way, he never fully embraced the call God had for his life. Joe had done something similar. He used the Bible for a temporary and unconventional fix. In doing so, he turned one of the greatest forces for good into a prop.

Recognizing his foolish mistake, Joe asked the pastor to pray with him before he left. After the pastor left, Joe dusted the Bible off and began to read. He recognized that God had used the situation to show him he needed the Lord above all else.

Prayer Focus
Lead the group in prayer and consider the following topics of focus:
- For God to help us rely on Him for our strength
- For God to help us never take our relationship with Him for granted

3.4

HELP TO UNDERSTAND GOD'S CALL

FOCUS VERSES
I Samuel 10:6-7
⁶ And the Spirit of the LORD will come upon thee, and thou shalt prophesy with them, and shalt be turned into another man.
⁷ And let it be, when these signs are come unto thee, that thou do as occasion serve thee; for God is with thee.

LESSON TEXT
I Samuel 10:1-24

TRUTH ABOUT GOD
God will speak into our lives and provide confirmation.

TRUTH FOR MY LIFE
I will counsel with godly leaders to help me understand God's call.

Thinking about Last Week:

Have students refer to their Daily Devotional Guide to answer the following questions:

1. What most affected you as you read through the Lesson Text and the Biblical Insights?
2. How did it shape your prayers and thoughts throughout the week?
3. Do you feel you grew closer to the Lord this past week? Why or why not?

SG TEACHING OUTLINE

Icebreaker: As a child, what did you dream about doing as an adult?

Lesson Connection: Share the Lesson Connection.

I. GOD CALLED SAMUEL

> *To whom can you turn for godly advice? What advice from them has helped you in the past?*

A. Samuel's Mother Dedicated Him to the Lord

B. When Samuel Heard God Speak, Eli Helped Him Understand God's Voice ⓘ

C. We Need the Ministry to Help Us Hear and Understand the Plan of God

> *What may be hindering you from hearing the voice or call of God?*

II. GOD CALLED SAUL

A. The Spirit Moved on Saul and God Gave Saul Signs to Confirm His Calling

B. We Must Allow the Spirit to Move in Our Lives

C. Saul Felt Reluctant to Accept His Call

D. Though I May Feel Inadequate, the Ministry Can Help Me Accept and Understand My Calling Ⓥ

> *What causes your reluctance to answer God's call in your life? How would a man or woman of God in your life respond to your reluctance?*

Internalizing the Message

Prayer Focus
Lead the group in prayer and consider the following topics of focus:
• For God to help us understand His call for our lives
• For God to help us respond to His call for our lives

LESSON CONNECTION

As we journey through life, some of us may have difficulty finding our calling. We may feel a twinge of envy when we hear others testify that they absolutely knew what God wanted them to do as a teenager or even a tween. We may wonder why we remain unsure about our spiritual future even though the Bible tells us to walk worthy of our calling (Ephesians 4:1). We may also face the very real possibility that God has already revealed our calling, but we have yet to realize it.

Such was the case with singer Connie Francis. Francis had achieved minimal success as a singer, but the lightning bolt of fame had yet to strike her and rocket her to the top of the charts. She wisely thought through contingencies. Having received a scholarship to New York University, Connie considered a career in medicine. Before heading off to college, her father insisted she give singing one last chance. She appeased him by recording "Who's Sorry Now?" in what she thought would be her very last recording session. She even argued so much with him during the recording that she barely had enough tape to complete the song.

Who's sorry now? Connie thought she knew the answer to that question. She was sorry for listening to her father. She was sorry for wasting time recording the song. She was especially sorry when the song seemed to take the same path as her other pieces, headed straight for music oblivion.

As Connie watched the show *American Bandstand*, she heard host Dick Clark praising an amazing girl and predicting her song would boost straight to the top of the charts. Connie felt envious, wishing she were that girl. Then she realized she was that girl. Clark played her song "Who's Sorry Now?" Suddenly Connie was no longer sorry. She was elated. Connie went on to have a successful career in music.

Connie seems a lot like young Samuel and Saul. They were not sure what they should do. They were surprised when they heard God's call that would change their lives forever. Their stories show that we all sometimes need help to understand God's call.

BIBLE LESSON

I. GOD CALLED SAMUEL

Samuel and Saul lived during a momentous time in Israel's history as the nation moved from the tumultuous days of the judges to kingship. The Book of Judges is full of increasing chaos and violence. As we move into the Book of I Samuel, we see God calling Samuel to be a prophet and so much more. He was a kingmaker, a priest, and the last judge of Israel. But the people grew weary of judges and God leading them. They desired a king like all the other nations. God warned them of their choice before giving them what they demanded. Samuel anointed Saul to become the first king of the nation (I Samuel 10:24).

Both Samuel's and Saul's stories reveal the importance of having godly ministers and spiritual advisors to help us make sense of God's call. Young Samuel relied on the wisdom of Eli to help him understand God called him to be a prophet. Samuel did not fully comprehend the voice of God, but Eli told him to talk with God. When Samuel presented himself, God called him to be a prophet (I Samuel 3:1–14).

Samuel used his prophetic gifts to pave the way for Saul to become king. At first, Saul was reluctant to accept the mantle of king, but the Lord helped him overcome his inadequacies. Saul started out well, but he should have paid more attention to the words of Samuel and allowed Samuel to mentor him.

To whom can you turn for godly advice? What advice from them has helped you in the past?

A. Samuel's Mother Dedicated Him to the Lord

Samuel might have felt like he had no choice but to accept his calling because his mother, Hannah, had dedicated him to the Lord before his birth (I Samuel 1). She was unable to have children, so Hannah prayed for a child when she was at the Lord's Temple in Shiloh. She vowed if the Lord would give her a child, she would dedicate him to the Lord.

The priest Eli watched her praying and mistakenly thought she was drunk. He even chastised her. Eli might have had good reason to suspect something nefarious going on in the house of the Lord. Many people came to the Temple to make sacrifices, but they also drank and feasted. But Hannah was not like other people. She had not been drinking. She told Eli her story. When he understood her sorrowful situation, he told Hannah to go in peace, and he prayed that the Lord of Israel would grant what she had been praying for.

Hannah no longer felt sad. She later conceived and gave birth to a son named Samuel. Fulfilling her promise to dedicate Samuel to the Lord, she weaned him and sent him to live in the Temple at Shiloh.

B. When Samuel Heard God Speak, Eli Helped Him Understand God's Voice

Other children may have also lived in the Temple. Parents may have left children there because they could not care for them. Other children may have sought refuge there as they fled war or famine. Yet other parents may have dedicated their children to the Lord as Hannah had done. Like his extraordinary mother, Samuel was not any ordinary child.

One night he heard a voice calling to him. Samuel had no idea what to do. The word of the Lord was rare in those days, so young Samuel had no point of reference. He thought Eli was calling for him, but Eli said he didn't call for him. Samuel returned to his room. The voice called out to Samuel twice more. On the third time, Samuel returned to Eli, and the priest realized the Lord was calling Samuel. He told Samuel to answer, "Speak, LORD; for thy servant heareth" (I Samuel 3:9).

Teacher Option: *Show image to either take the place of the question or to help illustrate it.* ▯

When Samuel answered the call, the Lord told him of his ministry and the fall of the house of Eli. God was going to do something great in Israel, and Samuel would play a vital role in it. Samuel spoke the word of God to the people, and the Lord confirmed every proclamation, not letting any of Samuel's words fall to the ground. As a result, everyone from Dan to Beersheba knew the Lord had established Samuel as a prophet. Dan was the northernmost part of Israel and Beersheba, the southernmost. A similar phrase might be "from coast to coast." Americans might say "from New York to L.A." God made Samuel's prophetic gifts well known, far and wide.

C. We Need the Ministry to Help Us Hear and Understand the Plan of God

Samuel's story teaches us the need for help from the ministry in discerning God's plan for us. We are all trying to listen for God's call, but sometimes we may find it difficult to understand. Hannah certainly struggled with her situation. She wondered why God had given other women children while seemingly abandoning her. But Hannah did not give up. She journeyed to the Temple and prayed.

While prayer is always a good place to start to understand the call of God, we also need men and women of God who can speak words of life to help us gain the understanding we need. Although the priest Eli misunderstood Hannah's desires at first, he later spoke a powerful message of hope to her.

Being raised by a godly mother, Samuel probably knew the importance of faithfulness and dedication, but he had never heard the voice of the Lord. We may find ourselves in similar situations. Those raised in church may look at their upbringing and wonder why they have difficulty understanding God's call despite their knowledge. Those not raised in godly homes may wonder if they missed out on something that would help them hear and understand God's call. In both cases, we should not focus on our inadequacies; we should focus on hearing the call of God. We should make time to talk with godly leaders and spiritual advisors to correctly respond to the call of God.

What may be hindering you from hearing the voice or call of God?

II. GOD CALLED SAUL

Samuel served as a faithful priest, prophet, and judge in Israel. He represented a quintessential minister, possessing all the best characteristics of any leader. He was also a prayer warrior. The people begged Samuel not to stop crying out to the Lord for them. Sadly, the people did not fully appreciate all Samuel had done for them. They demanded a king like all the other nations.

Part of the problem arose because Samuel's sons could not succeed him since they accepted bribes and could not be trusted. Although Samuel had a sterling and unimpeachable reputation, his sons did not. The people also wanted a stronger military. In the era of the judges, Israel's tribes acted as a loose confederation. A few united to defeat a threat but eventually went back to their own territories. A king could unite the tribes and truly make Israel a nation and defeat the menacing Philistines.

The timing also proved ripe for kingship because superpowers were having problems. The Hittite nation disappeared from history, and the Egyptians were weak. The issue of having a king, however, was not merely practical or strategic; it was spiritual. The people had not just rejected Samuel in their demands; they had rejected God (I Samuel 1:8). Therefore, the Lord told Samuel to choose Saul to be the first king of Israel.

A. The Spirit Moved on Saul and God Gave Saul Signs to Confirm His Calling

Samuel first encountered Saul when the soon-to-be king was searching for his father's lost donkeys. Samuel told Saul that the donkeys were found. The prophet then gave Saul food and a place to stay. Samuel took Saul to the outskirts of town and privately anointed him to be king.

Samuel told Saul of several signs that would confirm his calling. Each of those signs came true. Then the Spirit of the Lord rushed on Saul just like on Samson. But instead of receiving super strength, the Spirit moved on Saul and caused him to prophesy. The Spirit changed Saul and made him into a different person. (See I Samuel 10:6.) From that day on, people would ask whether Saul was one of the prophets due to the move of the Spirit in his life. (See I Samuel 10:10–12.)

B. We Must Allow the Spirit to Move in Our Lives

While we all have gifts that make us useful in the kingdom of God, we need something more than our own skills and abilities. We need to allow the Spirit of God to move in our lives to make us who we were truly meant to be. Like Saul, we must be open to becoming a different person.

The New Testament speaks of putting off the old nature through baptism (Romans 6). Baptism by water and baptism of the Holy Spirit help us take on a godly nature (Galatians 3:27). Although Saul lived long before the New Testament era, he experienced something very similar long before the Day of Pentecost in Acts 2.

Once Saul became king, the people saw him win many battles. They might have attributed these victories to his stature. The Israelites were looking for a king, and they wanted someone to be the "big man." Saul didn't think his height and physical appearance would make him a good king. In the early part of his calling to kingship, he recognized his need of the Spirit. Perhaps that is why he felt so reluctant to accept the call.

C. Saul Felt Reluctant to Accept His Call

Whenever we read of individuals being called in the Bible, we often see their reluctance. Moses told the Lord he had difficulty speaking (Exodus 4:10). Isaiah wondered how he could declare the Word of God as a man of unclean lips dwelling among a people of unclean lips (Isaiah 6:5). Jeremiah felt like his youth disqualified him (Jeremiah 1:6).

Saul expressed a similar reluctance when God called him. Samuel privately anointed Saul earlier, but Saul later had a public coronation as the Lord demonstrated to the people that Saul would be king. But at first no one could find Saul because he was hiding among the baggage (I Samuel 10:22). Ironically, a man who looked like a king due to his stature was trying to hide from the people.

D. Though I May Feel Inadequate, the Ministry Can Help Me Accept and Understand My Calling

We may all feel inadequate like Saul, Moses, Isaiah, Jeremiah, and many others. Humility is good when it comes to calling. Surprisingly, humility and exaltation are tied together in Scripture. In speaking to the ministry, I Peter 5:6 provides us with a promise: "Humble yourselves therefore under the mighty hand of God, that he may exalt you in due time." This verse reveals something ironic and spiritually powerful. Many people believe humility is not the path to promotion. That might be true on some level in the natural world, but humility is a spiritual requirement in the kingdom of God.

Teacher Option: A supplemental video is available in the Resource Kit. **V**

What causes your reluctance to answer God's call in your life? How would a man or woman of God in your life respond to your reluctance?

We must have the humility to focus on advancing God's kingdom and not our own. If we have humility that manifests itself in reluctance, we are in good company. But we should not ignore the call. Instead, we should seek the help of the ministry to assist us in understanding our call. Men and women of God can advise us on the next steps. They can pray with us and help us follow God's plan. They are good people to talk to because they have already walked the path of humility and exaltation.

INTERNALIZING THE MESSAGE

The basketball coach at a small but successful college prepared for his day. He had more than a five-o'clock shadow this morning, so he started shaving to make himself more presentable. He sprayed out the shaving cream and lathered up. After taking a few swipes at his growing beard with his razor, he heard his wife's voice from downstairs. There was a phone call for him. Since the story occurred in the days before cell phones, the coach needed to make his way downstairs to answer the landline tethered to the wall.

Wondering if he should even bother with the call, he asked his wife, "Who is it?" as he continued shaving. She replied, "Honey, it's *Sports Illustrated*." The surprising answer shocked the coach, causing him to cut himself while shaving. This was it. His big moment. He had worked so hard to improve his team. Even though most people did not give his program the time of day, one of the best sporting magazines on the planet recognized his coaching genius.

Wiping the blood from his cut face, the coach turned to sprint downstairs. He ran right into the wall, but the pain did not deter him. He rounded the corner and grabbed the handrail. His speed and exuberance nearly caused him to slide down the stairs. Thankfully, the rail saved him. He busted around the corner and hit his knee on the table. Grabbing his throbbing leg, he continued hopping toward the phone. He grabbed it and said, "Hello, *Sports Illustrated*?"

On the other line, a cheerful voice replied, "That's right! And for only a small monthly subscription rate, you can enjoy the very best *Sports Illustrated* has to offer." The dejected coach hung up the phone and slumped down next to the wall.

We may find ourselves in similar situations. No matter the outcome, we should answer the call with the same enthusiasm as the coach. Even if our calling sometimes fails to meet our expectations, we must focus on what God expects from us. While we read of Samuel's wondrous actions as a prophet, we may sometimes forget that he probably had to do seemingly menial chores in the Temple at Shiloh. Although Saul would win many battles as king, his road to the throne began with a search for donkeys.

So, let us answer God's call with enthusiasm. Let us rejoice even if our calling presents us with ordinary situations that may seem pointless to us at the time. If we are faithful, someday God will turn the ordinary into the extraordinary.

Prayer Focus
Lead the group in prayer and consider the following topics of focus:
• For God to help us understand His call for our lives
• For God to help us respond to His call for our lives

GOD'S WORD

FOR LIFE

ADULT LESSON GUIDE

SUMMER 2023

TABLE OF CONTENTS

1.1

AUTHORITY TO FORGIVE

FOCUS VERSE
Mark 2:10
But that ye may know that the Son of man hath power on earth to forgive sins, (he saith to the sick of the palsy,)

LESSON TEXT
**Mark 2:1–12;
Acts 5:29–32**

TRUTH ABOUT GOD
As God, Jesus has the power and authority to forgive sins.

TRUTH FOR MY LIFE
I will trust that God forgives my sins.

Series Overview:

This series, "The Power of Forgiveness," shows the mercy and grace of Jesus Christ on display through several accounts in the Gospels. These lessons highlight the authority of Jesus to forgive, His desire to forgive and not condemn, His command that we forgive others, and the hope that as long as we have breath, we can find a place of forgiveness. This series will help us activate the power of forgiveness in us and through us.

[SG] TEACHING OUTLINE

Icebreaker: What is the most crowded place you've ever been in?

Lesson Connection: Share the Lesson Connection.
> *What do you think the paralyzed man thought when he found out others were healed but he was still paralyzed?*

I. JESUS CAME HOME TO CAPERNAUM

    A. A Crowd Gathered to Hear Him Preach

    B. Four Friends Sought to Bring a Paralytic to Jesus [I]
> *How do you think the homeowner felt? What about the paralyzed friend?*

    C. Jesus Saw Their Faith and Forgave the Man's Sins

    D. I Will Bring My Needs to Jesus [V]
> *What testimonies do you have of God's healing touch? What testimonies do you have of God giving you grace as you wait for His touch?*

II. THE SCRIBES DOUBTED JESUS

    A. Jesus Confronted the Scribes
> *How would you have responded if you were in the crowd?*

    B. His Healing of the Paralytic Confirmed His Deity

    C. I Will Trust That God Forgives My Sins
> *Is it easier to believe God for physical healing or spiritual healing? Why do you think this is the case?*

Internalizing the Message

Prayer Focus
Lead the group in prayer and consider the following topics of focus:
- For God to give us faith to believe Him for whatever we need
- For God to use us to help others receive their miracles

LESSON CONNECTION

Jesus caused a great stir in Capernaum the first time He visited after beginning His ministry. Matthew 4:13 records He had recently moved there. On the first Sabbath after arriving back in town, He and four disciples—Peter, Andrew, James, and John—went to the synagogue where Jesus was given the opportunity to teach.

His teaching astonished the congregation. They had never heard anyone teach like Him before. But suddenly Jesus was interrupted. A man cried out, but the voice wasn't . . . human. A snarling, guttural, demonic voice shouted, "Let us alone; what have we to do with thee, thou Jesus of Nazareth? art thou come to destroy us? I know thee who thou art, the Holy One of God" (Mark 1:24). The crowd was stunned. They were expecting a nice service at synagogue, not an encounter with a demon.

Jesus had already amazed the crowd with His teaching. He amazed them even more with His power. He calmly looked at the man and commanded the demon, "Hold thy peace, and come out of him" (Mark 1:25). Immediately the demon came out. The crowd had never seen a man demonstrate such authority that a demon would obey a human being just because He told it to be quiet and leave. The congregation had a lot to talk about at lunch.

Later, Jesus gave them even more to talk about. When the service was over, He went to Peter's house and found Peter's mother-in-law sick in bed with a fever. With a simple touch, Jesus healed her. News quickly spread of this miracle and of what had happened earlier at the synagogue. That evening the whole town gathered where Jesus was and brought all who were sick or demon possessed to Him, and Jesus healed them all. Actually, there was at least one paralyzed man in town who may not have been carried to Jesus that evening.

This paralytic heard of how Jesus miraculously healed so many in town. He knew he should have been happy for those healed, but as he lay on his bed staring at his lifeless legs, he only felt bitter regret about not being healed himself. His regret increased when he heard Jesus had left town that morning. There would be no healing for him, at least not anytime soon. In that bitter moment, he resolved he would not miss another opportunity to be healed the next time Jesus came to town.

What do you think the paralyzed man thought when he found out others were healed but he was still paralyzed?

BIBLE LESSON

I. JESUS CAME HOME TO CAPERNAUM

After leaving Capernaum, Jesus traveled throughout Galilee preaching in their synagogues and casting out demons (Mark 1:39). Jesus finally made His way back to Capernaum with His disciples and went home. Maybe a nosy neighbor saw Him, but someone spread the news that the miracle worker was back.

A. A Crowd Gathered to Hear Him Preach

Before long, someone was knocking on Jesus' door. Then another and another. So many people showed up to hear Him that the crowd spilled out the door and into the street. Anyone else who showed up would just have to wait for another time to hear Jesus.

B. Four Friends Sought to Bring a Paralytic to Jesus

Soon someone came knocking on the door of the paralytic's house. Four of his friends came in excitedly and let him know, "Jesus is back." Each friend took a corner of the bed and carried him to the house where Jesus was. When they arrived, the crowd wrapped around the house. Some peered in the windows. These men would get nowhere near Jesus. Whatever disappointment they felt at first turned into determination to get to Jesus no matter what.

They did not wait for Him to finish teaching and talk to Him after service. This was their opportunity to see their friend healed. They did not know how many more opportunities like this they would get. One of them saw the stairs on the side of the house leading up to the roof, and a crazy thought came to him. *We could climb to the roof and lower him through it.* They had to be desperate and determined to come up with that idea. After all, this was someone else's house. How would they like strangers tearing off the tiles of their roof?

How do you think the homeowner felt? What about the paralyzed friend?

This idea sounded crazy, but they went for it. These four men hefted their friend in his bed up to the roof and went to work making a large hole to lower him through. A typical roof in Israel at that time was flat. Wooden support beams were put in place, matted branches laid across the beams, and a thick layer of clay piled on the branches. They would have made a raucous noise and major mess digging through all that. Finally the hole was large enough for one of them to peer through. There was Jesus, smiling. He was looking up and nodding His head in approval, maybe even laughing as these four men lowered their friend through the new hole in the roof and set him right in front of Jesus.

Teacher Option: *A supplemental image is available in the Resource Kit.* **I**

C. Jesus Saw Their Faith and Forgave the Man's Sins

This was certainly a first. Never had anyone expressed such determination and faith to get to Jesus. Clearly, these men had great faith, otherwise they would not have done what they did. When Jesus saw their faith, He did not immediately heal their friend. He spoke something altogether unexpected to the paralyzed man: "Son, thy sins be forgiven thee" (Mark 2:5).

Sins? He was not there for forgiveness; he was there for healing. We cannot know what was going on in this unnamed man's heart, but Jesus' actions reveal man's greatest need is not physical healing; it's spiritual healing. This man had been bound to his bed for a long time, but his need to be right with God was greater than his need to walk. The paralytic could have remained paralyzed but still be saved if his sins were forgiven. But what would he have gained if he was healed physically but lived and died unforgiven?

Jesus later asked, "For what shall it profit a man, if he shall gain the whole world, and lose his own soul?" (Mark 8:36). The man's soul was priceless to God, so Jesus dealt with his greatest need first and forgave his sins in response to his faith.

D. I Will Bring My Needs to Jesus

We all have needs. Some of us have great needs only God can meet. Some of us need healing in our bodies. All of us need healing in our souls that only comes through the forgiveness of our sins. We can bring all our needs to Jesus in faith. He can meet any need.

As Apostolics—being like the apostles and the first churches they started—we believe in, proclaim, and pray for physical healing. No Scripture text teaches that Jesus only healed when He physically walked this earth or that healing only occurred while the apostles were alive.

Teacher Option: *A supplemental video is available in the Resource Kit.* V

On the contrary, Jesus said in Mark 16:17–18, "And these signs shall follow them that believe; In my name . . . they shall lay hands on the sick, and they shall recover." Not only does Scripture declare healing is possible, but we also have personal testimonies of being healed. When we need healing in our bodies, we may bring that need to Jesus and believe He can heal us. If the healing doesn't happen immediately, we will keep asking, seeking, and knocking as we are taught in Matthew 7:7. May we have the same determination the paralytic and his friends had. Granted, that process can be difficult and discouraging as we wait for healing, but we pray for more grace to keep looking to God for His touch.

What testimonies do you have of God's healing touch? What testimonies do you have of God giving you grace as you wait for His touch?

Perhaps in certain circumstances God has a different plan for us than healing us of a particular issue. Perhaps God has different timing than ours. It is difficult to imagine a scenario in which healing would not be in our best interest. From our perspective, healing is always best. But we know God's ways are higher than ours, and God knows what He is doing, even when we don't. God will give us grace to keep our faith and believe He is still for us and will accomplish His purpose and be glorified even through our afflictions.

This story in Mark 2 teaches us that our most essential need is salvation. We need to be forgiven of our sins and made alive through the gift of God's Holy Spirit. We must know Jesus and be in right relationship with Him. Let's bring our needs for spiritual healing to Jesus. Through His grace and our faith, we will be made whole.

II.   THE SCRIBES DOUBTED JESUS

When Jesus forgave the paralytic's sins, he immediately felt an inner freedom, a cleansing. He felt something he hadn't felt in a long time: joy. But not everyone there was overjoyed. Some scribes who were experts in the law of Moses were shocked when Jesus dared to pronounce someone's sins forgiven. In their hearts they questioned, *"Why doth this man thus speak blasphemies? who can forgive sins but God only?"* (Mark 2:7). Jesus was presuming to do what only God could do. Exactly. How dare this blasphemer presume to act in God's stead and try to forgive sins? Who does He think He is?

A. Jesus Confronted the Scribes

Jesus knew what the scribes were thinking, and He addressed them head on. "And immediately when Jesus perceived in his spirit that they so reasoned within themselves, he said unto them, Why reason ye these things in your hearts?" (Mark 2:8).

Jesus knew why they were thinking what they were thinking. The Word of God teaches that no mere man could forgive sins; that was God's prerogative alone. The scribes were right about that, but they were wrong that Jesus was blaspheming because they did not understand who Jesus really was. They thought He was just a man—a wicked one at that—who dared to claim the attributes of God. They did not understand that He was the Son of God, God in flesh, who exercised all the authority of God.

Jesus also knew they would not believe that the paralytic's sins were forgiven, so He worked another miracle for the glory of God. Jesus proposed a simple test. "Whether is it easier to say to the sick of the palsy, Thy sins be forgiven thee; or to say, Arise, and take up thy bed, and walk? But that ye may know that the Son of man hath power on earth to forgive sins, (he saith to the sick of the palsy,) I say unto thee, Arise, and take up thy bed, and go thy way into thine house" (Mark 2:9-11).

The crowd gasped. Right before their eyes, the paralytic—now the former paralytic—stood up. Then he did exactly what Jesus told him to do. "Immediately he arose, took up the bed, and went forth before them all" (Mark 2:12). He might have wanted to stay and celebrate with Jesus and his friends, but if the one who just healed you tells you to get up and leave, you get up and leave. But he probably did not just calmly walk out. He likely leapt and joyfully headed out the door and toward home. As he walked away rejoicing, he heard voices in the house raised in praise to God. The crowd was amazed and glorified God. They had never seen anything quite like that.

How would you have responded if you were in the crowd?

B. His Healing of the Paralytic Confirmed His Deity

In this amazing miracle, we see that Jesus was not just a man but was God revealed in the flesh. Scripture reveals the deity of Christ in two main ways: by direct statements that testify Jesus was God in flesh and by examples of Jesus doing or saying things only God could do or say.

In this case of the paralytic, we see Jesus doing and saying something only God could do or say. If Jesus had just healed the man, that would not prove He was God in flesh because God can use us to lay hands on someone and help bring healing. By no means does this mean we are divine.

In this story, Jesus forgiving this man's sins and then healing him of his paralysis confirm Jesus' deity. The man's physical healing helped prove his spiritual healing. Jesus has the power to forgive, not as a man, but as God in flesh.

C. I Will Trust That God Forgives My Sins

Jesus is still forgiving sins today. Acts 5:31 tells us Jesus is seated in Heaven at the right hand of God, which means in the place of supreme authority, "to be a Prince and a Saviour, for to give repentance to Israel, and forgiveness of sins." Jesus made forgiveness of sins possible through His death on the cross to pay the penalty for our sins and through His resurrection and ascension to Heaven. Forgiveness becomes a reality for us when we turn to Jesus as our Lord and Savior in faith and repentance and call on His name in baptism. We can trust that Jesus will forgive our sins just as He forgave the man in Mark 2.

Forgiveness, of course, is not just a one-time experience. Repentance is not just a one-time act. Until the Lord returns and we are transformed to be like Him, we are liable to still sin even as we walk with God in a life of holiness. When we inevitably fall short of the glory of God and His perfect standard, let's be thankful we can turn back to Jesus and be forgiven again.

Is it easier to believe God for physical healing or spiritual healing? Why do you think this is the case?

May we never take His mercy and grace for granted, but when we need forgiveness, we are invited to come boldly to the throne of grace to obtain mercy and find grace to help in our time of need (Hebrews 4:16). He freely offers mercy and grace to those who have faith in Him like He did for the paralytic.

INTERNALIZING THE MESSAGE

What a celebration the former paralytic and his friends must have had later that day. They probably laughed at what they had actually done. "Man, we tore up the roof to get you to Jesus."

"Yeah, and now I get to help you repair it."

The former paralytic was thrilled to be able to walk with his friends to go repair the roof. Their determination and desperation to get to Jesus certainly paid off in more than one way. He received physical healing, which first caused him to seek out Jesus, and he received something much more significant: spiritual healing when Jesus forgave his sins. He just wanted to walk physically, but now he could walk with the Lord spiritually. He was restored in body and soul.

We learn so much from this story. Physical healing is possible through Jesus Christ. We should pray for people to be healed in their bodies. But spiritual healing is even more important; it should be our priority. Ideally, we'll experience both like the paralytic did, but should we remain unhealed physically, may God give us the grace to be grateful to receive what we need most and still make our priority our relationship with the Lord.

We also get a glimpse close to the beginning of Jesus' ministry that Jesus was not just a man; He was God in flesh. Jesus used physical healing as proof that He had the authority to forgive sins. By miraculously showing He had the authority to forgive sins, He revealed He was no mere man, but God in flesh. When we are healed physically, glory to God. And when we are not healed physically, glory to God. Let's be thankful we are saved, and let's exalt Jesus as God in flesh.

When we read this story, we likely tend to see ourselves in the role of the paralytic in need of healing. We should also seek to fulfill the role of the friends. The paralytic would have remained as he was, unhealed and unforgiven, if he had not had someone to bring him to Jesus. Jesus wants to use us to bring others to Him. It may be inconvenient. It may require us to do things we might not be inclined to do. These four friends weren't inclined to dig holes in someone else's roof. But what joy they experienced in being instrumental in their friend being forgiven and healed. The former paralytic never forgot what they had done for him. In the remaining time we have as we wait "for that blessed hope, and the glorious appearing of the great God and our Saviour Jesus Christ" (Titus 2:13), may God use us greatly to bring others to Jesus for healing, spiritually and physically.

Prayer Focus
Lead the group in prayer and consider the following topics of focus:
- For God to give us faith to believe Him for whatever we need
- For God to use us to help others receive their miracles

SERIES 1: THE POWER OF FORGIVENESS

1.2

GO AND SIN NO MORE

FOCUS VERSE
John 8:11
She said, No man, Lord. And Jesus said unto her, Neither do I condemn thee: go, and sin no more.

LESSON TEXT
John 3:17; 8:1–11; Romans 6:15–23

TRUTH ABOUT GOD
God desires to extend grace instead of condemnation.

TRUTH FOR MY LIFE
I will receive God's grace and choose not to continue in my sin.

Thinking about Last Week:

Have students refer to their Daily Devotional Guide to answer the following questions:
1. What most affected you as you read through the Lesson Text and the Biblical Insights?
2. How did it shape your prayers and thoughts throughout the week?
3. Do you feel you grew closer to the Lord this past week? Why or why not?

SG TEACHING OUTLINE

Icebreaker: Can you think of a time when you did the right thing with the wrong motive?

Lesson Connection: Share the Lesson Connection.

I. JESUS TAUGHT THE PEOPLE IN THE TEMPLE

    A. The Scribes and Pharisees Brought a Woman Caught in Adultery
       » *Does this situation seem suspicious to you? What do you think the scribes and Pharisees were after?*

    B. Jesus Ignored Her Accusers ⬛I
       » *What do you think Jesus wrote on the ground?*

    C. I Will Listen to Jesus Instead of My Accusers

II. AFTER CONTINUAL QUESTIONS JESUS FINALLY RESPONDED TO THE ACCUSERS

    A. "He That Is Without Sin . . . Let Him First Cast a Stone"
       » *How does this wisdom help to confirm Jesus' deity?*

    B. Jesus and the Woman Were Left Alone

    C. "Go, and Sin No More" ⬛V

    D. I Will Receive God's Grace and Choose Not to Continue in My Sin
       » *How does this story present the perfect balance of justice and mercy?*

Internalizing the Message
       » *How can we live in the divine balance of justice and mercy?*

Prayer Focus
Lead the group in prayer and consider the following topics of focus:
• For God to help us live to show mercy to those who sin
• For God to help us live above the power of sin

LESSON CONNECTION

These men wore their badges proudly. They were the self-commissioned purity police. They roamed around with their ticket pads open and pens drawn, ready to write anyone up who broke Moses' law. On that day they finally found the purity police's most wanted. They planned a raid to arrest her in the act, but they were not just after her. They wanted to use this opportunity to arrest Jesus.

They could hardly sleep a wink that night. As they tossed and turned, their ears rang with the blasphemous words of that carpenter saying, "If any man thirst, let him come unto me, and drink. He that believeth on me, as the scripture hath said, out of his belly shall flow rivers of living water" (John 7:37–38). They had heard worship as some of the crowd who was listening began believing. Some had even hailed Him as their Messiah. But He could not be their Messiah. He was just a carpenter, from Nazareth no less. They had studied the Law. They knew what the Messiah would be like, what He would do. They even knew where He would come from. He would come from Bethlehem, not Nazareth. This poor impostor was no Messiah.

Jesus had come to Jerusalem for the Feast of Tabernacles. During this holy feast, the Jews remembered the hardships their ancestors had experienced as they wandered through the wilderness after God set them free from Egyptian slavery. Jesus was ruining their holy festival. In the name of righteousness, they had to put a stop to His teaching, even if that meant putting a stop to Him. As they schemed, they finally fell asleep.

As the sun began to peek above the plain, Jesus was already up, headed down toward the city. Merchants in the marketplace were dabbing dew off their carts, opening up for the day. Jesus nodded at them as He headed for His house, the Temple. He was greeted warmly by a full house—some familiar faces, some new faces. Everyone was there to hear what this wonder worker would say. The day before, He had promised they could be filled with the Spirit of God. What would He promise this day? Some leaned against the outside walls with their arms folded, still not sure what to think but curious what He would say. Others sat close, hanging on every word, hoping to hear a specific word from Him for them. Suddenly they heard screams and shouts as the purity police paraded in, dragging a woman behind them. We pick up her story in John 8.

BIBLE LESSON

I. JESUS TAUGHT THE PEOPLE IN THE TEMPLE

A. The Scribes and Pharisees Brought a Woman Caught in Adultery

While Jesus taught in the Temple, somewhere else in Jerusalem scribes and Pharisees had arrested a woman caught in adultery. They brought this humiliated woman to the Temple. They interrupted Jesus' teaching, set her right in front of Him, and loudly announced they had caught her in the very act of adultery. This whole situation was suspicious. These scribes and Pharisees did not need to humiliate her and involve Jesus. To them, He was not the highest religious authority. They could have locked her in a cell until they could bring her before the Sanhedrin. Obviously, adultery involves two people, so where was the guilty man? If the man somehow escaped when the woman was arrested, they made no effort to arrest him. And how did they know when and where to go to catch her? This scene seemed like a setup.

Does this situation seem suspicious to you? What do you think the scribes and Pharisees were after?

The humiliated woman sat there as her accusers stood before Jesus. John 8:4-6 records their opening statements. "They say unto him, Master, this woman was taken in adultery, in the very act. Now Moses in the law commanded us, that such should be stoned: but what sayest thou? This they said, tempting him, that they might have to accuse him." John identified their motive. Their motive was not necessarily promoting righteousness; it was trapping Jesus. They were using the woman just to put Jesus in an impossible situation.

If Jesus replied, "Let her go," they could accuse Him of breaking the law of Moses, which clearly called for execution by stoning as the penalty for adultery. This response would turn the Jews against Him and His teaching. But if He replied, "Execute her," they could accuse Him of advocating they break Roman law. The Romans had stripped the Jewish authorities' right to execute people for religious crimes. He would end up being punished by the Romans. They could not lose. Jesus was as good as gone.

B. Jesus Ignored Her Accusers

Teacher Option: A supplemental image is available in the Resource Kit. **I**

However, He said neither. In fact, He said nothing. Jesus did not immediately respond to her accusers. He stooped down and wrote on the ground with His finger, like He did not even hear them. The Gospel writer did not tell us why Jesus wrote or what He wrote. Teachers and preachers have speculated for years what He wrote. Perhaps He was diffusing this dangerous situation by taking a breath and writing a few words. Or perhaps Jesus stooped down to show He was not standing over her in judgment. Some have suggested He began writing the names of women the accusers had inappropriate relationships with or that He wrote other sins they committed. For whatever reason, Jesus

What do you think Jesus wrote on the ground?

wrote what He wrote, and before long, the accusers pressed Him again for His response.

C. I Will Listen to Jesus Instead of My Accusers

Jesus had not liberated the accused woman yet, but He had not accused her either. Maybe Jesus' writing encouraged her and gave her hope. His behavior was not hostile toward her in any way, and He seemed to be concerned not to humiliate her any further. Perhaps when Jesus ignored her accusers and knelt down close to her, she fixed her eyes on Him and ignored them as well. Was there something in Jesus' eyes or facial expression that drew her to Him and allowed her to trust Him with her life?

To be in right relationship with God, we often have to ignore accusers. The devil will bring our sins and failures to our attention with great clarity to make us think there is no way God would forgive us. He might try to make us think, *I'm flawed. I always end up doing wrong—that's just what I am and do.* Other people may mock our attempts to live for the Lord and say it won't last. We really can't control what others might do or say. All we can do is ignore them and focus on the Lord and what He says about us.

In John 3:17, Jesus said, "For God sent not his Son into the world to condemn the world; but that the world through him might be saved." Jesus did not come just to proclaim we are sinners and guilty before God; He came to save us. Does this mean the woman's sin was no big deal? Of course not. Her sin and ours cost Jesus His life. Forgiveness for our sins and salvation for our souls are why He came. He came to pay the price for our sins so we may be saved.

II. AFTER CONTINUAL QUESTIONS JESUS FINALLY RESPONDED TO THE ACCUSERS

These prosecutors did not let Jesus off the hook. They demanded He pass His judgment on her and her sin. Finally, He stood up, wiped the dust off His hands, and in one sentence blew apart their entire scheme. Jesus responded, "He that is without sin among you, let him first cast a stone at her" (John 8:7).

A. "He That Is Without Sin . . . Let Him First Cast a Stone"

This was a divinely inspired response. Jesus did not urge them to violate the law of Moses. In fact, He gave them permission to carry out justice just as long as they never needed mercy. They could cast a stone if they were qualified, but that meant they were not guilty of her same sin or any sin. According to Moses' law, when someone was sentenced to death by stoning, one of the witnesses of that capital crime had to cast the first stone. Then the other witnesses could join in. Someone did not get to make baseless accusations against someone and be done; they had to be involved in carrying out the sentence. If they were caught lying, they suffered the same sentence they intended for the accused.

Jesus was not going to let them off the hook. If they were genuinely concerned for righteousness to prevail in Israel, they would have to carry out the sentence according to the Law right then. And since they were apparently so concerned about Jesus' views on the situation, He added the qualification for who could carry out this capital sentence: someone with no sin of his own. This stripped them of their hypocrisy. Surely they would not be unjust and call for her punishment while being guilty of sin themselves, and surely they wouldn't punish her while failing to also punish the other guilty party.

Jesus knew their motives. The accusers had not come to the Temple to punish a crime but to trap Jesus. In one brilliant sentence, He exposed their hypocrisy and true motives and destroyed their attempt to turn the Jews or the Romans against Him. The Jews would not be upset because Jesus supported the Law. The Romans would not be upset because Jesus made it impossible for the accusers to break their law.

How does this wisdom help to confirm Jesus' deity?

B. Jesus and the Woman Were Left Alone

After Jesus' response, He knelt down and wrote on the ground again. While He wrote, the accusers thought. And they fumed. His words pierced their consciences. They felt their own putrid hypocrisy. Then from the oldest—the ones with the longest record of sin to think about—to the youngest, they all left. All of them. It even appears all the people who came to hear Jesus also left.

C. "Go, and Sin No More"

When the final accuser and onlooker were far away, Jesus stood up and asked, "Woman, where are those thine accusers? hath no man condemned thee?" (John 8:10). Greatly relieved, she humbly replied, "No man, Lord." Jesus replied, "Neither do I condemn thee: go, and sin no more" (John 8:11). Many Christians have been troubled by this story, as if Jesus were treating sexual immorality as insignificant. But Jesus was not treating it that way. Remember, her sin and ours cost Him His life. Rather, Jesus stayed true to His mission, not to condemn, but to save.

Teacher Option: A supplemental video is available in the Resource Kit. **V**

He did not have to condemn her. Her conscience convicted her. She was ashamed beneath the full weight of her sin. She had a repentant heart, tender toward God in response to His grace. Standing there in the presence of grace in flesh, she was forgiven. She was set free. Salvation is not just about being forgiven or just being freed from the penalty of sin, such as condemnation and judgment. Salvation is also about being freed from the power of sin that controlled us and then seeking to live like Jesus wants us to according to His commands.

In the same moment Jesus offered her forgiveness, He also called her to stop living in sin and to start living a life of devotion to God—a life of repentance and holiness. The message of salvation is good news. That's why it's called the gospel. No matter how great our sin, God's grace is greater, and God will forgive those who turn to Christ to be saved. But let us not forget the second part of Jesus' sentence. We are called to go and sin no more. Just because God is so merciful and has given us so much grace does not give us a license to freely disregard God's Word. Paul wrote in Romans 6:15, "What then? shall we sin, because we are not under the law, but under grace? God forbid." According to the same chapter, if we continue to flagrantly sin and disregard God's Word, we are living like sin is our lord, rather than Christ. Living like that leads to death—eternal death separated from God. (See Romans 6:16, 23.)

But praise God for all who trust in Jesus for salvation and who, through the power of the indwelling Holy Spirit, live like Jesus is Lord and allow the Holy Spirit to make them holy. Praise God for the everlasting promise of everlasting life.

D. I Will Receive God's Grace and Choose Not to Continue in My Sin

When we have faith in Christ and repent, like the woman forgiven of adultery, the Lord floods our souls with grace and forgives us. Just as Jesus told the woman to go and sin no more, the same command comes to us. None of us will ever be perfect in this life, but by the power of God's Spirit that dwells in us, we can live a life marked by obedience and victory over sin, a life where we don't flagrantly disobey God and His Word. If we truly believe Jesus is Lord, we will seek to live like it.

Paul described Christians as those who have been graciously set free from the power of sin that was destroying their lives. We are like slaves who have been liberated from slavery that would have killed us. How should we live in response to that? We should live with thanksgiving for God's grace and His power that set us free. Let's make our best effort not to yield ourselves to our former master, sin, but yield ourselves only to the true Master, Jesus Christ. In other words, let us go and sin no more.

How does this story present the perfect balance of justice and mercy?

INTERNALIZING THE MESSAGE

Jesus handled this very difficult and tricky situation so graciously and wisely. In just a few minutes—with a single sentence—not only did He destroy His opponents' effort to discredit Him, but He also ministered to the woman and helped turn her from her sin and set her on the path of salvation.

The command to sin no more seems impossible, but she was not left on her own. Right before this suspicious scene in the Temple, Jesus taught, "If any man thirst, let him come unto me, and drink. He that believeth on me, as the scripture hath said, out of his belly shall flow rivers of living water" (John 7:37-38). After Jesus' resurrection, He would guide her so she could come to receive the Holy Spirit to give her new spiritual life and to empower her to walk with Him. His Spirit within her would be a continual source of spiritual life, vitality, and power to live the life He called her to live.

Thankfully, through the life-giving power of the Spirit, we too can drink more deeply of the Spirit in order to live a life above the bondage of sin. It's not complicated. Most of us already know what to do to open our lives wider to the working of the Spirit. Let's fill our days with daily prayer and Bible reading. Let's join together weekly with other believers in services for worship and to hear the Word proclaimed. And let's fast on a regular basis to disconnect from the world and draw closer to God. In calling us to heed Jesus' command, let's do what will enable us to do just that. And let us always remember we are living for our gracious and loving Lord, who is for us, who will help us, who will forgive us when we inevitably stumble, and who will pick us back up so we can keep walking.

How can we live in the divine balance of justice and mercy?

Prayer Focus

Lead the group in prayer and consider the following topics of focus:
- For God to help us live to show mercy to those who sin
- For God to help us live above the power of sin

SERIES 1: THE POWER OF FORGIVENESS

1.3

SEVENTY TIMES SEVEN

FOCUS VERSES
Matthew 18:21–22
²¹ Then came Peter to him, and said, Lord, how oft shall my brother sin against me, and I forgive him? till seven times?
²² Jesus saith unto him, I say not unto thee, Until seven times: but, Until seventy times seven.

LESSON TEXT
Matthew 18:21–35

TRUTH ABOUT GOD
A forgiving God requires us to forgive others.

TRUTH FOR MY LIFE
I must forgive others as Jesus has forgiven me.

Thinking about Last Week:

Have students refer to their Daily Devotional Guide to answer the following questions:
1. What most affected you as you read through the Lesson Text and the Biblical Insights?
2. How did it shape your prayers and thoughts throughout the week?
3. Do you feel you grew closer to the Lord this past week? Why or why not?

SG TEACHING OUTLINE

Icebreaker: How would you describe forgiveness to someone who has never heard of it?

Lesson Connection: Share the Lesson Connection. I

I. THE KINGDOM OF HEAVEN IS LIKE A CERTAIN KING

    A. The King Had Compassion and Chose to Forgive His Servant

        » *How would you respond if you were forgiven of a debt you knew you could not pay?*

    B. God Will Forgive Our Debts

        » *Why do we see our sins as small but others' as great? How does God see our sins compared to others' sins?*

II. THE KING'S SERVANT WAS UNGRATEFUL

    A. The Servant Refused to Forgive

        » *How would you have felt if you were this second servant? What if you were the other servants witnessing this ingratitude?*

    B. The King Condemned This Unforgiving Servant

        » *Do you feel this response by the king was just? Are you surprised the king rescinded his forgiveness and required his servant to pay the debt he previously forgave?*

    C. We Must Forgive Others as Jesus Has Forgiven Us

        » *What benefits have you felt from forgiving others?*

Internalizing the Message V

Prayer Focus

Lead the group in prayer and consider the following topics of focus:
- For God to help us forgive others
- For God to heal us from the hurts others have caused

LESSON CONNECTION

A supplemental image is available in the Resource Kit. (I)

Ｎew York City at Christmastime is breathtaking. Ryan and Ashley flew there from Florida to spend three days in Manhattan. It was beautiful and busy. One of their friends drove them around town. Traffic was so tightly packed, they felt like they could reach out the window and open the glove compartment of the car beside them. Yellow cabs with silver bumpers were everywhere. The bumpers used to be yellow, but it's not really a good day for a cabbie in New York unless they've traded a little paint.

One of the highlights of that trip was a little shopping trip to Chinatown. Ryan wanted a baseball cap, but he did not want to pay full price. Chinatown was famous for bargaining, but Ryan wasn't exactly the bargaining kind of guy. His friend coached him on how to get the best price.

They'll sell for high, but you offer low. They'll say no; you walk out. Then you meet in the middle. That was how the game was played. Ryan gave it a shot. He walked into a shop, saw the baseball cap on the shelf, and asked, "How much for the Braves hat?"

"Twenty bucks."

"Will you take fifteen?"

"Twenty."

"Sold."

Maybe next time. Everyone wants to pay as little as possible to get as much as possible. Peter was no better at the game than Ryan. Peter walked into the store and saw Jesus standing behind the counter. Mercy was sitting on every shelf, and on the counter, and on the racks, and in the windows. Mercy was everywhere in this shop, but Peter knew Jesus. He knew how much Jesus valued mercy, so rather than insult Jesus by asking to pay less for it, he offered Jesus above asking price.

The rabbis down the street were selling mercy for three bucks a day. They taught if a brother sins against you, God calls you to forgive him three times. After that, you're off the hook. But Peter knew Jesus was more merciful than most. In fact, He was more merciful than everyone. Peter opened up his wallet, pulled out three bills, then three more, and one more for good measure. He offered Jesus well above asking price.

"Jesus, if my brother sins against me, how many times should I forgive him? Up to seven times? You want me to be merciful, Jesus? Can do." Seven times seemed mighty merciful to Peter, especially since the going rate was three times. Jesus took a glance at mercy all throughout the shop and replied, "Not seven, Peter. Seventy times seven." Then Jesus told this story.

BIBLE LESSON

I. THE KINGDOM OF HEAVEN IS LIKE A CERTAIN KING

Jesus began in Matthew 18:23, "Therefore is the kingdom of heaven likened unto a certain king, which would take account of his servants." The king decided to review the accounting books to see who owed him money and how much they owed. Then it was up to his collections department to demand payment for all debts. That accounting audit revealed a debtor who owed him ten thousand talents.

A talent was a measurement of weight in silver or gold. We do not know exactly how much ten thousand talents might be in today's economy, but it would be in the millions of dollars. The amount the debtor owed was so great, he would never be able to pay back the debt he owed. Jesus and His audience knew what that meant for the man and his family. "But forasmuch as he had not to pay, his lord commanded him to be sold, and his wife, and children, and all that he had, and payment to be made" (Matthew 18:25).

Since the servant couldn't pay, the king sentenced him and his family to slavery and demanded all their possessions be sold and the proceeds given to the king. Unfortunately, this didn't come close to paying the full debt. Slaves at top price were sometimes sold for a talent each, but usually they were sold for a tenth of a talent.

A. The King Had Compassion and Chose to Forgive His Servant

In one last plea for mercy, the indebted servant fell to his knees and begged for more time. That made no sense. All the time in his lifetime would not be enough. But suddenly, Jesus' story took a surprising turn. "Then the lord of that servant was moved with compassion, and loosed him, and forgave him the debt" (Matthew 18:27). Just like that, his debt was gone. The king did not mock him; he forgave him. The king felt compassion for this man and didn't just lower his debt; he forgave it.

What overwhelming joy the servant felt. The crushing debt was gone. He and his family were safe, and his property was secure. They were saved. "Thank you, my king. I could never receive a greater gift than what you gave me." What joy, what rejoicing.

B. God Will Forgive Our Debts

How would you respond if you were forgiven of a debt you knew you could not pay?

This is a snapshot of the mercy of God when He forgives all our sins. Our sins are like a debt we owe to God. Our debt of sin is so huge, we can never repay it. Because we can't pay, we face great punishment, but God in His great compassion forgives us when we come to Him and freely acknowledge we have no means to pay. Thank God He forgives the debt we could never pay.

This story also gives us insight into how great our sins are from God's point of view. Many of us think of ourselves as pretty good, and we may be from our limited human perspective. We think we're better than most people in our world. We might not be great saints, but we're not great sinners. We tend to minimize our own sin by thinking it's not that bad. However, we have no accurate sense of the number of times we have failed to follow God's Word.

No matter how we feel about our sins, God is pure and sinless. He is holy. We are like poor servants owing a debt of ten thousand talents, an unpayable debt. Our only hope is for our gracious King to have compassion on us and announce, "I forgive your debt. You owe me nothing." The penalty for our unpaid sins is eternal death and separation from God in Hell. All we can do is bow our knees to our King and plead for mercy. When we do, we are sure to find a King, gracious and good, ready to forgive.

Jesus was sinless and didn't deserve to die, but He willingly died in our place. God said His death would be a substitute for ours if we turned to Jesus in faith. The Cross is all about Jesus paying the debt we could never pay.

> Why do we see our sins as small but others' as great? How does God see our sins compared to others' sins?

II. THE KING'S SERVANT WAS UNGRATEFUL

The story again took a surprising but unpleasant turn. Our friend, who was just forgiven of his unpayable debt, "went out, and found one of his fellowservants, which owed him an hundred pence: and he laid hands on him, and took him by the throat, saying, Pay me that thou owest" (Matthew 18:28). He ran out of the throne room and sought out a man who owed him a debt. He grabbed his debtor by the throat and choked him, demanding he pay back everything he owed.

This second debtor in Jesus' parable only owed his friend a hundred pence, which would take around three months to pay back. This debt was payable. It was pennies compared to the millions the first servant owed the king. The second servant responded just like the first servant. "And his fellowservant fell down at his feet, and besought him, saying, Have patience with me, and I will pay thee all" (Matthew 18:29).

A. The Servant Refused to Forgive

Here is the unpleasant turn. No matter how merciful the king had been to the first servant, his heart was unmoved by his fellow servant's plea for mercy. He threw his debtor into prison until he could pay the debt. He would remain imprisoned until family or friends could gather the amount of money owed or until the prisoner worked off all the debt.

This kind of shocking behavior could not remain hidden. Some of the king's other servants witnessed this ungrateful act and told the king everything they had seen. Doubtless these other servants heard of the extraordinary kindness the king had shown the first servant, so when they saw how cruelly he treated his fellow servant, they couldn't believe the hypocrisy and ingratitude. How could he possibly act that way after all he had been forgiven?

B. The King Condemned This Unforgiving Servant

When the king learned what the first servant had done, the king was shocked and furious. Matthew 18 reads, "Then his lord, after that he had called him, said unto him, O thou wicked servant, I forgave thee all that debt, because thou desiredst me: shouldest not thou also have had compassion on thy fellowservant, even as I had pity on thee? And his lord was wroth, and delivered him to the tormentors, till he should pay all that was due unto him" (Matthew 18:32–34).

The king summoned the servant to return to the throne room and called him wicked. The forgiven servant failed to show the same kind of mercy to others that he had received from the king. The king said, "You should have treated him as I treated you. You should have had mercy." But because the servant refused to be merciful, he disqualified himself from receiving mercy. His unpayable debt was his to pay. The first servant was thrown into prison himself until he could pay all his debt, but everyone knew he would die in prison.

C. We Must Forgive Others as Jesus Has Forgiven Us

In case we miss the point of this powerful story, Jesus made it very plain: "So likewise shall my heavenly Father do also unto you, if ye from your hearts forgive not every one his brother their trespasses" (Matthew 18:35). A forgiving God requires us to forgive others. I must forgive. You must forgive. Why? Our debt owed to God is infinitely greater compared to any debt a person could owe us. If God was willing to forgive us of our unpayable debt, we must be willing to forgive others their much smaller debts. And if we refuse to forgive—not just struggle but refuse to forgive—Jesus explicitly taught that God will not forgive us.

In Jesus' sermon in Matthew 6, He taught us to pray, "And forgive us our debts, as we forgive our debtors. . . . For if ye forgive men their trespasses, your heavenly Father will also forgive you: but if ye forgive not men their trespasses, neither will your Father forgive your trespasses" (Matthew 6:12–15).

Jesus is calling us to forgive, else we will not be forgiven. He's calling us to always be willing to forgive. Remember that Jesus was answering Peter's question about how often we are to forgive others by saying, "I say not unto thee, Until seven times: but, Until seventy times seven" (Matthew 18:22). This teaching is very difficult. Depending on the sin committed against us, it can be even revolting or offensive to us to think we need to forgive.

> How would you have felt if you were this second servant? What if you were the other servants witnessing this ingratitude?

> Do you feel this response by the king was just? Are you surprised the king rescinded his forgiveness and required his servant to pay the debt he previously forgave?

We might have difficulty with Jesus' teaching on forgiveness in this story because we don't believe our sins against God could be such a huge unpayable debt. As far as we know, we haven't really hurt someone else or been too wicked toward someone, so we can't believe our sins against God are quite as bad as someone's sin against us.

But in this story, Jesus was showing us how God views the situation. Our being born in sin and the cumulative sins we have committed against Him by breaking His law are greater than someone's sins against us. If God forgave us, we must forgive others, otherwise we disqualify ourselves from being forgiven by God.

Certainly, benefits come to us when we forgive others. Studies have revealed some of the benefits of forgiveness: improved mental health, less anxiety and stress, lower blood pressure, fewer issues with depression, and so forth. It's good to know and experience these benefits, but these potential benefits are not why Jesus commanded us to forgive; He commanded us to forgive because God has forgiven us. That is the right reason for forgiveness; no more, no less.

What benefits have you felt from forgiving others?

INTERNALIZING THE MESSAGE

A supplemental video is available in the Resource Kit. **V**

This teaching is hard, and depending on the situation, it may be extremely hard to follow. Forgiving someone does not mean that what the person did was okay, and in extreme situations such as abuse, consult the proper leaders or authorities. Yet the Lord is calling us to forgive—to release debt and put the person in His hands. You may not be able to imagine how you could forgive a particular person, but if you commit to forgive, God will help you through His Spirit to forgive. He will strengthen you in the journey of forgiveness until it is finished.

Forgiving is not pretending the wrong did not happen. Neither is forgiving allowing someone to continue willfully and maliciously harming us. Forgiveness is an act of the will. It happens when we consciously decide to cancel someone's debt, which means we will not hold the wrong over the person, actively seeking to punish or turn others against the person. When we forgive, we decide we will not retaliate or repay someone for what he or she has done. In doing this, we make space for God to avenge us if He thinks we need to be avenged. God's Word still declares, "Vengeance is mine; I will repay, saith the Lord" (Romans 12:19). Forgiveness gives God permission to fight our battles.

Let's not think of forgiveness as a feeling, especially at first. It is deeper than ceasing to feel angry, resentful, or hurt. It will likely be a long time before we can feel that way. Think of forgiveness as a commitment to act or not to act. Over time God will change our feelings, and they will soften and not sting quite as much. It may take a long time—perhaps a year or longer—but God can work on our hearts as we seek to obey Him. And God will heal our hearts, and we will be able to think of the person who hurt us without feeling hatred, anger, or bitterness. The sting will be gone.

Choosing to forgive takes a moment, but the process takes time. And we can know when the process is complete. We have fully forgiven when we no longer tell our story as the victim trying to get people to sympathize with us and turn against the person who hurt us. Further, we know we have forgiven when we no longer get pleasure or satisfaction when we hear something negative has happened to that person.

Forgiveness is not an option. If you've been hurt, forgive. Don't wait until the person comes to you seeking to make everything right. That may never happen. Our Lord commanded us to freely forgive—forgive without limits. The one who forgave our unpayable debt calls us to forgive the debts others owe us, and He stands ready to empower us and bless us as we seek to obey Him by forgiving others.

Prayer Focus
Lead the group in prayer and consider the following topics of focus:
- For God to help us forgive others
- For God to heal us from the hurts others have caused

SERIES 1: THE POWER OF FORGIVENESS

1.4

THE TALE OF TWO THIEVES

FOCUS VERSE
Luke 23:42
And he said
unto Jesus, Lord,
remember me when
thou comest into thy
kingdom.

LESSON TEXT
**Matthew
27:39–43; Luke
23:32–43**

TRUTH ABOUT GOD
God is always ready
to save.

TRUTH FOR MY LIFE
I can call on Jesus
and find a place of
repentance.

Thinking about Last Week:

Have students refer to their Daily Devotional Guide
to answer the following questions:
1. What most affected you as you read through
   the Lesson Text and the Biblical Insights?
2. How did it shape your prayers and thoughts
   throughout the week?
3. Do you feel you grew closer to the Lord this
   past week? Why or why not?

SG TEACHING OUTLINE

Icebreaker: If you have ever stolen anything, what is the least valuable item you stole?

Lesson Connection: Share the Lesson Connection.

I. JESUS WAS CRUCIFIED BETWEEN TWO THIEVES

    A. Jesus Was Mocked on the Cross

        » *In understanding Jesus died so we can live, how should that make us feel toward Him?*

    B. The King of the Jews Ⓘ

        » *How does God use the cross, a symbol of shame, as a symbol of hope for us?*

    C. I Will Choose to Worship Jesus as My Savior and King

II. THE UNREPENTANT THIEF

    A. "If You Are the Christ, Save Yourself and Us"

    B. We Must Choose Humility When Approaching Jesus for Forgiveness

III. THE HUMBLE THIEF

        » *How can multiple people hear the same message or encounter Jesus in the same way, yet one believes in Him while others remain hardened in unbelief?*

    A. He Admitted His Own Guilt and Turned to Jesus for Mercy

    B. "Today You Will Be with Me in Paradise" Ⓥ

        » *Some are offended that a thief could be with Jesus after only praying near the end of his life. Why do we feel like people need to earn their right to be saved?*

    C. We Can Call on Jesus and Find a Place of Repentance

        » *Have you already responded in this way to the gospel of Jesus Christ? If not, are you ready to turn to Jesus?*

Internalizing the Message

Prayer Focus
Lead the group in prayer and consider the following topics of focus:
• For God to help us always have a repentant heart
• For God to help us minister to those who need Him

LESSON CONNECTION

Matt and Lydia were heading out to dinner and maybe a little shopping on that Friday night. They motored down the main boulevard in their Dodge Spirit, looking for the right place for a dinner date. Since they were in Orlando metro, there were more restaurants than Disney has Dalmatians. Before long, they noticed police presence everywhere. Police cars sped by with lights flashing and sirens blaring. Police officers and sheriff deputies were on foot, shining flashlights as they searched the ditches. Helicopters circled overhead, shining their spotlights on the unsuspecting city below.

Matt and Lydia finished a delicious dinner and headed back toward their apartment. Even after hours of this countywide manhunt, the police were still searching for their suspect. Matt pulled the car in front of their apartment building and ran over to Lydia's side to open her door. Suddenly he heard some rustling in the woods just behind the apartment. He whispered to his wife, "I just heard something. It sounds like something or someone is in the woods." Before they had a chance to head up the stairs and into their apartment, Matt saw what he heard.

A young man in his twenties, wearing jeans and a dark T-shirt, was crawling out of the woods and into the clearing right behind the apartment building, right in front of Matt and Lydia. When the man made it to the clearing, he stood straight up and stared at the young couple. Everything started to make sense. That guy may be the guy the police were looking for.

Dozens of heavily armed, highly trained officers and deputies, canine units, and helicopter units were all looking for one guy. And there stood Matt—at 150 pounds soaking wet with keyrings in both pockets, he hadn't won an arm-wrestling contest in ten years. There he was looking right at the suspect, and the suspect was looking right at him.

Matt mumbled to his sweet wife, "We need to get out of here now." He and Lydia moved toward the trunk of the car, opened it up like they didn't see anyone out of the ordinary, and grabbed their shopping bags. Matt was trying to be cool and nonchalant, but inside he was screaming, "Help!" He closed the trunk. Together they walked toward the stairs and bolted up to their apartment, where Matt called 911 and waited for help to arrive.

That was how people felt around the two thieves we meet in Luke 23 and Matthew 27. They were probably not garden-variety thieves, boosting flat screens out of living rooms. For them to be crucified, those thieves either hurt someone in their burglaries or stole from someone powerful. They made their living off the dying. On that dark Friday, they were going to pay for their crimes, as both of those thieves found themselves crucified on crosses right next to Jesus.

BIBLE LESSON

I. JESUS WAS CRUCIFIED BETWEEN TWO THIEVES

In the final moments of Jesus' life on earth, the holiest Man who had ever lived died between two convicted criminals as if He Himself were a sinful lawbreaker. Luke called these two men who were with Him malefactors, a general term for a criminal. Matthew called them thieves. Since Jesus was crucified between them, His place in the center would have caused Him to be the focus and perhaps cause observers to believe Jesus was the worst criminal of them all.

A. Jesus Was Mocked on the Cross

From the earliest hours in the morning until Jesus died around 3:00 PM, the crowd continually mocked and abused Jesus. The Roman soldiers mocked Him by wrapping a scarlet robe around Him, shoving a crown of thorns on His head, and placing a reed in His hand like a scepter. They pretended to honor Him by kneeling before Him, saying, "Hail, King of the Jews." They mercilessly scourged Him, and then they crucified Him.

While Jesus was pouring out His love for all humanity as He was dying for all our sins—even dying for the people who hated Him and murdered Him—people still mocked and blasphemed Him. They should have honored and loved Him, especially since He was dying for them. Matthew transcribed their actual blasphemous words: "And they that passed by reviled him, wagging their heads, and saying, Thou that destroyest the temple, and buildest it in three days, save thyself. If thou be the Son of God, come down from the cross. Likewise also the chief priests mocking him, with the scribes and elders, said, He saved others; himself he cannot save. If he be the King of Israel, let him now come down from the cross, and we will believe him. He trusted in God; let him deliver him now, if he will have him: for he said, I am the Son of God" (Matthew 27:39–43).

The crowd and the soldiers shook their heads in scorn and blasphemed Jesus for actual truths, but they didn't realize it. Jesus was indeed the Son of God, the Savior, the King of Israel, someone who trusted in God and was accepted by God more than anyone else, but the mockers were blind to those truths. They claimed if Jesus would come down from the cross and save Himself, they would believe in Him since saving Himself would prove He really was the Son of God, the Savior, the King of Israel. But Jesus could only truly be their Savior if He refused to save Himself.

In understanding Jesus died so we can live, how should that make us feel toward Him?

B. The King of the Jews

After nailing Jesus to the cross, the Roman soldiers nailed a sign above Jesus' head on which they wrote what He was accused of: "THIS IS JESUS THE KING OF THE JEWS" (Matthew 27:37).

Teacher Option: *A supplemental image is available in the Resource Kit.* I

359

When someone was crucified, the charge against that person was first written down on a sign, and the criminal carried it or it was hung around his neck. Finally the sign was fixed to the cross, intending to deter anyone who was thinking about committing the same crime. The Romans were saying, "Do this, and this will be done to you."

The sign above Jesus was intended to be sarcastic. Neither the Jews nor the Romans were affirming Jesus as the king of the Jews. Rather, they were professing that the Romans rule the Jews, and this is what Roman power will do to anyone claiming or being proclaimed to be a king—a rival to Caesar.

Both the Romans and the Jews mocked Jesus because neither understood His kingship. Jesus had not come as a rival to Pontius Pilate, the Roman governor of Judea, or as a rival to Caesar himself. Jesus did not come to overthrow them or establish a new Jewish monarchy to throw off the yoke of Roman rule. One day Jesus will come again and be King over all the earth. Then He will overthrow all those opposed to God and His people, but in the first century land of Israel, Jesus came to die on the very cross that so many others thought discredited him.

How does God use the cross, a symbol of shame, as a symbol of hope for us?

C. I Will Choose to Worship Jesus as My Savior and King

Jesus' own people did not accept or honor Him because of the cross. However, His followers accepted and honored Him because of the cross and the price He paid for us there. To the Jews, the cross made Jesus repugnant and unworthy of their faith, but the cross makes Jesus beautiful and praiseworthy to us. Thanks to His love on Calvary's cross, I will choose to worship Him as my Savior and my King.

Our right response is to give thanks to Him as our Savior and to bow our knees in worship to Him as our King and our Lord. Worship is not just words of praise—although that's part of it—but worship is expressed in our actions and living our lives devoted to Him and following His Word. How could we do any less in light of the Cross?

II. THE UNREPENTANT THIEF

A. "If You Are the Christ, Save Yourself and Us"

One of the thieves lobbied for Jesus to save Himself and both criminals crucified with Him. In other words, "If you are the Messiah, our Savior-King, get to saving. If you have so much power, start using it. Start with yourself, and then save us too—if you really are what your followers say you are." But that is not how we approach Jesus for salvation. We don't demand Jesus prove Himself to us before we consider following Him. We don't bring our arrogance while ignoring our own sins and making demands of Him.

B. We Must Choose Humility When Approaching Jesus for Forgiveness

We come humbly before Him. We profess Him to be the Savior and recognize His greatness and grace in dying for us. We must recognize our sin nailed Him to the cross. We make no demands of Him because He doesn't owe us anything. There at the Cross, we humbly bow and confess our sins because only the humble, repentant heart finds forgiveness.

III. THE HUMBLE THIEF

In a remarkable turn of events, one of those thieves had a change of heart. At first he mocked and insulted Jesus along with his fellow criminal, but while he was nailed to his own cross, the second thief came to realize who Jesus really was. It's a mystery how belief enters a person's heart.

How can multiple people hear the same message or encounter Jesus in the same way, yet one believes in Him while others remain hardened in unbelief?

Second Peter 3:9 teaches us it is not God's will that any should perish but that all would come to repentance, but God does not force His will to prevail or force us to believe. He will move on us with His Spirit to bring us to a place where we can believe, but in the secret place of the human heart, one allows the Spirit to complete His work while another doesn't. On Calvary that day, one of the criminals responded to the Spirit's work in his heart, and he had a change of mind about Jesus. Humbly, he came to believe that Jesus really was the Messiah and Savior of the world. He even rebuked the other criminal who continued to insult Jesus.

A. He Admitted His Own Guilt and Turned to Jesus for Mercy

Luke recorded the conversation between the two criminals. "But the other answering rebuked him, saying, Dost not thou fear God, seeing thou art in the same condemnation? And we indeed justly; for we receive the due reward of our deeds: but this man hath done nothing amiss" (Luke 23:40–41).

This rebuke must have shocked the mocking thief. Maybe he noticed his criminal counterpart had stopped insulting Jesus, but he had no idea the Spirit of God was working on the other thief to bring him to faith in Jesus. The Spirit was causing him to truly recognize his own sin and see he was guilty and deserving of death, but Jesus was not.

In a moment of divine revelation, the Spirit led one of the thieves to see Jesus as the Savior and King and to see his need to be saved. This amazing grace and miraculous faith enabled him to turn to Jesus for salvation. God's Spirit brought him to faith and repentance as he cried out to Jesus, "Lord, remember me when thou comest into thy kingdom" (Luke 23:42).

B. "Today You Will Be with Me in Paradise"

Without hesitation, Jesus received the thief into right relationship with Him. Jesus replied, "Verily I say unto thee, To day shalt thou be with me in paradise" (Luke 23:43). In a moment the thief's sins were gone, and he was forgiven. He was saved and ready to enter Paradise. That's a bit of an odd couple: Jesus, the holy God of glory who had never done anything wrong, and a thief who seemingly had not done anything right, except cry out to Jesus for mercy, and it was enough.

Teacher Option: *A supplemental video is available in the Resource Kit.* **V**

We don't know exactly how long that thief—excuse me, child of God—lingered in life before he died. But knowing his death was not the end—he would soon be with Jesus in Paradise—certainly helped ease his pain. He likely continued to suffer physically until his lungs exhaled their final labored breath and his eyes closed in death. But in that moment of release, he opened his eyes in the world beyond and saw Jesus. Not the battered and broken Jesus he had seen on the cross, but the Lord of glory in shining splendor who gladly welcomed him into His presence.

Some are offended that a thief could be with Jesus after only praying near the end of his life. Why do we feel like people need to earn their right to be saved?

C. We Can Call on Jesus and Find a Place of Repentance

What wondrous grace Jesus offered this former criminal. If people believe they can't be forgiven because their sins are so great, or if they think it's too late for them to come to the Lord, we can point them to this former thief who now lives eternally with Jesus in Paradise. His sins were great; he even blasphemed Jesus on the cross. Yet God's grace was greater, and Jesus still forgave him.

Since he lived and died before Jesus died on Calvary and rose from the grave, the thief was saved immediately upon faith and repentance. But when Jesus poured out His Spirit on the Day of Pentecost in Acts 2, He inaugurated a brand new covenant for believers. Our experience with Jesus beautifully builds on faith and repentance as it leads us into covenant relationship with Jesus through water baptism in Jesus' name and being adopted into God's holy family through the indwelling Holy Spirit.

Have you already responded in this way to the gospel of Jesus Christ? If not, are you ready to turn to Jesus?

For those who have sinned and run from God all their lives, God is always ready and willing to save. Even at the end of our lives, as death draws near, Jesus is ever ready and will save us if we yield to the work of His Spirit and turn to Him in repentance so we can be born again of water and Spirit. Then we too can hear Jesus say, "Today you'll be with me in Paradise."

INTERNALIZING THE MESSAGE

God's grace and mercy are so much greater than we can imagine. This experience of the repentant thief gives us a glimpse of how limitless God's grace really is. The Lord takes great pleasure in saving those whose sins and failures were particularly abundant. We see that in this former thief, now child of God. We also see God's great grace in Simon Peter, who denied he even knew Jesus after the crowd arrested the Lord. We see it in Paul who hated Jesus and tried to destroy the church. God saved both of them and raised them into great saints and leaders in His newborn New Testament church. We see God's great grace in Mary Magdalene, who sinned so much she had been possessed by seven demons. But Jesus graciously and powerfully delivered her, and she became one of Jesus' most loyal followers. She stood by Jesus at the cross, and Jesus honored her by first appearing to her after He resurrected. All these flawed people are trophies of grace.

Thankfully, so are we.

Our experience may not be as dramatic as the thief's. Frankly, thank God for that. But in some fundamental ways, our experience is greater than the thief's or anyone's experience who died before Jesus' death, burial, and resurrection and before the outpouring of the Spirit on the Day of Pentecost. Truly the thief and others like him experienced salvation, but they didn't have the privilege to be baptized in water in Jesus' name and to be indwelled by the Spirit of God.

We get to experience that wonderful new birth ourselves and offer that opportunity to other people today. If through our testimony or through the message of a preacher, the Spirit moves on others to bring them to faith and a desire to be saved, we can lead them to the waters of baptism in Jesus' name and to experience the baptism of the Holy Spirit with the initial sign of speaking in other tongues. The thief didn't get to experience all that, but for those of us who do, one day we will be with Jesus—and with that thief—for eternity.

Prayer Focus
Lead the group in prayer and consider the following topics of focus:
- For God to help us always have a repentant heart
- For God to help us minister to those who need Him

2.1

THE LIFE GOD BLESSES

FOCUS VERSE
Matthew 5:6
Blessed are they which do hunger and thirst after righteousness: for they shall be filled.

LESSON TEXT
Matthew 5:1–12; Galatians 5:19–25

TRUTH ABOUT GOD
God desires to pour out His blessings on those who recognize their need of Him.

TRUTH FOR MY LIFE
I will acknowledge my need of God.

Series Overview:

This series, "Kingdom Living," looks closely at the Sermon on the Mount and the way Jesus calls us to live as His disciples. These lessons will investigate the life God blesses, the mission of every disciple, the disciplines of a disciple, the importance of seeking first the Kingdom, and the priority of obedience. The truths highlighted in the teachings of Jesus on the mount are crucial for the life and spiritual health of every believer. This series will encourage us to live as children of the King.

SG TEACHING OUTLINE

Icebreaker: What is the strangest craving for food or drink you have had?

Lesson Connection: Share the Lesson Connection.

I. BLESSINGS ON THE EMPTY

    A. Those Empty of Hope, Happiness, and Pride Ⓘ

        » *This sermon was Jesus' first as a new rabbi in Galilee. How do you think the crowd responded to His sermon that the poor are blessed?*

        » *How is meekness different from weakness? How do we exercise meekness to the glory of God?*

    B. I Will Trust God to Fill My Emptiness with Good Things

II. BLESSINGS ON THE FULL

    A. Those Full of Mercy, Purity, and Peace

        » *Have you ever noticed there is a connection in the Bible between purity and peace?*

    B. I Will Share God's Blessings in My Life with Others

        » *How can you bless someone with the blessings God has given you?*

III. BLESSINGS ON THE PERSECUTED Ⓥ

    A. For Righteousness' Sake

    B. For God's Sake

        » *What experiences have you had with ridicule or even persecution for your faith? How has that shaped your faith?*

    C. I Will Acknowledge My Need of God

Internalizing the Message

Prayer Focus
Lead the group in prayer and consider the following topics of focus:
• For God to empty us of what we don't need in our lives
• For God to fill us with all we do need in our lives

LESSON CONNECTION

A farmer and his young son who were working in the fields during a particularly dry summer. The sky had frequently been cloudy, but there had been no rain for weeks. Then suddenly, as it sometimes happens in the Midwest, the wind and sky took a sudden turn. "It is going to rain!" the farmer shouted to his son. "Let's head to the house." The pair ran across the field, traversing ditches and navigating around fenceposts. The rain had already started falling when the father and son reached the field near the house, but the dirt had quickly become muck. As the boy came around the corner to the front porch steps, he slipped and tumbled headlong into a puddle.

The father couldn't resist a chuckle as he quickly picked up his mud-caked son and carried him under the porch, safe from the rain. Inside, his mother cried out, "Do not track anything in here! I will get you both some towels. Just be patient." As the father and son stood shivering on the porch, the boy began to grumble his complaints as his father wiped the mess from his face and hair. "I hate the rain," the boy blurted out. "What is it good for anyway?" The father laughed again, empathizing with his son's miserable state. "Son, you have no idea how much good the rain does. The rain is a blessing for everyone and everything around here." The soaked and filthy boy was skeptical. "To everyone and everything? How so?"

"Well, you know the rain barrels by the house? Why, if it wasn't for the rain, we would not have any drinking water or water for baths. We are going to have full barrels of fresh, cool water tomorrow morning. And the crops need the rain too. If it did not rain, none of the vegetables would grow, and we would not have anything to feed ourselves or sell in town. And of course, all this rain will keep the weather cool for the animals. And while you might not like all this mud, the pigs are going to love it. And you know that brook you like fishing in? All this rain means that stream is going to run high the next few days, and there will be lots of fish. Plus the rain will clear a lot of the dust, making the air cleaner and easier to breathe. So you see, the rain benefits us in different ways depending on what is needed, but it is always a blessing."

BIBLE LESSON

I. BLESSINGS ON THE EMPTY

God loves to pour out blessings upon His children. But God has especially shown compassion on the pained, weary, and downtrodden. When Jesus began His public ministry, He read from Isaiah 61:1-2 in the synagogue and specifically mentioned His ministry was to the poor, brokenhearted, captives, blind, and bruised (Luke 4:18). These groups could be classified as those who feel empty, a nagging deficit deep in their souls. Jesus loved these groups dearly as evidenced by the crowds who followed Him: prostitutes, tax collectors, common fishermen, lepers, blind, lame, and others in need of healing. When challenged by the Pharisees why He associated with publicans and sinners, Jesus responded, possibly with a knowing smile on His face, "They that are whole need not a physician; but they that are sick. I came not to call the righteous, but sinners to repentance" (Luke 5:31-32).

A. Those Empty of Hope, Happiness, and Pride

Matthew 5:3-11 is famously known as the Beatitudes. It began Jesus' well-known Sermon on the Mount. The first group of Beatitudes could be categorized as empty: the poor in spirit, they that mourn, the meek, the hungry for righteousness. There is considerable debate concerning the phrase "poor in spirit." Matthew 5:3 is the only place in the Bible where this phrase is found. Even in Luke's version of this passage, the author omitted "in spirit," simply referring to the poor. (See Luke 6:20.) Being poor in spirit may refer to us when we see ourselves as we truly are—limited, inadequate beings in need of God's grace. We realize the absence of hope when we trust in our humanity alone. Once we realize our need of God and the insufficiency of our own humanity, God is able to fill us as sincere seekers with His Spirit, and we become heirs of Christ and inhabitants of His kingdom.

Throughout all our lives, we have identified with those who mourn. We often associate mourning with the death of a loved one, but any loss can result in mourning. Losing a job due to layoffs or a house to a fire can cause mourning. Parents can feel mourning when their last child leaves the house, and their home is now silent. Certainly we mourn when we realize how poor in spirit we are and how much our sin separates us from God. No matter the reason we mourn, we have the promise of God's comfort in the midst of our mourning. Jesus often referred to the Holy Spirit as a Comforter (John 14:16, 26; 15:26; 16:7). When we are filled with God's Spirit, we can be confident the everpresent Comforter dwells within us and will provide timely comfort during times of mourning.

This sermon was Jesus' first as a new rabbi in Galilee. How do you think the crowd responded to His sermon that the poor are blessed?

Not all emptiness is bad. To be meek is to be empty of pride and self, to be gentle and slow to anger. Meekness is not cowardice but is patience and longsuffering even in the face of persecution.

When we empty ourselves of pride and allow God's Spirit to help us be patient, even if the whole world is against us, Jesus promised we shall inherit the earth.

Teacher Option:
A supplemental image is available in the Resource Kit. ❶

God also promised to fill everyone who hungers and thirsts for righteousness. Those who have felt extreme hunger and thirst can testify how much these pangs overwhelm and preoccupy them. Because God honors sincere and holy desires, He promised to fill all people who hunger and thirst for righteousness. Interestingly, this infilling results in even more hunger and more infilling in an eternal cycle. God's righteousness should keep us wanting more and more. Thankfully, the more we desire, the more God will fill us.

How is meekness different from weakness? How do we exercise meekness to the glory of God?

B. I Will Trust God to Fill My Emptiness with Good Things

It is easy to give to the Lord the things we know we have; however, it is sometimes difficult to empty ourselves and trust God will be faithful to fill those empty spaces. When our spirits are downcast—when we grieve for lost loved ones or we struggle in the face of trials—we can be confident God will enter our empty spaces and fill us to overflowing with His Holy Spirit. God thrives on using empty vessels to perform His will.

II. BLESSINGS ON THE FULL

While God is especially concerned for the empty, His blessings are for all seasons of life. He is not just a "very present help in trouble" (Psalm 46:1), but He also "taketh pleasure in them that fear him" (Psalm 147:11). God is a fellow celebrator in good times just as He is a help in bad times. He desires for us to seek Him, not just to pray for our needs but also to rejoice over victories. Moreover, the longer we live faithfully for God, the more God's blessings seem to compound upon themselves and continue to grow.

A. Those Full of Mercy, Purity, and Peace

The next group in the Beatitudes could be classified as the full. These are people full of mercy, full of purity, and full of peace. Being full of mercy has a self-fulfilling promise: when we give mercy, we will receive mercy. This is connected to the principle of sowing and reaping found elsewhere in Jesus' teaching (Luke 6:38) and the writings of Paul (Galatians 6:7). Being pure in heart relates to sincerity and holiness, which results in seeing God. This passage is a helpful reminder that it is impossible to fully discover God until we know Him in purity and holiness. Pure in heart does not mean we're perfect and never make mistakes. Pure in heart means our heart is single, undivided. We're not living on the fence about our relationship with Jesus. Simply stated, pure in heart is living on the right side of the fence.

Have you ever noticed there is a connection in the Bible between purity and peace?

Jesus spoke a special blessing over the peacemakers. Those willing to make peace have the beautiful privilege of being called God's children. Being a peacemaker is not always easy, especially in a tumultuous and hostile world, but being full of

God's Spirit has always been a sign of belonging to God. When Jesus promised to send the Holy Spirit, He also promised, "Peace I leave with you, my peace I give unto you: not as the world giveth, give I unto you" (John 14:27). In another place, Jesus noted, "By this shall all men know that ye are my disciples, if ye have love one to another" (John 13:35). The way we will know who we are, whose we are, and the presence of the Holy Spirit within us is how we love and act in peace toward others.

B. I Will Share God's Blessings in My Life with Others

God's bountiful blessings are not given for the sake of blessing alone; God's blessings are designed to flow through us as well as into us. In the Book of Genesis, God gave Abraham a promise and a commission in the same sentence. "I will bless thee, and make thy name great; and thou shalt be a blessing" (Genesis 12:2). God's blessings were not for Abraham only but for everyone Abraham would encounter. Similarly, being full of mercy, peace, and purity are inherently for blessing others as well as ourselves. What good is having mercy if we don't interact with others who need it? What benefit is being full of peace if we do not speak into the tumult around us? What good is being full of righteousness and purity if it does not empower us to be distinctive witnesses in a world devoid of these things? Let us all pray for God to daily remind us that we are pipelines of God's blessing, not storage bins.

How can you bless someone with the blessings God has given you?

III. BLESSINGS ON THE PERSECUTED

The final group specifically mentioned by Christ in the Beatitudes were the persecuted. While persecution certainly looks different in the modern Western world than it did in Jesus' time, persecution certainly still exists. In some places around the world, this still includes violence, imprisonment, and even death. However, in all cultures this persecution might include the encroachment of ungodly ideologies, cultures, and mindsets upon the church. However, regardless of what persecution looks like, those who suffer can expect God's blessings too.

Teacher Option: *A supplemental video is available in the Resource Kit.* **V**

A. For Righteousness' Sake

Being persecuted is not unique to Christianity. Many groups around the world continue to suffer persecution based on race, ethnicity, gender, or religious beliefs, and these are all great injustices. However, there is something unique about suffering for righteousness' sake. Persecution happens when the good we do for God results in attacks from the enemies of our soul. For example, when we begin to exercise the fullness of mercy and peace, some will undoubtedly disagree and turn on the merciful and peacemakers. When we suffer for doing good, we will receive the same promise as the poor in spirit—for we shall inherit God's kingdom. However, we must be careful not to mistake all naysayers as persecution for righteousness' sake. If we are not exercising the fruit of the Spirit, we might receive persecution because we are actually acting ungodly, which will never be blessed.

B. For God's Sake

In addition to suffering for the sake of righteousness, it is also possible to suffer for the sake of Christ. While these two concepts are closely related, they are distinct. We can suffer for righteousness' sake simply by standing up for principles of goodness, truth, morality, and justice. However, suffering for God's sake is persecution directly related to our Christian beliefs. When we are mocked for our godly dress, our theological beliefs, or our testimony for Jesus, this is persecution for God's sake.

However, when we know we are in line with God's will for our lives and we are experiencing this type of persecution, our response should not be despair. Rather, Jesus encouraged His listeners to "rejoice, and be exceeding glad: for great is your reward in heaven" (Matthew 5:12). Perhaps this is why so many early Christian martyrs worshiped and thanked God even as they were burned on stakes and fed to lions. They viewed persecution for the sake of God as an honor, not a burden. They also understood that persecution for God's sake puts us in good company with the prophets who came before. Even more than the prophets, we also identify with Christ, who forewarned His followers, "If the world hate you, ye know that it hated me before it hated you. . . . If they have persecuted me, they will also persecute you" (John 15:18-20). Because Christ suffered first, we can trust that He will be able to empathize with our hurts and provide the comfort and strength needed to endure.

What experiences have you had with ridicule or even persecution for your faith? How has that shaped your faith?

C. I Will Acknowledge My Need of God

At different times we will all experience emptiness, fullness, and persecution. Some may experience all three at one time in varying degrees. At other times a local church may have a wide variety of members who are all in different seasons and each needing unique blessings. Fortunately, we serve a God who knows how to respond to everyone uniquely. He can bless the grieving soul in the same moment He blesses the rejoicing soul and the persecuted soul.

Although the seasons may be different, we do not have to approach a different Spirit in these different seasons. Just as rain produces a wide variety of benefits, the same Spirit can simultaneously bless a church full of people who each need something unique from God.

However, in order to receive these blessings, we must collectively and individually acknowledge our need of His blessings. God is a gentleman and will not bless those who do not wish to be blessed. We must humble ourselves and pray to receive God's great blessings.

INTERNALIZING THE MESSAGE

Although the story at the beginning of the lesson was fictional, the struggles we face daily are real. It is possible for a pastor to speak at a funeral (grieving), officiate a wedding (celebrating), and be mocked by coworkers for his faith at his part-time job—all in the span of a couple days. It is also common for Christians to go through seasons of mourning and seasons of celebration. Sadly, many do not realize they are in days of celebration until the days of mourning come. We must all stay in tune with God's blessings in our lives and continually communicate with Him.

Jesus told another better-known parable about fathers and sons in Matthew 7:7–12. Jesus spoke generally about the nature of fatherhood. What type of father would not give good gifts to his children? Moreover, if a father loves his children, he will certainly not give them anything that could harm them. Most fathers cannot imagine giving their hungry son a stone instead of bread or a dangerous serpent instead of some tasty meat. If this is true of earthly, flawed, imperfect fathers, think how much more this must be true of our perfect heavenly Father. God desires to bless us and has the ability to do so more than we could ever imagine. In order to receive these blessings, we must be willing to ask. God listens to those who cry out to Him. He promised, "Ask, and it shall be given you; seek, and ye shall find; knock, and it shall be opened unto you: for every one that asketh receiveth; and he that seeketh findeth; and to him that knocketh it shall be opened" (Matthew 7:7–8).

However, immediately after speaking about seeking for good things from God and reflecting on the nature of fathers giving gifts to their sons, Jesus gave the encouragement commonly known as the Golden Rule: "Therefore all things whatsoever ye would that men should do to you, do ye even so to them: for this is the law and the prophets" (Matthew 7:12). Even in a conversation about praying for and receiving good gifts from our heavenly Father, Jesus gave a poignant reminder that these gifts are not for our benefit only. The blessings we receive from God should cause us to grow in love, respect, and compassion for our neighbors. Only when we receive this revelation will we fulfill the command given to Abraham in which we are blessed to be a blessing.

Prayer Focus
Lead the group in prayer and consider the following topics of focus:
- For God to empty us of what we don't need in our lives
- For God to fill us with all we do need in our lives

2.2

THE MISSION OF A DISCIPLE

FOCUS VERSE
Matthew 5:16
Let your light so shine before men, that they may see your good works, and glorify your Father which is in heaven.

LESSON TEXT
Matthew 5:13–16; 28:16–20;
II Thessalonians 1:11–12

TRUTH ABOUT GOD
God's design for the church is to embody His glory.

TRUTH FOR MY LIFE
In every aspect of my life, I will demonstrate God's glory.

Thinking about Last Week:

Have students refer to their Daily Devotional Guide to answer the following questions:
1. What most affected you as you read through the Lesson Text and the Biblical Insights?
2. How did it shape your prayers and thoughts throughout the week?
3. Do you feel you grew closer to the Lord this past week? Why or why not?

(SG) TEACHING OUTLINE

Icebreaker: Share about a time when you lost electricity for days and had to be creative, living without artificial light.

Lesson Connection: Share the Lesson Connection.

I. METAPHORS OF MISSION

   A. Salt
   > » *Who in your life would you describe as a salt-of-the-earth child of God? How has this person's life helped bring flavor to yours?*

   B. City on a Hill Ⓘ

   C. Lamp in Darkness Ⓥ
   > » *Who was a light for you when you were making your way toward Jesus Christ? To whom are you being a light?*

   D. I Desire God to Be Present in Every Aspect of My Life

II. MY ROLE AS A WITNESS
   > » *Share an example of a time when you witnessed to someone of the goodness of God in your life.*

   A. The Witness of Evangelism

   B. The Witness of Separation
   > » *How can we live righteously without falling into the sin of self-righteousness?*

   C. The Witness of Incarnation

   D. In Every Aspect of My Life, I Will Demonstrate God's Glory
   > » *What areas of your life do you need to surrender to God for His glory? How will you do that?*

Internalizing the Message

Prayer Focus
Lead the group in prayer and consider the following topics of focus:
• For God to help us be salt, light, and a city on a hill
• For God to give us boldness to share our testimony as His witness

LESSON CONNECTION

Being called to be a witness in a court of law may be an anxiety-filled process. Witnesses are often called to testify in court for important reasons. When a witness is called forward, attorneys believe their witness's word can help make or break the case. The defendant is hoping to be saved by the witness; the plaintiff is hoping the witness will bring a conviction.

The process seems ceremonious and procedural. The witness must show up at the courtroom at the appropriate time, preferably dressed in a respectable manner. The witness must place one hand on the Bible and swear to tell "the truth, the whole truth, and nothing but the truth." Then the questions often come in rapid-fire succession. The witness tries to carefully remember all the details, knowing every word spoken will be analyzed. Even the witness's mannerisms will be critiqued. Was she nervous? Why did she say what she said and not something else? What about what the witness did not say? Was anything omitted or avoided? The witness might sit in her chair with her mind racing, realizing her words might forever change someone's life.

While being a witness for God should not produce this same level of anxiety, it should be treated with the same level of seriousness. We can quickly see many similarities to faith. Just as in a courtroom, a witness for God is expected to act and dress a certain way. If not, his character could be called into question. A good witness must have an answer ready. It would be foolhardy for him to arrive unprepared. The witness must be just as careful about what he says as what he does not say. Furthermore, what the witness does not say is almost as important as what he does say. A good witness does not add to or take away from the truth.

However, a major difference between God's witnesses and most courtroom witnesses is the empowerment that comes with the infilling of God's Spirit. Jesus Himself prophesied, "But ye shall receive power, after that the Holy Ghost is come upon you: and ye shall be witnesses unto me" (Acts 1:8). Christians do not need to be anxious about being witnesses because we know God has already granted every Spirit-filled believer the power necessary to be an effective witness.

BIBLE LESSON

I. METAPHORS OF MISSION

Jesus often used analogies and anecdotes that helped His listeners better understand His teaching. While many might not understand the contents of a scholarly theology textbook, most people have used salt, and all people who can see know the value of light. Jesus used these metaphors precisely so we could receive and understand His teaching easily. These metaphors describe the nature of the mission of every Christian witness.

A. Salt

Many who have cooked with others present have had some variation of the following happen. While the chef labors diligently cutting vegetables, organizing seasoning, and checking timers, rogue self-appointed taste testers enter the kitchen and step toward the pot on the stovetop with spoon in hand. While the aromas waft through the kitchen, the testers dip their spoons into the still-cooking meal and bring the portion to their lips. Then perfectly on cue, they comment, "Needs a little salt." Alternatively, sometimes the chef will request a friend try the meal to see if it needs more salt. This is because everyone who cooks knows the value of salt. Salt is a strong ingredient by itself (one can quickly tell if a dish is over-salted), but used in the right proportion, salt actually draws out flavors and elevates the taste of the entire dish.

Jesus described His people as the salt of the earth. True Christians draw out the essence of who people are supposed to be. Just as salt helps elevate true flavors, Christians on God's mission help draw people out of the world and help them to see who God intended them to be. All humanity was made in God's image, but unfortunately that image has been broken, abused, and watered down. But a salt-of-the-earth Christian can look past that brokenness, draw out the image of God in that person, and help restore that person to God's intentions. However, some Christians have lost their saltiness, or effectiveness. Jesus did not mince words when describing these Christians; He called them "good for nothing" (Matthew 5:13).

Who in your life would you describe as a salt-of-the-earth child of God? How has this person's life helped bring flavor to yours?

B. City on a Hill

Teacher Option: *A supplemental image is available in the Resource Kit.* [I]

Drivers who have taken a road trip with friends have experienced the frustration of too many "backseat drivers" in the car. One person recommends taking the highway while another insists he knows a shortcut through the country. Meanwhile, the GPS is recommending a third option that no one in the car likes. Traveling can be difficult, especially when so many different locations look the same. However, notable landmarks can make navigating a city easier. Denver, Colorado, is a great example of such a city. The mountains are always to the west, and the flatlands are always to the east. Between these significant markers, anyone remotely close to the city can quickly orient themselves.

Similarly, Christians on mission for God should stand out from the world around them. Just as a city on a hill is easily visible for miles around, it should be obvious that Christians are who they say they are. However, Christians should not just stand out for the sake of being different. We should stand out as a landmark for others to identify and orient themselves. When people are lost, they start looking for landmarks. In like manner, the church exists in a world full of confused and lost souls hoping for a solid landmark to look to. We should live in a way that God's kingdom is readily visible in our lives and in our communities to receive those sincere seekers.

C. Lamp in Darkness

Some do not cook, and many do not live near notable landmarks, but everyone who can see can testify to the value of light. In the darkest hours of the night, even the cheapest pen-lights can seem like a lifesaver. We now have flashlights built into our phones. These are invaluable to parents making midnight trips to check on the kids. Even the smallest light can cause a great effect. Lights shine brighter the darker the surroundings get. However, for a light to be useful, its rays cannot be inhibited. A hand placed over the front of the flashlight can once again plunge us into darkness.

We as Christians exist in a world that seems to grow increasingly darker as we approach the soon return of Christ for His church. We have an opportunity to shine brighter than ever. As the world gets darker, the more people gather around the light. We must make sure our light is shining brightly for all to see, beckoning lost and wandering souls into the light of God's salvation.

However, while the light of God's Word is never a problem, sometimes Christians entrusted with God's light can get in the way and cause a shadow to be cast that makes it difficult for God's light to be seen. True Christians desire for God's light to shine clearly through their lives and not be a distraction. Perhaps this is why Jesus concluded this analogy with the instruction to "let your light so shine before men, that they may see your good works, and glorify your Father which is in heaven" (Matthew 5:16). We know we are being effective witnesses in the world when the people seeing our good works turn their hearts and minds to glorify God. When people see our good works and praise us, we are doing these works for the wrong motivations and are actually preventing souls from reaching the true light of the world, Jesus Christ.

Who was a light for you when you were making your way toward Jesus Christ? To whom are you being a light?

D. I Desire God to Be Present in Every Aspect of My Life

The Christian faith must permeate the believer's entire life to be effective. One cannot expect to glorify God on Sundays only and still be an effective witness. We must desire God to saturate each aspect of our lives to the point nothing is neglected. Perhaps this is why the apostle Paul beseeched the Romans to "present your bodies a living sacrifice" (Romans 12:1). Nothing was more total and final in the Old Testament than animal sacrifice. The bull or sheep was slaughtered and burned; its entire body was offered as worship to God. Similarly, as living sacrifices, we must make regular trips to the altar to ensure every part of our lives is completely offered to God.

II. MY ROLE AS A WITNESS

Each analogy Jesus mentioned—salt, a city on a hill, and a light in the darkness—all describe the nature in which we are witnesses for Christ. Witnessing is more than an activity saved people do; we are called to be witnesses as part of our spiritual genetic makeup. By definition, witnesses tell the story of their experiences. Those who believe their witness are inherently called to action and persuaded to change their way of living. We witness through evangelism, through inward and outward holiness, and through the very image of God manifested in our daily lives.

Share an example of a time when you witnessed to someone of the goodness of God in your life.

A. The Witness of Evangelization

Evangelism is part of the Great Commission given by Jesus, in which He commanded the disciples to go, teach, and baptize (Matthew 28:19). We cannot properly fulfill these commands without going. Being a witness is active and intentional; it is not a passive activity. Furthermore, a witness must be willing to teach. Teaching in this sense does not have to be in a formal classroom setting, and the witness does not have to be a professional teacher. Rather, witnesses must simply be willing to share their personal testimonies and the gospel of Jesus Christ. Intentional lifestyle evangelism of this kind produces souls entering the kingdom of God through the wonderful gift of baptism in the name of Jesus Christ.

B. The Witness of Separation

A preacher once said Christians are to be insulated not isolated. Christians cannot reach the world while hiding from it. While we must exercise wisdom in exactly where we go (for example, it would not be wise for a Christian to frequent nightclubs to witness to the lost), a witness cannot remain quarantined from the world and expect to be a faithful witness.

However, being in the world does not mean we should act like the world. While the popular phrase "in the world but not of it" is not explicitly found in the Bible, its origins are found in the words of Jesus when He prayed, "I pray not that thou shouldest take them out of the world, but that thou shouldest keep them from the evil. They are not of the world, even as I am not of the world. Sanctify them through thy truth: thy word is truth. As thou hast sent me into the world, even so have I also sent them into the world" (John 17:15–18).

Jesus never called us to be removed from the world entirely when a large part of the reason we are here is to be witnesses. However, Jesus does call us out of the world and to sanctification for His glory. This sanctification is a call to be holy and more like Him, even if it means being separate from the ideals and values of the world. This type of separation includes distinction in many parts of our lives, including dress, speech, emotions, and even our thoughts. We must live holy in all these areas, and the world will recognize this distinction.

How can we live righteously without falling into the sin of self-righteousness?

C. The Witness of Incarnation

Perhaps the most powerful witness we have available is the act of being progressively formed into God's image. Paul prayed, "That the name of our Lord Jesus Christ may be glorified in you, and ye in him, according to the grace of our God and the Lord Jesus Christ" (II Thessalonians 1:12). Christ is glorified in our lives when we are made more like Him, and we are continually enveloped by His nature. Even though we will never attain perfection (only Christ is perfect), that does not mean we should not strive for perfection. This striving is not of our own power but through the transforming power of the Holy Spirit. We are to cooperate with the work of the Spirit.

Finally, since we are filled with God's Holy Spirit, we should expect the power associated with such an infilling to empower us to be witnesses. (See Acts 1:8.) Moreover, the image of Christ should be daily manifested in our lives through demonstration of this power. We should expect the supernatural to follow us, just as it followed the first disciples everywhere they went. (See Mark 16:20.)

D. In Every Aspect of My Life, I Will Demonstrate God's Glory

One might be surprised how much God's glory can be reflected in our lives when God is allowed to saturate and fill every part of our lives. It is easy to see how God can be reflected in our speech and dress, but God's glory should also be demonstrated in how we manage our finances, make business decisions, raise our children, and even drive in traffic. The process of being formed into God's image is lifelong and is only completed when we finish our course and are received into Heaven. Until then, we are in a continual process of self-examination, praying daily for God to keep molding and transforming us as a patient potter works unruly clay.

What areas of your life do you need to surrender to God for His glory? How will you do that?

INTERNALIZING THE MESSAGE

Part of being a good witness in a courtroom is seen in the attitude and demeanor of the witness. A flippant witness will not be taken seriously, but an arrogant witness will lose credibility. A witness who only pleads the fifth amendment and refuses to speak will be seen as useless. The words of the witness will not be viewed in a vacuum, as if they were words on a page. The witness's lifestyle will be just as relevant as his words, and his mannerisms could cause even a true testimony to be rejected.

An example of a true witness with a bad lifestyle was the demon-possessed woman who followed Paul and Silas as they witnessed in Philippi. The woman, described as a soothsayer, or fortune teller, followed them around screaming, "These men are the servants of the most high God, which shew unto us the way of salvation" (Acts 16:17). Interestingly, the words of this witness were true. Even though she was possessed by demons, she told the truth about Paul and Silas.

In this instance, Paul would not have agreed with the modern marketing adage that all publicity is good publicity. While Paul tolerated her antics for a few days, he must have been concerned that a woman filled with demons was their biggest source of advertisement in Philippi. Acts 16:18 records that Paul became grieved (greatly annoyed, NKJV) and cast the demons out of her. Even though her words were true, her lifestyle was not consistent with the message and promise of the gospel of Jesus Christ.

We must be very careful not to be guilty of speaking the correct words but living incorrect lifestyles. The Pharisees were also guilty of this habit. Jesus warned His disciples, "The scribes and the Pharisees sit in Moses' seat: all therefore whatsoever they bid you observe, that observe and do; but do not ye after their works: for they say, and do not" (Matthew 23:2-3). The Pharisees spoke one thing but lived another. Simply stated, they were hypocrites. May such a condemning statement never be said of our lives or our churches. A great tragedy in living for God is the near miss in which someone has all the correct information and knowledge about God but does not translate it into daily living. Just knowing is not enough; we must be the salt and light God intended.

Prayer Focus
Lead the group in prayer and consider the following topics of focus:
- For God to help us be salt, light, and a city on a hill
- For God to give us boldness to share our testimony as His witness

2.3

DISCIPLINES OF A DISCIPLE

FOCUS VERSES
Matthew 6:4, 6, 18
⁴ That thine alms may be in secret: and thy Father which seeth in secret himself shall reward thee openly.

. . . . .

⁶ But thou, when thou prayest, enter into thy closet, and when thou hast shut thy door, pray to thy Father which is in secret; and thy Father which seeth in secret shall reward thee openly.

. . . . .

¹⁸ That thou appear not unto men to fast, but unto thy Father which is in secret: and thy Father, which seeth in secret, shall reward thee openly.

LESSON TEXT
Matthew 6:1–18

TRUTH ABOUT GOD
God expects us to have the right motives when we give, pray, and fast.

TRUTH FOR MY LIFE
I will seek to honor the Lord through my daily spiritual disciplines.

Thinking about Last Week:

Have students refer to their Daily Devotional Guide to answer the following questions:
1. What most affected you as you read through the Lesson Text and the Biblical Insights?
2. How did it shape your prayers and thoughts throughout the week?
3. Do you feel you grew closer to the Lord this past week? Why or why not?

(SG) TEACHING OUTLINE

Icebreaker: Besides the devil, who do you see as the biggest villain in the Bible?

Lesson Connection: Share the Lesson Connection.

I.   GIVING (I)

   A. The Importance of Giving

     » *Why is the topic of giving sometimes difficult to address in our twenty-first century culture?*

   B. The Proper Motive for Giving

   C. I Will Honor the Lord through Giving

     » *How can we properly see giving as a privilege, not a burden or obligation?*

II.   PRAYING

   A. The Importance of Prayer

   B. The Proper Motive for Praying

     » *What has been your experience with prayer? Is prayer difficult or a joy for you?*

   C. I Will Draw Close to the Lord through Prayer (V)

III.   FASTING

   A. The Importance of Fasting

   B. The Proper Motive for Fasting

     » *How often should we fast? If we cannot fast meals because of medical conditions, what other ways can we fast?*

   C. I Will Honor the Lord through My Daily Spiritual Disciplines

     » *Which spiritual discipline helps you feel closest to God?*

Internalizing the Message

Prayer Focus
Lead the group in prayer and consider the following topics of focus:
- For God to help us see our spiritual disciplines like He sees them
- For God to help us to be faithful in our spiritual disciplines

LESSON CONNECTION

A bi-vocational pastor was working for a small, local health clinic. Since he was in a remote area, good-paying jobs were scarce. The pastor felt blessed to have a job that could support his family and allow him the flexibility to still pastor his church. However, despite enjoying the work and being well paid, the pastor had one major problem: his supervisor at the clinic was not overly kind, and that is saying it kindly. The supervisor frequently overburdened her employees by passing off her own work to them, and she had no problem harshly berating her subordinates publicly. Her language was foul, and her demeanor was arrogant. Many workers complained to human resources and upper management, but their efforts were in vain.

The pastor believed that prayer changes things, so he took this matter to the Lord in prayer. Months passed and his supervisor had not changed. In fact, she had gotten worse. The pastor committed to prayer even more, yet still nothing seemed to change.

After nearly a year, the health-care company offered to send several employees to a training seminar in another state for one week. The topic of the conference was "Working with Difficult People." Intrigued, the pastor volunteered to go. However, after a week at the conference, the pastor was discouraged. He had taken exhaustive notes but felt as though nothing could help his situation. On the last day of the conference, he approached the main speaker and relayed his situation. "I don't know what to do," he bemoaned. "I've tried everything."

The conference speaker offered an unexpected suggestion. "Have you tried buying her a gift and writing her a nice card?" The pastor was shocked. "Why would I do that?" he asked, incredulously. The speaker replied, "It sounds like she's stressed. She works in a remote area and is the only one within one hundred miles who can do her job. Perhaps if you work hard to treat her kindly, she will realize the error of her ways and treat you all differently."

The next week, the pastor convinced the entire office to chip in and buy their supervisor a card, a bouquet of flowers, and a gift certificate to her favorite restaurant. Within a month the entire office noticed a drastic change in the supervisor. She spoke softer and was more patient and sensitive to her employees' needs. In the end, the pastor was right that prayer did change things, but before God changed the supervisor's heart, God first had to change the pastor's own heart.

BIBLE LESSON

In His Sermon on the Mount, Jesus contrasted the behavior of hypocrites with how He expected His followers to live. Jesus taught His disciples proper motives for common spiritual disciplines. In this passage, Jesus did not overtly tell His disciples to give, pray, or fast; He simply assumed they already were. He constantly spoke of when they practiced these spiritual disciplines. They did not need instruction convincing them to give, pray, or fast, but Jesus knew they needed Him to show them the correct motives.

I. GIVING

Teacher Option: *A supplemental image is available in the Resource Kit.* 🔲

The first discipline Jesus mentioned was giving. Money and possessions are a sensitive topic, but Jesus did not shy away from difficult topics. However, this was more than just about giving. Many modern translations make it clear that Jesus was referring to "practicing your righteousness before other people" (Matthew 6:1, ESV). The practice of giving alms was traditionally associated with charitable donations to the poor and needy. Although the hypocrites were doing good by helping the poor, they were nullifying the spiritual benefit of their practices by broadcasting their goodness for all the world to see. Jesus said they already had the reward they were seeking—fame and recognition by other people. Instead of seeking God's approval, which is eternal, they sought man's approval, which is fleeting.

A. The Importance of Giving

The importance of giving cannot be overstated. Jesus was speaking about giving to the poor of the land who sat in public places and begged for alms, such as the man who sat at the Temple and sought something from Peter and John (Acts 3:2). However, this is not the only type of giving mentioned as normal and beneficial in Scripture. Many believers in the Book of Acts sold their possessions and gave gifts to the church to benefit the entire church body (Acts 2:45; 4:32-37). Church leaders also received a special offering for famine relief in Judea (Acts 11:27-30), similar to present-day churches giving in response to natural disasters, such as hurricanes or earthquakes. It was common for churches to support pastoral ministry financially (I Corinthians 9:13-14; I Timothy 5:17-18). Giving generously was normal for all New Testament Christians. It is impossible to be apostolic—living as the apostles did—without giving generously.

Why is the topic of giving sometimes difficult to address in our twenty-first century culture?

B. The Proper Motive for Giving

Just the act of giving is not sufficient. Jesus taught it is possible to do right with a wrong motive. Giving with a pure motive demonstrates and grows our faith and trust in God. When we give faithfully, consistently, and sacrificially, we grow in our trust in God as He continues to supply every need. Even if we do not experience wealth and prosperity, God will provide for every need.

Jesus encouraged those listening that God sees their good deeds. God is the only one we need to see our giving. The proper motivation for our spiritual disciplines is growing closer to God in relationship and likeness. Just as God has given bountifully to humanity, including sacrificing Himself on a cross, we are to imitate Him by giving selflessly to others.

C. I Will Honor the Lord through Giving

The principles of giving are closely related to the principle of sowing and reaping. Paul encouraged his readers, "But this I say, He which soweth sparingly shall reap also sparingly; and he which soweth bountifully shall reap also bountifully. Every man according as he purposeth in his heart, so let him give; not grudgingly, or of necessity: for God loveth a cheerful giver" (II Corinthians 9:6–7). The ESV translates part of this passage as "not reluctantly or under compulsion." Those who give because they feel obligated will not receive blessings for their giving. Giving is a privilege we have to honor the Lord and bless others. Giving should not be viewed as a burden but as an opportunity. We should purpose to honor the Lord through regular, generous, joyful giving and then note the change it makes in our lives.

How can we properly see giving as a privilege, not a burden or obligation?

II. PRAYING

Jesus also assumed His followers would be praying because He said, "When thou prayest" (Matthew 6:6). Although many people sincerely desire to pray, many are not sure where or how to begin. Jesus first addressed underlying motivations behind prayer, helped reveal the purpose of prayer, and then gave us an example of prayer. The passage commonly known as the Lord's Prayer is a helpful template for believers learning how to pray. Believers just beginning to pray would do well to use this prayer as a starting point as they grow more comfortable speaking with God on a regular basis.

A. The Importance of Prayer

By simplest definition, prayer is communication with God. For any relationship to thrive, there must be healthy communication. God speaks to us through His Word, but He also speaks to us through times of prayer. Healthy prayer is a dialogue where we commune with God and He communes with us. It would be foolish to think a marriage could thrive if there were no communication or if the conversation was all one-sided. In our relationship with God, we must learn to have two-way conversations called prayer. The more we practice prayer, the more we will become familiar with God's voice, and the better we will be able to discern His will and desire for our lives.

B. The Proper Motive for Praying

Since prayer is communication with God, prayer is an intimate practice. The hypocrites Jesus described prayed primarily to be seen by others. Their desire was not to speak with God as much as it was to perform in public. Those who pray to be admired by other people have the admiration they desire. However, those who pray to touch God's heart will have more than humanity could ever provide. It is far more important that God hears our prayers than for any human to hear our prayers. That is not to say that believers should not pray together. James encouraged believers to gather to pray (James 5:16). New Testament believers frequently gathered to pray, especially for urgent needs such as Peter's release from prison. (See Acts 12:12.) However, when we pray together, the focus must remain on God, not on people.

Those who have experienced the beauty and mystery of prayer can testify that prayer truly changes things. Prayer draws us closer to God, helps us better discern His voice, transforms hearts, changes circumstances, and results in countless, indescribable blessings. Perhaps this is why Paul encouraged Christians to "pray without ceasing" (I Thessalonians 5:17). Discovering the power of prayer should draw us to live a lifestyle where prayer is common and frequent.

What has been your experience with prayer? Is prayer difficult or a joy for you?

C. I Will Draw Close to the Lord through Prayer

The true story of the bi-vocational pastor and difficult supervisor testifies that continual, disciplined prayer will draw us closer to the Lord. Prayer changes things, but prayer first changes the heart and mind of the person praying. Those who do not allow prayer to transform them and continue to pray selfish prayers "ask amiss" when they pray (James 4:3). However, the wise believer does well to approach prayer with humility and servitude, not presumption and arrogance. Even Jesus concluded a prayer with "nevertheless not my will, but thine, be done" (Luke 22:42). True humility in prayer recognizes the superiority and sovereignty of God, the insufficiencies of human wisdom and knowledge, and the importance of being formed into God's image. Through humble and consistent prayer, we can daily draw closer to God.

III. FASTING

Teacher Option: A supplemental video is available in the Resource Kit. **V**

The final discipline Jesus mentioned in this section of the Sermon on the Mount was fasting. Fasting is mentioned multiple times in the Old Testament. Moses fasted forty days and forty nights while spending time with God on the summit of Mount Sinai. (See Exodus 34:28.) The Day of Atonement called all the congregation to afflict their souls, often a reference to fasting. (See Leviticus 16:29–30.) Jewish and rabbinical tradition called for even more fasting. However, fasting had become so commonplace that the people had forgotten its purpose. Jesus assumed His followers were already fasting, so He simply set out to correct their motivations.

A. The Importance of Fasting

Of the three disciplines we have covered, fasting might be the most uncomfortable because it goes against our basic biological instinct to eat. Fasting is inherently uncomfortable and undesirable. Our bodies need food to survive; that is part of God's design. God also designed humanity to know how to gather food and feed the body. However, the act of fasting causes us to remember that communion with God is even more important than our most basic human needs. As Job sat in his ash heap scraping boils from his skin, he reflected on how important God was to him. Job mused, "I have esteemed the words of his mouth more than my necessary food" (Job 23:12). Fasting reminds us that having a strong relationship with God will sustain us even better than food can.

B. The Proper Motive for Fasting

The Pharisees followed all the required fasts and more. They were judgmental of those who were not as fastidious as them. The Pharisees even distorted their faces to look weaker than they were, hoping their gaunt expressions would impress more people. Ironically, by fasting just to look better than others, the Pharisees fell into the same wrong motives as Old Testament Israel and earned a similar rebuke as them. "Behold, ye fast for strife and debate, and to smite with the fist of wickedness: ye shall not fast as ye do this day, to make your voice to be heard on high" (Isaiah 58:4). Fasting done for the purpose of strife and debate is never God's will.

The proper motive for fasting, as with all personal spiritual disciplines, must be to draw closer to God. Our flesh is weak and limited, but fasting reminds us we are more than flesh and blood. Fasting helps us to empty ourselves of selfish desires and helps bring our spirits more in line with what God is doing in our lives.

How often should we fast? If we cannot fast meals because of medical conditions, what other ways can we fast?

C. I Will Honor the Lord through My Daily Spiritual Disciplines

Giving, praying, and fasting are only some of the spiritual disciplines we can practice on a regular basis to draw closer to God. Regular study of God's Word and meditation on spiritual things are also biblically demonstrated disciplines. Even evangelism, service, and fellowship are forms of spiritual disciplines. Perhaps the most difficult of all disciplines are the practices of silence and solitude where we get alone with God, free from distractions, to meditate on Him and His Word.

Disciplines are not easy, nor are they instinctive; they must be developed and strengthened over time. Just as muscles do not grow with one trip to the gym, disciplines are not perfected in one day. Disciplines require consistency over time and may become a positive habit that daily draws us closer to God. God is honored when we faithfully make time to spend with Him, for He is always ready to meet with us. He honors our efforts every time we come to Him. In all our spiritual disciplines, we have this promise to remember from James: "Draw nigh to God, and he will draw nigh to you" (James 4:8).

Which spiritual discipline helps you feel closest to God?

INTERNALIZING THE MESSAGE

The bi-vocational pastor from our earlier story was immediately humbled when the speaker suggested his thoughts and actions should change toward his boss before he could expect her to change. The pastor reflected how he was a lifelong Apostolic, an ordained minister, and a believer who had spent over a year praying for this woman to treat him and his colleagues better, but he had never once considered treating her better. The pastor had spent so much time in his spiritual disciplines praying for God to change her, but he had not asked for God to change his own heart first.

As the pastor told this story, he was quick to clarify that it is certainly biblical to pray for situations or other people to change. However, if our prayers for change only include others and not ourselves, we are certainly praying amiss. The pastor realized his prayers were actually selfish because none of them were for this woman's salvation or well-being; his prayers were simply for his own convenience, comfort, and preference. He admitted he had not thought critically about how he prayed until the Lord revealed it to him.

One of the dangers of knowing truth is assuming we always handle the truth correctly and treat others as we should. Thankfully, Apostolics do have truth. However, as long as we are flesh and blood, we will not be perfect, and we cannot assume we are always correct or that we treat others correctly. There is a difference between having the truth as a piece of theoretical knowledge and actually walking daily in that truth.

There is also a difference between knowing about God and knowing God personally. The first requires memorizing and learning facts; the second requires daily, faithful spiritual disciplines. The first requires collecting knowledge; the second requires becoming a practitioner, applying this knowledge to daily life. Spiritual disciplines can help us discover new levels of spiritual intimacy with God we have never experienced before. Spiritual disciplines can move us from a spiritual astronomer (always looking up and studying the stars) to a spiritual astronaut who ascends into the heavens to get closer to God. When we learn to give, pray, and fast with faithfulness and cheerfulness, God will meet us in those disciplines to elevate us to new spiritual heights.

Prayer Focus
Lead the group in prayer and consider the following topics of focus:
- For God to help us see our spiritual disciplines like He sees them
- For God to help us to be faithful in our spiritual disciplines

2.4

THE KINGDOM FIRST

FOCUS VERSE
Matthew 6:33
But seek ye first the kingdom of God, and his righteousness; and all these things shall be added unto you.

LESSON TEXT
Matthew 6:25–33

TRUTH ABOUT GOD
God has promised to take care of all our needs.

TRUTH FOR MY LIFE
I will make the kingdom of God the first priority in my life.

Thinking about Last Week:

Have students refer to their Daily Devotional Guide to answer the following questions:

1. What most affected you as you read through the Lesson Text and the Biblical Insights?
2. How did it shape your prayers and thoughts throughout the week?
3. Do you feel you grew closer to the Lord this past week? Why or why not?

⟨SG⟩ TEACHING OUTLINE

Icebreaker: What were you worried about most as a child? What about now?

Lesson Connection: Share the Lesson Connection.

I. A WORLD OF WORRY ⟨I⟩
   » *What are some things you believe create frustration and worry in people today?*

   A. The Worries of the Inner Life ⟨V⟩
      » *What are some ways we can compensate for painful or abusive experiences of our childhood?*

   B. The Worries of the Outer Life
      » *Why are human relationships often challenging to manage? Can you think of some approaches to relationships that can help us navigate the difficulties they create?*

   C. I Will Not Let Worry Control My Life
      » *Why is it our responsibility to determine the kind of life we live? What are some positive actions we can take to counter stress and worry?*

II. THE CURE FOR WORRY

   A. The Premise of the Kingdom of God

   B. The Priority and Promise of the Kingdom of God
      » *How does a focus on adoring and worshiping God minimize or eliminate worry, stress, and challenges from our lives?*

   C. I Will Make the Kingdom of God the First Priority in My Life

Internalizing the Message

Prayer Focus
Lead the group in prayer and consider the following topics of focus:
• For God to help us make Him and His kingdom our priority
• For God to help us trust Him to provide for our needs

LESSON CONNECTION

A young woman sat weeping as she rocked in her chair near the roaring fire of the fireplace. A concerned family member was alarmed at her emotional distress and questioned her as to what was troubling her.

The woman explained, "I was just sitting here thinking about what if I were married and had a baby."

"Yes, go on," followed the concerned loved one. "There's certainly no reason to cry about that thought."

The weeping woman continued, "But what if I were sitting here rocking my baby near the fireplace and lost my grip, and my baby fell into the roaring fire of that fireplace?" she continued to cry between her words.

"That would be terrible!" exclaimed her relative. "What a terrible thought!"

"Yes," the woman continued. "I cannot bear to think about it, yet it is all I can think about." She broke out into uncontrollable sobs once again.

"But, Dear," the loved one exclaimed, "You have no child. You are not married. You are not engaged to be married. Why, you are not even dating anyone right now. Why would you be so troubled over such a thought?"

"I don't know," she sobbed. "I just can't help myself." The young woman continued to cry.

Something in the human psyche causes people to struggle with fear, anxiety, or worry. Some people deal with extreme concern that their clothes might not be impeccable or their house might not be perfect for company, all the while their clothes are fine and they are not even expecting visitors to their home. Too often we allow concerns and worries to trouble us when there is no cause to worry.

Is it possible that some people's worry stems from their failure to arrange their lives in proper order with biblical priorities? In this lesson we will consider what should be the top priority in our lives as believers. It might not prevent all concerns and worries in life, but it certainly can help us live without undue emotional stress as we pursue the kingdom of God above all other pursuits.

BIBLE LESSON

I. A WORLD OF WORRY

Teacher Option:
A supplemental image is available in the Resource Kit. **I**

Merriam-Webster defines *worry* as "mental distress or agitation resulting from concern usually for something impending or anticipated: anxiety; an instance or occurrence of such distress or agitation." Life has a way of presenting obstacles and challenges that create mental distress, agitation, or frustrations. How we deal with these challenges determines our level of mental anxiety. We cannot altogether eliminate these sources of worry, but we can take control of and responsibility for our mental state and choose to pursue the kingdom of God above all things.

What are some things you believe create frustration and worry in people today?

A. The Worries of the Inner Life

Our internal fears and concerns stem from our experiences, often beyond our choice and control. For instance, we do not choose the family we are born into, the economic state of that family, where we were raised, or the emotional conditions that surrounded us in childhood. Further, many people today come from broken homes and have even suffered mental, physical, emotional, and sexual abuse. It is a shame—and sometimes a crime—what many children suffer in their childhood. Those conditions and abuses do not come by the child's own choice or doing, but the child can overcome the lingering effects through great effort.

We often experience inner turmoil that grows out of the conditions of our childhood. Some individuals grow up with great insecurities—fear and worry over their ability to have enough to eat, to have the ability to achieve and excel, or to be worthy of acceptance and love. Since these concerns often grew out of childhood circumstances, these individuals cannot avoid them but must determine how they will deal with them and overcome them.

Children who seldom or never received affirmation may struggle with insecurity and find it difficult to believe in themselves as adults. They may think, *No one else believes in me so why should I believe in myself?* They often lack self-confidence; their self-worth is low; and their insecurity, which births anxiety and worry, is high. They cannot change their childhood experiences or undo their hurts, but they can discover deliverance from worry and hope for change all in the kingdom of God.

What are some ways we can compensate for painful or abusive experiences of our childhood?

B. The Worries of the Outer Life

As we reach adulthood, we discover life brings new struggles that go beyond our childhood experiences. We have pressures and stresses that come from our jobs, such as expectations and demands from supervisors and peers. We worry about social

Teacher Option:
A supplemental video is available in the Resource Kit. **V**

status, bills, and inflation. We experience all the typical upheavals of life through its mundane routines and uncharted twists and turns. Life is made of these kinds of challenges.

We encounter rigors and associated stresses that stem from changing relationships—family relationships, disagreements, and reunions. It's not always easy to maintain balanced relationships with the very people from whom we need love and acceptance the most. On the other hand, friends come and go in and out of our lives, which also creates expectations and challenges as we try to manage the nuances of human relationships.

Why are human relationships often challenging to manage? Can you think of some approaches to relationships that can help us navigate the difficulties they create?

Although these external pressures are common to all people, there is no one-size-fits-all template for managing and eliminating these stresses and the concerns they bring. We just faithfully ride the waves of life's circumstances and never lose the hope that life in Christ affords us. Kingdom life is the answer to dealing with all these stresses. It involves deciding not to allow the pressures of life to control us even when we cannot control the external and internal sources from which they flow. This is easier said than done, but with God's help we can change.

C. I Will Not Let Worry Control My Life

Ultimately, life is what we make it out to be. We can live a peaceful life filled with love and joy, or we can live a life of unbearable turbulence and torment. It essentially boils down to how we view the challenges and how we determine to deal with them. If we are to enjoy a peaceable life, we must refuse to allow worry to dominate us. We must choose to take responsibility and control our lives through the exertion of positive actions that counter the stress and worry.

Why is it our responsibility to determine the kind of life we live? What are some positive actions we can take to counter stress and worry?

Certainly, there are natural things we can do to help manage the pressures, stresses, and worries of life. We can eat a healthy diet, which will help to control our physical weight and balance our hormones. We can ensure our lifestyle affords us a restful night of adequate sleep daily, and we can refuse to overcrowd our schedules with useless or non-productive activities. We can practice relaxation techniques and exercise our bodies. All these have natural benefits and will aid us in managing the stresses of life. However, nothing compares with the importance of nurturing our spiritual health. Nurturing our spiritual health involves our connection to the kingdom of God; it is the only effective cure for worry.

II. THE CURE FOR WORRY

A. The Premise of the Kingdom of God

In Matthew's gospel, Jesus implores us to "seek ye first the kingdom of God, and his righteousness; and all these things shall be added unto you" (Matthew 6:33). He referred to many of the needs we all have, such as food, drink, and clothing. But Jesus pointed out that the birds that fly through the air do not worry about these basic needs and the heavenly Father still provides for them (Matthew 6:26). He was not suggesting we do not have these basic, human needs; rather, He was revealing that God is aware of our fundamental needs and is fully capable of caring for us.

Jesus was giving His disciples an approach to life wherein we do not have to worry about the basic needs of life, but through a divine relationship, God will supply all our needs. Neither the birds nor the flowers worry. Why should God's crowning work of creation—humanity—spend their days worried about their basic needs? In the kingdom of God, we can live in spiritual relationship with our divine Creator and find relief from the dissipating effects of worry.

B. The Priority and Promise of the Kingdom of God

Many ideas stem from the possible differences or similarities between the terms "kingdom of heaven" and "kingdom of God." However, while the term "kingdom of God" is used extensively throughout the New Testament, the term "kingdom of heaven" appears half as often and only in the Gospel of Matthew, which was written to a primarily Jewish audience. Most scholars believe that the term "kingdom of heaven" was the more palatable term for communicating to the Jewish mindset. For the purpose of this lesson, we will consider the two terms similar, and we will focus on the kingdom of God as the realm in which relationship with God exists and God's will and purpose are supreme in Heaven and on the earth. This idea of God's divine will should guide our prayers. We pray, "Thy kingdom come. Thy will be done in earth, as it is in heaven" (Matthew 6:10).

Jesus promised our basic needs would be supplied if we seek first the kingdom of God and His righteousness (Matthew 6:33). If we make the kingdom of God and His righteousness priority in our lives, we can be free from worrying about receiving the necessities of human life. Jesus was pointing out a new approach and kind of living in this world—a life focused foremost on God's kingdom with His will in perfect view.

How many people go from the cradle to the grave without ever really knowing God or His will for their lives? They may know about Him and even acknowledge His presence in the world, but have they really experienced His presence and allowed Him to impact their day-to-day existence? Have they even explored the possibilities of what entering into Kingdom life now might involve or how it could revolutionize their lives?

Some people even offer up routine prayers for what they desire from life. They talk to God, but do they allow God to talk to them? Do they hear and recognize His voice? Talking with God and hearing His voice through prayer are certainly important, but living the Kingdom life is so much more.

In his book *Hearing God: Developing a Conversational Relationship with God*, Dallas Willard writes, "Ultimately, we are to move beyond the question of hearing God and into a life greater than our own—that of the kingdom of God. Our concern for discerning God's voice must be overwhelmed by and lost in our worship and adoration of him and in our delight with his creation and his provision for our whole life." To Willard, entering into the kingdom of God involves an intimate relationship with God that overwhelms the mundane elements of our earthly existence. This appears to be the fulfillment of Matthew 6:33, which thrusts us into the kind of relationship with Jesus Christ that will manage—if not eliminate—the worries of life that proceed out of its many stresses and pressures.

Entering into this Kingdom life necessarily brings an individual into close contact and communion with the righteousness of God. Life in the kingdom of God is not consumed with worries about our essential physical needs but is overwhelmed by righteousness, peace, and joy in the Holy Ghost. (See Romans 14:17.) When we are in this kind of intimate relationship with Jesus Christ, we are so focused on adoration and worship that we often lose sight of our own worries. This focus is not reckless because our heavenly Father will provide for our needs. When we are consumed with worshiping God, we have little time for worry.

Jesus taught, "Labour not for the meat which perisheth, but for that meat which endureth unto everlasting life, which the Son of man shall give unto you: for him hath God the Father sealed" (John 6:27).

How does a focus on adoring and worshiping God minimize or eliminate worry, stress, and challenges from our lives?

C. I Will Make the Kingdom of God the First Priority in My Life

What is the solution for dealing with our frustrations and worry? We should make the kingdom of God our priority and pursue His righteousness. When we decide to make His kingdom our priority, we begin the process of clearing away the smoke of life's distracting challenges. We look worry in the eyes and declare that it will have no dominion over us. Making the kingdom of God our priority first looks like adoration and worship. The psalmist wrote, "Give unto the LORD the glory due unto his name: bring an offering, and come into his courts. O worship the LORD in the beauty of holiness: fear before him, all the earth" (Psalm 96:8–9).

As we pursue God through adoration and worship, our frustrations begin to dissipate and our worries become dim. The more we focus on God and pursue His divine purpose, the less we will think about the worries of this life. And amazingly, we will discover God is providing exactly what we need for abundant life in His kingdom.

INTERNALIZING THE MESSAGE

Adrian Rogers stated, "The scourge of the twenty-first century is half hearted Christianity. Half-hearted Christianity will not do it. It never could. But surely not in these times. Are you seeking for Christ with all your heart? Is there anything in your life you love more than the Lord Jesus Christ? If so, then my friend, that thing—whatever or whoever it is—has become an idol in your life. Realizing that, what steps can you take today to remove it from the throne and put Christ back in His proper place in your life?"

Let's take these steps to make God and His kingdom priority in our busy, complex lives.

1. Commit ourselves wholeheartedly to Jesus Christ and His kingdom—no holding back.

2. Spend quality time with the Lord Jesus every day—in prayer, in His Word, in reflection.

3. Focus on developing intimacy with Jesus every day. Talk to Him, allow Him to speak into our lives, and daily enjoy His presence.

4. Commit our schedule to the Lord. We know what is on our to-do list, but do we truly reflect God's priorities, or do we reflect our own? Let's daily align our priorities with God's priorities.

5. Refuse to worry about our challenges. Put our stresses and worries in God's hands every morning and trust He will provide what we need when we need it.

6. Find time for others throughout the day. The kingdom of God is lived out in community with the fellowship of believers. Make a phone call, drop a card in the mail, or send an email. Let others know they are important to us, and let godly brothers and sisters speak wisdom into our lives. Live Kingdom life together.

As we seek daily to grow in relationship with Jesus by living within His kingdom and pursuing His righteousness, Jesus will draw near to us. "Draw nigh to God, and he will draw nigh to you" (James 4:8). God desires relationship with us more than we could possibly know or imagine.

Prayer Focus
Lead the group in prayer and consider the following topics of focus:
• For God to help us make Him and His kingdom our priority
• For God to help us trust Him to provide for our needs

2.5

THE PRIORITY OF OBEDIENCE

FOCUS VERSES
MATTHEW 7:24;
25:24-25
[24] Therefore whosoever heareth these sayings of mine, and doeth them, I will liken him unto a wise man, which built his house upon a rock:

. . . .

[24] Then he which had received the one talent came and said, Lord, I knew thee that thou art an hard man, reaping where thou hast not sown, and gathering where thou hast not strawed:
[25] And I was afraid, and went and hid thy talent in the earth: lo, there thou hast that is thine.

LESSON TEXT
Matthew 7:21-27; 25:14-30

TRUTH ABOUT GOD
God's Word is the only sure foundation for the Christian life.

TRUTH FOR MY LIFE
I will rely on God and not on myself.

Thinking about Last Week:

Have students refer to their Daily Devotional Guide to answer the following questions:
1. What most affected you as you read through the Lesson Text and the Biblical Insights?
2. How did it shape your prayers and thoughts throughout the week?
3. Do you feel you grew closer to the Lord this past week? Why or why not?

(SG) TEACHING OUTLINE

Icebreaker: Where would you live if you could live anywhere in the world?

Lesson Connection: Share the Lesson Connection.
» *In what ways can we be more sensitive and obedient to God that may bless the kingdom of God?*

I. THE WISDOM OF OBEDIENCE

A. The Insufficiency of Just Hearing God's Word
» *Why do you think God was so upset over Saul's disobedience? Was this Saul's first instance of disobeying God's word?*

B. The Necessity of Obeying God's Word

C. I Will Demonstrate Faith through My Obedience
» *What are some ways our faith in God and His Word are demonstrated through obedience to God?*

II. THE PARABLE OF THE TALENTS

A. A Blessing for Obedience Not Outcome (V)
» *How can you use the gifts and abilities God has given you for His glory?*

B. Self-Reliance, the Enemy of Obedience
» *How can self-reliance lure us away from obedience to God? Why must we be certain to keep our talents dedicated to the call of God?*

C. I Will Rely on God and Not on Myself

Internalizing the Message (I)

Prayer Focus
Lead the group in prayer and consider the following topics of focus:
• For God to help us hear and obey His Word
• For God to help us use the gifts He gave us for His glory

LESSON CONNECTION

The late pastor James Kilgore told the story of a Sunday school girl who wanted to have something to give in the offering at church, but she had no money. She was likely one of the children who rode the bus to Life Tabernacle. But something was different about this girl; she was not content just to let the offering plate pass her by. Before she boarded the bus, she found a single bloom from a solitary stem of a flower. That tiny flower would be her offering in Sunday school.

Can you imagine the delight she must have felt placing her tiny bloom into the offering plate that morning? There is something satisfying about giving what we have to God even when it seems insignificant to others. She gave with her childlike excitement. A sensitive Sunday school teacher observed her giving that morning and thought, *I must take this flower to Pastor Kilgore and tell him the story.* When he received the tiny bloom and heard the touching story, the Holy Spirit nudged the pastor to share the story in the service that morning. As he was obedient to the prompting of the Spirit, an atmosphere of giving swept across the congregation.

Perhaps it was Pastor Kilgore's idea to auction the flower for missions or possibly a sensitive soul in the congregation offered to purchase the flower, but the church auctioned off that single bloom for tens of thousands of dollars for the cause of Global Missions. It all happened because a little girl was obedient to her desire to give something in the offering, because of the obedience of a Sunday school teacher in her prompting to share the story and flower with the pastor, and because of a sensitive pastor who shared the story and raised many thousands of dollars for missions. Like the widow woman who cast in her two mites—which was all she had—the Sunday school girl gave more than everyone gave that day.

What a blessing obedience to God is in our own lives and in the lives of others who are touched through our acts of obedience, whatever they might be.

In what ways can we be more sensitive and obedient to God that may bless the kingdom of God?

BIBLE LESSON

I. THE WISDOM OF OBEDIENCE

A. The Insufficiency of Just Hearing God's Word

Jesus was finishing His Sermon on the Mount. From there He would go down that mountain and begin walking toward the Cross. As He closed this sermon, He told a story of two builders. They both scoped out the land to find the perfect place to set up a home and settle down. One of the builders looked down at his feet and saw sand. He unloaded his pack and passed up his pick axe, chisel, and hammer. He picked up the shovel and dug a few feet until he was satisfied. Then he unpacked his hammock, poured some lemonade, and smiled at how easy this was. But Jesus said, "And every one that heareth these sayings of mine, and doeth them not, shall be likened unto a foolish man, which built his house upon the sand" (Matthew 7:26).

Perhaps Jesus thought about some of the Old Testament prophets who had preached the Word, but their audience did not listen. Every true prophet of the Old Testament and every minister of the gospel in the New Testament knew what it was like to deliver God's inspired message for a specific occasion only to watch some souls reject the message and walk away unchanged. It is painful to watch people reject God and His Word. It is a privilege to hear the message God sends to us, but we are only blessed through our obedience to His message.

King Saul missed out on God's blessings because he did not obey God's command to utterly destroy the Amalekites (I Samuel 15:2-3). Saul and his army captured and spared the Amalekite king, Agag, and the best of the sheep, oxen, fatlings, lambs, and all that was good (I Samuel 15:9). The Lord sent His prophet Samuel to rebuke King Saul. Samuel asked him, "Hath the LORD as great delight in burnt offerings and sacrifices, as in obeying the voice of the LORD? Behold, to obey is better than sacrifice, and to hearken than the fat of rams. For rebellion is as the sin of witchcraft, and stubbornness is as iniquity and idolatry. Because thou hast rejected the word of the LORD, he hath also rejected thee from being king" (I Samuel 15:22-23).

Why do you think God was so upset over Saul's disobedience? Was this Saul's first instance of disobeying God's word?

B. The Necessity of Obeying God's Word

The other builder looked down at his feet and smiled. He knew building his house on a rock would keep his house standing when today's gentle breeze grew into tomorrow's violent gale. Jesus said, "Therefore whosoever heareth these sayings of mine, and doeth them, I will liken him unto a wise man, which built his house upon a rock" (Matthew 7:24). Jesus gave the same weather forecast to both builders. "And the rain descended, and the floods came, and the winds blew, and beat upon that house" (Matthew 7:25, 27). Both houses faced the same forecast, but only one house still stood after the storm because it was built on a rock. Jesus likened this house to whosoever hears His Word and obeys it.

It is impossible to claim to be a Christian who loves and serves Jesus Christ but refuses to hear and obey the Word of God. It is an oxymoron to claim to follow a leader but refuse to follow where the leader is leading. God sent stern words of warning to the people of Israel through His prophet Ezekiel concerning hearing and doing His words. "And they come unto thee as the people cometh, and they sit before thee as my people, and they hear thy words, but they will not do them: for with their mouth they shew much love, but their heart goeth after their covetousness" (Ezekiel 33:31).

C. I Will Demonstrate Faith through My Obedience

Obedience to God is necessary first because Jesus Christ commanded it. "If ye love me, keep my commandments" (John 14:15). Our obedience to God demonstrates our faith in God and our worship of Him. If we believe something to be true, we will act accordingly because actions demonstrate true belief. That is the essence of faith: acting upon what we believe to be true. E. L. Holley illustrated this principle in a memorable way. If someone runs into a crowded room to announce the building is on fire and the crowd must evacuate immediately, only those who truly believe the building is on fire will evacuate. However, if someone in the crowd exclaims, "I believe!" but does not begin moving toward the exit, his actions belie his words. Faith in God and His Word are intimately associated with obedience.

What are some ways our faith in God and His Word are demonstrated through obedience to God?

II. THE PARABLE OF THE TALENTS

Jesus told another parable related to this principle. Matthew 25:14–30 relates what has come to be known as the Parable of the Talents. Jesus told of a man who was preparing to leave on a distant journey. The man anticipated he would be gone for a while, so he distributed talents to three servants. A talent was a large sum of money. Some scholars believe each talent was equivalent to twenty years of wages. He gave these talents to his servants according to their ability—five talents to one servant, two talents to another servant, and one talent to a third servant. The man anticipated these servants would put these talents to work to grow his wealth during his absence.

After a long time, he returned and settled accounts with his three servants. The servant who had received five talents returned them to his master along with five additional talents he had gained through trading. The servant who had received two talents gained an additional two talents and returned all four to his master. The third servant who had received one talent only returned the lone talent. Scripture reveals the servant was fearful and hid the one talent instead of investing it. "I was afraid, and went and hid thy talent in the earth: lo, there thou hast that is thine" (Matthew 25:25).

The lord was pleased with the increase realized by the servant in charge of five talents and the servant who had been left with two talents. However, the servant who fearfully hid his one talent faced the wrath of his master in the time of reckoning. His lord called him a "wicked and slothful servant" (Matthew 25:26). He should have put the one talent to work and earned interest from the investment. Consequently, the unprofitable servant lost all he had.

A. A Blessing for Obedience Not Outcome

The Lord does not measure the outcome of our lives based on production but on obedience. The man who left his three servants in charge of his wealth was just as pleased with the servant who returned four talents as he was with the servant who returned ten. The servant with one talent was not condemned because of lack of production; he was condemned because of lack of obedience or effort. He did nothing to grow what his lord had left in his charge. God knows our abilities and talents. He does not expect us to do more than we are able to do, but He does expect us to do what we are capable of doing based on the talents He has given us. We all come from different backgrounds of life and circumstances, and the Lord is fully aware of our differences. He plans for us to use our life situations and abilities for His glory. Some servants will be missionaries to nations all over the planet; some will be pastors in North America; some will be faithful laborers in their own hometowns, using their abilities within various endeavors of industry; but all will have the ability to contribute to and bless the kingdom of God. Our Lord desires and requires faithfulness, not just results. "Moreover it is required in stewards, that a man be found faithful" (I Corinthians 4:2).

Some people worry because they feel their giftings do not match the abilities of others. Some believers even excuse themselves from doing anything at all because they cannot do what others can do. God's blessings are not based on production in the Kingdom but on our obedience to God's call on our lives.

B. Self-Reliance, the Enemy of Obedience

God gave us gifts and talents, but He does not expect us to operate strictly out of our human strength and abilities. He desires us to submit our human faculties and abilities to Him and allow Him to use us as we serve in His kingdom. The proper key to the effective use of our human abilities is to rely on the strength of God rather than on our own human strength. When we rely on Jesus Christ, we can accomplish anything He desires us to do for His kingdom. Sadly, some people become so reliant on their own human abilities that they lose sight of the empowerment of Christ and may even turn away from the commandments of the

Teacher Option: *A supplemental video is available in the Resource Kit.* **V**

How can you use the gifts and abilities God has given you for His glory?

How can self-reliance lure us away from obedience to God? Why must we be certain to keep our talents dedicated to the call of God?

Lord. It is dangerous to become so self-reliant that we fail to live a life of obedience to God and His plan for our lives.

C. I Will Rely on God and Not on Myself

We should focus on obeying the Word of God no matter what that may entail. Rather than fretting over our perceived inabilities, we should rely completely on God's assistance. Since our achievements in His kingdom are not anchored to our abilities alone, we should refrain from self-reliance. God wants to bless the gifts and abilities He has given us, but He can only bless what we put in His hands. In the Parable of the Talents, the lord promised an increase of responsibility to the servants who had labored and increased the value of what he had left in their charge. To each of those two servants, he promised similar blessing. "His lord said unto him, Well done, good and faithful servant; thou hast been faithful over a few things, I will make thee ruler over many things: enter thou into the joy of thy lord" (Matthew 25:23).

If we desire more giftings and abilities to use for the glory of God, we must first be faithful in the talents He has already given us. The key to such spiritual success in God's kingdom comes by relying on the empowerment of the Holy Spirit in our lives. We make a mistake if we assume the limited or seemingly small gifts and talents God has given us are so insignificant that we should just bury them and let others serve in the kingdom of God. In the day of reckoning, God will not compare our accomplishments with those of others we deemed to be more talented. He will compare our achievements with what He initially put in our hands. He wants and expects us to use what we have all for His glory.

INTERNALIZING THE MESSAGE

A supplemental image is available in the Resource Kit. ⓘ

In his book *A Call to Excellence*, Gary Inrig tells the story of Bertoldo di Giovanni, whom he says "is a name even the most enthusiastic lover of art is unlikely to recognize. In his time, he was an important sculptor but none of his work has lasted. His chief claim to fame is as a historical connector. He was the pupil of Donatello, the greatest sculptor of his time, and the teacher of Michelangelo, the greatest sculptor of all time.

"Michelangelo was only fourteen years old when he came to Bertoldo, but it was already obvious that he was enormously gifted. Bertoldo was wise enough to realize that gifted people are often tempted to coast rather than to grow, and therefore he kept trying to pressure his young prodigy to work seriously at his art. One day, he came into the studio to find Michelangelo toying with a piece of sculpture far beneath his abilities. Bertoldo grabbed a hammer, stomped across the room, and smashed the work into tiny pieces, shouting his unforgettable message: 'Michelangelo, talent is cheap; dedication is costly!'"

The gifts and talents God bestows on us are only a blessing to us and to others when we devote their use to the Lord and His kingdom. If we assume they are too meager or insignificant to bless anyone or bless the kingdom of God, they will remain dormant, unused, and small. When we obey God and entrust their usefulness to His hand, these gifts and talents become significant and helpful in His kingdom. If we bury them like the servant with one, solitary talent, we will stand before God in shame and judgment. But if we put them to use in obedience to our Lord, we will become increasingly effective within His kingdom, and He will increase our usefulness and Kingdom responsibilities.

Prayer Focus
Lead the group in prayer and consider the following topics of focus:
- For God to help us hear and obey His Word
- For God to help us use the gifts He gave us for His glory

3.1

I WILL BUILD MY CHURCH

FOCUS VERSE
Matthew 16:18
And I say also unto thee, That thou art Peter, and upon this rock I will build my church; and the gates of hell shall not prevail against it.

LESSON TEXT
Matthew 16:13–20; Luke 5:1-11

TRUTH ABOUT GOD
Jesus calls disciples to follow Him.

TRUTH FOR MY LIFE
I will be a disciple of Jesus.

Series Overview:

This series, "A Glorious Church," presents the church as one of God's greatest gifts to His people. These lessons will show God's plans for His church by declaring He would build His church, the purpose of the church, the church in action, and the beautiful bride of Christ. This series will give us a greater appreciation for the church and the important role it should play in our lives. Jesus is coming soon. And when He returns, He is coming for a glorious church.

[SG] TEACHING OUTLINE

Icebreaker: What are your favorite outdoor hobbies?

Lesson Connection: Share the Lesson Connection

I. JESUS WENT LOOKING FOR DISCIPLES

A. Jesus Entered Peter's Boat and Taught the People. [I]

B. Peter Launched Out into the Deep and Let Down His Net

C. The Miracle of Fish Revealed Jesus' Identity
    » *Have you had an encounter with God like Peter did? What feelings or thoughts did it evoke within you?*

D. I Will Worship Jesus for Who He Is
    » *What have you left behind to follow Jesus?*

II. JESUS CAME LOOKING FOR US

A. Jesus Came to Build His Church
    » *What does it mean to be called out and called together? How do you practice faith as a community of believers rather than an individual attending church services?*

B. His Church Is Built Upon the Revelation of Who He Is

C. We Are His Church; It Is Not a Building [V]
    » *How can you intentionally share church with others besides inviting them to your local place of worship?*

D. I Will Be a Disciple of Jesus

Internalizing the Message
    » *Has God tried to speak with you, but you responded about another person or situation instead of the condition of your own heart, soul, or spirit?*

Prayer Focus
Lead the group in prayer and consider the following topics of focus:
• For God to help us follow Him with our whole heart
• For God to help us make other disciples for Him

LESSON CONNECTION

Brett went deep-sea fishing once in Florida. He and his friends were all having a good time, but all that ended for Brett when the fishermen started catching fish. They pressed out into deep waters, and the ship captain began to cast the poles out of the boat. Almost immediately they began reeling in beautiful blue and green mahi-mahi. The trip was fun, new, and exciting. Then the men threw their ocean catches into a cooler right by Brett. His heart wouldn't let him fish anymore. He sat atop the cooler to keep the lid closed, and all he could hear were fish begging for their lives, beseeching someone to have mercy. They were flopping around like fish out of water.

Brett was conflicted. He had come all this way and spent all this money to catch fish for dinner, but he just could not sit there and let them slowly die. He wanted to jump up, commandeer the boat, open the cooler, and throw every single fish back into the ocean. But he'd have to explain to his former friends why they spent hundreds of dollars to go deep-sea fishing so he could return their spoils to the ocean and spoil their trip. He stayed there and painfully listened as the ruckus quieted down and he realized it was too late.

Brett was a softie when it came to fish. He tried to go fishing another time. One of the men in the church was going to show him how to hook the minnows. The gentleman held up a hook with one hand and a live minnow in the other. Then he said, "You get yourself a hook, and then you get yourself a minnow. And you drive that hook right through that minnow's eye." Brett was going to be sick. He's just not a fisherman.

Brett would have embarrassed Simon because Simon was a fisherman. He looked the part with tan, leathery muscles. He smelled the part, just ask Mrs. Simon. And he lived the part. After the sun disappeared each night, he met up with his colleagues and headed for the boats to see what gifts the ocean had to give. Simon had the "I'd rather be fishing" bumper sticker on his mule. But one day he met Jesus who called him to something higher than just fishing for fish; Jesus called Simon to fish for men.

BIBLE LESSON

I. JESUS WENT LOOKING FOR DISCIPLES

A. Jesus Entered Peter's Boat and Taught the People

Teacher Option:
A supplemental image is available in the Resource Kit. **I**

That day Simon, also called Peter, was fishing on the Sea of Galilee. Luke 5 presents Jesus preaching at the selfsame sea to a great crowd. Perhaps due to the large crowd, Jesus asked this fisherman, Simon Peter, who did not appear to be part of this large crowd, if He could borrow his boat. After Jesus climbed into the fishing boat, Peter pushed the boat out into the sea and became a member of Jesus' crowd (Luke 5:3).

B. Peter Launched Out into the Deep and Let Down His Net

After Jesus' message, He approached Peter and instructed him to take his boats out into the deep where they would catch fish (Luke 5:4). This was an odd way of paying for a boat rental. Surely Jesus saw the obvious; they had just returned from fishing and had caught nothing. But Peter agreed and took two boats out to deep water based on Jesus' word. On the way, Peter may have said to himself, "What does this preacher know about fishing? We fished all night and caught nothing. Now He thinks there will be fish there just because He said so? I can't wait to see the look on His face when we come back empty again." Peter and his associates, James and John, cast their net. They heard the distinct sound of their net tearing (Luke 5:6). What was happening?

C. The Miracle of Fish Revealed Jesus' Identity

If the lurch of the fishing boat was not enough, the number of fish Peter saw as he lifted the net assured him he was experiencing a supernatural event. Peter did not know how the fish got there or how Jesus knew they would be there; Peter just knew he had experienced something that defied all of his previous experiences. Such is the outcome of encounters with God. Perhaps Peter remembered the contempt and doubt through which he had viewed Jesus' instruction. The awe swiftly drained from his face as dread took its place. Peter knew Jesus was more than just a man. Even the rabbis could not perform such a feat. At the least, Jesus had to be a prophet. When Peter arrived at the shore to face Jesus, he collapsed to his knees and prayed, "Depart from me; for I am a sinful man, O Lord" (Luke 5:8).

Have you had an encounter with God like Peter did? What feelings or thoughts did it evoke within you?

D. I Will Worship Jesus for Who He Is

The Old Testament prophet Isaiah had a similar experience. One day Isaiah had a vision of God positioned on a throne within the Temple in Jerusalem. Angels were singing around the throne. The entire Temple began to shake violently. Isaiah cried out, "It's all over! I am doomed, for I am a sinful man. I have filthy lips, and I live among a people with filthy lips. Yet I have seen the

King, the LORD of Heaven's Armies" (Isaiah 6:5, NLT). Much like Peter, Isaiah was confronted with his sinfulness upon seeing God manifested in power. Isaiah saw the Lord on His throne; Peter saw a net bursting with fish that only divine intervention might explain. These divine encounters portray an important truth. When we see God, the views of ourselves, others, and the world are radically altered.

Rather than deny their sinfulness or attempt to absolve themselves, Peter and Isaiah owned their sinfulness. Likewise, both left their encounters commissioned into God's service. Isaiah became Jehovah's prophet to the kingdom of Judah; Peter became a fisher of men. Encountering Jesus causes a radical paradigm shift in our lives. When we meet Jesus, our values change as we realign our lives to match His holy purpose. Peter began fishing for fish, but he left fishing for men.

What have you left behind to follow Jesus?

II. JESUS CAME LOOKING FOR US

A. Jesus Came to Build His Church

The word *church* has become connected with a gathering place for Christian services, but it has lost the original meaning the earliest Christians attributed to it. If Jesus came to build His church and plans to have us play a role in it, we must understand what Jesus came to build. If Jesus came to build physical meeting places for Christians across the world, His mission is almost complete. However, Jesus' mission is about building a spiritual kingdom.

The word *church* in our English translation of the New Testament comes from the Greek word *ekklesia*, literally meaning "to call out of." The disciples knew this word frequently referred to the people of Israel in the *Septuagint*, the Greek translation of the Old Testament. In Greek culture, *ekklesia* referred to an assembly of male citizens over the age of twenty who lived in the same city. They were called out of their homes and called together to determine the best interests of their city. Similarly, the church consists of those who have been called out of the world and called together into Christ's kingdom that will one day be inaugurated upon the earth.

What does it mean to be called out and called together? How do you practice faith as a community of believers rather than an individual attending church services?

B. His Church Is Built Upon the Revelation of Who He Is

Since we are a group of people called out of the world and called together by Christ, we must be directly connected to the person of Jesus Christ. The mission of Christ is the mission of the church. Jesus gave the clearest and most precise definition of His mission in Luke 4:18–19: "The Spirit of the Lord is upon me, because he hath anointed me to preach the gospel to the poor; he hath sent me to heal the brokenhearted, to preach deliverance to the captives, and recovering of sight to the blind, to set at liberty them that are bruised, to preach the acceptable year of the Lord."

Jesus was quoting a prophecy from Isaiah, and He announced the fulfillment of that prophecy. He clearly identified the purpose of His ministry. If Jesus were running for political office, this passage could be His platform. We cannot separate the person of Christ from the work of Christ; we cannot understand one without the other. Jesus described Himself as anointed because of the Spirit of the Lord upon Him. The title *Christ* means "the anointed one"; it represents the Hebrew word *Messiah*. Jesus' last name was not Christ; rather, it was the title that recognized Jesus as anointed by the Spirit of the Lord for specific tasks such as those listed in Luke 4:18–19.

As Jesus' disciples, we are called to continue Jesus' ministry and extend it to the ends of the earth. (See Acts 1:8.) Luke provided a subtle hint to this in the first verse of the Book of Acts. While speaking of his previous volume, the Gospel of Luke, he stated his Gospel detailed "all that Jesus began both to do and teach" (Acts 1:1). The Gospel of Luke was the beginning of Jesus' ministry, but it is not the end. The Book of Acts is the continuation of Jesus' ministry through His disciples. Through us, Jesus is still doing and teaching in our world.

Long after that boat rental on the Sea of Galilee, Peter recognized Jesus for who He really was. According to Matthew 16:16, Simon Peter confessed Jesus as the Christ, the Messiah. While many people have recognized Jesus as an important teacher, leader, even revolutionary, Jesus' messiahship is a spiritual revelation that comes from God alone. As we have seen, Luke 4:18–19 reveals the Messiah's ministry. In the Book of Acts, believers continued that ministry. We should see the continuation of that same ministry in our local churches today. When we understand who Jesus is and what His mission is, we go and do likewise.

C. We Are His Church; It Is Not a Building

Teacher Option: *A supplemental video is available in the Resource Kit.* **V**

The term *ekklesia* always referred to people, not a building. The earliest gathering places for worship were believer's homes, outdoors, and in extreme cases, the catacombs. When we understand the humble beginnings of the Christian faith and the view Christians had of themselves as a group, it is hard to see how churches have become multimillion dollar buildings. While these buildings can be tremendous assets, we live in a world where instead of *being* the church, believers *attend* church. The church has become a place we go and a thing we do. There is little emphasis in the public consciousness of being the church.

Instead of sharing our personal testimonies of the gospel, many have settled for inviting people to "church." We should invite people to visit a place where the church gathers, but we as believers bring church to people everywhere we go. We must reflect on what kind of church we are bringing to our coworkers, family members, and friends. Regardless of our level of awareness and intentionality, we are bringing church to them. Just inviting people to a building reveals how we may have limited divine encounters to the physical location for the local church. Can God move at your workplace, the store, or a house, or is He limited to the building where the church meets? Perhaps the most dangerous thing about a church building is it has caused us to relegate faith to a place rather than to people. The church is people, not a building. We must retain our corporate identity as the body of Christ and be the church God is calling us to become.

How can you intentionally share church with others besides inviting them to your local place of worship?

D. I Will Be a Disciple of Jesus

Disciples have committed to follow the teaching and example of another. The relationship between a martial arts student and his teacher (sensei) provides a contemporary example of the relationship between disciple and master. If students just learn knowledge and skills from their sensei but not how to apply them in real life, they are left immature and defenseless. Instead, senseis get personal, shaping students at their level. They lead students into comprehensive training in a variety of ways to shape students holistically and prepare them for real-life scenarios. Traditionally teachers may provide knowledge and skills to students to shape their minds primarily; however, the master and disciple relationship provides something deeper—that sensei model of holistic transformation.

Jesus offers us a similar relationship that distinctively sets us apart as Christians. Jesus' love makes this relationship unique. His love is not based on our worthiness or ability to return the love. When we love others as Jesus has loved us, God abides with us and is perfected within us. (See I John 4:7–12.)

INTERNALIZING THE MESSAGE

In John 21, we see a situation similar to Luke 5. Peter, James, John, and other disciples were near the Sea of Galilee after Jesus had risen from the dead. Peter decided to go fishing, and the other disciples decided to accompany him. They fished all night but caught nothing, and a man appeared and instructed them to cast their net on the right side of the boat where they would catch fish. When they obeyed, they caught a tremendous number of fish. Suddenly, the disciples recognized that the man on the shore was Jesus. Peter quickly jumped into the sea and swam toward Jesus. Instead of speaking with Jesus upon arrival, Peter dragged the net of fish up to the shore by himself. The disciples ate together, but Jesus and Peter had still not spoken. Finally, Jesus spoke to Peter and asked him three times, "Do you love Me?" This was reminiscent of the three times Peter denied Jesus outside His trial.

Jesus came specifically for Peter to restore him to his position as a disciple. Jesus' focus was not on Peter's knowledge and abilities but on restoring the relationship from which Peter's future ministry would flow. Jesus knew exactly where Peter was and responded to Peter in a specific way that would speak to Peter's heart. Jesus finished His talk with Peter by saying, "Follow Me." Then Jesus prophesied to Peter about his death as a martyr when Peter was old. Peter may have lost his faith when he was younger, but he would cling to it when he was old. Peter responded in the most inappropriate, irreverent, human way. He looked back to see John following and asked Jesus, "What about him, Lord?" In the middle of an intimate moment with Jesus, Peter turned the attention away from himself and onto John.

Jesus calls us to focus on our individual calling, ministry, and soul. Instead of communicating with God, we sometimes drag up another person and situation, offer God excuses, or become easily distracted. Our human nature has a terrible habit of hiding and blaming others when God comes seeking us. (See Genesis 3.) Our God has an intentional plan to develop a relationship with us, help us grow, and discover our callings. To facilitate this process, we must allow the Spirit to guide us closer to Him instead of moving away from Him.

Has God tried to speak with you, but you responded about another person or situation instead of the condition of your own heart, soul, or spirit?

Prayer Focus
Lead the group in prayer and consider the following topics of focus:
- For God to help us follow Him with our whole heart
- For God to help us make other disciples for Him

SERIES 3: A GLORIOUS CHURCH

3.2

THE PURPOSE OF THE CHURCH

FOCUS VERSE
Acts 4:20
For we cannot but speak the things which we have seen and heard.

LESSON TEXT
Acts 4:13–35

TRUTH ABOUT GOD
God established His church to come together and reveal Him to the world.

TRUTH FOR MY LIFE
I will testify to others about the things I hear and see God do.

Thinking about Last Week:

Have students refer to their Daily Devotional Guide to answer the following questions:
1. What most affected you as you read through the Lesson Text and the Biblical Insights?
2. How did it shape your prayers and thoughts throughout the week?
3. Do you feel you grew closer to the Lord this past week? Why or why not?

SG TEACHING OUTLINE

Icebreaker: If you could witness any miracle, what would it be?

Lesson Connection: Share the Lesson Connection.

I.   THE BOOK OF ACTS CHURCH

    A.   The Disciples Ministered to Others and Operated in the Miraculous
       » *What is the connection between church unity and church growth? How can a church grow in unity and extend that unity to those outside the faith community?*

    B.   The Disciples Were Determined to Testify of Jesus

    C.   The Church Prayed Together and Cared for One Another
       » *How does your church see itself? How does that affect the behavior of the church?*

    D.   I Will Testify to Others about the Things I Hear and See God Do
       » *How is your church encouraging a culture that values community despite the heavy cultural emphasis of individualism in the world?*

II. THE CHURCH TODAY

    A.   The Miraculous is Still Available to the Church Today ⓥ
       » *How does your church intentionally construct an atmosphere where the miraculous can happen at any time in any place?*

    B.   We Are Not to Forsake Gathering Together for Worship and Prayer

    C.   We Are Called to Care for One Another and Minister to Others
       » *How is your church currently ministering to the most vulnerable groups in your community? If your church is not providing a ministry to any vulnerable groups, identify the vulnerable groups and discuss a plan to effectively minister to them in their greatest need.*

    D.   I Will Help to Fulfill the Purpose of the Church
       » *How can your local congregation intentionally build a community of faith that equally values the contributions of every member?*

Internalizing the Message Ⓘ

Prayer Focus
Lead the group in prayer and consider the following topics of focus:
• For God to unify us as a church
• For God to use us to minister to our community together

LESSON CONNECTION

After the miraculous Day of Pentecost, the number of Jesus' disciples ballooned from 120 in Acts 1 to 3,120 in Acts 2. That is rapid church growth. These two chapters set a precedent for how faithfully practicing the ordinary can lead to extraordinary moves of the Spirit. In Acts 1, the disciples met together to pray frequently. They also determined to fill Judas' vacant position as a disciple. They nominated two candidates and prayerfully cast lots, akin to our flipping a coin. Since they prayed before casting lots, God directed the outcome. Essentially, the church had their first business meeting in Acts 1 where they selected a new disciple for the First Pentecostal Church of the New Testament. These seemingly ordinary events led to the supernatural outpouring of God's Spirit on the Day of Pentecost.

This same precedent can be seen at the end of Acts 2. After the Day of Pentecost, Luke recorded, "And they continued stedfastly in the apostles' doctrine and fellowship, and in breaking of bread, and in prayers" (Acts 2:42). After a tremendous revival, the new Christians devoted themselves to ordinary Christian practices as a community. But the outcome was far from ordinary. Luke reported miraculous wonders and signs (Acts 2:43) and supernatural compassion for each other (Acts 2:44–45). Believers volunteered their money, property, and other resources to the community of faith and to those in need. All this happened as a result of faithfully practicing the ordinary disciplines of worship and fellowship within the newborn New Testament church.

Their faithfulness attracted God's attention and blessing. Acts 2:47 reads, "And the Lord added to the church daily such as should be saved." The result of the ordinary practices of prayer, fellowship, and worship along with extraordinary miracles and ministries was salvation regularly extended to others. Such was the humble, but powerful beginnings of God's Spirit-filled, Spirit-led church.

BIBLE LESSON

I. THE BOOK OF ACTS CHURCH

A. The Disciples Ministered to Others and Operated in the Miraculous

The miraculous healing of a lame beggar provides an example of how commonplace the ministry of the early church operated in Jerusalem. They did not need to invite the crippled beggar to their church; Peter and John took church to him. After this miracle and Peter's follow-up sermon, the number of Christians grew to roughly five thousand members (Acts 4:4). When we take church to others, we can impact them significantly through the ministry into which God calls each believer.

What is the connection between church unity and church growth? How can a church grow in unity and extend that unity to those outside the faith community?

B. The Disciples Were Determined to Testify of Jesus

Peter and John's prayer for the lame beggar as well as Peter's sermon garnered the attention of the Sanhedrin, the ruling religious council of Jews. This council of elite Jews brought Peter and James in for judgment. Although the Romans were the political rulers of the Palestine region and beyond, they attempted to avoid settling religious disputes. This afforded the Sanhedrin tremendous power, even under Roman government.

The Temple guard jailed Peter and John overnight and took them before the Sanhedrin the following morning. The public gathered to support Peter and John in the trial. The man who was formerly lame was also standing with them. Consider the tension Peter and John might have felt as they stood before many of the same men who had sentenced Jesus to crucifixion. Peter responded to the Sanhedrin boldly, emphasizing how the power manifested through the name of Jesus caused healing to occur, for "neither is there salvation in any other: for there is none other name under heaven given among men, whereby we must be saved" (Acts 4:12).

The Sanhedrin removed Peter and John from the chamber while they conferred. The council feared public punishment would heighten the religious fervor of these Christians and cause a widescale rebellion in the city. When the council allowed Peter and John to return, they commanded them to cease speaking and teaching in the name of Jesus. Peter and John replied, "Whether it be right in the sight of God to hearken unto you more than unto God, judge ye. For we cannot but speak the things which we have seen and heard" (Acts 4:19–20). Like other Christians in their community, Peter and John were committed to sharing what they had seen and heard regarding Jesus Christ.

C. The Church Prayed Together and Cared for One Another

These two returned to the Christians as soon as they were released and informed the community of the Sanhedrin's ruling. Many of the church—which was over five thousand members strong—came together in unity and prayer. During their prayer, they recited the first two verses of Psalm 2. This citation allows us to see how early Christians saw themselves, the Jews, the world, and their place in God's plan. Psalm 2 is a royal psalm that discusses the opposition Israel faced from the nations, such as Assyria, Babylon, Egypt, and so on. Since God set His chosen king in Jerusalem, Israel cannot be overcome by the nations (Psalm 2:6). The early Christians quoted this psalm because it displayed how the meaning had been transformed for them due to Jesus' ministry. Early Christians saw the Jews as the nations and Jesus as God's chosen messianic king.

Although the Sanhedrin opposed the Christians, the church had unshakable faith that God's Messiah would overcome. They began to see the Sanhedrin's opposition as futile. Due to this and the power of the community they all shared, they were prepared to continue practicing their faith with boldness.

How does your church see itself? How does that affect the behavior of the church?

D. I Will Testify to Others about the Things I Hear and See God Do

Despite a traumatic arrest, incarceration, and judgment from the Sanhedrin, Peter and John rejoined the community and ignited it with further zeal for the work of the Lord. Early Christians did not practice an individualistic type of Christianity, which is often practiced in North America. Rather than praying for God to strengthen them as individuals or the other apostles to perform ministry, the Christians prayed for the Spirit to strengthen the community. They understood their ability to testify and share the gospel was not based on individual merit or ability but on the health of their community.

The emphasis of the community over the individual is clear in how believers shared hearts and minds as well as money, property, and food. When their church service was over, the Christians did not return to their homes, care for their families, and plan for a big service next Sunday. Rather, they came together to mutually provide for themselves and others who were in need. Such a community could not be organized solely through the efforts of men. Often societies have tried to organize a comparable movement, and the outcome has been failed socialist states. However, when God is leading and individuals abandon individualism to embrace community through free will, the outcome will be miraculous signs and ministries. Just as we practice oneness in doctrine, we must also be one in practice. The community of faith, rather than the individuality of faith, is a major part of what makes Christianity a powerfully transformative experience.

How is your church encouraging a culture that values community despite the heavy cultural emphasis of individualism in the world?

II. THE CHURCH TODAY

A. The Miraculous Is Still Available to the Church Today

One key doctrine that separates the Pentecostal faith tradition from Reformed and mainline Protestant traditions is the doctrine of cessationism. As the name suggests, cessationism is the teaching that the gifts of the Spirit, as listed in I Corinthians 12 and 14, have ceased. This doctrine was initially formulated by John Calvin and reasserted by a Reformed theologian, B. B. Warfield. Warfield likely reasserted this doctrine in direct response to the modern Pentecostal movement that began in the early twentieth century.

The lack of spiritual gifting and the activity of the Holy Spirit in other faith traditions is not only a matter of theological doctrine but also a lack of experience. When Christians do not seek the gifts of the Spirit, those gifts do not appear. When Christians began seeking the gifts of the Spirit during the latter half of the nineteenth century, they reappeared. The opposite of cessationism is continuationism, which argues that the gifts have continued without end since the Day of Pentecost. The Pentecostal experience is the living embodiment of continuationism as we strive to continue the practice of Christianity as presented in the Book of Acts.

Teacher Option: *A supplemental video is available in the Resource Kit.* **V**

How does your church intentionally construct an atmosphere where the miraculous can happen at any time in any place?

B. We Are Not to Forsake Gathering Together for Worship and Prayer

Oneness Pentecostals see the example of the early church rather than church tradition, ecumenical creeds, or popular theories on leadership as normative practice for all churches. Essentially, the record of the church presented by Luke in Acts is a historical document; however, it is much more than just history. The Book of Acts also contains a template for an Apostolic church and the knowledge, practices, and structure needed to sustain it. While we must recognize emerging differences, such as culture, advancements in science and technology, and changes in people's worldviews, many of the practices of the Apostolic church will remain the same as the Book of Acts.

As early Christians encountered persecution and other obstacles, they never abandoned gathering together for fellowship, worship, and prayer as a united community of faith. Conducting church services during the COVID-19 pandemic was difficult. To maintain safety many churches had to adapt their services to teleconferencing and livestreaming. Churches recognized the need to maintain the continuity of the community and found creative ways to stay connected. To effectively serve the Lord, our brothers and sisters, and the surrounding community, adaptations are something necessary and beneficial. No matter what it takes, we should never allow anything to disrupt the community of faith.

C. We Are Called to Care for One Another and Minister to Others

As the early church continued to grow and face further persecution, the responsibility to care for those in need became great and time-consuming. In Acts 6, the apostles recognized this need and appointed seven individuals to distribute food to those in need. Keep in mind the early church did not choose between advancing the gospel and caring for the physical needs of its community; they continued ministry on both of these essential fronts.

The Epistle of James teaches believers that "pure religion and undefiled before God and the Father is this, To visit the fatherless and widows in their affliction, and to keep himself unspotted from the world" (James 1:27). It is not enough to maintain and pursue doctrinal integrity through teaching and preaching. We preach not to allow the world to corrupt the church, but we should also preach that the church should bless and better the world. What we truly believe is best displayed by how we care for the most vulnerable in their distress. Since the ancient world was largely a patriarchal culture where women and children could not own property or find legitimate employment, orphans and widows were the most vulnerable and distressed individuals in society.

> How is your church currently ministering to the most vulnerable groups in your community? If your church is not providing a ministry to any vulnerable groups, identify the vulnerable groups and discuss a plan to effectively minister to them in their greatest need.

James did not specify that believers care only for *their* orphans and widows. These Christians likely cared for orphans and widows, whether or not they were a part of the faith community. If we only care for those who think, act, look, and talk like us, we have set conditions on whom we love, and Jesus' love has no such parameters. Timothy Bollmann, who served as a professor in Bible college, said it this way: "We are most like Jesus when we lose our ability to choose whom we love."

D. I Will Help to Fulfill the Purpose of the Church

The early church did not see preaching as more valid, necessary, or important than food distribution. Rather the church recognized that people with certain skill sets and giftings need to be used where they are most useful. That is why the apostles appointed these seven deacons to oversee food distribution so the apostles could focus on their specific callings and unique skills, the Word, and prayer (Acts 6:4). The early church used the metaphor of a body to better understand the composition and function of the church. Because the church is the body of Christ, it consists of many members suited to different tasks. (See I Corinthians 12:12.) The eye is not suited for the same tasks as the foot, neither is the foot suited for the tasks of the eye. However, both are necessary for the body to function completely. The church functions best when members are in the right place performing the tasks most suited to their particular callings.

> How can your local congregation intentionally build a community of faith that equally values the contributions of every member?

Since the church is the body of Christ and a body is composed of many members, one individual cannot fully represent all attributes of Christ alone. The physical manifestation of Jesus is His church. When people encounter the church, they should leave the encounter as if they have experienced the hands, feet, eyes, and heart of Jesus in action. We cannot do it alone. We need each other to be the body of Christ that continues the mission of Christ.

INTERNALIZING THE MESSAGE

A supplemental image is available in the Resource Kit. Ⓘ

Stephen Hawking was a renowned modern scientist whose popularity has endured due to the inspirational nature of his life and his contributions to science. Hawking was diagnosed with Lou Gehrig's disease in 1963 at the age of twenty-one years old. He had just begun his graduate studies. Over time, Lou Gehrig's disease gradually paralyzed Hawking. Although his intellect was strong as ever, his body struggled with essential tasks. He used a speech-generating device that responded to his finger and later his cheek once he could no longer move any muscles in either hand. Hawking accomplished more with his disabled body than many accomplish with their functional bodies. Despite his drive to overcome adversity, his struggle illustrated just how difficult it is to lose the function of one's body. If the parts of the body of Christ are present but not functioning, the effectiveness of the church's ministry will not reach its full potential.

There are a few reasons some parts may not be functioning. Some members may be overworking and not allowing other members to obtain competency in their specific ranges of functionality. Hands and mouths can both communicate; however, a mouth that speaks too often may not allow hands to be utilized when necessary. Also, a church may not value certain ministries equally. A church may not hold jail ministry and children's ministry at the same level of importance. But if they are glorifying God and working to make disciples for Him, they are equally valuable to the kingdom of God.

Finally, members of a body may not be growing appropriately to perform their key functions within the body. Cancer is a form of growth in the body. Cancer grows when the DNA in a cell has been changed and replaced with contrary instructions. The results are useless masses with no benefit and are ultimately a detriment to the entire body. These cancerous parts of the body are removed to preserve the health of the entire body. When growth occurs contrary to the body of Christ's DNA, surgical removal through the Spirit of God may be the necessary remedy.

Christians must grow by the Scripture, the influence of the Holy Spirit, and the work of the fivefold ministry (Ephesians 4). This ensures that all members of the body of Christ experience healthy growth, are utilized regularly, and develop competency within their unique range of calling and giftedness. If we have accepted the calling to be the church, we must acknowledge the need of every member of the body and incorporate each member into the life and service of the church. We must not allow churches to become dysfunctional, disproportionate, or diseased. Let's be intentional about pursuing healthy communities of faith where non-Christians can experience the manifestation of Jesus within the body of Christ.

Prayer Focus
Lead the group in prayer and consider the following topics of focus:
- For God to unify us as a church
- For God to use us to minister to our community together

3.3

THE CHURCH IN ACTION

FOCUS VERSES
Matthew 28:19–20
[19] Go ye therefore, and teach all nations, baptizing them in the name of the Father, and of the Son, and of the Holy Ghost:
[20] Teaching them to observe all things whatsoever I have commanded you: and, lo, I am with you alway, even unto the end of the world. Amen.

LESSON TEXT
Matthew 28:16–20; Mark 16:15; Luke 24:44–53; Acts 1:1–8

TRUTH ABOUT GOD
Jesus commissioned His disciples to take the gospel everywhere to everyone.

TRUTH FOR MY LIFE
I will proclaim the gospel to everyone I can.

Thinking about Last Week:

Have students refer to their Daily Devotional Guide to answer the following questions:
1. What most affected you as you read through the Lesson Text and the Biblical Insights?
2. How did it shape your prayers and thoughts throughout the week?
3. Do you feel you grew closer to the Lord this past week? Why or why not?

(SG) TEACHING OUTLINE

Icebreaker: Besides the gospel, what is the best news you have heard in your life?

Lesson Connection: Share the Lesson Connection. (I)

I. BEFORE HIS ASCENSION, JESUS REMINDED THE DISCIPLES OF HIS PURPOSE

   A. He Had to Suffer, Die, and Rise from the Dead
      » *What does it mean to live your life intentionally and purposefully for Jesus?*

   B. He Was the Gospel That Was to Be Preached (V)
      » *What does it mean for God to uphold justice and also show mercy? Why did God choose to do this?*

   C. I Will Remember Jesus' Purpose
      » *How does God's Spirit heal the harm caused by sin and evil in our world? What hinders us from performing such ministry?*

II. JESUS DECLARED TO THE DISCIPLES THEIR PURPOSE

   A. Preach the Gospel to Every Creature
      » *What are some ways you could extend the good news to all creation in your community?*

   B. Teach All Nations

   C. Baptize

   D. I Will Proclaim the Gospel to Everyone I Can
      » *What social or political issues can limit us and how often we share the gospel with others?*

Internalizing the Message

Prayer Focus
Lead the group in prayer and consider the following topics of focus:
• For God to give us gratitude for the gospel
• For God to use us to share the gospel with others

LESSON CONNECTION

A supplemental image is available in the Resource Kit. ⓘ

In 490 BC the Persians invaded Greece to bring Greece under the control of the Persian Empire. Although there were several Greek city-states, the Athenians were most impacted by the invasion. The Battle of Marathon was a key battle that turned the tide of the first Greco-Persian War. The defeat did not critically wound the Persians; however, it significantly increased Athenian morale. Their victory proved the Greeks could resist the Persians and even defeat them on the battlefield.

Marathon was located approximately twenty-five miles from Athens. Legend states that a messenger, named Pheidippides (pronounced fai-dip-pa-des), was commissioned to carry the good news of the victory back to the Athenians. Pheidippides swiftly ran south to Athens, but after he arrived, he collapsed and died immediately once he shared the good news. While the Athenians lamented his death, they were relieved to know their enemy was defeated. Pheidippides's good news brought the Athenians relief and comfort.

This story is more than just a brief lesson in Greek history. The New Testament was written in Greek rather than Hebrew to communicate the gospel with as many people as possible. Alexander the Great's army conquered much of the known world and painted the world Greek between 336–323 BC. The Greek language became an important means of communication across the new empire. When the Romans conquered the Greeks in 146 BC, they recognized the usefulness of the Greek language and continued speaking and writing it. As a result, the New Testament was strategically written in Greek.

Greek words with biblical significance would have been used to describe Pheidippides. Since his message was good news, the Greek word *euangelion* was likely used. This word is usually translated *gospel* in our English translations, and it denotes good news and victory. New Testament authors used *euangelion* to present the message of Jesus overcoming the forces of sin and death; His victory is good news for all humanity.

When Jesus commissioned His disciples to preach the gospel, He called them apostles, or *apostolos*, in Greek. The Greeks regularly used *apostolos* to refer to a messenger or someone sent forth with orders. Just as Pheidippides was sent forth as a messenger carrying good news, Christ has sent us into the world as messengers with His good news. We are heralds of a new kingdom, the kingdom of God. And we proclaim this kingdom's victory over the forces of evil, death, and sin.

BIBLE LESSON

I. BEFORE HIS ASCENSION, JESUS REMINDED THE DISCIPLES OF HIS PURPOSE

A. He Had to Suffer, Die, and Rise from the Dead

In the synoptic gospels—Matthew, Mark, and Luke—Jesus' ministry turned toward Jerusalem after the twelve disciples discussed His identity as Messiah. (See Matthew 16; Mark 8; Luke 9.) Along this journey Jesus' encounters with various Jewish sects, such as Pharisees, Sadducees, and Herodians, became more frequent and rigid. In Luke 9, after Peter confessed Jesus as the Messiah, Jesus predicted His death to the disciples (Luke 9:18-22). Then while Jesus was speaking to a much larger crowd, He invited believers to take up their cross daily and follow Him. The cross has been romanticized by modern Christians as a symbol of the Christian faith and hope. But to Jesus' audience, taking up your cross reminded them of the parade of condemned individuals bearing their crosses upon which they would soon die the Roman death penalty.

Then Luke recorded the miracle on the Mount of Transfiguration. Peter, James, and John saw Jesus glorified as He prayed. Moses and Elijah appeared alongside Jesus and spoke to Him about His death that would happen soon. On the mountain the disciples heard God's voice from Heaven say, "This is my beloved Son: hear him" (Luke 9:35). Jesus' mission was to die in Jerusalem, and the Spirit of God was confirming His mission to the disciples. Sadly, they did not listen.

As we close Luke 9, Jesus resolutely set out for Jerusalem. Jesus' ministry as Messiah and suffering servant had been confirmed. He was fully aware that He was heading to Jerusalem to be betrayed, tortured, and killed. Rather than His disciples being supportive, they fell asleep at inappropriate times (Luke 9:28-36), argued over which of them would be the greatest (Luke 9:46-48), rebuked others inappropriately (Luke 9:49-50), and offered to misuse their authority against the Samaritans (Luke 9:51-56). Jesus' twelve disciples completely missed His mission although they traveled with Him for three years. We can be in the church all our lives and altogether miss what Jesus has commissioned us to do and be.

What does it mean to live your life intentionally and purposefully for Jesus?

B. He Was the Gospel That Was to Be Preached

To truly understand how Jesus' death, burial, and resurrection are good news, we must understand the bad news that confronts us all. Certainly Jesus is our Savior, but that inherently means we must be saved from something. When a firefighter rescues someone trapped in a burning building, the firefighter saves the person from being burned alive. In like manner Jesus has saved us from the guilt of sin. Sin is contrary to God's law, and since God is just, His standard is perfect. The Greek word for

What does it mean for God to uphold justice and also show mercy? Why did God choose to do this?

sin, *hamartia*, implies an archer "missing the mark." If the archer misses the target completely or just by a few inches, the archer missed the mark. We have all missed the mark; therefore, each of us bears the guilt of sin. (See Romans 5:12.) But thanks be to God, the guilt of sin is removed because God has "forgiven you all trespasses; blotting out the handwriting of ordinances that was against us, which was contrary to us, and took it out of the way, nailing it to his cross" (Colossians 2:13-14). Jesus frees us from the guilt of sin because He bore the wrath of God for us.

C. I Will Remember Jesus' Purpose

Jesus' purpose was not just to deliver us from the guilt of sin and the wrath of God; Jesus also broke the power of sin through His resurrection. The gospel promises the power of sin is continually being broken through the infilling of the Holy Spirit. In Colossians 3, Paul made key arguments about how the power of sin is broken. Paul saw believers as being raised to new life with Christ. Since he spoke in the present tense, he was speaking of how believers are raised into new life through the Holy Spirit.

Although Christ has raised us to new life, lingering effects of sin still remain within us and may even remain with us for life. We are called to play an active role in putting these sinful behaviors to death (Colossians 3:5). In doing so, we daily become more like Jesus, put on His nature, and are renewed as we learn to know Him and become like Him.

How does God's Spirit heal the harm caused by sin and evil in our world? What hinders us from performing such ministry?

The gospel also empowers us to aid others to overcome the guilt and power of sin in their lives. Jesus brought good news to the poor, proclaimed the release of the captives, gave sight to the blind, brought oppression to an end, and announced that the time of the Lord had come (Luke 4:18-19). These miracles are available physically and spiritually. Jesus liberated people held in physical and spiritual bondage and blindness. We continue Jesus' mission by allowing Him to do the same through us for others.

II. JESUS DECLARED TO THE DISCIPLES THEIR PURPOSE

A. Preach the Gospel to Every Creature

Sin fractured the entire creation, not just humanity, to its core. Therefore, the gospel does not just affect humanity but also works to mend all creation. Paul explored this theme in Romans 8:18-23. He discussed how creation was subjected to sin and its negative effects—such as death, dysfunction, disconnection—through the Fall. Yet creation eagerly waits in hope for its day of redemption, much like believers also eagerly wait. Paul used pregnancy as a metaphor, explaining all creation groans in childbirth for the day of its deliverance (Romans 8:22).

Even though we are experiencing salvation, we still will be saved from much more. Our physical bodies, earth, and all creation will be redeemed and restored for the glory of God. All the lingering power of sin as well as the damages caused by sin will be removed from creation. When we share the gospel, we are not only teaching people about Jesus but also proclaiming His glorious good news to the entire creation.

What are some ways you could extend the good news to all creation in your community?

B. Teach All Nations

Each account of the Great Commission featured Jesus' commission to preach the gospel to all nations (Matthew 28:18, Mark: 16:15, Luke 24:47). Jesus made it clear how this would happen according to Acts 1:8. After receiving the Holy Spirit, believers would spread the gospel in Jerusalem (Acts 1-7). The gospel would spread to the regions of Judea and Samaria (Acts 8-12). Later, believers would preach the gospel to the Gentile nations, eventually ending in the empire's capital, Rome (Acts 13-28).

Peter and John were sent to Samaria after the apostles heard the Samaritans had received the gospel message. Peter and John needed to see the Samaritans' experience. The apostles had likely only shared the gospel with fellow Jews. Since Heaven is made up of people from every tribe, nation, and language (Revelation 5:9), we must not discriminate. It took an angel, a vision, and an escort to get Peter to preach to Cornelius, a Gentile, in Cornelius's home. May it never take this much for us to share the gospel with anyone, especially people from a different nation, culture, or religion than our own.

C. Baptize

Jesus also commissioned us to baptize in His name. Without insight into historical background, it can be difficult to see why John the Baptist caused such a ruckus. His message of repentance was an affront to the religious leaders. Baptism predated the New Testament and involved a ritual washing that Gentiles received alongside circumcision if they wanted to fully convert into Judaism. This ritual was performed to wash away the filth of the Gentile world so the new Jewish converts would be clean.

But John preached the baptism of repentance to all Jews in Israel. This teaching emphasized that their birth as Jews was not enough. All people, including Jews, needed to repent of their sins, so being baptized by John was a public sign of their confession and dedication to amend their sinful behavior. The Pharisees and Sadducees attended one of John's baptismal services, but only to watch. John promptly confronted them (Matthew 3:7-10). The Pharisees and Sadducees banked on their genealogy for their righteousness, but the kingdom of God is not something we are born into naturally. God has no grandchildren; we must all be born again into the kingdom of God.

Likewise, Christians join a new community also. In baptism we are initiated into God's new covenant. Since all of the apostles were

Jews, they were familiar with Jewish proselyte baptism, John's baptism, and what each represented. When Jesus instructed the apostles to baptize, they understood baptism in this context. When Cornelius and his household received the Holy Spirit, Peter equated their experience with his own. Because of this, Peter baptized Cornelius and his household in Jesus' name into the covenantal community, and they were recognized as full members of the body of Christ (Acts 10:47–48). Through baptism in Jesus' name, we obtain access to a new and better covenant in Jesus Christ.

D. I Will Proclaim the Gospel to Everyone I Can

Just before Jesus ascended, the disciples asked Him, "Lord, wilt thou at this time restore again the kingdom to Israel?" (Acts 1:6). The apostles still did not understand. Likewise, we also may be led astray by social or political matters. The goal of Jesus' commission is not to advance the kingdoms of this world but to advance Christ's kingdom. This happens when we extend the values, service, and hope of the Christian community to all. Every believer is a minister, called to share Jesus' kingdom with others.

For some, the ministry will become a professional vocation. Missions, for example, was not just something Paul did; it was part of his identity. Some may not embrace ministry as a professional vocation; however, it remains a large part of their lives. Aquila and Priscilla helped establish and maintain churches in Corinth and Ephesus and helped lead Apollos to the Christian faith. Many theologians suggest Apollos is the author of the Epistle to the Hebrews. Without Aquila and Priscillia's ministry, Apollos may not have been saved.

While Jesus has a specific calling for each of us, our general calling is to share the gospel with others. God has commissioned and equipped us to go out into the world just like He sent the apostles. When we follow God's general calling, He leads us into our individual calling, uniquely specialized for our skills, personalities, and life experiences.

What social or political issues can limit us and how often we share the gospel with others?

INTERNALIZING THE MESSAGE

The original audience of the Epistle of Hebrews is unknown. Some suggest the epistle was written to Jewish Christians living in Rome, while others suggest it was written to the church in Jerusalem. However, based on references within the letter, the audience was Jewish (1:1), immature in their faith (5:12), experiencing persecution (10:32–35), and wavering in their commitment to their faith (10:26–27). The writer wrote to help them grow in their faith, despite their intense persecution.

The writer of Hebrews invited his audience to consider the individuals who previously suffered for following the will of God. Although Hebrews 11 is often considered highlighting the heroes of faith, a more fitting description might be highlighting persons who suffered immensely for the faith. Hebrews 12:1 encourages believers to lay aside our setbacks, particularly the sins that ensnare us, "seeing we also are compassed about with so great a cloud of witnesses" (Hebrews 12:1). These witnesses are those who have lived the life of faith before us. Their faithfulness bears witness to our faithfulness to God. By their example and encouragement, we patiently run our race set before us.

This race is not only won by endurance and faithfulness but also by keeping our eyes on Jesus, "the author and finisher of our faith" (Hebrews 12:2). The NLT calls Jesus "the champion" of our faith, meaning He successfully ran and completed this race without any errors. Jesus endured all the hostility, shame, and pain of the cross by focusing on the tremendous power of the gospel to save us. When we err, we are encouraged to focus on the faithful testimony of believers and on what gave Jesus strength. Hebrews advocates that we must be other-focused rather than self-focused. It is not about our strength or ability but how we are empowered by the community of faith.

When Jesus comes and we meet the saints who have gone before us, instead of us asking them their stories, they may ask us our stories. Consider the joy and excitement shining on their faces as we testify of the great work God did through His Spirit. We are and will continue to be witnesses of what Jesus has done and continues to do. We will tell our stories.

Prayer Focus
Lead the group in prayer and consider the following topics of focus:
• For God to give us gratitude for the gospel
• For God to use us to share the gospel with others

3.4

THE BRIDE OF CHRIST

FOCUS VERSE
Ephesians 5:27
That he might present it to himself a glorious church, not having spot, or wrinkle, or any such thing; but that it should be holy and without blemish.

LESSON TEXT
Genesis 24:45–67; Ephesians 5:25–27

TRUTH ABOUT GOD
Jesus is coming for a church without blemish.

TRUTH FOR MY LIFE
I will prepare myself to be part of the bride of Christ.

Thinking about Last Week:

Have students refer to their Daily Devotional Guide to answer the following questions:
1. What most affected you as you read through the Lesson Text and the Biblical Insights?
2. How did it shape your prayers and thoughts throughout the week?
3. Do you feel you grew closer to the Lord this past week? Why or why not?

SG TEACHING OUTLINE

Icebreaker: What is the most humorous wedding story you have heard?

Lesson Connection: Share the Lesson Connection

I. A BRIDE FOR ISAAC

    A. Abraham Sent His Servant to Find a Bride for Isaac. Ⓘ

    B. Rebekah Came to the Well
       » *If you have ever prayed a prayer to know God's plan, how did God answer your prayer? Did you believe the answer as it came?*

    C. Rebekah Was Willing to Leave Her Home for Canaan

    D. I Will Leave the Familiar to Pursue a Relationship with the Lord
       » *Did you have to leave behind something familiar and safe to go where Jesus was calling you? What was that experience like for you?*

II. THE BRIDE OF CHRIST

    A. Jesus Came to Find a Bride for Himself
       » *How can a healthy marriage be a way to display the love of Jesus to others?*

    B. The Church Will Be Glorious, Without Spot or Wrinkle
       » *How does your relationship with Jesus help the church grow as a body of believers?*

    C. This World Is Not Our Home

    D. I Will Prepare Myself to Be a Part of the Bride of Christ Ⓥ
       » *How does your faith serve as a lamp to help you find your way to Jesus in a spiritually dark world? How does it serve as light to guide others?*

Internalizing the Message

Prayer Focus
Lead the group in prayer and consider the following topics of focus:
• For God to help us live as the betrothed bride of Christ
• For God to help us be ready for His coming

429

LESSON CONNECTION

Ancient Israel had unique wedding customs during biblical times. Marriages were arranged years before the wedding ceremony and could even occur when the bride and groom were still children. The betrothal process involved an agreement between two families. These marriages were not necessarily made for love, but the parents hoped the groom and bride would love each other. Marriages were often arranged to benefit both families.

After initial consultation between the families, the groom's father paid a bride price to purchase the right to wed the bride to his son. Unfortunately, in the patriarchal culture of the ancient Near East, women were viewed as part of their father's or husband's property. In addition to the dowry, the groom often presented a gift of his own to the bride. This gift became part of the property the bride brought with her into the marriage.

When the terms and conditions of the marriage were agreed upon by both families, they formed a marriage contract, completing the betrothal process. Then the groom returned and built a room onto his father's house where he and his new bride would live as husband and wife. By this point the groom and bride were legally considered each other's betrothed. From the perspective of the law, the betrothed couple was married, even though they had not yet had a formal ceremony or consummated their marriage.

When Mary became pregnant with Jesus, Joseph, a righteous man, sought to put her away quietly and spare her whatever public disgrace he could (Matthew 1:19). Divorce was required to break off an engagement. How shameful would it be for a betrothed bride to have a sexual relationship with someone else while her betrothed groom was away building them a home? The amount of social disgrace on Mary was tremendous.

The marriage process of the ancient Near East is featured multiples times in Scripture. A few different times, Jesus used the historical background of betrothal and marriage to reveal theological truths. Paul also wrote to Christians about marriage, both to reveal theological truth and to ensure husbands and wives engage in healthy relationships. This will help us all better understand the engagement between Isaac and Rebekah.

BIBLE LESSON

I. A BRIDE FOR ISAAC

A. Abraham Sent His Servant to Find a Bride for Isaac

Teacher Option: *A supplemental image is available in the Resource Kit.* **ⓘ**

Abraham was around 120 years old and wanted his son Isaac to get married, but he did not want Isaac to marry one of the local Canaanite women. Abraham asked his servant Eliezer to travel to Abraham's homeland in Mesopotamia, modern-day southwestern Iraq (Genesis 24:4). This journey was around 3,400 miles and would have taken him nearly 170 days if he traveled twenty miles each day. By the time he returned, he would have been traveling for nearly a year.

But Abraham was not asking his servant to do something he had not done himself. Abraham had made this selfsame journey almost fifty years earlier. His body was weary with age, but his faith was as strong as ever. He sent Eliezer with ten camels to carry supplies for the journey and gifts that would pay the bride price for Isaac's future wife. The length of the journey and the risk of being robbed made it dangerous. But Abraham had faith in his servant, and his servant had faith in Abraham.

B. Rebekah Came to the Well

When the servant finally arrived, he stopped his camels near the outskirts of town. It was almost time for women to come to the well to collect their water in the evening. He waited by the well and whispered a prayer asking the Lord to give him a sign that he was choosing the right bride for Isaac. If a woman offered to give him and all his camels water, she was the one. As he finished praying, he saw a woman carrying a water pot on her shoulder. Rebekah offered to give Eliezer a drink of water, and she offered to water all his camels (Genesis 24:18). Was she the one for Isaac?

If you have ever prayed a prayer to know God's plan, how did God answer your prayer? Did you believe the answer as it came?

When Rebekah finished, the servant offered her jewelry as a gift of gratitude, and then he asked about her family. Rebekah revealed that Nahor, Abraham's brother, was her grandfather. God had guided Eliezer directly to Abraham's relatives, just as Abraham had requested (Genesis 24:26–27).

Rebekah ran home to tell her family the good news. Laban, Rebekah's brother, met and escorted Eliezer inside their home. The servant told Rebekah's family about his mission and how Rebekah was the woman God selected to be Isaac's wife. Eliezer, Laban, and Rebekah's father all agreed on a marriage contract for Rebekah, the servant provided several gifts as a bride price, and his mission was nearly complete.

C. Rebekah Was Willing to Leave Her Home for Canaan

Rebekah's family asked the servant to stay for ten more days, but he didn't want to delay the long journey. Rebekah's family agreed to let Rebekah decide. She told them she was ready to leave right away. The family said their goodbyes, and Rebekah, her servants, and Abraham's servant mounted the camels and departed (Genesis 24:55-60). That day Rebekah made life-altering decisions. Genesis does not record whether Rebekah ever returned to see her family again. We presume this goodbye was final. Rebekah was leaving her family behind to join another family through marriage to a man she had not met.

This story is shocking to readers today, but this practice was normal in Rebekah's culture. That doesn't mean it was easy for Rebekah. But despite any difficulty, Rebekah was not so comfortable where she was that she could not move to where her calling led her next. The watering maiden was willing to become the wife of a patriarch, whatever that would entail.

D. I Will Leave the Familiar to Pursue a Relationship with the Lord

The call to leave behind what is familiar to follow God's plan is a common theme in Scripture. The familiar brings security and safety because it is known and understood. When we leave that behind, we leave the comfort of knowing where we are and our understanding of how things function. Rebekah walked into the unknown trusting God rather than trusting her fear. Faith is not the absence of fear; faith is the choice to trust despite the presence of fear. God calls us to embrace the unknown alongside Him by walking in faith in the presence of fear.

God is not asking us to do something He has not done Himself. While God knows what a human being is thinking, He could not fully experience humanity without living as a human. Through the Incarnation, the incorporeal became corporeal, the infinite became finite, the divine became earthly.

Did you have to leave behind something familiar and safe to go where Jesus was calling you? What was that experience like for you?

All the Godhead was manifested in Jesus Christ (Colossians 2:9). Hebrews reminds us Jesus was like us in every way, except He did not sin (Hebrews 4:15). God understands our human experience because He experienced it. God embraced the unknown by walking into the human world as a human. Now He calls us to walk in the human world while being filled with the Holy Spirit. One glorious day He will transform us and this world into a new creation perfected by the ministry of Christ and the kingdom of Heaven.

II. THE BRIDE OF CHRIST

A. Jesus Came to Find a Bride for Himself

The church is referred to as the bride of Christ in Revelation 19. We see a snapshot of the marriage banquet between Christ and His church celebrated. Biblical authors may have embraced the language of the church as Christ's bride to explain Jesus' first and second comings. During Jesus' first coming, the Father paid the price, resulting in the gift of salvation to the bride. Because of Jesus' first coming, the church is His betrothed. During Jesus' second coming, He will celebrate His marriage banquet with His bride as they come together to abide with one another forever. Between now and His second coming, Jesus is preparing a room for us in His Father's house (John 14:1-4).

Christian marriage is significant because God chose to use marriage to reveal His love to us. The love between a husband and wife makes Christ's love manifest to others. While marriage is not required to faithfully serve God, Christians who are married should allow the love that exists between spouses to reveal the love of Christ to others. Their marriage may be one of their best or worst witnesses of their faith. Paul set the bar high for husbands and wives. Husbands are to love their wives as Christ loved the church, and wives are to follow their husbands just as the church follows Christ. Faithfully living this way displays the love and devotion of Jesus for others to see.

How can a healthy marriage be a way to display the love of Jesus to others?

B. The Church Will Be Glorious, without Spot or Wrinkle

Everyone has probably grumbled or complained about the church at one point or another. Dr. Jim Littles, professor emeritus at Urshan Graduate School of Theology, often humorously states, "Be careful about griping to Jesus about His church. It's His lady and He's crazy about her." We often fail to live up to our calling, which is to be without spots, wrinkles, and blemishes (Ephesians 5:27). Nevertheless, we aspire to this high calling just as husbands and wives aspire to love their spouse despite hurt or fear of rejection.

Jesus does not love the church because it is perfect. However, within His love is the driving force of redemption. Jesus' love moved Him to give "himself for it; that he might sanctify and cleanse it with the washing of water by the word" (Ephesians 5:25-26). Jesus' sacrifice was not just to save us but also to cleanse us. The church must embrace her Bridegroom and allow His love to heal and grow her into a bride without spots, wrinkles, and blemishes.

How does your relationship with Jesus help the church grow as a body of believers?

C. This World Is Not Our Home

Think of someone with a remarkable testimony of transformation. It is what Jesus will do with the earth on a much larger and grander scale. Although we live here, this world is not our home. Since we were born again, our source of life is from Heaven, not from here. We are in this world but not of it. We are just pilgrims and strangers passing through this land on the way to a better land, a city not made with men's hands. While we are here, we must live to glorify God and make disciples as we make our way from here to Heaven.

D. I Will Prepare Myself to Be Part of the Bride of Christ

In Matthew 25, Jesus shared a parable referred to as the Parable of the Ten Virgins, or the Ten Bridesmaids. These ten bridesmaids were friends of the bride, the groom, or both. Each had a lamp to help her find her way in the dark. Unfortunately, the bridegroom was delayed. Only five of the ten virgins had brought additional oil for their lamps.

At midnight they heard that the bridegroom was coming; all the bridesmaids went out to meet him. Only the five wise women had enough oil to keep their lamps lit for the wedding ceremony. The foolish bridesmaids asked the wise to share, but the wise knew if they shared their oil, they would not have enough for themselves. The foolish ran out to buy oil while the wise waited for the bridegroom and his attendants. When the foolish returned, they found the door locked. They knocked on the door, but the bridegroom replied that he did not know them. Jesus offered one final verse to interpret this parable, saying, "Watch therefore, for ye know neither the day nor the hour wherein the Son of man cometh" (Matthew 25:13).

Teacher Option: *A supplemental video is available in the Resource Kit.* **V**

Although Jesus told this parable about bridesmaids, we understand the church's role in the relationship is to be the bride. However, Jesus will not have many brides, just one. His church will be His bride. This parable reminds us that we must be ready because we do not know exactly when Jesus is coming back for His church. The church's goal is to be ready to meet Jesus, just as the five wise bridesmaids were ready. Since we live in a time of spiritual darkness, the lamp of the Word and Spirit help us find our way and help us to be a light in our darkened world.

How does your faith serve as a lamp to help you find your way to Jesus in a spiritually dark world? How does it serve as light to guide others?

434

INTERNALIZING THE MESSAGE

Another of Jesus' parables that predominantly features the betrothal and wedding customs of biblical times is the Parable of the Wedding Feast found in Matthew 22:1-14. This parable used Israelite betrothal and wedding customs to explain the Marriage Supper of the Lamb (Revelation 19:6-10). The historical-cultural context of betrothal and wedding customs is necessary to appropriately understand this parable.

This parable featured a king who prepared a lavish, sumptuous wedding feast for his son's marriage. However, none of the invited guests attended. The king sent out his servants to the guests, but they either ignored the servants or killed them. The king was furious. Instead of wasting the feast, he bid his servants to invite "both bad and good" (Matthew 22:10) to the feast. While the king was touring his banquet hall brimming with guests, he spotted a guest who was not dressed appropriately for the wedding. The king confronted this man about his inappropriate attire, and the man was speechless. The king ordered his servants to bind the man and throw him into "outer darkness" (Matthew 22:13). Jesus concluded the parable with a chilling statement, "For many are called, but few are chosen" (Matthew 22:14).

Jesus appealed to the wedding feast to explain certain aspects of the coming kingdom of Heaven. The king is God. The king's son is Jesus, the Son of God. The guests who were initially invited but later attacked the king's servants were the Jews. The guests who were later invited were the Gentiles. The man without the wedding garment was an attendee who had not come prepared for the feast. Jesus demonstrated that both bad and good will be coming to the banquet, representing the many who are called. However, others came prepared for the son's wedding, even though they were not originally invited. Those who were prepared represent the few who are chosen.

We should all put on the wedding garment—through God's beautiful plan of salvation—and attend the Marriage Supper of the Lamb. In that day we will finally be with the one who paid the price for us, built a home for us, and came back for us. And so shall we ever be with the Lord.

Prayer Focus
Lead the group in prayer and consider the following topics of focus:
- For God to help us live as the betrothed bride of Christ
- For God to help us be ready for His coming

Fall 2023

Series 1: David and Solomon

This series follows Israel's second and third kings from the day David was anointed until the day Solomon prayed for wisdom to lead God's people. Between those two signal moments, we will watch David run onto the battlefield to fight Goliath, and with the help of Nathan the prophet, collect the supplies his son Solomon needs to build the Temple for the God's glory.

Series 2: Jesus Responds to Faith

This series will look at Jesus' nighttime meeting with Nicodemus as well as the riverside meeting with John the Baptist. Then we follow Jesus to an unexpected conversation at a well and finally to a centurion who needed a miracle. We will see Jesus' grace-filled and powerful response to faith, and humanity's faith-filled, expectant response to Jesus' grace.

Series 3: Parables of Jesus

This series will walk us through four parables Jesus taught in the Gospel of Matthew. We will see a sower sow seed, a shepherd find a lost sheep, laborers working in the vineyard, and a king throw a banquet for his son. Each of those parables possessed a spiritual meaning and application for Jesus' first-century audience and our twenty-first century audience.

Winter 2023–24

Series 1: Holiness

This series begins when Isaiah sees God for how holy He is. We will look at the call of God to the children of Israel before they crossed the Jordan River into the Promised Land, and we will see how the same God who empowered the three Hebrew children in Babylon and forgave the woman caught in adultery empowers us to live a holy life for His purpose.

Series 2: God Is Faithful

This series highlights the unfailing faithfulness of God to Ruth and Naomi, despite the famine and deaths in their family. God was equally faithful to Jonah in the belly of a whale, Daniel in a den of lions, and Esther in a kingdom with a government official bent on killing all the Jews in Persia. Although life is sometimes unkind and unjust, we know God is faithful.

Series 3: The Bread of Life

God calls us to know Him beyond just enjoying the good gifts He gives. We will see a blind man see and five loaves and two fish feed a multitude. We will stand with the disciples in a storm-tossed boat as Jesus calms the sea—once by speaking to it, once by walking on it. Then we will hear the altar call He gives to follow Him just because of who He is: the Bread of Life.

Spring 2024

Series 1: John
Through this series in the Gospel of John, we will witness Jesus' compassion for the lost and hurting. We will observe John see Jesus for who He really is. We will witness the love that drove Jesus to the cross and watch from a well as Jesus points to the coming harvest. Finally we will witness Jesus leave the crowds to find and rescue one lost sheep.

Series 2: Worshiping Our Sovereign God
In this series, the disciples truly see Jesus for who He is. We will stand on the Mount of Transfiguration; then we will stand wide-eyed in the boat as the wind and waves obey Jesus. We will watch as Jesus calms an unridden colt and humbly, yet triumphantly rides into Jerusalem. Finally, we will gather around the throne to worship the one who sits on the throne.

Series 3: Elijah and Elisha
This series will follow the powerful ministries of two powerful men of God. Elisha joins Elijah and follows him all the way until the time he is translated into the presence of God. Then God uses Elisha to perform twice as many miracles as his mentor, including healing a leprous, even skeptical Syrian general because of the faith-filled counsel of his Hebrew maid.

Summer 2024

Series 1: Jesus Teaches Us to Pray
"Jesus Teaches Us to Pray" shows us four examples where Jesus prayed or taught us to pray. We begin in Matthew 6 with the "Lord's Prayer" and move to Matthew 9 to Jesus' command to pray Kingdom prayers. We will hear Jesus pray for us to take His yoke on us, and we will finish by seeing Jesus in the Garden of Gethsemane praying for God's will to be done.

Series 2: "I Am" Sayings
Four passages in John's Gospel identify Jesus with the I AM of Exodus 3. Jesus proclaimed, "I am the light of the world." In John 10, Jesus said, "I am the door." We continue to Jesus' exclusive statement, "I am the way, the truth, and the life." Finally, we hear Jesus proclaim, "I am the true vine." Each of these sayings helps us see Jesus as the incarnate I AM.

Series 3: Fruit of the Spirit and Gifts of the Spirit
This series provides two lessons to learn the fruit of the Spirit and two lessons to learn the gifts of the Spirit. We will study the time Jesus cursed the fig tree, while the second lesson looks closely at each fruit of the Spirit. The remaining two lessons examine the spiritual gifts to demonstrate how God wants to use the spiritual gifts to glorify Him and edify His church.

Apply the Apostolic Message

Somewhere between a verse-by-verse commentary and the Apostolic Study Bible, the eight volumes in the Apostolic Handbook Series bring a two-to-four-thousand-year-old text to life with fresh application to our lives and the church today. You will find insights on the culture, language, and history of Israel, the gospel of Jesus Christ, and the church of the first century, thoroughly grounded by Apostolic writers. The complete set includes:

- Handbook on the Historical Books
- Handbook on the Book of Acts
- Handbook on the Epistles of Paul
- Handbook on the Gospels
- Handbook on the Pentateuch
- Handbook on the General Epistles and Revelation
- Handbook on the Psalms and Wisdom Literature
- Handbook on the Prophets

pentecostalpublishing.com

Study the Apostolic Message

SCAN TO PURCHASE

The Deluxe Edition of the Apostolic Study Bible features a premium genuine leather cover plus:

- Study notes written exclusively by Oneness Pentecostal scholars
- Special emphasis given to passages of Scripture that are important to the Apostolic message
- Book introductions and outlines that call attention to key Apostolic insights as well as theme, authorship, date, and other significant information
- Feature articles on Pentecostal distinctives of holiness, the new birth, living in covenant, miracles, and more by scholars such as David K. Bernard, Daniel Segraves, and David Norris
- 8 pages of maps
- Word Aflame Press Concordance created with emphasis on key words significant to Oneness Pentecostals

pentecostalpublishing.com

DISCIPLESHIP NOW

Unlock an Incredible Library of Apostolic Media

DOWNLOAD THE APP TODAY

 App Store · Google Play · **ROKU** · tv · androidtv · fireTV

Discipleship Now is the platform that puts Apostolic content into the palm of your hand. Get access to video studies and devotional content that will enrich your home, your relationships, and your own walk with God.

Personal and church accounts are available at discipleshipnow.com.

DISCIPLESHIPNOW   **UPCI**